Wanted

NUMBER ELEVEN
CLAYTON WHEAT WILLIAMS TEXAS LIFE SERIES

Historic County Jails of Texas

Edward A. Blackburn Jr.

Texas A&M University Press
College Station

Copyright © 2006 by Edward A. Blackburn Jr.
Manufactured in the United States of America
All rights reserved
First edition

The paper used in this book meets the minimum requirements
of the American National Standard for Permanence
of Paper for Printed Library Materials, z39.48-1984.
Binding materials have been chosen for durability.
∞

Library of Congress Cataloging-in-Publication Data

Blackburn, Edward A., 1923–
    Wanted : historic country jails of Texas / Edward A. Blackburn, Jr. — 1st ed.
      p. cm. — (Clayton Wheat Williams Texas life series ; no. 11)
    Includes bibliographical references and index.
    ISBN 1-58544-308-5 (cloth : alk. paper)
    ISBN 1-58544-498-7 (pbk. : alk. paper)
    1. Jails—Texas—History.   2. Jails—Texas—Pictorial works.   I. Title: Historic
county jails of Texas.   II. Title.   III. Series.
   HV8746.U62T425   2006
   365′.9764—dc22
                          2005010243

Unless otherwise noted, all photos are by Edward Blackburn Jr.

To my wife, Sadie Gwin Blackburn, whose fifty-eight years of love,
counsel, and encouragement were the inspiration for this work,
and to Stanley Gilbert, classmate, friend, and travel companion
to 254 Texas counties.

Contents

Preface

"JAIL" IS A FOUR-LETTER WORD. As such, writers of early Texas architectural, political, and social history have avoided the subject. They consider courthouses, personalities, and battles safer ground. An integral part of every nascent community, the jail was often built even before the courthouse. The place of incarceration went by a variety of names such as calaboose (a corruption of the Spanish *calabozo* ("dungeon, cell"), hoosegow, cooler, pokey, clink, and slammer. As Willard B. Robinson emphasizes in his classic books on Texas architecture, the presence of a substantial courthouse and jail gives communities an aura of permanence, safety, and law and order.

As I traveled about Texas doing the research for this book, I was struck by the beauty and magnificence of many of the nineteenth-century courthouses and jails that today seem ornate and overstated. In reality, the structures were an expression of the pride and power felt by early Texas pioneers. Talented authors such as Mavis P. Kelsey, Donald Dyal, June Rayfield Welch, and Clark Counsey have duly documented the courthouses. Indeed, the idea of visiting and documenting the county jails was suggested by Kelsey, who, while researching his book on the courthouses, had already noticed the interesting architecture hiding in the shadows of their larger companion houses of justice.

This book focuses on the period from 1840 to 1940, which I chose largely because of the jail architecture of the time. In 1840 the newly organized Republic of Texas had solved some of its most pressing problems—issuing currency, selecting officials, and defining county responsibilities. Over the next hundred years, Texans would tame the frontier and develop the industries of ranching, farming, lumber, and petroleum, as well as the infrastructure—railroads and highways—to serve them.

The decade of the Civil War, followed by Reconstruction, set the scene for widespread lawlessness. The Indians on the frontier, emboldened by the absence of settlers who had gone East to fight the war, created a problem that would take about ten years to solve. This period was witness to the restless western migration by Northern and Southern families. Previously law-abiding people who were dislocated from the farms and land that bound them together were on the move. The restraints and discipline of community were often lost, giving rise to a breed of desperate renegades and gunmen. The rapid creation of courthouses and jails was the first step in the return to a civilized society.

The renaissance in courthouse and jail construction, stimulated by timely legislation, began in the 1880s and lasted until the onset of the Depression in 1928. This period produced new county courthouses and jails by an emerging group of talented architects. The buildings designed by these artists would last almost seventy years, through the lean times of the Great Depression and the beginning of World War II, when materials and manpower were diverted into the life-and-death struggle to preserve the Western system of law and rule by consensus.

After the war, evolving architectural ideas and the nature of new materials permanently changed the looks of municipal buildings; however, the trend toward standardized materials that fit the four-by-eight-foot module limited the stylistic variations. Central heat and air-conditioning made tall ceilings and open windows for ventilation passé, and the end of local county executions in 1923 precluded the need for gallows towers, ornamental or otherwise.

The concept of punishment also changed. In 1840 there was very little consideration for the prisoners' comfort, and jails were primitive indeed. The need for sanitation, heating, cooling, ventilation, and security gradually began to be addressed and influenced the design and quality of jail buildings. Outwardly, these facilities became "government standard"—utilitarian and efficient—but lost much of the architectural character that fascinates people who find comfort in traditional form. Because of the increasing numbers of lawbreakers, buildings for confinement were often moved away from the courthouse square to a remote area of each county.

The preliminary search for material on Texas county jails was disappointing. I found several good magazine articles and a well-written graduate thesis by Craig M. Cowden from Texas Tech University, which proved immensely valuable. Cowden's thesis and three books on contemporary and historic Texas architecture by Willard B. Robinson, late professor of architecture at Texas Tech University, provided a working foundation. Because this volume has been designed to recount a few of the historical highpoints of each county's background followed by the history of the jails there, I have repeatedly used the six exemplary volumes of the *New Handbook of Texas* from the Texas State Historical Association as a valuable resource. County histories, both old and new, generated by local authors have also been very useful and, whenever possible, I have interviewed local historians.

The journey to all 254 Texas counties took three and a half years and required more than thirty-five thousand miles of air and automobile travel. Astonishingly, the travel time went by rapidly and was great fun, mainly because of the companionship of Stanley Gilbert, my 1948 medical-school classmate from the University of Texas Medical Branch at Galveston. The enjoyment of recollections of common experiences is a great cure for fatigue. Stanley's death from cancer in August 2000 slowed and encumbered the completion of the book, and I have missed his wisdom and humor.

The diversity of the state of Texas is a remarkable thing. The marvelous assistance and friendly cooperation rendered to us in our search for jailhouse history by members of the Texas Historical Commission, courthouse officials, historians, librarians, museum directors, and local citizens made this work a joy. Following each county's description, I have made an effort to list the many helping hands, but the narrative by the local consultants was often taken verbatim. The cheerful and warm reception and cooperation by all of the people we met validated our good luck in being Texan.

My debt to contributors would be too long if listed separately. For this reason, sources, especially interviews, have been included with each county's information. Special thanks, however, are due to Will Howard, Doug Weiskoph, Ellen Hanlon, and Ann Douglas in the Texas Room of the Houston Public Library for their cheerful help.

Assistance in identifying the jail architects came from Stephen Fox, Architectural Historian at Rice University and Fellow of Anchorage Foundation of Texas. Marvin Kruger of Southern Steel Co. of San Antonio helped in documenting the various jail cell manufacturers. Tom Shelton at the Institute of Texan Cultures in San Antonio found some very useful photographs. Architect David Bucek, who has pursued his own exhaustive research on Houston architect Eugene Heiner, generously provided text and photos of all of Heiner's known jails. Curtis Tunnell, former Director of the Texas Historical Commission, made the resources of the commission available to me. I would make special mention of the advice and wisdom provided to me by Ron Tyler, Director of the Texas Historical Association. My friend, Dr. Mavis Kelsey, gave the encouragement, guidance, and wisdom so essential to novice authors as the work progressed. Susan Cowles, my secretary extraordinaire, offered her computer skills and performed relentless verification of factual material.

Finally, great credit must be given to my wife, Sadie Gwin, a published author in her own right. She edited and re-edited my manuscript and labored to confirm the subjects and credits for the illustrations. Her support assured my continued effort while weeks and months turned into years. After Dr. Gilbert's death she managed to put her own projects aside long enough to drive with me to some of the counties for additional information.

Edward A. Blackburn Jr.

Wanted

Introduction

TRADITIONALLY THE COUNTY JAIL and the county sheriff have been the fulcrum of state law enforcement at the local level. When a territory became a county with newly designated boundaries, the organization led directly to the task of law enforcement. The election of judges, commissioners, and a sheriff was followed by the construction of a courthouse and a jail. After annexation to the United States, the new state of Texas amended its constitution to state that counties were to provide a courthouse, a jail, and bridges. In the early days on the frontier, houses needed to be built, while crops were planted and harvested, and some areas witnessed ongoing skirmishes with hostile Indians. In Baylor County, for instance, settlement had to be abandoned for several years because of the frequency and strength of Comanche Indian attacks. Pioneer families who immigrated to the new territory demanded jail facilities to deal with an onslaught of outlaws and drifters. In several instances, the great need for a jail meant that its construction took precedence over the courthouse. For example, in Anderson County, the first jail was built in October 1846, while the residents were still using a rented house for a courthouse.

When a jail was not available, citizens managed to find a sturdy tree and chained wrongdoers to it for safekeeping until punishment was determined. Most courthouse squares in the western counties had a windmill for public water supply, and the structure was also used to fetter prisoners overnight. Most counties built a substantial log building called a dungeon to serve as a lockup. These dungeons were often two stories and had double or triple walls. The strongest hardwood available was oak, and it was generously used to make these jails.

Judge R. E. B. Baylor's 1843 description of the early jail in Brazos County is typical of the dungeons widely used from 1840

Reagan County
calaboose, 1904–
1911, Stiles, Texas.

to 1870 (reprinted in *Bryan Eagle,* June 24, 1962). The commissioners' court minutes of other counties prescribed similar, if not as detailed, specifications for proposed dungeons. The Brazos County specifications called for a 12′ square, two-story log building constructed of fitted timbers hewn from oak. The floor and foundation consisted of two layers of 10′ square timbers with 2″ of oak planking on top. The dungeon featured three-layer oak walls. The inner and outer layers were made of 10′ square horizontal oak timbers and were separated by 8′ vertical timbers. The dungeon room, or ground level, had a 10′ ceiling made of 10′ square timbers. It had no windows or doors.

The only entrance was through a 30′ square trapdoor on the second floor. Prisoners were let down into the jail room by a ladder, which was then withdrawn. There was no heat, light, or plumbing. The top floor, built of single walls of 10′ timbers, could be used as sheriff's quarters or a confinement area for female prisoners. It had two small windows with 1′ iron bars and a single heavy oak door to the outside, accessed by a stairway on the exterior of the building. The pitched roof was made of shingles. Some similar dungeons had stone foundations, which were

Coryell County dungeon, 1858–1875. Double log crypt. Coryell County Museum, Gatesville, Texas.

buried below grade to discourage prisoners from digging out. To deter diggers, some builders used iron plates to line the floor, ceiling, or door. The corners were cleverly dovetailed to make a sturdy, secure joint that was, in some cases, additionally reinforced with 2′ dowels (Jordan-Bychkov, 152).

Farther west, large trees (such as oak or pine) were unavailable, so other materials were used. Some counties, such as Shackelford and Tom Green, built "picket" buildings, in which the logs of smaller trees were lined up vertically and fastened together stockade fashion to create a confinement wall. Later, as milled lumber became available, 2″ by 4″ or 2″ by 6″ (and, in one case, 2″ by 12″) lumber was laid flat and fastened with many large nails. At least eighteen counties used this expedient, and, in two instances, the building was sold secondhand to a younger county after a few years. None of these jails was escape-proof, and when time and materials became available, stone replaced wood.

Nevertheless, some of the wooden jails lasted for thirty years. The museum at Gatesville in Coryell County has preserved an original log jail built in 1858. Since the first-story dungeon was originally below ground, it gives a good idea of the craftsman-

The old "Bat Cave," on Military Plaza, San Antonio, Texas, used for Police Headquarters and City Jail. Photo by Brack, in 1890.

Bexar County jail, 1850–1879, inside courthouse wall, San Antonio, Texas. Photo courtesy of Elaine Davis, Aniol Collection 39/12, Daughters of the Republic of Texas Library, San Antonio.

ship of the pioneer carpenter. The building concept did not die out when stone became the material of choice. In San Antonio, Bexar County, the famous "bat cave" perpetuated the doorless and windowless first-floor cell, albeit on a grander scale. The second story of that prison had two small windows, properly barred. Sanitation was problematic in these prisons. In Orange County, the difficulty was solved by building the wooden jail out over the Sabine River.

The sophistication of jail construction varied across Texas. From east to west, the older communities of East Texas and along the Gulf Coast procured better facilities earlier on. For example, Galveston built a brick prison as early as 1848, whereas, from 1917 to 1925, Bailey County, in the Panhandle, used a second-hand wood jail bought from Parmer County. There were, of course, isolated exceptions in the western counties, such as Bexar County, where a stone jail was built in 1850, and in San Elizario, El Paso County, where an adobe home from the 1820s became a courthouse and jail in 1850. As Willard Robinson points out, the quality of the public buildings, including jails, was a function of the maturity of the community. Secondary factors such as the availability of materials and local economic conditions were just beginning to improve in Texas when the Civil War began. Nascent railroad routes and public building construction were, for all practical purposes, halted until the 1870s.

In 1869 E. J. Davis, a Republican Reconstruction figure, was elected governor. He deplored the condition of the Texas jails (see W. Robinson 1983, 44). Undoubtedly the jails were harsh punishment when new, and by 1870 they were mean in every sense of the word. After the war, westward migration began, and law enforcement under the Reconstruction government was inadequate, uneven, and prejudiced against anyone who had served in the Confederate Army. The population, previously family oriented and bound to the land, was uprooted, and the territory was flooded with new waves of settlers from Southern and Northern states alike. The stage was set for a period of lawlessness, and the population of the state penitentiary nearly trebled in one year alone.

In 1870 Texas was readmitted to the Union; that same year, the controversial state police force was formed at the behest of Governor Davis, who, as Walter Prescott Webb says (Webb, 220), may have felt the need for extra enforcement to ensure his tenure in office. The state police were a mixed bag. Adj. Gen. James Davidson embezzled thirty-seven thousand dollars in state funds. In addition, Capt. Jack Helm was accused of murdering prisoners before he was discharged, and a warrant was issued for his arrest (*New Handbook of Texas,* vol. 6, 75). These may be the worst examples, but the sobering fact is that abuses were tolerated. In 1873 the state police were disbanded, and the Frontier Battalion of Texas Rangers (which had been disbanded during Reconstruction) was reorganized in 1874. The Texas Rangers' new assignment was to deal with the rampant disorders along the Texas-Mexico border as well as the outlaw element within the state. This vast, underpopulated area recognized no state or law and was the realm of bandits and cattle rustlers. Pacification would bring well-deserved fame and some criticism to the Rangers, but their reorganization was a step in the right direction. Under Reconstruction, the U.S. government had forbidden the formation of any organized group of armed citizens in Texas.

Even before the Civil War, legislation was passed requiring the counties to provide "clean and healthy" jails, but because no provision was made to finance the improvements, the laws received little attention. The state constitution of 1876 compelled counties to provide detention facilities but still provided no funding. In that same year, the Fifteenth Legislature authorized Blanco County and "certain other counties" to levy a special tax for the years 1876, 1877, and 1878 to construct courthouses (Moursund, 49). At the time, individual counties had to petition the legislature for the right to finance such construction. In 1881 the legislature passed a law to allow each county to sell bonds to finance courthouse construction, but not until 1884 was the law broadened to include jail construction (W. Robinson 1983, 86).

The stage was then set for the creation of new jails by almost every county in Texas. The building process would last into the first part of the twentieth century and would spell busy times for architects, builders, and jail manufacturers such as Diebold Safe and Lock Company of Canton, Ohio, Pauly Jail Manufacturing of St. Louis, and Southern Steel of San Antonio. At last, jails and law enforcement were considered important. Expanding their talents, architects designed penal institutions to stand beside the more imposing courthouses, which often simulated medieval castles or fortresses and later reflected popular Victorian or French styles.

The role of the few jail-cell manufacturers varied considerably, from complete service (including architects, materials, builders, and providers of furnishings for the iron cells) to provision of only the prefabricated cells. The standard jail was two or three stories tall and had sheriff's quarters on the first floor and free-standing iron cages on the second and third floors. Some had a gallows or hanging tower, complete with a double trapdoor and a ring in the ceiling to hold the rope. Seldom were these facilities for execution used, however. Jails that lacked a gallows would, if necessary, build a scaffold on the courthouse lawn, so the hanging was public in the true sense. The Archer County jail had a special room—facing the gallows—for witnesses, but the structure was never used.

In the beginning, jails were separate from the courthouse and were located either on the corner of the town square or a block or two away. Occasionally they were connected to the courthouse by a catwalk, as in Bastrop County and Angelina County. After 1900, architects began to incorporate the jail

Callahan County
jail, 1880–1898.
In 1883 the jail
was moved and
reconstructed
in Baird, Texas.
Photo courtesy
of the Institute of
Texan Cultures
at the University
of Texas–San
Antonio.

within the courthouse, sometimes in the basement but usually on the third or fourth floor. There was some advantage in having the prisoners close to the courtroom, but it was soon discovered that the inmates could frustrate the county's entire machinery by flushing pillows and linens down the toilets, thus stopping up the plumbing for the whole courthouse. Since the end of World War II, the trend has been to locate jail buildings in some remote corner of the county seat.

Jail construction gradually slackened during the first part of the twentieth century as counties completed the transition to more permanent structures. The 1920s saw some new construction of jails, especially in the western counties as they caught up with population growth. The Depression years brought limited funding, however. By the end of the 1930s, it was growing evident that the war raging in Europe would soon involve the United States. Frantic rearming and the ever-increasing demand for military materiel and personnel put jail construction on hold.

The end of World War II on V-J Day found many counties still using their nineteenth-century prisons. Although substantial in structure, some of these jails were nearly sixty years old

San Augustine
County jail, 1883–
1919, San Augus-
tine, Texas. (The
building is now an
architect's office.)

and were not up to code in the view of then modern penologists. The period of postwar jail construction would become
another interesting story, as the jails deteriorated and overcrowding became a serious problem in the 1960s. The Texas
Department of Corrections (TDC) soon became involved in
precedent-setting litigation in the *Ruiz v. Estelle* class-action suit
against the TDC (Kemerer, 361). The outcome would have a
long-term effect, as counties began tearing down old jails and
building new ones to comply with the mandates of the new
Texas Commission on Jail Standards, which was formed by the
Sixty-fourth Legislature in 1975. The result has been the loss of
many historic buildings. Recent years have seen an enlightened
consciousness, and some counties have preserved their old jails
and converted them into museums, libraries, or civic centers.

THE BUILDERS

The construction of jails varied across the state and over
time—from the simplest log cabin without plumbing in
the 1840s to modern buildings with all utilities by 1940. The

philosophy of punishment changed as well, gradually becoming
more humane, and this was reflected by the early dungeons' giving way to more sanitary, better lighted, and more spacious cells.
Early jails were the homemade product of citizens who had limited time and little sympathy for the convicted, in contrast to the
plethora of penologists, social workers, psychologists, lawyers,
and media personalities whose vocation is now to plead the prisoners' case. Today we are taken aback by the swift, often harsh,
punishment that was meted out in the absence of facilities required for long-term incarceration. Flogging, confinement, and
doubtless some unjustified hangings were the expedient punishments. Jail development depended on three professions: architects, builders, and jail-cell manufacturers.

The Architects

Jail architects first came to Texas probably in the late 1870s
(I have been unable to document the work of any architect before 1879). The cornerstones on many jails and courthouses,
however, show no architects' names, even though the designs of
the buildings speak clearly of professional talent. The stones always clearly define the names of the county commissioners and
the county judge who doled out funds from the county coffers,
but they are silent on the subject of the architect.

Nine architects each designed at least one jail during the
1870s, and Jacob Larmour and E. H. Klerk planned two: the
Travis and Milam county jails. During the next twenty years,
thirty-one architects created some of the most interesting and
remarkable structures built in the state. Eugene T. Heiner
(1852–1901), Houston architect, alone planned and supervised
sixteen new jails between 1880 and 1900. Two brothers, Frederick Ruffini (?–1885) of Austin, and Oscar Ruffini (1858–1957)
of San Angelo, designed five jails each.

During the next forty years, more than one hundred architects would design and build in excess of 160 jails, not counting
those that were built by the jail-cell manufacturers using their
own designers. For instance, Pauly Jail Building and Manufacturing Company of St. Louis designed fourteen jails that they
also built, complete from top to bottom, including bricks, mortar, cells, and keys. Jails were suddenly big business, and it is
small wonder that the manufacturers would design lockups to fit

their fabricated cells and ironwork. Diebold Safe and Lock Company designed and contracted two buildings, and a late-comer, Southern Structural Steel Company of San Antonio, founded in 1898, designed and built four (appendix B).

The Contractors

After the architectural plans were completed, contractors were asked to bid on a project. Usually a local contractor was able to win the contract: Ninety-seven contractors each built one or two jails in their own area. The big exception was the firm of Martin, Byrnes, and Johnson, which built twelve jails between 1877 and 1906. It seems that much of their work was done without the benefit of an architect, although they apparently had some design help in certain cases. In this book I have made no distinction between jails built with architectural assistance and those built without.

Pauly Jail Building and Manufacturing Company won seventeen contracts for construction and ironwork, and Diebold Safe and Lock Company provided the construction and cells for twelve counties. The records I consulted did not always specify the division of responsibilities since the makers of the cells were capable of carrying out any or all of the aspects of the project.

Jail Manufacturers

In the beginning, the ironwork that was used to confine prisoners was simple and consisted of steel bars of variable quality over the windows and doors. The earlier dungeons had no windows or at best a single, small barred window high up beyond the prisoners' reach. As time passed, jail manufacturers' products became more sophisticated, and the quality of the steel improved.

Peter Joseph Pauly, born in 1832 in Coblentz, Germany, founded Pauly Jail Building and Manufacturing. At age fourteen, he moved to America and became a blacksmith's apprentice in St. Louis at three dollars per month. He worked as a machinist and blacksmith from 1849 to 1856, when his brother John joined him as steamboat blacksmith. In 1870 the brothers began to manufacture prison and jail equipment. As their business grew, they began calling themselves the Pauly Jail Building and Manufacturing Company and moved their quarters to include a whole block on DeKalb Street in St. Louis. The jail cells were designed, constructed, and assembled at the plant, then disassembled and shipped to the new or remodeled jail, where they were reassembled in place. Within a few years Pauly dominated the market for jail equipment, and the company's products were sold all over the United States. Pauly products were used in fifty-eight Texas county jails. In 1889 founder P. J. Pauly died, but the business continued under the leadership of his son, P. J. Pauly Jr. The company's only serious competition was Diebold Safe and Lock. Pauly continued to sell jails in Texas through the first quarter of the twentieth century until a new company, Southern Structural Steel in San Antonio, began to control the Texas market. As new jail construction slowed down during the Depression and World War II, Pauly began to falter and finally declared bankruptcy in 1964.

In 1887 Pauly developed an invention by W. H. Brown and Benjamin Haugh called a rotary jail. It consisted of a central steel arbor around which pie-shaped prison cells were mounted. As a hand crank rotated the arbor, each cell would come into alignment with a single vestibule into which the prisoner could enter from his cell. A number of these carousels were sold in the Midwest and one each to Grayson and Ellis counties in Texas. Because of mechanical problems, the concept did not catch on, and those counties soon replaced these units with a more traditional jail.

Karl Diebold founded Diebold Safe and Lock in 1859 for the manufacture of safes. In 1872 the company moved to Canton, Ohio, where the expanded facility allowed the business to begin manufacturing bank vaults and jail cells. Like Pauly, Diebold manufactured, assembled, and then disassembled jails for shipment. Diebold also made iron jail doors and trapdoors for gallows. The company invented the "link lever lock" system, which allowed the jailer to open individual cell doors from outside the cell block. By the turn of the century, the company had phased out this division of its operation and begun to concentrate on bank vaults, safes, and locking devices. L. T. Noyes was Diebold's agent in Texas, and he built or provided the prison equipment for at least eighteen jails there.

Southern Steel Company was founded in San Antonio, Texas, in 1897 by David Franklin Youngblood (1869–1954). Originally Youngblood Brothers Steel, the company changed its name first to Southern Structural Steel in 1903, Southern Prison Company in 1927, and finally Southern Steel in 1943. At age fourteen, Youngblood began working for Hull Construction, a manufacturer of jails, in Troy, Alabama, where he learned the business. In his early twenties he developed tuberculosis and was advised by his doctor to move to a dry climate. He applied to the Pauly Company of St. Louis to be their sales agent in Texas but was turned down because of his poor health. Youngblood then moved to Uvalde, Texas, but within a year relocated to San Antonio, where he started his own firm in 1897.

He bought five hundred acres of land on the southern edge of San Antonio and built a plant for the manufacture of steel products—steel vaults, bridges, and jails. Soon his two brothers joined him to form a partnership, and in 1927 the three discontinued the construction business and focused on manufacturing jails. They developed several patents for jail cell doors and locking mechanisms. One interesting innovation in jail bars was the development of a hollow cylinder with a loose steel bar in the center. The company boasts that not one of its bars has ever been compromised. When an effort was made to saw through a bar, the loose core bar turned inside and was not cut. By 1940 Southern Steel had built or provided jail equipment for at least thirty-nine jails in Texas and had developed a national market.

A note on sources to the armchair or roadside historian

The invaluable *New Handbook of Texas* (1996) is cited in every entry that follows. Also very useful are the *Texas Almanac,* published biennially in odd-numbered years by the *Dallas Morning News,* and Leon Metz's *Roadside History of Texas* (1994).

Almost all of the 254 counties noted in this book have local museums or libraries that are devoted in part to law enforcement. They are too numerous to list, and their hours of operation are flexible. Check with the local visitor's bureau or chamber of commerce for more information.

The
County Jails
of Texas

Anderson County (Palestine)

Anderson County was named for Kenneth Lewis Anderson, vice president of the Republic of Texas from 1844 to 1846, when Texas was annexed to the United States. The county seat was named for Palestine, Illinois, a local minister's hometown. Nearby was Fort Houston, one of a few stockade forts built in 1836 by early Texas Rangers for protection against Indians.

On October 4, 1846, the county commissioners ordered a jail to be built. The county had no courthouse—only a rented house or temporary building. The jail was the dungeon type, which had a first floor accessible only by a trapdoor in the second story. Typically the dungeon was a 20′ by 20′ structure with double walls of 12″ square oak timbers with a 6″ space between them filled with 5″ vertical logs. (Specifications for this jail were changed to 18″ square in November 1846; rock was placed one foot above and below ground.) The first story was 10′ high. The lower room had two 18″ square windows that were double barred both inside and out, with 1″ thick iron bars placed 4″ apart. The upper story was reached by out-side stairs through a door of a strength proportional to the building. The floor of the second story was made of 10″ square oak timbers crossed with 2″ oak planks secured with 4″ iron spikes. The second floor had a double trapdoor, opening

Anderson County jail, 1879–1931, Palestine, Texas. Designed by architects Clayton and Lynch. Photo courtesy of David Andrews, director, Museum of East Texas Culture, Palestine, Texas.

down into the dungeon with a ladder to admit or withdraw prisoners. The outer wall was built on a 4' stone foundation extending 3' below grade. By February 22, 1847, the jail was complete at a cost of $1,037.50. In January of that year, bids were taken for a courthouse to be completed by May 1847.

In 1879 the county commissioners decided that a new jail was needed. The resulting building indicated the growing wealth of the region and the development of architectural specialization in public buildings. A two-story jail—18' square—of limestone laid one foot above and below ground was constructed diagonally across the street from the courthouse square. The architects were Clayton and Lynch of Galveston. The contractors, Jones and Ligon, built the structure, complete with a clock tower, in six months for $19,379.80. The Pauly Jail Building and Manufacturing Company provided architectural advice as well as cells. The clock in the tower was maintained and wound weekly by P. A. Kolstad, a local jeweler. In 1931, the old 1879 jail was replaced on its original location with a new lockup that was used until 1982. Currently the facility is empty and unused, though for a brief time it served as a juvenile detention center.

Interview conducted by the author: David Andrews, curator, Museum for East Texas Culture.
Other resources: Tyler, Barnett, and Barkley, eds., *New Handbook of Texas*, vol. 2, 1105, 1112; Neyland, *Anderson County Courthouse; Dallas Morning News, Texas Almanac, 1998–1999.*

Andrews County (Andrews)

Andrews County was created in 1876 but not organized until 1910. At that time, the population was 975. The county was named for Richard Andrews, a Fort Bend County pioneer who was the sole Texan fatality at the battle of Concepción on October 28, 1835 (the preamble to the battle of San Antonio).

The first jail, built in 1930, was a modest two-story rectangular building of yellow brick in Texas Renaissance style. The sheriff's quarters were on the first floor, but the edifice had no gallows since it was built after state legislation was passed in 1923 forbidding executions in the local counties. When the facility was built, Andrew

Andrews County jail, 1930–1956, Andrews, Texas. Designed by architects Becker and Dixon. Photo by Stanley Gilbert. From the author's collection.

County's population was 736, although oil production would increase the population over the next few years. The firm of Becker and Dixon provided architectural services; the cells, ironwork, and probably architectural advice, however, were supplied by the Southern Prison Company of San Antonio. The structure was used until 1956, when the courthouse was remodeled and the jail cells were moved to the second and third floors. Now considered unsafe, the jail building is unoccupied.

Interview conducted by the author: Sheriff Wayne Farmer.
Other resources: Tyler, Barnett, and Barkley, eds., *New Handbook of Texas,* vol. 1, 178, and vol. 2, 255; Kelsey and Dyal, *Courthouses of Texas;* Kingston, Harris, and Bailey, eds., *Texas Almanac, 1984–1985; Dallas Morning News, Texas Almanac, 1996–1997;* William C. Davis, *Three Roads to the Alamo;* DeLorme Mapping, *Texas Atlas and Gazetteer.*

Angelina County (Lufkin)

Angelina County was created and organized in 1846. The county (population 1,845 in 1850) was named after Angelina, an Indian woman who was baptized by Spanish priests and later served as an interpreter for Louis Juchereau de St. Denis's expedition into East Texas in 1716 and 1717. It has had four county seats: Marion, 1846; Jonesville, 1854; Homer, 1858; and finally Lufkin, 1892. Marion, known in 1828 as

Angelina County jail, 1925–1955, Lufkin, Texas. (The cat-walk to the courthouse was removed in 1951.)

McNeill's Landing, is located about thirteen miles east of Lufkin, near the Angelina River; until 1882, it was the northern terminus of regular steamboat service from the Sabine Pass and the Gulf of Mexico. The town of Lufkin was founded in 1882 as a stop on the Houston and East and West Texas Railroad line to Shreveport. The town was named after E. P. Lufkin, an engineer who was working on the construction of the railroad.

The first jail in Angelina County was in Homer. According to legend, the survey crew routing the new railroad planned to go through the town. One Saturday night the crew celebrated too much in Homer, and Constable W. B. Green put them in jail. The next morning they paid a fine and were released, but the survey superintendent was so infuriated that he changed the route to bypass Homer and go to Denman Springs, later called Lufkin.

In 1892, a jail was built in Lufkin on the southeast corner of the courthouse square, facing south. That facility served for thirty-four years until replaced in 1926 by a new building on the north side of the courthouse, facing north. The 1926 jail, which still stands, was built by Southern Structural Steel of San Antonio and cost fifty-nine thousand dollars. It originally had a catwalk connecting it to the second floor of the courthouse, but the walkway was removed during remodeling in 1951. In 1955, the jail was moved to the top floor of the new county courthouse, but that lockup has now been replaced by a new facility.

Interviews conducted by the author: Texas Historical Commission; Bonnie Killiam, historian; Edward T. McFarland, county judge; Nancy Croom Wilson, curator, Photo Collection, Museum of East Texas; Margaret Bullock; Franklin Weeks, president, Angelina County Forum; John Wilkins, librarian, Kurth Memorial Library.

Other resources: Tyler, Barnett, and Barkley, eds., *New Handbook of Texas,* vol. 1, 180, vol. 4, 510, and vol. 5, 755; DeLorme Mapping, *Texas Atlas and Gazetteer;* Wortham, *History of Texas;* Commissioners' Court Record, D 158–66, F 122; Haltom, *History and Description of Angelina County, Texas.*

Aransas County (Rockport)

Aransas County was created in 1871 and organized in 1872. The county was carved out of Refugio County, one of the original counties formed by the Republic of Texas in 1836. Rockport, previously the county seat of Refugio County, was made county seat of the new Aransas County.

Throughout its history, Aransas County has witnessed its share of interesting events. It is believed that the area was visited by Alonso de Piñeda, a Spanish explorer, in 1519; by Cabeza de Vaca in 1528; and by René-Robert Cavelier, Sieur de La Salle, in 1685. During the early nineteenth century, it was the export and import facility for the towns of Bexar and Refugio. The Spanish briefly fortified Live Oak Peninsula (near present-day Aransas County airport), but Indian raids led to its abandonment. Zachary Taylor is said to have established his main camp on Live Oak Peninsula before moving against Mexico during the Mexican War. The first jail of record—

designed by James Riely Gordon in 1890—was built with an elaborate courthouse. That edifice, described by Willard Robinson as "Moorish Stylistic,"

Aransas County jail (right background), 1890–1955, Rockport, Texas. Designed by architect J. Riely Gordon. Photo courtesy of the Texas State Historical Association, Austin.

was unusual and attracted national attention for its architect. The sheriff's quarters were on the first floor; the ironwork and cells for prisoners on the second floor were probably provided by the P. J. Pauly Company of St. Louis.

In 1919 a severe hurricane struck Rockport, and for several weeks the lockup provided refuge for a number of families. Nell Mundane Reed lived in the jail from 1941 to 1955, while her father was deputy sheriff. She recalls "playing school" with the prisoners, who were locked up on the second floor. Nell would place her "desk" on the lawn below the windows and pass papers up and down to the prisoners by a string so she could grade their work. On one occasion, she remembers, her father heard a strange noise at night and, upon investigation, found that several prisoners had dug through the brick wall and were about to lower themselves on a rope made from bedsheets. The two-story brick jail was used until 1955.

Interviews conducted by the author: Genevieve Hunt, Nell Mundane Reed.

Other resources: Tyler, Barnett, and Barkley, eds., *New Handbook of Texas*, vol. 1, 217, and vol. 5, 638; *Dallas Morning News, Texas Almanac, 1996–1997;* Kelsey and Dyal, *Courthouses of Texas;* DeLorme Mapping, *Texas Atlas and Gazetteer;* W. Robinson, *People's Architecture.*

Archer County (Archer City)

Archer County was created in 1858 and organized in 1880, when it had a population of 596. Archer County was part of the Peters colony, a grant in 1841 by the Republic of Texas to twenty English and American investors headed by William S. Peters. The colony's troubled history was aggravated in 1845, when the company hired Henry O. Hedgecoxe, an abrasive Englishman, as its agent. Finally, in 1852, armed and disgruntled colonists drove Hedgecoxe out in what was known as the Hedgecoxe War.

The first jail, built in 1882, was a 16' square wooden structure of 4" by 6" pine boards laid on top of one another and nailed down with large spikes. A small window in each of two walls provided ventilation, and the entrance was closed with a steel door. This facility was used until replaced by a stone jail in 1910; the original structure was then used as quarters for the courthouse janitor.

The second jail, built in 1910, was

Archer County jail, 1874–1910, Archer City, Texas. Photo by the author.

a three-story sandstone building with living quarters for the sheriff on the ground floor. It cost $17,250.50 and had a gallows complete with an observation room for witnesses. In 1911, however, Archer County passed an ordinance prohibiting hanging, thus preempting the Texas state law of 1923 outlawing executions at the county level. The architect is unknown; the manufacturer of the jail cells is uncertain, but a plaque on the cell-locking mechanism says "Lever Locking System Sliding Door Pat. June 25 1918." This suggests that modifications were made after the jail was completed. The first prisoner to "enjoy" the new accommodations was a man who had been arrested for horse theft, a serious offense in those days. The jail was used until 1974 and held more than eight thousand prisoners during those sixty-four years.

Interviews conducted by the author: Lavell Beesinger, secretary to Archer County Judge Paul O. Wylie; Deputy Clerk Vickie Ross Lear, Archer County; Delores Cox, Archer County Museum.

Other resources: Tyler, Barnett, and Barkley, eds., *New Handbook of Texas*, vol. 1, 224, and vol. 5, 167; W. Robinson, *People's Architecture*; Cowden, *Historical Texas County Jails*.

Armstrong County (Claude)

Armstrong County was created in 1876 and organized in 1890, when the population was 944. Claude (originally Armstrong City), Texas, grew up along the Fort Worth and

Armstrong County jail, 1894–1953, Claude, Texas.
Equipped by Pauly Jail Manufacturing. Photo courtesy of
Jean Dobbs.

Denver City Railway built across the northern part of Armstrong County in 1887. In 1890, Claude was declared the county seat after Charles Goodnight, the famous early rancher, broke a tie vote. The first jail was a wooden calaboose—Texas slang for the Spanish word *calabozo,* meaning "prison." In 1894 the calaboose was replaced by a two-story stone structure built by Pauly Jail Company for $14,000. Stone was quarried fourteen miles south of Claude and hauled to the site by wagon and mule for $1.50 per day. The walls of the building are said to have been twenty inches thick. The Romanesque Revival edifice with its domed tower faced southeast, one block west of the town square. The tower held a water tank that was filled from the public well on the square, then piped to the kitchen and the bath upstairs. In 1954, the old jail was torn down, and a modern two-story structure was built using the original stone and cells. The cost was $40,000. In 1970, the *Amarillo Daily News* interviewed Mrs. Tiny McFarland about living in the old jail when her father, Pat Lynch, was sheriff. Her mother cooked for the family and the prisoners, too, so they all enjoyed the same menu. Her mother washed the jail laundry, often with the help of a trustee. Mrs. McFarland and the other children were not allowed on the second floor, but they would talk to the inmates from the yard below and sometimes pass candy up to them by a string. During the fifty-eight years that the jail was in use, only three prisoners escaped. One Chinese inmate, when released, returned to China and periodically sent gifts back to the McFarlands.

Interviews conducted by the author: Kim Wright, Texas Historical Commission; Ardyth Bagwell, historian; Sheriff Carmella Jones.

Other resources: *Dallas Morning News, Texas Almanac, 1996–1997;* Tyler, Barnett, and Barkley, eds., *New Handbook of Texas,* vol. 2, 144.

Atascosa County (Jourdanton)

A*tascosa,* the Spanish word for "boggy," was used as a name for south central Texas as early as the mid-eighteenth century. In fact, it describes much of the county, especially the southern part. The area was organized in 1856, and Navatasco, now nonexistent, was made the county seat. Pleasanton became the seat of government in 1858 and remained so until the seat was moved to Jourdanton in 1910.

According to court testimony by P. B. Winn, age seventy-five in 1937, the first jail he remembered as a child in Pleasanton was a log building in which he lived when his father was the jailer. The 1872 *Western Stock Journal* describes a jail, probably the same

Atascosa County jail, 1915–1952, Jourdanton, Texas. Designed by architect Henry T. Phelps.

one, as a 12' deep hole with a roof and a trapdoor over it. Another jail, built in 1875, measured 22' by 28' with two stories. On the first floor were two cells with a walk-around; the jailer's quarters were on the second floor. A third keep was built about 1890 with sheriff's quarters on the first floor. This was a two-story, brick-and-stone building in the French Third Empire style. The similarity of this structure and the one by Eugene Heiner in Bee County suggests that Heiner was the architect.

After the county seat moved to Jourdanton in 1910, a rental house served as a jail until a new lockup was built in 1915 at a cost of twenty thousand dollars. Henry T. Phelps of San Antonio designed the facility, which was constructed by Southern Structural Steel of concrete with brick veneer. On the first floor were offices and sheriff's quarters; cells were located on the second floor; and the third floor contained a gallows with trapdoor. The gallows was never used. The jail still stands today and is used as a juvenile probation center, having served its primary purpose until 1982, when a modern facility was built.

Interviews conducted by the author: Judge Taylor Brite; Christopher Hill, juvenile probation officer; Peggy Steinle, Texas Historical Commission; Phyllis Metcalf of Lockhart, Texas, historian.

Other resources: *Dallas Morning News, Texas Almanac, 1996–1997* and *1998–1999;* Tyler, Barnett, and Barkley, eds., *New Handbook of Texas,* vol. 1, 157, 273; W. Robinson, *People's Architecture;* Atascosa County Court Record, Jan. 25, 1875; District Court Record, 1937; Atascosa Historical Committee, *Atascosa County History.*

Austin County (Bellville)

Austin County, with a population of about fifteen hundred in the mid-1830s, was one of the original counties created by the Republic of Texas in 1836. The area was within the original land grant to Moses Austin in 1820 and was organized by his son, Stephen Austin, in 1822. The grant extended from the Lavaca River in the west to the Trinity River in the east and from the Gulf of Mexico to the Old San Antonio Road.

The first county seat was San Felipe de Austin, near present-day Sealy, Texas, which was the site chosen by Stephen Austin in 1823 for the

Austin County jail, 1896–1982, Bellville, Texas. Equipped by Pauly Jail Manufacturing.

place of government for his colony. It became the county seat of Austin County when Texas became a republic in 1836. Texas was annexed by the United States in 1846, and in 1848 the Austin County seat was moved to Bellville. The new seat of government was named for Thomas B. Bell, an early settler and one of Stephen Austin's Old Three Hundred families.

A wooden jail was built in 1854 by James Ervin and used until 1879. A second keep is said to have existed before 1896, but this is not confirmed. In February 1896, an ad was run in the *Galveston Daily News* for bids to build a new prison. In March 1896, two bids were received, one from Pauly Company for $19,970 and the other from Diebold Safe and Lock of Canton, Ohio, for $19,840. Pauly was awarded the contract, possibly because the company had built an almost identical jail for Milam County in 1895. A Pauly architect drew the plans and subcontracted the construction to F. B. and W. S. Hull Brothers of Dallas.

The three-story Bellville building, with a gallows on the fourth floor, was built of red brick and accented with white stone lintels. The first floor contained an office and living quarters for the sheriff; cells were on the second floor. According to Pearl Meyer, who lived in the jail with her husband, Deputy Sheriff Cotton Noviskie, the jail could accommodate thirty-two prisoners with four to each cell. As was the custom at that time, Pearl Meyer cooked for her husband as well as the prisoners. The jail was remodeled in 1921 by Southern Struc-

tural Steel Company and was used until 1982. It is currently a
museum.

Interviews conducted by the author: Pearl Meyer, Austin County Jail
Museum; Robert A. Neely, historian.

Other resources: *Dallas Morning News, Texas Almanac, 1996–1997;* Tyler,
Barnett, and Barkley, eds., *New Handbook of Texas,* vol. 1, 303–304, and
vol. 5, 840; Kelsey and Dyal, *Courthouses of Texas;* W. Robinson, *People's
Architecture.*

Bailey County (Muleshoe)

Bailey County was created in 1876, but it was not organized until forty-one years later—in 1917. The county
was named for Peter J. Bailey, defender of the Alamo. The
population grew very slowly because the XIT and other large
ranches controlled most of the county. In 1900 the county
population was 4, and in 1920 it was 517. In 1919 Muleshoe
was voted the county seat, and in that same year, the commissioners' court approved spending one hundred dollars to buy
and move a twelve-year-old secondhand wooden jail from
Parmer County. Roy Barber was paid fifteen dollars to deliver
it to Muleshoe. It is said that in 1919, Sheriff H. A. Douglas
had the new jail moved close to his house so he could watch it
and take care of the prisoners at the same time.

Bailey County's second and present jail was incorporated
into the new brick courthouse built in 1925 for sixty thousand
dollars. McButler and Company of Lubbock was the architectural firm; the ironwork and cells, however, were built by
Southern Structural Steel. The Bailey County jail has been
troubled in recent years by a ghost that the inmates see from
time to time. Stories of the phantom began in 1979, when a
prisoner who was being held for the murder of his girlfriend
hanged himself in a cell. *County Magazine* (July–Aug. 1997)
has a full account of this troublesome specter, a problem that
Sheriff Jerry Hicks was not able to put to rest. Sheriff Hicks
has now retired, but it is said that the prisoners still insist that
the light be left on at night.

Interview conducted by the author: Sheriff Jerry Hicks.

Other resources: *Dallas Morning News, Texas Almanac, 1996–1997;* Tyler, Barnett, and Barkley, eds., *New Handbook of Texas,* vol. 1, 338; James Haley, "The XIT Ranch of Texas," *County Magazine* (July–Aug. 1997); County Commissioners' Court Minutes, June 11, 1919.

Bandera County (Bandera)

Bandera County was organized in 1856 and named for either the historic Bandera Pass or the Bandera Mountains, which dominate the topography of the county. It is unclear why *bandera,* the Spanish word for "flag," was given to the area. The pass was a historic trail between the Medina and the Guadalupe rivers, used by the Indians, the Spanish, Texas Rangers, and the U.S. Army. In 1842, Comanche Indians at Bandera Pass ambushed Texas Rangers under Jack Hayes. The Rangers defeated them with the Colt revolvers they had inherited from the Texas Navy.

The first jail in Bandera County, date unknown, was located on the site presently occupied by the Bandera County Library. It was a 14' square building built of 6" square cypress timbers and had one small window at the top but no door. Access was by ladder to a flat roof fitted with a trapdoor. Prisoners were first taken up the outside ladder; the ladder was then raised and put down through the trapdoor for them to descend. Afterward, the ladder was pulled up and the trapdoor closed. Difficult prisoners were chained to an iron ring bolted to the floor. It is said that no one ever escaped from this

Bandera County jail, 1881–1930, Bandera, Texas.

jail. Texas Ranger Jim Gillett, reminiscing about 1877 events surrounding the old log structure, said, "I remember a scout over in Bandera County. In one week's time, we caught ten or twelve fugitives and literally filled the little jail in Bandera."

The 1881 jail was designed by architect Alfred Giles, and the contractor was James A. Courtney. In the middle of the large central room was a double-deck cage. Prisoners were apparently allowed out of the cages and into the room at large for exercise. The door to the cells could be operated and secured from outside the central room. Mellie Ruth Smith Weed, whose father, Sam Smith, was the popular sheriff from 1905 to 1917, lived next to the jail as a child. She recalled helping her father feed the prisoners and sometimes, though forbidden to do so, sneaking in and talking to them.

About 1930 a new jail, a single-story concrete building with stucco finish, was built east of the courthouse. Other details are not now available because that facility was incorporated into a new law enforcement building in 1970. From the outside, there is no evidence of the old jail.

Interviews conducted by the author: Allen Mansfield, historian; Peggy Tobin, Bandera County historian.

Other resources: Jones, *Texas History Carved in Stone;* Gillett and Quaife, *Six Years with the Texas Rangers;* Haven and Belden, *History of the Colt Revolver;* W. Robinson and Webb, *Texas Public Buildings of the Nineteenth Century;* Weed, "Mellie Ruth Smith Weed"; Cowden, *Historical Texas County Jails.*

Bastrop County (Bastrop)

Bastrop County was one of the original twenty-three counties formed by the Republic of Texas in 1836. It was known by the Mexican designation "Mina municipality" until 1837, when the name was changed to Bastrop in honor of Baron de Bastrop (whose real name was Philip Bogel). Bastrop, or Bogel, had fled from Holland when he was accused of embezzling tax funds. He had helped Moses Austin obtain his Spanish land grant for colonization in 1820. The

area now
known as
Bastrop
County
was part of
Austin's sec-
ond land
grant, that
of 1831.

The first
jail in Bas-
trop County
was built in

Bastrop County jail, 1891–1974, Bastrop, Texas. Designed
by architect Eugene Heiner.

1839. It was supposed to have been a two-story 11' by 18' log
building that may have been in the traditional dungeon design.
In 1851, the county approved spending five thousand dollars
for a courthouse containing a lockup. Apparently the commissioners grew weary of the prisoners' proximity to the court
while in session, so in 1859 they ordered a separate 36' by 40'
jail, two stories high and with brick walls eighteen inches thick.

Presently standing on the courthouse square is the beautiful
1891 jail, which was used until 1974. When built, the 1891 jail
cost $15,312, including $2,540 for iron prison cells that were
provided by the Pauly Company. The architect was Eugene
Heiner of Houston; the contractor was Martin, Byrnes, and
Johnson. This Second Empire design has three floors with
sheriff's quarters of five rooms, bath, and kitchen on the first
floor. The second and third floors contained prison cells and
were said to be capable of holding sixty convicts before the
regulations put forth in the prison reform of the 1970s.

The 1891 jail did not contain a gallows, but the third floor
had a space where a temporary one could be constructed. A
ring for the rope was affixed to the rafters in the steeple and
suspended over the space for the platform, allowing for a drop
of eight feet. In 1892, an African American, who proclaimed
his innocence to the last, was hanged for murder, and in 1893
another African American was also hanged for murder. A third
man, who was white and described as an outlaw who had

killed thirteen people, was hanged on an unknown date. The historic building has been well restored, and some of the old cells have been preserved. The building is now used for the Bastrop Chamber of Commerce, certain county offices, and storage.

Interview conducted by the author: Valerie Johnson, Bastrop Historical Commission.

Other resources: McCollum, *Discover Bastrop's Historic Old Jail; Dallas Morning News, Texas Almanac, 1996–1997;* Tyler, Barnett, and Barkley, eds., *New Handbook of Texas,* vol. 1, 412; Kelsey and Dyal, *Courthouses of Texas;* W. Robinson, *People's Architecture;* W. Robinson and Webb, *Texas Public Buildings of the Nineteenth Century.*

Baylor County (Seymour)

Organized in 1879, Baylor County was named for H. W. Baylor, who practiced medicine in LaGrange, Texas, until he enlisted as a private in the Texas Rangers during the Mexican War. He participated in the assault on Monterrey, after which he was made regimental surgeon and remained with the Monterrey garrison. Later he practiced in Independence, Texas.

As was true in many of the western counties, hostile Indians prevented settlement or even exploration until 1853. Fort Belknap on the Brazos River in Young County was founded in the summer of 1851 as part of a string of forts to protect settlers against the Indian raids. The fort, though modest and troubled by a poor water supply, remained open until it was abandoned during the Civil War. Col. C. C. Mills led a group of settlers to the region in 1863, but the occupation failed because of repeated Indian raids, which grew in intensity in the absence of U.S. military forces during the Civil War.

Seymour was designated the county seat in 1879. The town was originally named Oregon City, but the name was changed in 1879 to honor a local cowboy, Seymour Munday. Built in 1883, Baylor County's first jail was used until it was demolished in 1967. Baylor County Sheriff Arch Holmes was resting at home in Seymour on a hot day in July 18, 1934, listening to Fort Worth radio station WBAP. The noon broadcast was about W. Lee O'Daniel's Light Crust Doughboys band (O'Daniel was governor of Texas from January 1939 through July 1941 and served in the U.S. Senate in 1941 and 1942). The station interrupted the program to announce that the bank at Albany had been robbed and that the robbers were headed north toward Seymour. Sheriff Holmes quickly grabbed his rifle, got in his car, and headed south looking for the crooks. Recognizing the car described in the announcement, the sheriff turned in pursuit. What followed was a high-speed chase over back roads, a change to another car, and pursuit through two counties, all the while exchanging gunfire with the bandits. Finally they were cornered at the end of a dead-end road on the Knox and Baylor county line. The fugitives, Jimmy Lucas and Jack Hardin, were wanted in several counties, but first option went to Shackelford County, where they were placed in the county jail. Court was in session, and both men pleaded guilty and received life sentences.

The three-story Baylor County jail was built in 1883 of local limestone and served the county until about 1970. It had sheriff's quarters on the first floor. Details about the architect and builder are unavailable.

Interviews conducted by the author: L. D. ("Jack") Jones; Doris Rushing, county clerk; Ellen Arnold, librarian.

Other resources: Jack Jones, *Baylor County Museum News,* Aug. 27, 1998; Tyler, Barnett, and Barkley, eds., *New Handbook of Texas,* vol. 1, 426; Kelsey and Dyal, *Courthouses of Texas;* DeLorme Mapping, *Texas Atlas and Gazetteer;* Hart, *Old Forts of the Southwest;* C. Robinson, *Frontier Forts of Texas.*

Bee County (Beeville)

Bee County was created in 1857 and organized in 1858, when the population was about six hundred. Beeville, on Medio Creek about ten miles east of present-day Beeville, was made the county seat, but the seat of government was

Bee County jail, 1893–1936, Beeville, Texas. Designed by architect Eugene Heiner. Photo courtesy of Sheriff Robert L. Horn.

moved west to Maryville in 1859. Shortly afterward, the name was changed to Beeville-on-the-Poesta.

According to Bee County historians, before the first jail was built, local citizens were paid to guard prisoners. The first jail of record was a frame double-walled building of board-and-batten construction built in 1874 at a cost of $1,381.74. An iron box near the single door has a "Pauly of St. Louis" plaque on it, but it is unclear when the sign was installed. In 1893, Bee County built a beautiful French Second Empire–style jail designed by Eugene Heiner, with cells and ironwork by Pauly. The structure cost $16,540 and served for forty-three years. That building was demolished in 1936, however, to make room for a new two-story lockup built by Southern Prison Company (also known as Southern Structural Steel). Although the 1936 structure was remodeled in 1979, it was finally replaced by a modern law enforcement facility in 1989.

There is a record of two public hangings in Beeville, one in 1871 and another in 1877, but these hangings did not occur in the jail. The scaffold for these executions was built on the west lawn of the courthouse.

Interviews conducted by the author: Sheriff Robert L. Horn; David Bucek, architect and historian.

Other resources: Ezell, *Historical Story of Bee County;* Tyler, Barnett, and Barkley, eds., *New Handbook of Texas,* vol. 1, 459.

Bell County (Belton)

Some settlement took place in Bell County as early as 1830 but was abandoned during the "Runaway Scrape" in April 1836. After the battle of San Jacinto, the county was re-occupied. In June 1836 the settlers fled again after a Comanche raid on Fort Parker in Limestone County. In the fall of 1836, however, George Erath built a fort on Little River, and settlers gradually returned. The following two years, 1837 and 1838, were troubled by four major Indian battles. These and the Bird's Creek fight between an estimated 240 Indians and thirty-five Texas Rangers in May 1839 caused the abandonment of the Little River Fort and a general withdrawal from the area. The Bird's Creek battle resulted in sizable losses for the Indians as well as seven Rangers dead and three wounded. It was 1843 before occupation of Bell County resumed. In 1850 the county was organized, and Nolan Springs (Nolanville) was designated county seat. The name was changed to Belton in 1851.

Bell County's first jail, constructed in 1854, was a typical dungeon type, built on lot 4, block 22, which is now 210 North Pearl Street. The specifications called for a two-story, 12' square building with double walls of 10" square logs set on a 5' foundation of stone. The stone foundation was set 3' into the ground and extended 10' out from the walls. The first story had no door and only two 10" square windows with bars. An outside stairway led to the second story. Access for prisoners was by a

Bell County jail, 1872–1883, Belton, Texas. The facility has been remodeled and is now a residence.

trapdoor in the center of the second-story floor. The second lockup was built in 1872 on the same site as the first facility, but this two-story structure was built of stone. One year later, nine horse thieves were caught and put in a large cell on the first floor. That night a mob of about three hundred citizens broke in and systematically shot and killed all nine prisoners. Their graves can be seen today in the South Belton Cemetery.

In 1883, a third jail was built on West Central Avenue for thirty-five thousand dollars. The architectural firm of J. N. Preston and Son of Austin designed it; the steel cages and ironwork were made by Pauly Brothers. That jail was used until 1950, but it has now been razed to make room for new construction.

Interviews conducted by the author: Wayman Wallace; Reba Robertson; C. E. Cox, Bell County Sheriff's Department; Vada Sutton, county clerk, Bell County; Lucille Morton, Conroe, Texas.

Other resources: Tyler, Barnett, and Barkley, eds., *New Handbook of Texas,* vol. 1, 450, 472, and vol. 2, 1112; W. P. Webb, *Texas Rangers;* Tyler and Ramsdell, *History of Bell County; Dallas Morning News, Texas Almanac, 1996–1997.*

Bexar County (San Antonio)

It is difficult to recount the history of Bexar County inasmuch as it is lengthy and at the same time central to all of Texas history. Domingo Terán de los Ríos, who found Indian encampments along the San Antonio River, explored the site of San Antonio in 1691. With the arrival in 1731 of immigrants invited by Spain from the Canary Islands, it became the first Spanish municipality in Texas. By 1740, in spite of hardship and epidemics, there were also five self-supporting missions in the area. After 1772 the Spanish missions in East Texas were abandoned, and many of their inhabitants moved to San Antonio. The descendants of the Canary Islanders, however, controlled the best land and became the new aristocracy. The rapidly growing community of San Antonio soon became the center of trade and traffic between Texas and Mexico.

As early as 1778, Father Agustín Morfi complained of the

noise of the
sentinel in
the guard-
house, a
military
stockade
(built about
1764) near
the gover-
nor's palace.
In 1793,
the Alamo
Mission was
secularized,
and part of

The old "Bat Cave," on Military Plaza, San Antonio, Texas, used for Police Headquarters and City Jail. Photo by Brack, in 1890.

Bexar County jail, 1850–1879, San Antonio, Texas (behind the "bat cave" courthouse), on the northwest corner of Military Plaza. Photo courtesy of the Institute of Texan Cultures, University of Texas–San Antonio.

it seems to have been used as a prison in the early nineteenth century.

The Council House, on the northeast corner of Main Plaza and Market Street, was the site of the infamous Council House Fight with the Comanche Indians in 1840, during the days of the Texas Republic. After the fight, the captured Indians were put into a part of the building that was known as the calabozo, which was used as a jail until 1850, when a new courthouse and stone lockup were built on the northwest corner of Military Plaza near the site of the old guardhouse.

The 1850 courthouse was separated from the jail by a two-foot-thick wall that stood fifteen feet high. In time, this courthouse and jail became infested with bats between the walls and in the ceiling and thus came to be called the "bat cave." The jail contained four cells, two upstairs and two down, the lower level poorly ventilated and without drainage, a condition not uncommon in the dungeons widely used at that time.

In 1879 a new jail was built as a result of agitation on the part of the *San Antonio Express*. Originally it had two floors, but in 1911, a third floor complete with a trapdoor and gallows was added. The gallows was used on several occasions, the last time in 1923. After a fourth floor was added in 1926, the original limestone was modernized with a brick veneer, although some of the old stone still remains visible when viewed from a side perspective. This jail was used until 1962, when a new combined city and county jail was completed.

Interviews conducted by the author: Mary Ann Noonan Guerra, San Antonio Conservation Society; Lewis Tucker; Elaine Davis, Daughters of the Republic of Texas.

Other resources: Tyler, Barnett, and Barkley, eds., *New Handbook of Texas,* vol. 1, 517; Mayhall, *Indian Wars of Texas*.

Blanco County (Johnson City)

Created and organized in 1858, Blanco County was named after the Blanco River, which flows through the area. The original county seat was in the town of Blanco. The old Blanco County stone jail, which was originally built on the Blanco courthouse square in 1876 at a cost of $1,500, still stands across the street from the 1885 courthouse. The east side of the facility, however, has been converted into a storefront, so it is not recognizable. The old stone building, 18′ by 14′ and now visible only from the alley to the west, had two rooms. The foundation, sunk 4′ below the ground, was made of 36″ stones and had stone walls that were 21″ thick. The window bars were set 1′ into the stone walls. The door was clad on both sides with solid iron. The first level contained two rooms, and in one of them was a large stone with an iron ring imbedded in it with which to chain unruly prisoners. T. R. Pullis of St. Louis provided the cells and other ironwork for $819; these cells were later moved to Johnson City when the county seat was relocated.

The move to Johnson

Blanco County jail, 1894–present, Johnson City, Texas.

City had both a geographical and a personal basis. After the Civil War, some Blanco County land was taken away while other land was added, thereby removing the town of Blanco from the center of the county. In 1879, James Polk Johnson had founded Johnson City on the Pedernales River. Years of petition and agitation finally resulted in a vote to move the county seat to Johnson City when the new courthouse in the town of Blanco was only five years old.

When the county seat moved to Johnson City in 1890, the basement of the James P. Johnson Building (present site of the Johnson City Bank) was used as a jail at first. In 1893, after three years of dealing with a damp lockup and sick prisoners, the commissioners' court ordered a new jail to be built for $6,450 by Diebold Lock and Safe. Diebold, as prescribed in the contract, employed J. E. K. Dildime of Johnson City to build a new stone structure that was to contain new cells as well as some of the old ones brought from the town of Blanco. That two-story jail on the corner of Pecan Street and Avenue G remains sturdy and is still used for its original purpose, although the interior ironwork has been changed.

Interviews conducted by the author: Joel Honeycutt, Blanco County Historical Association; Roy Byers; Bonnie Riley, Blanco (owner of the 1876 jail).

Other resources: Tyler, Barnett, and Barkley, eds., *New Handbook of Texas*, vol. 1, 583; Moursund, *Blanco County History;* Cowden, *Historical Texas County Jails*.

Borden County (Gail)

Borden County was organized in 1891, fifteen years after it was carved out of Bexar County. There were 222 people in the area at that time, averaging a little more than four square miles per person. The county was named for Gail Borden Jr., the inventor of evaporated milk and founder of the Borden Company, still a producer of milk products today.

Borden County's first and only jail was built in 1896. Earlier prisoners were held in Big Springs in Howard County, about forty-five miles away over primitive roads. One can

imagine how many hours the sheriff spent delivering prisoners to Big Spring and returning with them to the Borden County courthouse

Borden County jail, 1896–1972, Gail, Texas. Photo by Stanley Gilbert. From the author's collection.

for trial. Eventually the county commissioners signed a contract with Diebold Safe and Lock to build a jail for forty-five hundred dollars. Limestone was quarried from nearby Gail Mountain and hauled to the southwestern corner of the courthouse square. The final one-story building was square, with 24″ thick walls. The floor was ⅓″ steel with a 6″ stone subfloor, and the ceiling was made of the same steel. The cell cages, which were set in the center of the room, were made of case-hardened steel plate with 2″ holes cut out to make a latticework. On the outside of the cages was a walkway to allow the jailer to inspect the entire unit.

Not a lot of crime took place in Borden County, and it was only in 1935 that the first murder trial occurred there. In 1940, when the lockup was undergoing remodeling to install plumbing, it was necessary to dig up the floor to install a pipe to run into the cesspool. Before the job was completed, one of the town's regular "customers," who tended to tipple a little too much, happened to get locked up. Discovering himself in jail, he peered into the deep excavation and fell in. Unable to climb out, he crawled along the trench and finally fell into the cesspool outside the keep. The next morning, the sheriff found him sitting on the steps of the building. He said, "Sheriff, I did not mean to break out. I just fell out of jail."

The lockup was used until 1972, when it became more practical to send prisoners to Jones or Dawson County for safekeeping. The facility is no longer approved by the Texas Commission on Jail Standards and is used only for storage.

Interview conducted by the author: Kenneth Bennett, county treasurer, tax collector, and deputy sheriff.

Other resources: *Borden Citizen* 2(4); Tyler, Barnett, and Barkley, eds., *New Handbook of Texas,* vol. 1, 644; Kingston, Harris, and Bailey, eds., *Texas Almanac, 1984–1985; Dallas Morning News, Texas Almanac, 1996–1997;* Metz, *Roadside History of Texas.*

Bosque County (Meridian)

In 1836, the Republic of Texas created twenty-three counties, and two of the largest of these were Bexar and Milam counties. Both were destined to be subdivided, and Bosque County was carved out of Milam County in 1850. The area was organized in 1854, when the population was a little less than two thousand. *Bosque* is Spanish for "woods," and the Bosque River was so named by early Spanish explorers in 1821. Surveyor George Erath laid out a township that was called Meridian after nearby Meridian Creek, which Erath had previously named.

The first Bosque County jail was a 14′ square two-story log building built in 1855, one year after the courthouse was completed. The lower level was buried 4′ below grade. The description suggests that the lockup was of the dungeon type. The log structure was used until 1875, when a new and larger keep, probably of wood, was built.

The 1875 structure was the scene of a double murder on the night of Sunday, December 15, 1878. Tom Horrell and Mart Horrell, suspects in

Bosque County jail, 1895–1979, Meridian, Texas. Photo courtesy of Elizabeth Torrence, Bosque County Collection.

the murder and robbery of J. F. Vaughan, were locked up. Vaughn had been a popular storekeeper who often kept money for other people in his safe. It is said that about fifteen men broke into the jail and threatened to burn the place down, thus persuading the guards to allow them access to the cell containing the two Horrell boys. Many shots were fired into the helpless prisoners. The mob, estimated at between one hundred and three hundred, then rode off into the dark.

A limestone jail built in 1895 was the third prison in Bosque County. John Drew was the contractor who built the two-story building with locally quarried white stone. The cells and ironwork were made by Diebold Lock and Safe. In 1978 the building was bought by Ralston Purina and, despite being registered as a historical marker, was razed in 1979.

Interviews conducted by the author: Elizabeth Bosque Torrence, County Historical Commission chair; James H. Colquin, Waco; Ken Holmes, Dallas historian.

Other resources: Tyler, Barnett, and Barkley, eds., *New Handbook of Texas,* vol. 1, 643; W. Robinson, *People's Architecture;* DeLorme Mapping, *Texas Atlas and Gazetteer;* Sonnichsen, *I'll Die before I'll Run;* Cowden, *Historical Texas County Jails.*

Bowie County (Boston)

Bowie County was formed from part of Red River County in 1840. In the 1830s, Red River County was thought to be part of the state of Arkansas and therefore a part of the United States, causing some confusion in the settlement process. The first county seat of Bowie County, although temporary, was in DeKalb, Texas, twelve miles west of present-day New Boston. Today Boston is the official county seat of Bowie County, even though in 1986 a new county courthouse was built and dedicated in New Boston.

First-time visitors to Bowie County will almost certainly be confused by the names of three towns: Boston, Old Boston, and New Boston. Boston, founded in 1841, was named after a local merchant, W. J. Boston, and not for Boston, Massachusetts. When construction of the Texas and Pacific Railroad

passed four
miles north
of Boston
in 1876,
citizens
arranged
to build a
depot near
the tracks,
and "New
Boston" was
born, al-
though the
county seat

Bowie County jail, 1891–1984, Boston, Texas. Designed by
architect Harry R. Taylor. Photo by Stanley Gilbert. From
the author's collection.

remained at Boston. About 1885, the county seat was moved
to Texarkana but then shifted once again in 1890 to a new site
one mile south of New Boston. Shortly thereafter, the post
office and the name "Boston" were moved to the new site,
and the original community came to be called "Old Boston."

The old Bowie County jail, built in 1891, is perhaps the
main historic feature in Boston, Texas, today. The three-story
brick structure is still standing on the southeast corner of the
old courthouse square and was used until 1984. The 1889
courthouse is gone, having been destroyed by fire in 1986, but
the square has been nicely landscaped by civic-minded Bosto-
nians. The relic jail is said to have been designed by Harry R.
Taylor and built by contractors Sonnefield and Emmons at a
cost of $10,250. It was later remodeled by Southern Prison
Company. It had an adjacent cottage for the sheriff or jailer,
and it contained a gallows as well. Because of the three tiers of
cell blocks it seems large for its time, but it must be remembered that the population in early East Texas was greater than
in the rest of the state. The jail is not used today except on
Halloween, when the school children decorate it for parties.

Interviews conducted by the author: Maryleen Megason, county clerk;
R. L. Anderson; Christine Woodrow, New Boston.

Other resources: Tyler, Barnett, and Barkley, eds., *New Handbook of
Texas,* vol. 1, 658, vol. 2, 566, and vol. 4, 986, 1132; Kelsey and Dyal,
Courthouses of Texas; Cowden, *Historical Texas County Jails.*

Brazoria County (Angleton)

Brazoria County, like Bexar County, played an important part in early Texas history. The area was part of Austin's colony, and many of the Old Three Hundred took land grants there. Stephen Austin's choice for his own land was in Brazoria County, about ten miles south of Brazoria Town on the west bank of the Brazos River. The plantation, called Peach Point, was occupied by his sister, Emily Austin Bryan, and her husband. Brazoria County was one of the original twenty-three counties created by the provisional government organized at San Felipe in November 1835. Henry Smith of Brazoria was elected the first provisional governor of Texas at the Consultation of 1835, and after the battle of San Jacinto, the town of Velasco, at the mouth of the Brazos River, became the seat of the provisional Texas government. On May 14, 1836, Santa Anna signed a peace treaty with Texas at Velasco, so the agreement came to be known as the Treaty of Velasco. Brazoria County was organized on December 20, 1836, and Brazoria became the county seat.

Anticipating the need for a lockup in 1837, the county commissioners directed a two-story jail to be built with double-crib walls of logs, 8″ in diameter, separated by vertical 10″ hewn timbers between the cribs. The jail was large— 44′ by 20′. Though not specified, access to the lower-floor dungeon was typically by a trap-door in the floor of the second story.

The first permanent

Brazoria County jail, 1897–1916, Angleton, Texas. Photo courtesy of Brazoria County Historical Museum.

jail built in Brazoria in 1854 was used until the county seat was
moved to Angleton in 1897. During the early years, both the
county and the city of Brazoria thrived; by 1860 the county
had a population of 7,143. During the Civil War, the Dance
Brothers operated a small-arms manufacturing plant at Brazoria on the banks of the Brazos River and at East Columbia.
These factories were a significant source of small arms for the
Confederacy.

   After the county seat moved to Angleton, a two-story
brick jail was built there. It was replaced in 1916, however,
by a jail on Cedar and Chenouga streets. This was also a two-
story brick building, and it served until 1940, when a new
courthouse with a jail on the fifth floor was constructed.

   Interview conducted by the author: Jamie Murray, librarian.
   Other resources: Kingston, Harris, and Bailey, eds., *Texas Almanac,
1984–1985; Dallas Morning News, Texas Almanac, 1996–1997;* Tyler, Barnett,
and Barkley, eds., *New Handbook of Texas,* vol. 1, 708, vol. 5, 105, and
vol. 6, 718; Wiggins and Sylvia, *Dance and Brothers;* Pierce, *Texas under
Arms;* DeLorme Mapping, *Texas Atlas and Gazetteer;* W. Robinson and
Webb, *Texas Public Buildings of the Nineteenth Century.*

Brazos County (Bryan)

Brazos County was organized in 1843 and named for the
Brazos River, which marks its southwest boundary. The
first county seat was Booneville, which occupied one hundred
acres that were purchased in July 1841; the town was laid out
about three miles east of the present city of Bryan. In 1841,
the county was called Navasota, but the name was changed to
Brazos County in 1842. The jail was built in 1843, three years
before the first courthouse was constructed.

   The 1843 jail in Booneville was a two-story dungeon built
by John C. Crawford for one thousand dollars to be paid in
county bonds. The construction of the log jail is interesting. It
was basically two stories, the first story of which was a double-
walled room within a room, with an 8″ gap between the walls.
The walls were made of 10″ square hand-hewn post oak logs,

and the gap was filled with vertical 8″ post oak logs. The foundation was a double layer of 10″ square post oak hewn logs side by side, covered by a flooring of 2″ oak planks nailed down to the oak timbers. The first story had no door or window, and access was by a 30″ square trapdoor in the center of the floor of the second story. The timbers of that floor lay on top of the two walls of the first story, and the walls were of post oak timbers similar to those in the first story, except that they were only one wall thick rather than two.

During its lifetime, the jail was said to have held only five Brazos County citizens, but it was occupied from time to time by numerous prisoners from surrounding counties. One murder suspect from another county escaped during a severe thunderstorm but returned after several weeks when the court was in session again. He asked the judge to either set bail for him or try him because he would rather hang than spend another night in the dungeon with the millions of fleas that filled every crack and crevice.

Bryan, Texas was founded in 1859 in anticipation of the construction of the Houston and Texas Central Railroad. When building crews reached Millican, Texas, however, work stopped because of the Civil War and did not resume until 1866. That year the county seat moved to Bryan, and a mass movement of people followed from Booneville and Millican to Bryan. The Booneville jail and courthouse were sold, the town gradually died, and today the only thing that remains is the cemetery.

The 1878 jail in Bryan was a two-story castlelike brick structure, complete with turrets, towers, and machicolations above the second floor. It was situated on the courthouse square at 25th and Washington streets. In 1954 it was demolished when a new courthouse with a lockup on the fourth floor was built.

Interviews conducted by the author: Ann Peterson, Bryan Library; Charles R. Schultz, chair, Brazos County Historical Commission.

Other resources: Tyler, Barnett, and Barkley, eds., *New Handbook of Texas,* vol. 1, 641, 712; Van Bavel, *Birth and Death of Booneville;* Roemer, *Texas.*

Brewster County (Alpine)

Brewster County was created out of Presidio County in
1887 and organized that year with Alpine as the county
seat. Alpine began as a tent city called Osborne on a spring
creek near a railroad that was under construction. The name
was changed first to Murphyville in 1883 and then to Alpine
in 1888. Two other adjacent counties, Buchel and Foley, were
also created in 1887, along with Brewster, but were never
organized. Finally those counties were added to Brewster
County in 1897.

The Alpine jail, built in 1887 and used until 1995, was a
two-story red-brick Victorian building with contrasting white
stone arches over the windows. It was built by Diebold Safe
and Lock for twenty-seven thousand dollars. The sheriff's
quarters were on the first floor, and the sheriff's wife cooked
for the prisoners as well as for her family. Southern Prison
Company manufactured the present ironwork. The jail was
remodeled sometime after 1901. Since the Southern Prison
Company began business in 1897 as Young Brothers Steel
Company, the cells in the Alpine lockup were evidently installed at the time of the remodeling, and the original Diebold
cells were likely then made available to the Marathon jail,
which had become a holding prison for Brewster County.

Marathon had been designated the county seat of Buchel
County in
1887, al-
though it
lost that sta-
tus when
the Buchel
area became
part of
Brewster
County in
1897. The
first "jail" in
Marathon,

Brewster County jail, 1887–1995, Alpine, Texas. Built by
Diebold Safe and Lock.

as in some other counties, was the leg of a windmill to which prisoners were chained. Later, an adobe house was used, but prisoners tended to escape from it. A stone jail was later built in Marathon, and two cages manufactured by Diebold Safe and Lock were brought from the Alpine jail about 1901 and installed for increased security. During the Mexican Revolution in 1911, the U.S. Army stationed troops in Marathon, first under Capt. Douglas MacArthur and later under Lt. George S. Patton.

Interviews conducted by the author: Frank W. Daugherty, Texas Historical Commission; Robin Lee Hughes, Center for Big Bend Studies, Sul Ross State University.

Other resources: Tyler, Barnett, and Barkley, eds., *New Handbook of Texas,* vol. 1, 129, 729, 800, and vol. 4, 498; *Dallas Morning News, Texas Almanac, 1996–1997;* Cowden, *Historical Texas County Jails.*

Briscoe County (Silverton)

Briscoe County was organized in 1892 and named for Andrew Briscoe, a Texian soldier. In 1835, John Davis Bradburn, a colonel in the Mexican Army at Anahuac, imprisoned Briscoe for refusing to pay an import duty. In a confrontation with Bradburn, William Barret Travis released Briscoe. Briscoe later fought in the battle of Concepción under James Bowie, the siege of San Antonio under Ben Milam, and the battle of San Jacinto. He became the first county judge of Harris County when Houston was the capitol of the Republic of Texas.

Briscoe County jail, Silverton, Texas. Designed by architect G. L. Lamar and built in 1894.

Thirteen miles southwest of the Briscoe county seat of
Silverton is a spring-fed creek called Los Lingos. Here the caprock falls away rapidly into the Valley of Tears below, which
legend says was named for the tears of white mothers and children, prisoners of the Comanche Indians, who regularly
brought their captives here to trade to other tribes and to the
Comancheros.

The architect and builder of the first jail in Briscoe County
was G. L. Lamar. It was constructed in 1894 for $2,487. Stone
was cut from Tule Canyon seven miles away and hauled by
wagon to Silverton, where cowboys, using hatchets, shaped
the stone. The cells and ironwork were provided by Herring-
Hall Safe and Lock Company of St Louis. The jail, which
stands on the courthouse square, is not used today but remains
in good condition, ready to be put to use if needed.

Interview conducted by the author: Beth McWilliams, county clerk.
Other resources: *Dallas Morning News, Texas Almanac, 1996–1997;* Tyler,
Barnett, and Barkley, eds., *New Handbook of Texas,* vol. 1, 739, 741, and
vol. 6, 691; Briscoe County Commissioners' Court Record, vol. 1, 125,
Aug. 25, 1894; DeLorme Mapping, *Texas Atlas and Gazetteer.*

Brooks County (Falfurrias)

Brooks County was created from San Patricio County,
which was one of the original counties created by the
Republic of Texas. San Patricio County was a vast area of
Texas south of San Antonio, west of the Gulf of Mexico, and
east of the Rio Grande; it was subsequently divided and subdivided into the counties of South Texas along the Rio Grande.
Brooks County was created in 1911 from parts of Hidalgo,
Starr, and Zapata counties. It was organized in 1912 with Falfurrias as the county seat.

The first jail, designed by Alfred Giles, was built in 1913,
one year before the completion of the courthouse. The two-
story brick structure, located one block east of the courthouse,
continues to stand and, as of this writing, is still in use. Southern Structural Steel Company built its iron cages. The gallows
had a trapdoor in a small room over the stairwell; in the ceiling

Brooks County jail, 1913–present, Falfurrias, Texas.
Designed by architect Alfred Giles.

was a steel loop where a hangman's rope could be attached, put around a prisoner's neck, and the prisoner then dropped through the trapdoor at the top of the stairwell. The hanging apparatus over the stairwell is still present but has never been used, according to the sheriff's department.

Interviews conducted by the author: Enola Garza, Ed Rachal Memorial Library; Ann Vallely, Brooks County Heritage Museum.
Other resources: Tyler, Barnett, and Barkley, eds., *New Handbook of Texas,* vol. 1, 752; Kelsey and Dyal, *Courthouses of Texas.*

Brown County (Brownwood)

Brown County was created in 1856 and organized in 1858, when the population of the area was about 244. It was named after Capt. Henry Stevenson Brown, veteran of the battle of Velasco, on June 26, 1832. Admission to the United States was supposed to gain help from U.S. troops—it did, but the years 1848–1858 were a bloody time, as the Texas Rangers and the U.S. Cavalry tried to protect citizens against bandits and Indian attacks along the Rio Grande and the frontier. In 1858, newly elected Gov. Hardin R. Runnels was determined to bring the Indians under control. He commissioned Ranger John S. ("Rip") Ford as supreme commander of all of the state's forces with broad powers of recruitment of new men to lead the action.

The withdrawal of the U.S. Army after the beginning of

the Civil War left the Rangers hard-pressed to cover such a vast area. During Reconstruction, which forbade the assembly of any armed

Brown County jail, 1902–1981, Brownwood, Texas.

group, the Rangers were disbanded. A breed of gunfighters, such as John Wesley Hardin, arose and went unchecked. In 1874, Hardin shot and killed the popular Brown County deputy sheriff, Charlie Webb, in Comanche. Though wounded in the hip by Webb's bullet, Hardin managed to escape the posse that hunted for him. Nevertheless, he was finally arrested by Texas Ranger John B. Armstrong in a dramatic confrontation outside Pensacola, Florida. Hardin was brought back to Texas and held in an Austin jail until he was tried, convicted, and sentenced to prison for twenty-five years. His brother, Joe Hardin, and several of Hardin's associates were arrested and put in the Comanche jail. A large crowd attacked the lockup at night and, after threatening to burn it down, removed the prisoners and hanged them.

A new, two-story log courthouse was built in 1870, and the jail occupied the first floor. In March 1880, the building was set on fire by a prisoner who managed to escape during the excitement. The second jail, a two-story stone structure, was built and used until the presently standing detention center was built in 1902. Local information is that the walls of the second jail had old cannonballs placed between the stones to enhance stability and prevent prisoners from removing the stones to escape. Martin and Moodie built this new jail, which was quite similar to the Comanche County keep, at a cost of eighty-six thousand dollars. The sheriff's quarters were on the first floor, and there was an upstairs gallows that was never used. This facility is now a museum.

Interviews conducted by the author: Ronnie Lapp, justice of the peace, Texas Historical Commission designee; Harriette Graves, *Brownwood Bulletin;* Pauline Hochhalter, Brown County Historical Society; Ross McSwain, San Angelo.

Other resources: Tyler, Barnett, and Barkley, eds., *New Handbook of Texas,* vol. 1, 769, and vol. 3, 453; DeLorme Mapping, *Texas Atlas and Gazetteer;* Map Ink, *Outlaws and Gunfighters of Texas Map;* Cunningham, *Triggernometry;* Sonnichsen, *I'll Die before I'll Run;* W. Robinson, *People's Architecture;* Havins, *Something about Brown;* Bishop, *In the Life and Lives of Brown County People.*

Burleson County (Caldwell)

In 1713 Louis Juchereau de St. Denis, on orders from the French governor of Louisiana, blazed a trail for trading purposes from Natchitoches in Louisiana to the Rio Grande near present-day Eagle Pass. A similar trail, some of it over the same ground, had been explored in 1690 by Alonso de León, who, coming from Mexico to counteract the French incursion, passed through East Texas searching for La Salle's Fort St. Louis near La Vaca Bay. After burning the remnants of the fort, de León continued to East Texas to establish missions among the Indians. These and other similar routes in time became part of the Old San Antonio Road in present-day Burleson County. In 1840, a trading post and community were established where the road crossed Davidson Creek. That same year, George Erath surveyed a town site that would become Caldwell, eventually the county seat of Burleson County. Today Texas

Burleson County jail, 1887–1955, Caldwell, Texas. Designed by architect Eugene Heiner. Photo courtesy of Sandra Balcar.

State Highway 21 more or less follows the route of the Old San Antonio Road.

Burleson County—named for Edward Burleson, a soldier of the Texas Republic and veteran of the battles of San Jacinto and Plum Creek—was created in 1846. Caldwell, the seat of government, was named for Mathew Caldwell, "the Paul Revere of Texas." Anticipating the battle of Gonzales, Caldwell rode to Bastrop calling Texans to arms.

The first jail in Burleson County was an 1848 log structure situated across Fox Street from the courthouse. The first prisoner, appropriately named Mr. Crooks, was also the first escapee. While incarcerated for horse theft, Crooks made a saw from a tin drinking cup and sawed the doorjamb loose, allowing him to slip away. Information about the second lockup is missing, but a third jail, a two-story brick-and-stone building, was constructed about 1887 on the corner of Fox and Echols streets. Eugene Heiner designed the structure, which was built for forty thousand dollars. It had sheriff's quarters on the first floor and cells by Pauly Jail Building and Manufacturing on the second. That facility remained in use until after World War II.

Interviews conducted by the author: Catherine Alford, president, Burleson Texas Historical Commission; Dennis Beran and Sue Beran.

Other resources: Tyler, Barnett, and Barkley, eds., *New Handbook of Texas,* vol. 1, 840, 845, vol. 2, 580, and vol. 4, 1139; DeLorme Mapping, *Texas Atlas and Gazetteer;* J. Williams and Neighbours, *Old Texas Trails;* Weddle, *Wilderness Manhunt.*

Burnet County (Burnet)

Burnet County, in Central Texas about fifty miles northwest of Austin, was created in 1852 and named for David G. Burnet, the provisional president of the Republic of Texas. Later that year, when the county was organized, one hundred acres were donated by Peter Kerr, and the community of Hamilton was chosen for the county seat. In 1858, the name was changed to Burnet since there was another post office in Texas by the name of Hamilton.

The first courthouse was a one-story frame building built

Burnet County jail, Burnet, Texas. Designed by architect
Frederick Ruffini and built in 1884.

in 1854 on the southwestern corner of the courthouse square. It contained a one-room jail, a courtroom, and an office. The structure burned in 1874, after which court was held under the trees on the square until a new courthouse with a jail was built that same year. The second lockup was built into the northeast corner of the 1874 courthouse and was used until 1884. The contractors for the courthouse and jail were G. F. and W. S. Vickers; the combined cost was $13,400. Noted occupants were John Beard, George Gladden, and Scott Cooley, all three of whom were involved in the Mason County War. That "war" was between "the Americans" and "the Germans," an outgrowth of the refusal of the German community to support the Southern cause in the Civil War.

The third jail, built in 1884, is a free-standing rectangular limestone building, showing exquisite craftsmanship; it has two stories, with the sheriff's quarters on the first floor and jail cells on the second. Designed by Frederic Ruffini of Austin, the structure was built on the corner of Washington Street and Pierce by J. T. Woodward at a cost of $9,365. The price did not include the cost of the cells and ironwork, which is unknown. The old lockup still stands today and is now an adult probation office.

    Interviews conducted by the author: Darrell Debo, Burnet County Historical Association representative; Cookie Wallace, director, Hermann Brown Free Library.
    Other resources: Pierce, *Texas under Arms;* Tyler, Barnett, and Barkley, eds., *New Handbook of Texas,* vol. 1, 850, and vol. 2, 1105; Debo, *History of Burnet County;* W. P. Webb, *Texas Rangers.*

Caldwell County (Lockhart)

Caldwell County lies in the watershed of the San Marcos River and Plum Creek. It was created in 1848 from parts of Bastrop and Gonzales counties and organized that same year. The county seat, Lockhart, is near the site of the famous battle of Plum Creek, where, in the summer of 1840, eighty-seven pioneers defeated about four hundred Comanche warriors. The area of Caldwell County was part of the Green De-Witt colony and was named for Capt. Mathew ("Old Paint") Caldwell, a popular Indian fighter and veteran of the Plum Creek fight.

The first jail in Caldwell County was built of oak logs in 1855, with the first floor partially underground. This structure burned in 1858, and for the next fifteen years, the keep was in the basement of the new 1858 limestone courthouse. That three-story building, including the basement, measured 40' by 65'; it was an impressive structure and served for thirty-four years.

The crowding and lawlessness of the post–Civil War period, however, required a new lockup; in 1873, the commissioners built their third jail of hand-cut stone, 50' square, on the corner of Main Street and Walnut. That structure divided the two-story building differently. The first floor had two cells and a kitchen, while the second floor had an additional two cells and the sheriff's quarters.

The fourth jail in Caldwell County, still standing on the corner of South Brazos and East Market Street, was built in 1910 for twenty-five

Caldwell County jail, 1910–1983, Lockhart, Texas. Designed by architect Thomas Hodges.

thousand dollars. It is a red brick building of five stories, including the basement, with sheriff's quarters on the first floor. The three stories above the ground floor contained nine large cells that were subdivided into smaller units. A gallows, originally included, was removed during the 1930s. The architectural style used by Thomas Hodges was Norman castellated; the contractors were Martin, Byrnes, and Johnson. The structure was used until 1983 and now houses the Caldwell County Historical Museum.

Interviews conducted by the author: Phyllis Metcalfe; Jeanna Navarro, Caldwell County Library; Aileen S. Bodeman.

Other resources: Tyler, Barnett, and Barkley, eds., *New Handbook of Texas,* vol. 1, 896, vol. 4, 256, and vol. 5, 242; W. P. Webb, *Texas Rangers;* O'Banion, "History of Caldwell County"; Conner and Yena, *Battles of Texas.*

Calhoun County (Port Lavaca)

Calhoun County was created in 1846 and named for statesman John C. Calhoun. The community of Lavaca, later Port Lavaca, became a refuge for survivors of an 1840 Comanche raid on Linnville, three and a half miles to the north. That raid was neither the first nor the last of a series of disasters that would plague would-be colonists in the area. Disasters go back further: In 1685, Sieur de La Salle wrecked two of his four ships within eighteen miles of Lavaca. The other ships had already returned to France. La Salle built Fort St. Louis on Garcitas Creek, twelve miles to the north of the future Port Lavaca. Somewhat later, the fort was sacked by Indians and finally burned by the Spanish. In 1846, the town of Indianola was founded at Indian Point on the western shore of Matagorda Bay, five miles south of Port Lavaca. The town prospered and in 1852 became the county seat. In addition to the ever-present rattlesnakes and mosquitoes, the next thirty-six years also brought four epidemics of deadly yellow fever, two epidemics of cholera, and then two devastating hurricanes—one in 1875 and the other in 1886. Although Indianola had been designated the county seat and briefly enjoyed the optimism and prosperity of a deep-water port, the de-

struction
wrought by
the 1886
tidal wave
dampened
investors'
enthusiasm
for rebuild-
ing. The
county seat
was re-
turned to
Port Lavaca
in 1887.

Calhoun County jail, 1896–1959, Port Lavaca, Texas.
Designed by architect H. M. White.

The first jail in Calhoun County was a wooden house in
Port Lavaca. When the county seat moved to Indianola in
1852, a new lockup was built, and the courthouse was constructed a couple of years later. Not until it became necessary
to carry out a death sentence was a gallows constructed—in
1855—for the hanging of a man named O'Conner.

In 1875 the Sutton-Taylor feud spilled over into Indianola,
when Bill and Jim Taylor ambushed and murdered Bill Sutton
and Gabriel Slaughter as they boarded a ship for Galveston. A
posse in Cuero later killed Jim Taylor. Bill Taylor was arrested
in Cuero by Marshal Reuben Brown and transferred to the jail
in Galveston. In September of 1875, his trial was held in Indianola during the time of the big hurricane. Since Brown was
in jail in Indianola as the storm was rising, the district attorney,
unable to get the deputy to release him, took the keys, opened
the door, and let Taylor and two other prisoners go. Taylor is
said to have repeatedly plunged into the raging surf and saved
a number of citizens before escaping with another prisoner on
the sheriff's horse.

Eleven years later, in 1886, Indianola was hit by a second
big storm and a tidal wave that washed the village away. The
county seat was then moved back to Port Lavaca, where a new
jail, designed by H. M. White, was built in 1896 and used until 1959. The builders were Martin, Byrnes, and Johnson. The
brick building with crenellated battlements and a round tower
at the corner cost fourteen thousand dollars. It contained a gal-

lows, which was used just once to execute an African American, Henry Wilson, in December 1914. The jail is now a museum at the corner of Ann and Leona streets.

Interviews conducted by the author: George Fred Rhodes, museum director; Noemi Cruz, Calhoun County Public Library.

Other resources: Calhoun County Historical Commission, *Shifting Sand of Calhoun County;* Calhoun County Historical Survey Committee, *Indianola Scrapbook;* Sonnichsen, *I'll Die before I'll Run;* Malsch, *Indianola;* Tyler, Barnett, and Barkley, eds., *New Handbook of Texas,* vol. 1, 900, and vol. 3, 831, 832; Weddle, *French Thorn.*

Callahan County (Baird)

Callahan County remained mostly unpopulated until after the Red River Wars and the defeat of the Comanches at Palo Duro Canyon. The county was created in 1858, but its first town, Belle Plain, was not laid out until 1875. When the county was organized in 1877, the town of Callahan was designated as the county seat, but an election three months later changed the seat of government to Belle Plain. After the Texas and Pacific Railroad bypassed Belle Plain, the new town on the railroad, Baird, was voted county seat in 1883.

The first jail in Callahan County was built in Belle Plain in 1880 by Martin, Byrnes, and Johnson for sixty-five hundred dollars. In the interval between 1877 and the completion of the new jail, prisoners were sent to Shackelford County for safekeeping; payments had to be made for that and also to certain officers for guarding the prison-

Callahan County jail, 1898–present, Baird, Texas. Designed by architect J. E. Flanders. Photo by Stanley Gilbert. From the author's collection.

ers. Construction on the Belle Plain jail began in January 1880. The building was a 28′ by 30′ rectangle. It had sheriff's quarters on the first floor and cells on the second. The stone, quarried locally, was 20″ thick, and each stone had an 8″ cannonball inserted between it and the next stone to prevent prisoners from slipping out a stone and escaping.

After the county seat was moved to Baird, citizens agreed to underwrite the cost of moving the stone jail from Belle Plaine to the new courthouse square in Baird, six miles away. J. H. Milliken and Company agreed to do the task for two thousand dollars. They were to dismantle the jail, haul it on wagons, and reassemble it at the new site. It was worth the effort since the jail was used until 1898, when a larger lockup was needed. The old building still stands rock solid and has been made available to the Boy Scouts for their meetings.

In 1898 the county built a new building. The two-story brick structure, designed by J. E. Flanders, was built by Sonnefield and Emmons of Dallas for $12,481. The first floor has quarters for the sheriff, and the second story has cell space for ten prisoners. Upon acceptance of the new lockup, the court ordered that, among his other duties, "the Sheriff is charged with the duty of oiling the windmill." No chore was too mundane to put on the shoulders of the guardian of the peace.

The 1898 jail is one of the oldest lockups in the state still certified by the Texas Commission on Jail Standards. Originally, the building had a gallows, which was used only one time, in 1907, when Alberto Vargas was hanged for the murder of Emma Blakley.

Interviews conducted by the author: Allen Wright, county attorney; Anita Mays, deputy sheriff; Lee Abernathy, Callahan County Historical Commission; Tom Ivy, Veterans Service Office.

Other resources: Tyler, Barnett, and Barkley, eds., *New Handbook of Texas,* vol. 1, 342, 475, 906; Settle, "Early Days in Callahan County."

Cameron County (Brownsville)

Cameron County, at the southernmost tip of Texas and separated from Mexico by the Rio Grande River, was originally part of gigantic San Patricio County. Cameron

Cameron County jail, 1913–1978, Brownsville, Texas. Designed by architect Atlee B. Ayres. Photo by Stanley Gilbert. From the author's collection.

was subdivided from Nueces County in 1848. The area seems to have been heavily occupied in prehistoric times but then sparsely populated up to the nineteenth century. The county was named for Capt. Ewen Cameron of the ill-fated Mier expedition.

When the county was organized in February 1848, the seat of government was Santa Rita, five miles upstream from Brownsville. (The river had changed course in 1830, and the village, originally in Mexico, became part of Texas.) After only eleven months, however, in December 1848, voters changed the seat of government to Brownsville, and it is said that Santa Rita citizens put their houses on wheels and moved there.

Three formal jails have been recorded in the history of Cameron County. According to the commissioners' court record, at first there was too little money to build a lockup, so the court rented houses around town to hold prisoners. After four years of disagreement, the county bought a lot on the corner of Tenth Street and East Levee and built a courthouse and small wooden jail on the site. That structure, a tiny half-floored single room, often holding fifteen to forty prisoners of both sexes, served Cameron County for more than thirty years.

In September 1859 the jail became a scene of violence. Legendary Juan Nepomuceno Cortina—a sometime-bandit and sometime-Robin Hood—made a night raid on Brownsville with forty or fifty followers and terrified the populace for several hours. He emptied the calaboose, then took supplies, guns, and ammunition, for which he paid the storekeepers. He killed four people, however, including the jailer. Cortina had been a law-abiding, well-to-do rancher in South Texas until the results of the Mexican War placed his ranch in the United States, changing both his culture and his inheritance. For many years he successfully eluded both the U.S. Army and the Texas Rangers. He died peacefully in Mexico City in 1894.

The second jail, designed by J. N. Preston and Son of Austin, was built in 1882 on the corner of East Madison and Twelfth Street, adjacent to the site of the planned new courthouse. This little structure served the county for thirty years.

Cameron County's third lockup, planned in 1911, was designed by San Antonio architect Atlee B. Ayres and was finished in 1913. The three-story concrete-and-brick building faces Van Buren Street at the corner of Twelfth Street. It was remodeled and expanded three times before being replaced in 1978. Currently it has been renovated to serve as an office building.

Interviews conducted by the author: Mitchell C. Chaney; Maria Watson Pfeiffer; Bruce Aiken, Texas Historical Commission.
Other resources: Tyler, Barnett, and Barkley, eds., *New Handbook of Texas,* vol. 1, 918, 776, and vol. 4, 888; Bay, *Historic Brownsville.*

Camp County (Pittsburg)

After the battle of San Jacinto, immigrants and settlers began to migrate from Alabama, Georgia, and Tennessee to the territory that would become Camp County. Created in 1874 and organized that same year, the county was named for John Lafayette Camp, a Texas legislator. Pittsburg, which had begun as a small community in 1850, was chosen to be the county seat in 1874. The original name was spelled "Pittsburgh," but in 1893 the "h" was officially dropped. The town was incorporated in 1891.

Camp County has had five jails. The first was a one-story, 18' by 20' wooden building built in 1878 at a cost of $700. When the old jail burned in 1893, a new, very substantial structure was built east of the courthouse. This second facility consisted of two stories of brick and cost $7,000. It was used until 1916, when a third lockup was built on the west side of the courthouse. In 1928, a new courthouse was built, and a fourth jail was built southwest of it. A fifth jail was completed north of the courthouse in 1967.

The last public execution in Camp County occurred in 1903, when a farmer, George Harkey, was hanged for the murder of a neighboring farmer, Gip Wright. The execution was carried out in Pittsburg before a large crowd. The sheriff declined to spring the trapdoor, so a man from Mount Vernon was brought over to do the job. After the execution, physician R. Y. Lacy pronounced Harkey dead, but the next morning, rumor had it that the dead man's family had fed him biscuits and milk all night and that he had recovered. The sheriff called Lacy, and the doctor dutifully went to the house, opened the casket, and pronounced George Harkey dead a second time.

Interviews conducted by the author: Mayor Dave Abernathy; Vernon Holcomb, Camp County Museum Association.

Other resources: Tyler, Barnett, and Barkley, eds., *New Handbook of Texas,* vol. 1, 934, and vol. 5, 222; Spencer, *Camp County Story.*

Carson County (Panhandle)

Carson County was created in 1876 and organized in 1888. Settlement began slowly because of a shortage of water and the complete absence of wood, either for construction or for fireplaces. The county was named for S. P. Carson, secretary of state of the Republic of Texas.

Charles Goodnight and John G. Adair formed a partnership to create the J. A. and Turkey Track ranch, the largest in the area. By 1887, when it was divided, the "J. A." comprised 1,335,000 acres of land in five counties. The Southern Kansas Railroad reached Panhandle City in 1888, while the much anticipated Fort Worth and Denver City Railroad, instead of routing through Panhandle City, passed eighteen miles south, through Claude in Armstrong County.

Panhandle was the only town in Carson County in 1888, and the entire population consisted of fewer than four hundred people. Water, chronically in short supply, was brought to Panhandle by railroad, put in barrels, loaded on wagons, and hauled to the ranches. In 1887, after several failed attempts, underground

Carson County jail (right), 1909–1950, Panhandle, Texas. Designed by architects J. C. Berry, Kerr, and Kerr. Photo courtesy of Carson County Square House Museum.

water was discovered, and direct-drive Eclipse windmills were used to bring the precious liquid to the surface.

The first jail in Carson County, a frame building, was built in 1888 at a cost of $175. The architects were Martin, Byrnes, and Johnson, and the builders were McKenzie and Pearce. The structure lasted until 1909, when a new brick jail was built for $10,000. That facility, designed by J. C. Berry, Kerr, and Kerr, had two stories, with the sheriff's quarters on the first floor.

O. L. Thorp was elected sheriff in 1922, just in time for the oil boom. By 1930, the population reached an all-time peak of 7,745. The Thorps lived on the first floor of the jail, and Mrs. Thorp cooked for the prisoners. This could be quite a demanding job because, at one time, the jail is said to have held sixty-four inmates; "standing room only" was the local saying. There was only a single jail break—one in which two prisoners escaped. They, however, failed to persuade the trustee, Mrs. Thorp's helper in the kitchen, to join them. The lockup was used until 1950, when it was replaced by a new building.

Interviews conducted by the author: Georgia Lane, registrar, Carson County Square House Museum; Paul Katz.

Other resources: Kingston, Harris, and Bailey, eds., *Texas Almanac, 1984–1985; Dallas Morning News, Texas Almanac, 1998–1999;* Tyler, Barnett, and Barkley, eds., *New Handbook of Texas,* vol. 1, 246, 994; J. E. Haley, *Charles Goodnight;* Randel and Stocking, *A Time to Purpose,* vol. 1.

Cass County (Linden)

Originally part of the Paschal judicial district, Cass County was created in 1846 and named for Lewis Cass, a U.S. senator and later secretary of state. The town of Jefferson was originally chosen as the county seat, but in 1852 the voters moved the seat of government to Linden. In 1860, the southern portion of Cass County was separated and named Marion County, with Jefferson as the county seat. In 1861, the name of the town was temporarily changed to Davis, for Jefferson Davis.

There is no standing historic county jail in Cass County. The 1916 jail, however, was used until 1992. The sheriff's quarters occupied the front of the building, and the lockup was placed at the back.

Cass County has been primarily a farming area since before the Civil War. The war and the consequent loss of manpower, due in part to the emancipation of slaves, precipitated a decline in agricultural production of cotton and corn, as well as a drop in property values. The arrival of the Texas and Pacific Railroad during the 1870s helped with the movement of forest and farm products. Oil production in this region began during the 1930s.

Cass County jail, 1916–1992, Linden, Texas. Photo courtesy of Custom Studio, Atlanta, Texas.

Interview conducted by the author: Gary Walker, photographer and historian.

Other resources: Tyler, Barnett, and Barkley, eds., *New Handbook of Texas,* vol. 1, 1012, vol. 2, 202, and vol. 3, 924; *History of Cass County.*

Castro County (Dimmitt)

Castro County was created in 1876. To encourage
settlement of its Panhandle lands, which were newly
won from hostile Indians in the Red River Wars of 1874
and 1875, the 1887 Texas legislature authorized the sale of
one section, 640 acres, to each person for $2 per acre. The
population of Castro County in 1890 was nine. The area was
organized in 1891 and named for Henri Castro, consul general to France during the days of the Republic of Texas.
(Castro later founded Castroville, west of San Antonio.) The
severe drought of 1892–1893 so discouraged settlers that the
1895 legislature offered four sections for a dollar per acre. Even
so, the 1900 census for Castro County listed a population of
only 400.

The county seat, Dimmitt, was named for the Rev. W. C.
Dimmitt, a partner in the Bedford Town and Land Company, which had organized and platted the county seat in
March 1890. There was no jail in the early days. C. I. Bedford
was the first sheriff, and in the absence of a detention center,
he took prisoners home with him to keep overnight. If a prisoner proved troublesome, Bedford would handcuff himself to
the convict and sleep that way.

The courthouse, completed in December 1892, was struck
by lightning in August 1906 and burned to the ground. The
court records show no suggestion of any jail until the second
courthouse was built in 1908. That facility was less than secure.
Sometimes the sheriff would lock up a prisoner only to encounter him on the street a few hours later. If unobserved,
the captive would usually return to eat his meals or spend the
night.

The second jail, on the third floor of the courthouse, was
built in 1940. The structure, designed by Townes and Funk,
was built of sandstone with Work Projects Administration
(WPA) help for $99,700. The courthouse was extensively re-
modeled in 1971, and new jail facilities were placed on the
first and second floors. Since then, the old third-floor lockup
has been used for storage.

Interviews conducted by the author: Clara Vick; Sheriff C. D. Fitzgerald. Other resources: Tyler, Barnett, and Barkley, eds., *New Handbook of Texas,* vol. 1, 1022, and vol. 2, 650; Kingston, Harris, and Bailey, eds., *Texas Almanac, 1984–1985; Dallas Morning News, Texas Almanac, 1998–1999;* Kelsey and Dyal, *Courthouses of Texas;* Hunter, *Moving Finger;* Tise, *Texas County Sheriffs.*

Chambers County (Anahuac)

The first jail in Chambers County was a wooden structure built by the Mexican garrison at Fort Anahuac in 1830. William Barret Travis was incarcerated in Fort Anahuac in 1832, not in the wooden lockup but in an abandoned brick kiln "because the jail was not secure enough." Col. Francis Johnson rescued Travis after a skirmish with the garrison.

Chambers County was organized in 1858, and Wallisville became the county seat. A courthouse fire in 1875, a deadly smallpox epidemic in 1877, and hurricanes in 1875, 1900, and 1915 plagued the area. Nevertheless, the county prospered. Historical records show that, in 1906, Wallisville passed an ordinance forbidding "free-ranging swine," making it unlawful to allow pigs to roam free in the streets. While this may have pleased the health department, the citizens decided it was time to move the county seat. An election held in 1907 designated

Chambers County jail, 1894–1911, Wallisville, Texas. Photo courtesy of Wallisville Heritage Park.

Anahuac as the seat of government, and the records were re-moved from Wallisville in 1908.

There is no documentation of a jail in Wallisville before 1878 because an 1875 courthouse fire destroyed all records. The first jail of record was a two-story brick lockup built in 1878 by contractor Charles Hankamer at a cost of fifteen hun-dred dollars. After seventeen years, this keep was replaced in 1894 by an impressive brick structure that had an imposing tower for a gallows, which was never used, and sheriff's quar-ters on the first floor. Diebold Safe and Lock Company pro-vided the iron cages. The stone foundation of the jail can be seen today among the tall weeds south of Interstate 10.

The similarity of the Chambers County jail to the 1892 Crockett County lockup is remarkable. It is quite possible that the former was also designed by architect Oscar Ruffini of San Angelo. Unfortunately, the new jail in its splendor and strength was seriously damaged by a severe hurricane that struck the Gulf Coast near Galveston in 1915. The county seat, however, had already been moved to Anahuac, where a brick prison had been built in 1911. It served until 1935, when another hurricane destroyed the courthouse and damaged the jail. Nevertheless, the structure served as a temporary court-house until new facilities (with cells on the third floor) were completed in 1937. That building would serve the needs of Chambers County law enforcement until 1983.

Interviews conducted by the author: Kevin Ladd, Wallisville Heritage Society; Jackie Wheat, Chambers County Sheriff's Department; John Middleton, historian.

Other resources: Tyler, Barnett, and Barkley, eds., *New Handbook of Texas,* vol. 1, 158, vol. 2, 33, 1085, and vol. 6, 813.

Cherokee County (Rusk)

Cherokee County was organized in 1846. Selection of the county seat involved a choice between Rusk and Cook's Fort. Joseph Thomas Cook had established Cook's Fort in 1839 as protection against Indians. It became a community

Cherokee County jail, 1941–present, on top floor of court-
house, Rusk, Texas. Photo from *Courthouses of Texas: A
Guide,* by Mavis Kelsey Sr. and Donald H. Dyal (College
Station: Texas A&M University Press, 1993).

of about
250 people,
and Joseph's
son, James,
farmed
nearby.
James, when
offered the
county seat,
declined
because it
would in-
terfere with
his farming
operation.

The alternate county seat, Rusk, was named after Thomas Jefferson Rusk, a Texas pioneer and veteran of San Jacinto.

The county was named, of course, after the Cherokee
Indians. In February 1836, the Houston-Forbes Treaty was
signed with Chief Bowles to ensure Cherokee neutrality in
exchange for designated lands for the Cherokee people. The
Texas senate, however, never ratified the agreement. Ever-
increasing incursions of settlers into the Native Americans' territory resulted in an Indian uprising led by Vincente Córdoba,
previously the *alcalde* (mayor) of Nacogdoches under the
Mexican government. With the support of officials in Mexico,
in October 1839, Indians attacked the settlement of Isaac
Killough and his relatives, killing eighteen people, an event
that became known as the Killough Massacre. This aroused the
citizen militia under Gen. Thomas Rusk and resulted in the
expulsion of the Cherokee from Cherokee County.

As early as 1847, a contract was let to build a log jail on lot
1 of block 15 in the town of Rusk. Lawlessness must have been
rampant because only eight years later, in 1855, another contract was let for the construction of a larger, two-story jail
for $4,250 — a big price for a jail at the time. The prison was
probably a formidable dungeon type.

In 1883, Rusk became the location for the second state

penitentiary (the first was in Huntsville), where it remained until 1917. A third lockup had been built on the northeast corner of the courthouse square in 1882. Unfortunately, no pictures of any jails are available, and only the scantiest descriptions appear in contemporary writing. In 1941, however, a new courthouse with a jail on the top floor was completed with WPA funds.

Interview conducted by the author: Susan McCarty, Chamber of Commerce.

Other resources: *Dallas Morning News, Texas Almanac, 1998–1999;* Tyler, Barnett, and Barkley, eds., *New Handbook of Texas,* vol. 2, 59, 309, vol. 3, 1095, and vol. 5, 726; Metz, *Roadside History of Texas;* Roach, *Hills of Cherokee;* Kelsey and Dyal, *Courthouses of Texas.*

Childress County (Childress)

Created in 1878 and organized in 1879, Childress County was named for the author of the Texas Declaration of Independence, George C. Childress. Childress City was chosen to be the county seat in 1887, but incentives from the Fort Worth and Denver City Railroad caused the citizens to move the seat of government to Henry, four miles from Childress City, because it was on the railroad right of way. Subsequently, the town of Henry was renamed Childress and incorporated in 1890.

The first murder trial in Childress occurred in 1888, when G. W. Clement

Childress County jail, 1939–present, on fourth floor of courthouse, Childress, Texas. Designed by architects Townes and Funk.

was accused of the crime. Temple Houston, son of Gen. Sam Houston, defended Clement. The defendant was found guilty, but a second trial found him innocent.

The first jail was a wooden structure built by B. T. Williams in 1887 on the corner of Third Street and Avenue D, where it served until l9o5. In 1905, a jail annex was built next to the 1892 courthouse on the northeast corner of the courthouse square; it was an attractive white two-story masonry building with imposing columns in front. The jail annex was used until a new courthouse containing a jail on the fourth floor was built by the WPA in 1939. Southern Prison Company of San Antonio provided the ironwork and cells.

Interviews conducted by the author: Sheriff Darin Smith; Jenny Lou Taylor, Childress County Heritage Museum; Lois Stiner, Childress County Museum.

Other resources: Kelsey and Dyal, *Courthouses of Texas;* Ehrle, *Childress County Story;* Tyler and Tyler, *Texas Museums;* Tyler, Barnett, and Barkley, eds., *New Handbook of Texas,* vol. 2, 80, 81; Metz, *Roadside History of Texas.*

Clay County (Henrietta)

Clay County was created in 1857 and organized in 1861. With the onset of the Civil War and the consequent withdrawal of federal troops from the frontier, Indian dep-redations in Clay County caused the 109 residents to depart for a safer area. No population figures are available for 1870, but reoccupation was

Clay County "dungeon jail," c. 1874–1878 (restored), Henrietta, Texas. Photo courtesy of Clay County Historical Society.

under way, and reorganization occurred in 1873 with the selection of Cambridge as the county seat. In 1882, the Fort
Worth and Denver Railroad passed through the abandoned
prewar town of Henrietta. Soon people moving in from Cambridge rejuvenated the railroad town of Henrietta; the community was incorporated and became the county seat.

The first jail in Henrietta was a two-story wooden dungeon built in 1874. It may have been replaced by a one-story
wooden jail, according to Katherine Douthitt's *Romance and
Dim Trails*. The one-story building she refers to, however, may
have been an 1893 structure ordered by the commissioners'
court for use on the county farm three miles northeast of
Henrietta. That jail was 20' by 23' and consisted of 2" by 6"
beams stacked one on top of another and nailed down. In 1878,
the county commissioners made a contract with J. S. Thomas
of Fort Worth to build a two-story square stone fortress for
seven thousand dollars. It is said to have been the first lockup
in the county to have steel cages for holding prisoners.

In 1890, the stone jail was replaced by a brick prison built
by the Pauly Jail Building and Manufacturing Company. It sat
on a stone foundation and had very generous sheriff's quarters
attached. The structure, built at a cost of twenty-four thousand
dollars, is on the corner of Graham and Ikard streets in Henrietta. In 1929, both the jail and the quarters were remodeled
and stuccoed; they continued in use until 1973, when they
were replaced. Today the 1890 building serves very nicely as
a museum.

Interview conducted by the author: Lucille Glasgow, historian.
Other resources: Tyler, Barnett, and Barkley, eds., *New Handbook of
Texas,* vol. 2, 146; Hurn, *Clay County,* vol. 1; Earle, *History of Clay County
and Northwest Texas;* Douthitt, *Romance and Dim Trails;* W. Taylor, *History
of Clay County.*

Cochran County (Morton)

Cochran County, on the far western edge of the Texas
Panhandle, shares a border with New Mexico at about
the same latitude as Lubbock. The Texas legislature created the

Cochran County jail, 1926–1968, in basement of courthouse, Morton, Texas. Photo courtesy of James St. Clair, office of the county judge.

county in 1876, after the completion of the Red River War. The population there grew very slowly, probably because of the remote location and the presence of several giant ranches, including part of the three-million-acre XIT ranch. As late as 1920, the total census was sixty-seven. Cochran County was organized in 1924, although in the beginning, all of the court proceedings were conducted in the adjacent Hockley and Lubbock counties.

In 1926, the new Cochran County courthouse in Morton was completed after much controversy and delay. It included a jail in the basement. Southern Structural Steel Company—now the major provider of jail products in Texas—provided the ironwork at a cost of $25,513. One would not now recognize the old 1926 courthouse and jail since it was expanded and completely modernized in 1968. The basement facilities have been converted to a detox tank, and the regular jail has been moved to the first floor.

Interview conducted by the author: Ethyl Smart, secretary to County Judge Robert Yeary.

Other resources: *Dallas Morning News, Texas Almanac, 1998–1999;* Tyler, Barnett, and Barkley, eds., *New Handbook of Texas,* vol. 2, 181; Kelsey and Dyal, *Courthouses of Texas.*

Coke County (Robert Lee)

Coke County was created in 1889 from Tom Green County and was organized that same year. The first county seat was Hayrick, but in 1891 the seat of government was moved to Robert Lee, a new town named for Gen. Robert E. Lee on the banks of the upper Colorado River. Coke County was the site of one of the

Coke County jail, 1907–1970, Robert Lee, Texas. Built by Southern Structural Steel.

early confrontations between landowners who installed barbed wire around their property and free-range ranchers. Rancher L. B. Harris suffered a loss in the 1880s, when free-range people burned six thousand dollars worth of new fencing materials. Wire cutting was a similar problem, which was finally settled by a new state law and the Texas Rangers.

In 1907 the Southern Structural Steel Company built a two-story stone jail with sheriff's quarters and a trapdoor gallows that was never used. Bill Allen, whose childhood home was next door to the lockup, recalls that one of the cells was a padded compartment. He and the sheriff's son, Will Percifull, who lived next door, found that the padded chamber was their favorite place for "rasseling." Sheriff Frank Percifull was a popular sheriff and seldom put anyone in jail. When one of the citizens had a little too much to drink, he simply took them to his home for safekeeping.

Eddie Good, whose father, Paul Good, was sheriff following Sheriff Percifull's retirement, lived in the Coke County Jail. He recalls that his father once arrested a large woman for bootlegging and, in the process of escorting her to jail, noticed a strange shape in her bodice. When questioned about it, she reached down into her dress and retrieved a full-sized army .45-caliber pistol and handed it to Sheriff Good. She told him she carried it to protect herself against other bootleggers. Local lore also has it that Sheriff Good was once called to investigate a suspicious truck that had been parked all day at E. V. Spence

Lake. When he approached the truck, he noticed many boxes that were partially covered with a fine net in the back. When questioned, the driver said that he was transporting his bees and beehives from South Texas to Colorado for the summer. He said that he was watering and refreshing his bees at the lake and that, when they came back at dusk, he would be on his way.

Violators of the law in Coke County are now sent to San Angelo for processing, and the jail in Robert Lee is no longer in service. The building now houses a museum.

Interviews conducted by the author: Bill Allen; Eddie Good; Lana Richards, Texas Historical Commission; Conita Copeland, historian.

Other resources: Tyler, Barnett, and Barkley, eds., *New Handbook of Texas,* vol. 2, 193, vol. 3, 581; *Dallas Morning News, Texas Almanac, 1998–1999;* Metz, *Roadside History of Texas.*

Coleman County (Coleman)

Coleman County was created in 1858 and organized in 1864. It was named for Robert M. Coleman, an aide to Gen. Sam Houston at the battle of San Jacinto. The first county seat was Camp Colorado, a U.S. Army post from 1857 to 1861; it was moved twice, finally to Jim Ned Creek in northern Coleman County. When the cavalry moved out during the Civil War, the Texas Rangers occupied the camp.

Coleman County jail, 1890–present, Coleman, Texas. Designed by architect Eugene Heiner. Photo courtesy of David Bucek.

In 1876 the citizens of Coleman County voted to move the seat of government ten miles south to donated land at Hord's Creek. There they

laid out the new town and named it Coleman. The first order
of business was to build a jail, which was done in 1879. That
jail was made of stone and consisted of two stories with a flat
roof. The courthouse was completed five years later in 1884.
The courthouse was better constructed; although extensively
remodeled in 1952, it is still in use today. The old lockup,
which "leaked" prisoners, was condemned in 1886. The new
facility, thought to have been designed by architect Eugene
Heiner, was completed in 1890 at a cost of $15,575. It is an
impressive two-story native-stone building and originally contained a gallows. Diebold Safe and Lock Company manufactured the cells. This building is still used as a detention center.

Interviews conducted by the author: Ronald W. Owens, historian;
David Bucek, historian.
Other resources: Tyler, Barnett, and Barkley, eds., *New Handbook of
Texas,* vol. 1, 932, and vol. 2, 201; Tyler and Tyler, *Texas Museums;* Kelsey
and Dyal, *Courthouses of Texas;* DeLorme Mapping, *Texas Atlas and
Gazetteer;* G. N. Hunter, *Historically Speaking.*

Collin County (McKinney)

Collin County was created from Fannin County in 1846
and named for Collin McKinney, signer of the Texas
Declaration of Independence. Buckner was first chosen as the
county seat. In 1848, however, the seat of government was
changed to McKinney, also named for Collin McKinney.

Collin County voted against secession but joined the Confederacy once the die was cast. There was, however, a smolder-
ing animosity, and a few citizens from the county participated
in the "great hanging" in Gainesville, when forty suspected
Unionists met their end in October of 1862. Even after the
Civil War, the Lee-Peacock feud in Hunt County spilled over
into Collin County, resulting in ambush and murder.

The Collin County jail was finished and accepted by the
commissioners in 1882. It was designed by Frederick E.
Ruffini of Austin, who designed a similar, if not identical,
facility for Comal County in 1878. The keep is a three-story
limestone building of nineteen thousand square feet. It is un-

Collin County jail, 1882–1979, McKinney, Texas. Designed by architect F. E. Ruffini. The jail is now a restaurant. Photo by Stanley Gilbert. From the author's collection.

usual in that it has a T-shaped floor plan and certain architectural enhancements, such as stilted and Roman arches and pilasters. It was a good design, one that served the county for ninety-five years until replaced by a modern jail in 1979.

One of the jail's more memorable guests was Raymond Hamilton, renowned bandit of the Bonnie-and-Clyde era in the early 1930s. Hamilton escaped by cutting through the bars and then shooting his way out. He was, however, recaptured shortly afterward. On another occasion, one very small prisoner, using a spoon, dug his way to freedom, but the other prisoners were too big to get through the hole. The jail was equipped with a gallows, and the last execution occurred in November 1922, when Ezell Stepp was hanged for murder.

Some repair work had been done on the 1882 jail by the WPA in 1938, but in 1979, the keep was finally replaced by a modern structure. The building retained its value, however. At the ripe old age of 114 years, it was sold at auction for almost ten times the $9,900 paid by the county taxpayers in 1882. It currently serves as a restaurant.

Interviews conducted by the author: Helen Hall, McKinney Memorial Public Library; Mary Dickerson, historian; Martha West Bacon, Collin County historian; Shirlene, McKinney, Memorial Public Library.

Other resources: *Dallas Morning News, Texas Almanac, 1998–1999;* Tyler, Barnett, and Barkley, eds., *New Handbook of Texas,* vol. 2, 214, and vol. 5, 204; Sonnichsen, *I'll Die before I'll Run.*

Collingsworth County (Wellington)

Collingsworth County—named for James Collinsworth, the first chief justice of the Republic of Texas—was created in 1876 and organized in 1890. The legislature misspelled his name and never corrected it, but the thought was there. The English owners of the Rocking Chair Ranch named the county seat, Wellington, for the Duke of Wellington. The Texas Panhandle was slow to develop until after the Indians were defeated in the Red River War. In 1880, the Collingsworth County population numbered only six. The area was home for several huge ranches, such as the Diamond Tail Ranch (partially in Donley and Childress counties as well) and the Rocking Chair, between the North Fork and the Salt Fork of the Red River (also partially in Wheeler County).

The first jail in Collingsworth County was on the first floor of the county courthouse, which was completed in 1893 at a cost of thirty-one thousand dollars. Shortly after its completion, the prisoners were threatened by a mob. The sheriff, who barricaded the courthouse doors, successfully defended the uprising. Later a second, temporary jail, which was used until 1912, was constructed on the courthouse lawn.

The third Collingsworth jail was a two-story brick Texas Renaissance building with two crenellated towers, located on West Street at Fourth Street. It was built in 1912 at a cost of nine thousand dollars, financed by a bond election. It had twelve cells plus a

Collingsworth County jail, 1912–1962, Wellington, Texas. Equipped by Pauly Jail Manufacturing. Photo courtesy of Collingsworth County Museum.

maximum-security compartment in the center provided by
Pauly Jail Manufacturing. There was a gallows, consisting of an
iron ring in the ceiling of the second floor with a trapdoor below, but there is no history of its ever having been used. The
1912 lockup was replaced by a modern facility in 1962.

During the 1930s, Texas was subjected to severe dust storms.
During such a storm in 1930, two prisoners escaped and hid
in a culvert in front of the jail. After two days of a statewide
manhunt, the two gave up for lack of water and food and
turned themselves in.

In 1934, the notorious Bonnie and Clyde were in the area
and ran off a bridge that had recently washed out. Unharmed,
they went to a nearby farmhouse and terrorized the family that
lived there. One of the farmhands slipped away and informed
the sheriff and his deputy in Wellington. The two law enforcement officials, not suspecting big-time criminals, soon found
themselves facing a machine gun. They were then cuffed with
their own handcuffs and taken to Oklahoma in their police
car. Once there, the sheriff and deputy were left tied to trees
with wire but otherwise unharmed. The infamous couple
never saw the Collingsworth County Jail.

Interview conducted by the author: Loretta Wright, Collingsworth
County Museum.
Other resources: Tyler, Barnett, and Barkley, eds., *New Handbook of
Texas,* vol. 2, 215, 630, and vol. 5, 635, 700; Kelsey and Dyal, *Courthouses
of Texas; Dallas Morning News, Texas Almanac, 1998–1999;* Phillips, *Running
with Bonnie and Clyde;* Flores, *Caprock Canyonlands.*

Colorado County (Columbus)

The area that was to become Colorado County began to
see Anglo settlers as early as 1821. It was part of the colony that was settled by Austin's Old Three Hundred. Originally, its administrative center was to be on the Colorado
River at the Atascosito Crossing, nine miles downstream from
Columbus, but this location was later changed to San Felipe
on the Brazos. Colorado County was one of the twenty-three
original counties created in 1836. As early as 1823, a commu-

nity that
eventually
became
known as
Columbus
had devel-
oped on the
Colorado
River. Co-
lumbus was
not incor-
porated un-
til 1866.

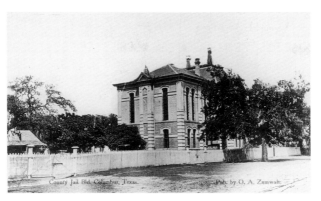

Colorado County jail, 1890–1941, Columbus, Texas.
Designed by architect Eugene Heiner. Photo courtesy
of Nesbitt Memorial Library, Columbus, Texas.

The first jail in Colorado County was a log building built
in 1838 for eight hundred dollars, but the citizens refused to
pay the builder, and it took him ten years to collect his money.
Meanwhile, in the absence of a county jail in which to keep
prisoners, Judge J. W. Robinson sentenced Wilson H. Bibbs to
receive thirty-nine lashes on his bare back and to be branded
with a "T" on his right hand. Bibbs had pleaded guilty to theft
and "thrown himself on the mercy of the court."

In 1847, Colorado County's second courthouse was built
with cells in the basement. A separate jail building was completed in 1858, and six thousand dollars was appropriated to
move the cages from the courthouse to the new structure. The
Victorian Italianate–style building was quite a contrast to previous facilities for confinement.

The 1858 jail seems to have been less secure than the courthouse jail because escapes occurred with great frequency. In
1866, one white man, accused of horse theft, and three freed-
men escaped. That did it. The citizens were concerned, so bids
were taken to build still another jail. The proposals were considered too high, so the compromise was to chain the prisoners
to a "bull ring" (probably a large stone) placed in the 1858 jail.

It is unclear what manner of incarceration was used until
a substantial jail, designed by Eugene T. Heiner of Houston,
was finished in 1890. The lockup was used until 1941, when it
was replaced by a modern facility. The old building was razed
in 1947.

Interviews conducted by the author: Bill Stern, Nesbitt Library, Columbus; David Bucek, author of Eugene Heiner collection, Houston; Cathy Searls Johnson Mahoney, granddaughter of Eugene Heiner.

Other resources: Tyler, Barnett, and Barkley, eds., *New Handbook of Texas,* vol. 2, 224, 235; Commissioners' Court Record Book 1862–1876, 86, 99, 116, 158; *Dallas Morning News, Texas Almanac, 1998–1999.*

Comal County (New Braunfels)

In March 1845 German settlers, under the auspices of the *Adelsverein,* or Society for the Protection of German Immigrants in Texas, began arriving in large numbers on the banks of the Comal River in what would become Comal County. The colonists had arrived in December of the previous year at Indianola, known at that time as Carlshafen, where a point of disembarkation had been arranged by Prince Carl of Solms-Braunfels of Germany. Other land arrangements had been made to the west, but because they were deep in Comanche country, the prince purchased two leagues of land, about eighty-eight hundred acres, around Comal Springs and named the area New Braunfels. Prince Carl had planned to build a castle for Princess Sophia, his fiancée in Germany, but she declined to come to Texas. As a result, Prince Carl turned the project over to John O. Meusebach, later the founder of Fredericksburg. The prince returned to Germany and married Sophia but never returned to Texas.

The first jail was built in 1853. It was made of 7″ by 12″ oak logs and had both an inner and an outer door. Further de-

Comal County jail (in the courthouse), 1898–1985, New Braunfels, Texas (jail is in the lower right corner). Designed by architect J. Riely Gordon.

tails are missing. The second lockup was a limestone building designed by F. E. Ruffini of Austin and completed in 1878. A similar, if not identical, jail was later built by Ruffini in Collin County in 1882. The Pauly Company of St Louis manufactured the cells in the Comal County detention center. In 1898, when the new courthouse was built, a jail was included in the building. That jail was expanded and remodeled by adding an annex in 1931, and the facility remained in use until 1985.

Interviews conducted by the author: Becky Lombardy and Michelle Oatman, Sophienburg Museum and Archives.

Other resources: *Dallas Morning News, Texas Almanac, 1998–1999;* Tyler and Tyler, *Texas Museums;* Tyler, Barnett, and Barkley, eds., *New Handbook of Texas,* vol. 1, 30, vol. 2, 237, vol. 4, 649, 987, and vol. 5, 1141; Rawson, *History of New Braunfels.*

Comanche County (Comanche)

Comanche County was created in 1856 and organized in that same year. Cora, sixteen miles to the southeast of the town of Comanche, was chosen as the county seat. The seat of government, however, was moved to Comanche in 1859. The population in 1860 was 709, but the withdrawal of federal troops during the Civil War resulted in widespread Indian depredations, and by 1866 the population had fallen to only 60. Comanche was incorporated in 1873 and eventually became a trade and transportation center.

Comanche County's 1903 jail is a remarkable Romanesque Revival stone building; it resembles a medieval castle and in its original form was complete with tower and battlements. It bears a striking resemblance to the Brown County jail, but the identity of the architect is unclear for either of these buildings. A projected jail design by J. Riely Gordon for Duval County was never built but bears such a resemblance to the Comanche County and Brown County jails that Gordon may have done all three. The contractor for the Comanche County lockup was Martin and Moodie, and the cost was twenty-seven thousand dollars. When a modern detention center was completed in 1988, the old Comanche jail was modestly remodeled to serve as a law and abstract office; fortunately, the building still retains much of its original character.

Interview conducted by the author: Christopher Till.
Other resources: Tyler, Barnett, and Barkley, eds., *New Handbook of Texas,* vol. 2, 240, 322; Tyler and Tyler, *Texas Museums;* Kelsey and Dyal, *Courthouses of Texas;* Cunningham, *Triggernometry;* Sonnichsen, *I'll Die before I'll Run;* W. P. Webb, *Texas Rangers.*

Concho County (Paint Rock)

Concho County, named for the river that runs through it, was created from Bexar County and organized in 1879. *Concho,* Spanish for "shell," is appropriate inasmuch as the river contains a large variety of clams, some of which produce beautiful Concho River pearls. The shells were prized by the Indians and widely traded, and the clams themselves were an important food for native tribes. Paint Rock got its name from the plethora of prehistoric Indian pictographs on a nearby Concho River bluff.

The first courthouse (1879) was a wooden building. In May 1882, various plans were submitted for a new jail. Those by Martin, Byrnes, and Johnson for a two-story jail were accepted, and a payment of fifty dollars was made for them. The jail, also built by Martin, Byrnes, and Johnson, had a stone foundation, and its first-floor iron cage had a stone floor as well. It was completed by 1884, but for some reason, repairs on the roof were necessary as early as December of that year.

In May 1911, bonds were authorized in the amount of fifteen thousand dollars for a new lockup. There are no photographs of the jail, but William Warren, son of W. E. Warren (sheriff from 1927 to 1935), has described it as being built of large limestone blocks and two stories high. It had an outside wooden stairway to the second floor but no inside stairs. There were no iron cells inside, and restraint was dependent on "huge iron doors," separate for the first and second floors. Heat was provided by a stove fueled by wood that the trusties cut. The 1911 jail is attributed to architect Oscar Ruffini of San Angelo, brother of F. E. Ruffini, an Austin architect.

Interviews conducted by the author: Carolyn Moody, Texas Historical Commission; William Warren, son of Sheriff W. E. Warren; Barbara Hoffman, county clerk; Cora Ellen Campbell, Paint Rock Ranch.

Other resources: Tyler, Barnett, and Barkley, eds., *New Handbook of Texas,* vol. 2, 256, and vol. 5, 14; Kirkland and Newcomb, *Rock Art of Texas Indians;* Kelsey and Dyal, *Courthouses of Texas; Dallas Morning News, Texas Almanac, 1998–1999.*

Cooke County (Gainesville)

Named for Capt. W. G. Cooke, a veteran of the Texas Revolution, Cooke County was created in 1848 and organized in 1850 with Gainesville as the county seat. Gainesville was named after Gen. Edmund Pendleton Gaines of Virginia, who arrested Aaron Burr in 1807 and was a witness at his trial for treason. He had also served in the Mexican War.

There is no official record of a jail in Cooke County for the first eight years after the county was created. In May 1857, however, the court ordered lot 1 of block 16 set aside for a lockup. The first jail of record was built in 1858 under a contract to F. N. Hackney for sixteen hundred dollars. Double walls were built on a rock foundation 3′ wide and 2′ high. The walls were of hewn timber, and the second floor was 9′ above the first. The double walls were separated by a space of 6″ filled with 6″ side-by-side oak timbers. All floors were to be of 2″ plank-ing that was "well nailed down." Each room, up and down, was to have one 12″ by 12″ window. Access to the upper floor was by

Cooke County jail, 1915–1981, Gainesville, Texas. The jail is now an adult correctional center. Photo by Gene's Photos, Gainesville, Texas.

outside stairs, and the only entry to the lower room was a 30″ square trapdoor and a ladder that could be withdrawn. During the Civil War, forty-two men were tried by a "citizens court" for being Union sympathizers. They were found guilty and hanged. It is not known whether the men were held in the jail during the irregular process.

In 1870, a visitor, W. O. Davis, said, "There was no jail. When the sheriff arrested a man, he turned him over to a deputy, who guarded him with a pistol, [but] very often the prisoner had the pistol and was gone a short time after his arrest."

In 1874, a second jail was built, described as a 14′ square oak box with windows. The third jail, built in 1884, was a brick building that included a fire station on the first floor. The second floor contained the city hall and a calaboose in the back. It was designed by architect J. J. Kane. Today it has been extensively remodeled and serves as the Morton Museum of Cooke County. The fourth jail, built in 1915 of red brick, was next door to the former lockup. It too has been remodeled and now serves as a community correction center.

Interviews conducted by the author: Patty Tucker, county clerk; Rebecca Larson, assistant county clerk.

Other resources: Tyler and Tyler, *Texas Museums;* Metz, *Roadside History of Texas;* Tyler, Barnett, and Barkley, eds., *New Handbook of Texas,* vol. 2, 308, and vol. 3, 41, 47; *Dallas Morning News, Texas Almanac, 1998–1999;* Kelsey and Dyal, *Courthouses of Texas;* Jones, *Early Days in Cooke County;* Smith, *First One Hundred Years in Cooke County;* Welch, *Historic Sites of Texas.*

Coryell County (Gatesville)

Named after pioneer James Coryell, Coryell County was created and organized in 1854. Coryell, a Texas Ranger, was killed by Indians while raiding a bee tree near the Brazos River in 1837. Gatesville, which was incorporated in 1870, is a community that grew up five miles west of old Fort Gates (1849–1852).

Located on a lot behind the present National Bank of Gatesville, Coryell County's first jail was a typical, although small, dungeon with double-log oak walls. The cell was a subterranean excavation 4½ feet deep, accessed only by a trapdoor. Understand-

Coryell County jail, 1934–present, Gatesville, Texas. Designed by Birch D. Easterwood.

ably, the wooden jail, when occupied, often required one or two guards, who were paid $1–$3 per day to keep their eyes on the prisoners. The jail was used for twenty years before being replaced. The Coryell County Museum has managed to preserve this sole-surviving dungeon jail in Texas.

In 1875 the commissioners' court contracted with P. J. Pauly and Brothers to build a second lockup. It was designed by W. P. Ingraham, for which he was paid $100. The facility was a two-story castle on South Seventh Street, and the cost of construction was $10,900. The structure had no gallows, but in 1891 two outdoor wooden gallows were constructed nearby for the execution of two men by the names of Leeper and Powell, who had murdered a man named John T. Matthes during a robbery. Matthes had lived long enough to say who had shot him before he died. The killers were tried, convicted, and hanged.

In 1897 once again P. J. Pauly was summoned to build a jail, which was to have a capacity for thirty prisoners with the usual sheriff's quarters on the first floor. Pauly was capable of undertaking all aspects of the job—design, construction, and installation—and apparently did so for this structure.

In the 1930s, however, because the 1897 jail was declared "structurally insecure," a fourth lockup was planned. Birch D. Easterwood drew the plans, and the building was constructed by Johnson Construction Company of Waco. Southern Prison Company provided the prison cells needed to supplement the Pauly compartments brought from the old jail.

Interviews conducted by the author: Jimmy L. Wood, justice of the peace; Helen Swift, Coryell Museum of History; Barbara Simpson, Coryell County clerk; Jenny Hendrickson, Coryell County Museum.

Other resources: Tyler, Barnett, and Barkley, eds., *New Handbook of Texas,* vol. 2, 344, 345, 1101, and vol. 3, 116; Mears, *Coryell County Scrapbook;* Scott, *History of Coryell County, Texas.*

Cottle County (Paducah)

In 1876 the Texas legislature created Cottle County from Fannin County. The area was organized in 1892 and named for George W. Cottle, a defender of the Alamo. The 1880 census of Cottle County was fourteen but ten years later had grown to 290 souls. In 1893, the legislature authorized a bond issue for financing a jail for the young county.

The first lockup was a two-story limestone structure built with the twelve-thousand-dollar proceeds of a bond sale. The structure was to have walls 22″ thick and to include a bell tower with a bell that "could be heard for three miles." When the building was finished, it officially opened for business on January 1, 1894, and served the county well until 1921, when a new structure was built. This second facility was a two-story rectangular building made of red brick in a simple utilitarian design. The architect is unknown. The lower level was five bricks thick, and the second level was three bricks thick. The ceiling of the first floor was made of concrete 2′ thick, while that of the second level was 3′ thick, both reinforced with ¾″ steel. Southern Structural Steel Company provided the cells. There was a trapdoor for a gallows, said to have been used

Cottle County jail, 1921–1998, Paducah, Texas.

once in 1921. The sheriff's quarters were in an adjacent build-ing. This edifice was remodeled in 1980 and used until the spring of 1998, when it was closed. Cottle County prisoners are now kept in Childress, Texas.

Interviews conducted by the author: Richard Burton; Sheriff Roy LeHew; Jimmye C. Taylor.

Other resources: *Dallas Morning News, Texas Almanac, 1998–1999;* Tyler, Barnett, and Barkley, eds., *New Handbook of Texas,* vol. 2, 350; Metz, *Roadside History of Texas;* C. T. Bennett, *Our Roots Grow Deep.*

Crane County (Crane)

Crane County was created from Tom Green County in 1887 but was not organized until 1927. It was named for long-time minister and president of Baylor University, William Carey Crane. Due to its remote location and scant rainfall (annual average 12.97 inches), the area remained relatively unpop-ulated through the first quarter of the twentieth century. The discovery of oil in 1926, however, made the arid and treeless territory the place where everyone wanted to be. Suddenly the county was organized, and the community of Crane, es-tablished in 1908, became the county seat. In 1920 the area's population was 37, but by 1930, it had grown to 2,231. There was only one problem: no water. What water there was, was reserved for cooking and making homemade whiskey. The women sent their laundry to El Paso rather than use the scarce resource for washing. The nearest water was from a well seven miles away and cost $1 per barrel, but good water came from Alpine, Texas, at $2.25 per barrel.

Jail? Who needs one with only thirty-seven people in the county? The truth is that in 1918 there were no roads in the area, so how was a prisoner going to escape? Once organized, though, a self-respecting county needs a jail, so in 1927 the commissioners made a deal to buy a secondhand lockup from Ector County for $175. This was a one-story, two-cell wooden affair made of 2″ by 4″ pieces of lumber stacked flat, one on top of the other, and nailed together. Ector County had built the jail in 1904 and used it for twenty years before retiring it in 1924.

Crane County's second jail was a little more formidable. It was a reinforced poured-concrete building with sheriff's quarters on the first floor and three cells upstairs: one for women, one for isolation, and one for everyone else. The facility was finished with white stucco. Crane County has no jail as of this writing, and no one is certain of the fate of the old building.

Interviews conducted by the author: Chief Deputy Sheriff Donnie Henderson and Sheriff Danny Simmons, both of Crane County; David Greer, Crane County Museum.

Other resources: Kelsey and Dyal, *Courthouses of Texas; Dallas Morning News, Texas Almanac, 1998–1999;* Tyler, Barnett, and Barkley, eds., *New Handbook of Texas,* vol. 2, 391; W. Robinson, *People's Architecture.*

Crockett County (Ozona)

Crockett County was created in 1875 and organized in 1891. Settlement was slow until after the Civil War. It was then that three battalions of Texas Rangers were deployed into the area to help control the Indian menace that had gone unchecked during the war. Camp Melvin was established at the Pecos River crossing near present Iraan, Texas. Although only intermittently occupied, the camp served as a defense. When Crockett County was first formed, it included Schleicher, Sutton, and parts of Val Verde, Edwards, and Kinney counties.

After organization, the community of Powell Well, named for the strong water well dug by E. M. Powell, was chosen as the county seat. In addition, land

Crockett County jail, 1894–present, Ozona, Texas. Designed by architect Oscar Ruffini. Photo courtesy of John Webel Lambeth.

was given for a courthouse, church, school, park, and jail. Soon
the name was changed to Ozona, and people began to buy
lots and develop a settled community. Curiously, Ozona is not
incorporated and in fact is the largest unincorporated town in
Texas. It happens to be the only town in Crockett County and
is managed by county government.

In 1891 the new commissioners' court met under a large
live oak tree and, among other things, ordered a set of handcuffs and two pairs of leg irons. That live oak tree is still standing. The land designated for the jail was soon occupied in
1892 by an artistic limestone building designed by Oscar Ruffini
of San Angelo. The lockup had sheriff's quarters on the first
floor, which are still used today for the sheriff's office. The
second floor held the cells for the prisoners, and there was
a tower for a gallows, although it was never equipped with the
trapdoor that gallows usually had.

There is a favorite local story that, during the 1900s, a
member of the sheriff's family noticed a blanket waving outside a window. Investigation revealed that some prisoners
had sawed through the cell bars, cut their way up through the
metal roof, and were letting themselves down with a rope
made from blankets. There was no joy for the prisoners that
night. They were returned to their cells forthwith.

Interviews conducted by the author: Johnnie Lambeth, Dripping
Springs, Texas; Genice Childress, Crockett County Museum.
Other resources: Tyler, Barnett, and Barkley, eds., *New Handbook of
Texas,* vol. 1, 942, vol. 2, 410, and vol. 4, 1192; Tyler and Tyler, *Texas
Museums;* Metz, *Roadside History of Texas.*

Crosby County (Crosbyton)

Named for Texas land commissioner Stephen Crosby,
Crosby County was created in 1876 but was not orga-
nized until 1886. Early settlement was slow due to widespread
Comanche, Kiowa, and Kickapoo Indian raids on isolated
farms and ranches. After the Civil War, the army sent Col.
Ranald S. Mackenzie, along with other military personnel, to
Texas to deal with the problem. Mackenzie became obsessed

Crosby County jail, 1914–1934, Crosbyton, Texas.
Designed by architect M. L. Waller. Photo courtesy of
Verna Anne Wheeler, director and photographer for the
Crosby County Pioneer Memorial.

with crushing the threat to the westward movement in frontier Texas and aggressively pursued the Indians of the Panhandle. In 1871, he fought a skirmish in Blanco Canyon a few miles southeast of where Crosbyton would later be founded. In 1874, he finally caught the Indians in Palo Duro Canyon, destroyed their horses, and ended the Red River War. Mackenzie slaughtered 1,048 horses and mules, salvaging only a few for use by his troopers. He well knew that the Indians' existence depended largely on horses.

Crosby County had three seats of government: Estacado in 1886, Emma in 1891, and finally Crosbyton in 1912. After the county seat was moved to Crosbyton, the Emma courthouse and jail were sold to Julian Bassett for fifteen hundred dollars. Using the proceeds, a courthouse could then be built in Crosbyton. The architectural firm of M. H. Waller of Fort Worth drew the plans for the courthouse, which was completed in 1914 with a jail in the southeast corner of the basement. In 1934, when the courthouse was remodeled, the lockup was moved to a different location. There is no known photograph of the 1934 freestanding jail. In 1965, the 1934 facility was remodeled, and sheriff's quarters were added; the original building is now hardly discernable.

Interviews conducted by the author: Verna Ann Wheeler, Crosby County Pioneer Museum; Kenneth Witt, county judge.

Other resources: Tyler, Barnett, and Barkley, eds., *New Handbook of Texas,* vol. 1, 582, vol. 2, 416, and vol. 4, 416; Kelsey and Dyal, *Courthouses of Texas; Dallas Morning News, Texas Almanac, 1998–1999;* Hall, *Early History of Floyd County;* Mayhall, *Indian Wars of Texas.*

Culberson County (Van Horn)

Culberson County was created from El Paso County in 1911 and organized in 1912. The highest point in Texas, Guadalupe Peak (8,751 feet), is found here. The county seat was named for Maj. Jefferson Van Horn, the discoverer of the most valuable commodity in those parts: a dependable water supply. The specific site of that discovery was called Van Horn Wells. In 1880, Maggie Graham and her wagon train were attacked by Apache Indians near the wells, about ten miles south of present-day Van Horn. Maggie was killed as she walked alongside her wagon and is buried in a poorly marked grave near the old stage station at Van Horn Wells. Her husband, though wounded, survived. As for the Indians, Texas Rangers caught up with them in the Diablo Mountains and killed everyone.

Before Culberson County was organized, the county jail for the area was in El Paso. During that time, there was a holding cell in Van Horn that consisted of a 12′ by 14′ room made of railroad ties. Because of the great distances in West Texas and since transportation was usually by horseback or wagon, strategically placed holding cells were necessary for managing and moving prisoners.

In 1912 a jail was built in Van Horn. It was a very modest, flat-roofed 16′ by 20′ brick building with two cells. There were eight barred windows and an iron door—a total of nine openings through which a resourceful prisoner could seek freedom—and, according to history, they did. The brick walls were thin, and detainees regularly escaped by dislodging bricks or, according to one source, "by breaking the windows." That facility was used until 1964, when a new courthouse was built that included a lockup. The 1912 jail is not used now, although the Culberson County Historical Commission has maintained the old structure.

Interview conducted by the author: Noble Smith, Culberson County Historical Museum.

Other resources: *Dallas Morning News, Texas Almanac, 1998–1999;* Tyler, Barnett, and Barkley, eds., *New Handbook of Texas,* vol. 2, 437, and vol. 6, 437; Metz, *Roadside History of Texas;* Reading, *Arrows over Texas.*

Dallam County (Dalhart)

Like so many other Texas Panhandle counties, Dallam County was created by the Texas legislature in 1876. Located in the extreme northwest corner of the Panhandle, it was remote and subject to Indian occupation until the end of the Red River War. It was organized in 1891. In 1901, the Chicago, Rock Island, and Pacific Railroad met the Denver and Fort Worth Railroad at a place called "Twist in the Panhandle." In true railroad tradition, it became Twist Junction and later became the town now known as Dalhart. The main business in early Dallam County concerned its part of the three million acres of Texas land traded for the construction of a new state capitol in Austin. This land ended up as the famous XIT Ranch. Sadly, the state capitol building in Austin, completed in 1854, burned in 1881. It is interesting to note, however, that, as early as 1879, the legislature had already appropriated the three million acres to raise the money for a new capitol building.

The original county seat was Texline, founded in 1888 as a division point for the Denver City and Fort Worth Railroad. The first county jail was built simply of 2″ by 4″ lumber, stacked flat side against flat side and nailed down. It was a 6′ by 8′ building with a flat roof, a wooden door, and two 4″ by 8″ windows for "air conditioning." The building still stands, though in near-demolished condition, in a vacant lot. In October 1892, a new single-story stone jail was completed at a cost of fifty-nine hundred dollars. It was used until the county seat was moved to Dalhart in 1903.

That same year, a courthouse was built on the north side of Dalhart. In 1906, bids were taken, and a lockup was erected next to the courthouse. The cells from the Texline stone jail were brought to the construction site and used in the new facility. Some of its cells were built by Diebold and some by Pauly, and it is unclear which cells came from Texline. The 1906 structure was used until 1922, when a new courthouse was built, including a jail on the third floor. The 1922 jail seemed to serve well until new requirements by the Texas Commission on Jail Standards mandated that a larger, improved detention center be built in 1982. The lockup was then moved out of the courthouse.

Interviews conducted by the author: Sheriff E. H. Little; Nick Olson, director, XIT Museum; Dallam-Hartley Counties Historical Association; Nicky Olson, curator, XIT Museum.

Other resources: *Dallas Morning News, Texas Almanac, 1998–1999;* Tyler, Barnett, and Barkley, eds., *New Handbook of Texas,* vol. 2, 476, and vol. 6, 1101; Metz, *Roadside History of Texas.*

Dallas County (Dallas)

In 1846 the Texas legislature formed Dallas County from Nacogdoches and Robertson counties. It is thought that it was named for George M. Dallas, who served as vice president under Pres. James K. Polk. In 1841, John Neely Bryan built a log cabin on the east bank of the Trinity River at a ford that had served Indian travelers for centuries on their east-west trade route. The site was soon crossed as well by a north-south road otherwise known as the Preston Road, which ran from Austin to the Red River. The Indians were troublesome until Sam Houston met with nine tribes at Fort Bird (later Birdville, east of Fort Worth) and secured a peace treaty. After organization, Dallas was made temporary county seat in 1846. Four years later, in 1850, an election was held to choose between Dallas and Hord's Ridge as the county seat. Dallas became the permanent county seat, and Hord's Ridge eventually became known as Oak Cliff.

In December of 1850, Dallas built its first county jail, which was a one-story, double-walled box, each wall made of 8″ hewn oak, separated by an 8″ space filled with vertical 8″ timbers. The building was 16′ square and 9′ high, containing one iron-encased window that measured 10″ by 16″. The door was 3½′ wide by 5′ high, cased in 6″ oak, double planked, with one side swinging in and the other swinging out. The window was barred with 3½″ iron bars, leaving very little room for the passage of air. It is unclear how long the log jail was used.

A two-story courthouse had been built on the courthouse square in 1871, and there may have been a jail in that structure. The building burned in 1880, but it was rebuilt with an

Dallas County jail, 1915–present, Dallas, Texas.
The jail is on the sixth floor of the Criminal
Courts Building. Photo by Stanley Gilbert.
From the author's collection.

additional floor and a tower. In 1892 the county built a three-story jail on Houston Street near the viaduct and Jackson Street. Sometime after 1893, the lockup was razed, and a post office was built on the site. Union Station stood nearby to the south.

In 1892, a new courthouse was built after the old 1871 courthouse burned a second time. Designed by Orlopp and Kusener, the courthouse has become a landmark on Houston and Main streets in downtown Dallas. It was built on the spot originally designated by John Neely Bryan as public ground and at the site of the first log courthouse in 1846.

The jail in the 1892 courthouse served until in 1915, when a larger criminal courts building with jail, designed by H. A. Overbeck, was completed across the street. This edifice is nine stories tall and has space for two hundred prisoners. To minimize escape, entrance to the lockup is by elevator only. It is a classic, early-twentieth-century Renaissance Revival building in red brick trimmed with terra cotta and white marble. The cells and ironwork were provided by the Pauly Jail Building Company. There are ninety-six cells on the sixth floor, arranged three tiers high. The jail has its own hospital, operating room, jailer's quarters, and barber shop. It is still in use today.

Interviews conducted by the author: Ken Holmes, historian; Billy D. Martin, maintenance supervisor of George Allen Courts Building; Paul

Bentley, Dallas Police Department, retired; Jim Foster, photo archivist, Dallas Public Library, Texas and Dallas History and Archives Division.

Other resources: *Dallas Morning News, Texas Almanac, 1998–1999;* Tyler, Barnett, and Barkley, eds., *New Handbook of Texas,* vol. 2, 478, 484, 1088; Robinson, *Gone from Texas;* Kelsey and Dyal, *Courthouses of Texas; Memorial and Biographical History of Dallas County, Texas.*

Dawson County (Lamesa)

Dawson County, named after Nicholas M. Dawson, veteran of the battle of San Jacinto, was created in 1876 and organized in 1905. Howard County handled its administrative and judicial chores in the interim. Col. William Shafter explored the area in October 1875 and found an Indian encampment at Laguna Sabrina, a shallow lake twenty miles west of the future Lamesa. The Indians departed to the west, but it was evident that this was a regular campsite. After 1875, as the buffalo began to be killed off and as the Native Americans were removed to Indian territory, ranchers began to move in to take advantage of the tall luxuriant prairie grass.

When founded, the county seat was named Chicago, but the name was changed to Lamesa when the post office was granted. The name no doubt derives from *la mesa,* Spanish for "table," which somewhat describes the flat, tablelike land in the area.

In May 1905, the court ordered an election to issue bonds to build a courthouse and jail. The measure passed in December 1905, and F. C. Maupin was awarded a contract to build the edifice for $2,849. The frame building was completed in 1906, but today no one remembers the location of the jail cell.

A second courthouse, designed by Sanguinet and Staats of Fort Worth, was built in 1917. It was a three-story brick building with a jail on the third floor. In 1952, an annex was added to the courthouse, and the jail was moved into the addition.

Interview conducted by the author: Wayne C. Smith, director, Lamesa Area Chamber of Commerce.

Other resources: *Dallas Morning News, Texas Almanac, 1998–1999;* Tyler, Barnett, and Barkley, eds., *New Handbook of Texas,* vol. 2, 540, and vol. 4, 47; Metz, *Roadside History of Texas;* Tyler and Tyler, *Texas Museums;* Lindsey, *Trail of Years in Dawson County, Texas.*

Deaf Smith County (Hereford)

Deaf Smith County was created in 1876 and organized in
1890. The county was named for Sam Houston's famous
scout, who, among other things, destroyed the bridge over
Vince's Bayou before the battle of San Jacinto, thereby pre-
venting reinforcements from joining Santa Anna. In the beginning, large ranches dominated the county, but these gradually
gave way to farms and the production of wheat.

In 1890, when the county was organized, the town of
Grenada, created by the XIT Ranch, was made county seat
in a close election. The name was changed to La Plata, which
soon had a courthouse, post office, school, jail, and saloon.
The lockup was said to have been a single iron cell of indeterminate manufacture in a modest building, perhaps the courthouse. La Plata remained the county seat for nine years before
a variety of difficulties arose: A serious drought set in from
1891 to 1894, then in 1897 a twenty-one-day blizzard buffeted
the county. The final blow came when the Pecos and Northern Texas Railroad bypassed La Plata in favor of a new community, Bluewater. In 1899, Bluewater was voted in as the
new county seat, but its name was changed to Hereford in rec-
ognition of the thousands of Hereford cattle in the area.

Deaf Smith County's second keep was immediately planned,
and the
necessary
taxes were
levied for a
jail, court-
house, and
school. The
cage from
the jail at
La Plata was
moved to
Hereford to
be used un-
til the sec-
ond lockup

Deaf Smith County jail, 1899–?, Hereford, Texas. Photo
courtesy of Deaf Smith County Historical Museum, Hereford, Texas.

was built. The new structure was a substantial two-story brick building with sheriff's quarters on the first floor. Ed F. Connell was sheriff from 1906 to 1910, and he and his family lived in the jail. Mrs. Connell cooked for the prisoners as well as for her family, and they all ate the same food. Sheriff Connell had been a Texas Ranger and had served as sheriff in La Plata before the move. His daughter, Eddie Connell Trussell, told about life in the Deaf Smith County lockup. At the time, the county was on the fringe of civilization, and if someone got sick, a note explaining the symptoms would be sent to the doctor in Amarillo. The forty-eight-mile trip by a cowboy on horseback took a day or two, and he would return with a diagnosis, medicine, and instructions. When one of Sheriff Connell's prisoners came down with abdominal pain, the doctor arrived with a diagnosis—appendicitis—so he performed an appendectomy on the second floor of the jail in the "run-around," the walkway around the cells in the center of the jail area.

Interviews conducted by the author: Donna Brockman and Paula Edwards, Deaf Smith County Museum.

Other resources: Tyler, Barnett, and Barkley, eds., *New Handbook of Texas*, vol. 2, 546; Metz, *Roadside History of Texas;* Tyler and Tyler, *Texas Museums;* Kelsey and Dyal, *Courthouses of Texas;* B. Patterson, *History of Deaf Smith County;* Deaf Smith County Historical Society, *Land and Its People*.

Delta County (Cooper)

Delta County was created and organized in 1870. It was so named because of its triangular shape, defined on its north and south borders by the North and South Sulfur rivers, which join at its eastern edge. Together, these rivers and "Jernigan's Thicket" on the west isolated the area in such a way that, before the Civil War, it became a refuge for desperados seeking a place that was beyond the reach of the law. After the war, as the thicket gave way to croplands, the outlaws began to go elsewhere, and the county enjoyed a period of prosperity brought on by the production of corn and cotton.

Delta County's first jail was a log and plank building located one block north of the courthouse square on Marshall Street. In 1876, following a long series of moves across Texas ahead of lawmen, Wild Bill Longley, using an assumed name, settled in Delta County long enough to do some farming for a "Parson" Lay. In storybook tradition, he fell in love with Lovenia Jack, the lovely sixteen-year-old daughter of a man named Jack, who had befriended him. Most of the stories agree that, after raising a crop on shares for Lay, a dispute occurred. Lay made the mistake of having Longley arrested and placed in the Delta County jail. This offended Longley, and, in June 1876, he set fire to the keep, escaped, borrowed a shotgun, and shot Parson Lay. The jail recovered and was rebuilt, but the preacher succumbed. Longley resumed his travels but was arrested in Louisiana in the summer of 1877. He was tried for the murder of Wilson Anderson in Giddings, Texas, and sentenced to hang. After thirteen months in the Giddings and Galveston jails, he was hanged on October 11, 1878. According to the *Austin Statesman,* Longley had killed thirty-two men. He was twenty-seven years old.

After repair of the fire damage, the 1871 wood jail lasted until 1889, when the second jail, a two-story brick building, was put up. That jail had cells and ironwork that were provided by the Pauly Company and a gallows that was used only once, when Jim Fisher was hanged for the murder of Austin Hardy. The 1889 jail was used until 1940, when a new detention center, now known as the Law Enforcement Building, was completed. The 1940 jail was replaced in 1994.

Interview conducted by the author: Sheriff Bennie Fisher.

Other resources: Tyler, Barnett, and Barkley, eds., *New Handbook of Texas,* vol. 2, 579, and vol. 3, 933; Cunningham, *Triggernometry; Dallas Morning News, Texas Almanac, 1998–1999;* Wax, *Dead Man on the Bayou?;* Kelsey and Dyal, *Courthouses of Texas.*

Denton County (Denton)

In 1841, the Texas congress made a land grant to the Peters colony, otherwise known as the Texian Land and Immigration Company, an investment group of English and Ameri-

can busi-
nesspeople.
The area
comprised
some four-
teen hun-
dred square
miles south
of the
Red River,
including
the future
Denton
County. In

Denton County jail, 1891–1964, Denton, Texas. Photo
courtesy of the Denton County Historical Museum.

1846, Denton County was created, and Pinckneyville was made
the county seat. Within ten years, the seat of government was
moved twice, finally to Denton, and named for John Bunyan
Denton, a preacher, Texas Ranger, and Indian fighter who
was killed in the battle of Village Creek near present-day Ar-
lington, Texas.

The first jail in Denton County was built in 1861 and was
located at North Locust Street and McKinney. It was a typical
dungeon—two stories, with walls of hewn logs, three logs
thick, and no door into the ground level. Access to the ground
level, where the prisoners were kept, was through a trapdoor
in the center of the second floor. Some dungeons had one
or two heavily barred 12″ by 12″ windows. The jail burned
in 1867, leaving Denton County with no detention facility;
prisoners thus had to be kept in neighboring counties. In
1868, when Sheriff Matt Daugherty was escorting a man from
McKinney back to Denton to be tried for murder, he was held
up by a gang of armed men and forced to release his prisoner.
That incident led to the construction in 1870 of a second jail,
a two-story sandstone building on the east side of the courthouse square. J. C. McDermott of Jacksboro built the jail for
thirty-six hundred dollars with bricks made by R. B. Harris at
the Bushey Plant southeast of Denton. The facility proved to
be too small and insecure to hold prisoners and was replaced
in 1878. The new lockup was a one-story edifice at 402 North
Elm Street, just north of the old facility. The design was of

shallow depth but displayed a long front dimension. Denton County's fourth jail—two stories—was built of brick and stone in 1891. It served the county until it was replaced in 1964.

Interview conducted by the author: Holly Hervey, Denton County Historical Museum.

Other resources: Tyler, Barnett, and Barkley, eds., *New Handbook of Texas,* vol. 2, 599, and vol. 5, 167; *Dallas Morning News, Texas Almanac, 1998–1999;* Bridges, *History of Denton, Texas.*

DeWitt County (Cuero)

DeWitt County, named for impresario Green DeWitt, was created from Gonzales, Goliad, and Victoria counties and organized in 1846. DeWitt went to Mexico City to obtain the right to introduce colonists into Texas. With Stephen Austin's help, he was granted a land concession between the Guadalupe and LaVaca rivers, extending from the Old San Antonio Road on the north to a line ten leagues (about thirty miles) inland from the Gulf of Mexico on the south. In 1825 DeWitt had a community surveyed that would later become the town of Gonzales, but Indian raids postponed settlement until 1834. DeWitt brought in 531 immigrants, and the community became the gathering place for the Texian military during the fight for independence from Mexico in 1835 and 1836. More than fifty men from Gonzalez made their way through Santa Anna's forces into the Alamo in response to Travis's call for help and of course were lost. After the county was organized in 1846, the county seat was changed four times before Cuero was finally designated in 1876.

DeWitt County jail, 1917–1960, Cuero, Texas. Photo courtesy of Patsy Goebel.

DeWitt County was the theater for one of the famous Texas disputes: the Sutton-Taylor feud, which lasted for ten years and resulted in twenty-two killings, many by ambush or lynching. Essentially, this was a post–Civil War conflict between the Taylor family and the abusive Reconstruction state police of Gov. Edmund Davis.

There were probably jails in the several early county seats of DeWitt County, but the first one for which records still exist is the Cuero jail built in 1877 at 208 Live Oak Street, across the street from the courthouse. That structure was built of brick and stone on a stone foundation three feet thick. The builder was Edward Northcraft of Hays County, and specifications called for cell-locking mechanisms and iron bars by Pauly Brothers. Some of the ironwork was to be manufactured locally. The cost was $16,000. The courthouse burned in 1894, but the jail lasted until replaced in 1917 by a three-story brick lockup built by Janssen Brothers for $18,745. That structure had cells and ironwork provided by Southern Structural Steel Company for $11,888. It was a formidable building and served the county until 1960.

Interviews conducted by the author: Frank B. Sheppard; Patsy Goebel; Verna Smith, DeWitt County Museum.

Other resources: *Dallas Morning News, Texas Almanac, 1998–1999;* Kelsey and Dyal, *Courthouses of Texas;* Frantz, Cox, and Griffin, *Lure of the Land;* Tyler, Barnett, and Barkley, eds., *New Handbook of Texas,* vol. 2, 617; Metz, *Roadside History of Texas;* Tyler and Tyler, *Texas Museums.*

Dickens County (Dickens)

Dickens County was created in 1876 and organized in 1891. It was named for J. Dickens, hero of the Alamo. The several large ranches in the county, including the Spur Ranch, the Pitchfork, and the Matador, dominated most of the county's early history. The town of Espuela became the temporary county seat. The voters, however, changed the seat of government to Dickens in March 1892.

In May 1892 the commissioners' court voted to issue $20,000 in bonds and levied a tax to build a courthouse; a contract was made with E. L. Aiken to construct the building.

Dickens County jail, 1909–present, Dickens, Texas. Built by Southern Structural Steel. Photo by Stanley Gilbert. From the author's collection.

The jail was a different story. In November of that year, the court passed an order to issue $11,000 in bonds to be delivered to Aiken to build a jail, but either carelessly or intentionally, the court failed to pass a tax to pay the interest and principle on the bonds. In 1893, after the jail was finished, the court decided that it would not accept the building and then repudiated the bonds. The record is unclear, but Aiken must have given or sold the jail to a J. L. Wells, who, incidentally, was on Aiken's bond. Wells then made an agreement to rent the jail to Dickens County for $10 per month for the "confinement of prisoners." Aiken's story has not as yet been heard. The jail served well enough until the next keep was built in 1909. Oral history says that there was a wooden jail that burned before the 1909 jail was built, but it is unclear whether this was the structure that Aiken had built.

In 1909 Southern Structural Steel Company built a lockup made of limestone for Dickens County, which is the third oldest jail still in use in the state and still certified by the Texas Commission on Jail Standards. The cost was nine thousand dollars. This structure was apparently secure, but folks tell about the time during Prohibition when three prisoners broke out through the roof during the night. They caught a ride to town with a bootlegger, bought several bottles of wine, and broke back into the jail, where they drank the wine and went blissfully to sleep. In another jailbreak, Sheriff W. B. Arthur was killed by prisoner Virgil Stallkup with a gun that had been smuggled into the lockup. Stallkup escaped but was later caught and given the death penalty.

Interviews conducted by the author: Rita Brendle; Sheriff Ken Brendle.

Other resources: *Dallas Morning News, Texas Almanac, 1998–1999;* Metz, *Roadside History of Texas;* Tyler, Barnett, and Barkley, eds., *New Handbook of Texas,* vol. 2, 633; Arrington, *History of Dickens County;* Dickens County Historical Commission, "Dickens County, Its Land and Its People," *Sesquicentennial Issue.*

Dimmit County (Carrizo Springs)

Dimmit County—named for Phillip Dimitt, hero of the Texas Revolution—was created in 1858 and organized in 1880. The misspelling of the name was a clerical error at the time the county was created. The arid and harsh country of Dimmit County was in the disputed territory between Texas and Mexico south of the Nueces River and became a sanctuary for desperados from both countries. They, along with hostile Indians, caused the territory to be only slowly settled until after the Civil War. Shortly after the war, John Townsend, a black man from Nacogdoches, tried to settle several families, but harassment by the Indians caused them to abandon the effort and move to Eagle Pass. After the war, pacification by Texas Rangers and U.S. troops led to settlement in the area. In 1884, discovery of artesian water gradually began to convert part of the county into a "garden district" for the production of vegetables.

The first jail in Dimmit County was on the site of the present detention center. It was built about 1885 from stone left over from the construction of the 1884 courthouse. Older citizens recollect that the sheriff always kept a pile of rocks in the field next to the jail and would exercise the prisoners by having them break the large stones into small ones.

The second jail was

Dimmit County jail, 1937–present, Carrizo Springs, Texas.

built in 1937 of poured, reinforced concrete and is still used today. It has sheriff's quarters on the first floor. The jail was the scene of a breakout and shootout in 1970, when four prisoners attacked Deputy Sheriff Coleman Lansford and took his keys. Once they entered the sheriff's quarters, they found Coleman's pistol and took his wife hostage. Before the day was over, Deputy and Mrs. Lansford had escaped, and the jail was under siege by Texas Rangers, the Department of Public Safety, city police, and the border patrol. All of the prisoners, one of whom was seriously wounded, surrendered. Even today a few bullet holes from this battle can be seen around the doors and windows.

Interviews conducted by the author: Gene Rodriquez, Sheriff's Department; Kathleen Farris, librarian; Vernon Lee Bell; David Thomas Farris, editor, *Carrizo Springs Javelin.*

Other resources: Tyler, Barnett, and Barkley, eds., *New Handbook of Texas,* vol. 2, 645; John Leffler wrote a chapter for "A History of Dimmit County," which can be found in the files of the *Carrizo Springs Javelin;* Tidwell, *Dimmit County Mesquite Roots,* vol. 1.

Donley County (Clarendon)

Donley County was created in 1876 and organized in 1882. It was named for Texas Supreme Court Justice Stockton P. Donley. The original county seat was at Old Clarendon, six miles north of the present town. In 1887, the Fort Worth and Denver City Railroad passed six miles south of the old town, so the entire population moved south and built a new Clarendon. The site of the old town is now covered by Greenbelt Reservoir. Old Clarendon was founded by a Methodist minister, Lewis Henry Carhart, who set out to create a Methodist colony that would be completely free of alcohol. In 1878, an English investment group, the Clarendon Land Investment and Agency Company, backed the community— much to its benefit. The rowdier cowboys of the area, however, called it "Saint's Roost."

The first jail in the new Clarendon was a cell in a house next to the railroad. According to retired Judge W. R. Christel, dynamite for the work crews was stored in the building, which was known as the "powder house." Perhaps the prisoners,

under these circum-
stances, refrained from
rough or disorderly
behavior while held
there. The cell from
the powder house has
been preserved on the
courthouse lawn.

In 1910, a small
brick jail that would
hold six to eight pris-
oners was built. A. C.
Greene recounts a

Donley County jail, 1910–1970, Clarendon,
Texas. Photo courtesy of Maggie Stewart.

story about G. R. Miller, who worked near Childress. It seems
that Miller dynamited a home in Childress, jumped a freight
train, and shot two young boys on the train. He was put off of
the train but somehow got on again, still headed west; he then
shot two more boxcar passengers. He was caught and jailed at
Clarendon. Miller avoided a lynch mob only because Sheriff
James T. Patman secretly transferred him to the jail at Claude
in Armstrong County. Following conviction and two escape
attempts, he was hanged at Clarendon on June 3, 1910.

The 1910 jail was used until 1970, when the state would
no longer certify the facility. Since that time prisoners have
been farmed out to neighboring counties on a contract basis.
The 1910 lockup was razed in 1980.

Interviews conducted by the author: W. R. Christel, county judge; Fan
Vargas, county clerk; Maggie Stewart.

Other resources: *Dallas Morning News, Texas Almanac, 1998–1999;* Tyler,
Barnett, and Barkley, eds., *New Handbook of Texas,* vol. 2, 129, 676; Kelsey
and Dyal, *Courthouses of Texas.*

Duval County (San Diego)

Duval County was formed by the Texas legislature in 1858
and organized in 1876. Like so many of the counties
between the Nueces River and the Rio Grande, the country
was wild and lawless until after the Civil War. The last major
Indian raid—by some forty Apaches—occurred as late as the
spring of 1878.

Duval County jail, 1885–1938, San Diego, Texas. Photo courtesy of the Institute of Texan Cultures, University of Texas–San Antonio.

In 1873, Mexican outlaw Alberto Garza set up shop in Duval County and began to trade in stolen horses. Garza sent word to the citizens of San Diego to "bring enough money to buy the stolen hides or enough men to skin the hide peelers." This, it seems, was just the kind of challenge the Anglos in San Diego liked, so they chose to skin the hide peelers and followed up with a raid that scattered the bandits.

Duval County's first jail, built about 1885, was on the southwest corner of the courthouse square and was constructed of brick with a stucco finish. It was a two-story rectangular building with a flat roof. A new courthouse was built in 1916, but the old jail continued in use until 1938, when the 1916 courthouse was remodeled with a new lockup included. In 1983, that jail was expanded to its present size and configuration.

Interview conducted by the author: Tom Shelton, Institute of Texan Cultures at San Antonio.

Other resources: *Dallas Morning News, Texas Almanac, 1998–1999;* Tyler, Barnett, and Barkley, eds., *New Handbook of Texas,* vol. 2, 742; Kelsey and Dyal, *Courthouses of Texas.*

Eastland County (Eastland)

Eastland County was created in 1858 and organized in 1873. It was named for William Mosby Eastland, the only Texan officer to be executed during the Mier expedition

in March of
1843. The
first county
seat was in
Merriman,
but in 1875
the voters
moved the
seat of gov-
ernment to
Eastland.
The jail
in Eastland

Eastland County jail, 1897–1980, Eastland, Texas.

County was built in 1897. It was a three-story brick and stone
building with sheriff's quarters on the first floor. The lockup
became famous as the jail involved in the so-called Santa Claus
bank robbery. That story begins in Cisco, ten miles west of
Eastland. Four less-than-sophisticated robbers drove into Cisco
on the morning of December 23 in a stolen new 1927 Buick.
Marshall (his given name) Ratliff, who was well known in
Cisco, wore a complete Santa Claus costume to avoid recogni-
tion. The action began at noon, when the four thieves entered
the bank with guns drawn. Within four minutes, shooting
began by robbers, law enforcement officers, and citizens, some
of whom were armed with guns and ammunition from the
nearby hardware store.

A chase began after a wild shoot-out in the alley behind
the bank, where the getaway car was parked. The robbers and
two hostages piled into the car and careened away. Suddenly
the robbers realized that the gas gauge was on empty. In desperation, they hijacked an Oldsmobile from a passing family.
The family's thoughtful fourteen-year-old, however, snatched
the keys as he fled. By now, hard-pressed by the posse, the
robbers got back into the Buick but, in their haste, left behind
both the loot and the hostages. The thieves, two of them
wounded, spent the next six days moving through the Brazos
River bottoms, mostly on foot but occasionally by car. Ratliff
was caught near South Bend in Young County, and the others
were apprehended the next day, hungry and exhausted, in

Graham, Texas. One was tried and given ninety-nine years, but he escaped twice, was recaptured both times, and was finally paroled. He is said to have lived out his life as a good citizen. Another, Henry Helms, was sentenced to death and executed in Huntsville. Ratliff was moved back to the Eastland jail, where he killed Tom Jones, the popular deputy sheriff, in an unsuccessful jailbreak. The next night, a large, irate mob broke into the lockup, dragged Ratliff out, and hanged him from a nearby utility pole.

In 1934, the jail was remodeled and expanded, incorporating the original structure within it. The ironwork and cells were provided by Pauly Brothers of St. Louis. The jail was used for prisoners until 1980. It is now being made into a museum with emphasis on the famous Santa Claus bank robbery.

Interview conducted by the author: Sheriff Bob Richardson.

Other resources: *Dallas Morning News, Texas Almanac, 1998–1999;* Tyler, Barnett, and Barkley, eds., *New Handbook of Texas,* vol. 2, 765; Metz, *Roadside History of Texas;* A. C. Greene, *Santa Claus Bank Robbery.*

Ector County (Odessa)

Named for Matthew Duncan Ector, a brigadier general during the Civil War, Ector County was created in 1887 and organized in 1891. In 1886, the Odessa Land and Townsite Company tried to promote the area that was to become Ector County as farmland despite the scant annual rainfall of 13.1 inches. Because there were few buyers, the company went bankrupt. The country eventually proved to be fine ranch land, however, and, when augmented by the big oil boom of 1926 and 1927, Ector County became established on a sound economic basis.

The county's first jail was built in 1904 on the northwest corner of the courthouse square. It was a rectangular one-story building with two rooms made of 2″ by 4″ planks laid flat and nailed down. The building appears to have been 20′–24′ long and perhaps 10′ from floor to ceiling. Each of the two rooms contained an iron cage and one 12″ window. The structure served for about twenty years despite the fact that several prisoners tried to escape by setting the building on fire. In 1927, Ector County sold its old, slightly singed, jail to Crane County for $175.

Ector County's second jail, in service from 1924 to 1938, was a small, white, reinforced concrete building built behind the courthouse. When the keep was moved into the third floor of a new courthouse in 1938, the old facility became a library and was so used until 1942. Southern Prison Company provided the cells in the new structure. The courthouse building and jail were designed by Elmer Withers; this building, however, was extensively remodeled in 1964 and was incorporated within a modern concrete and steel building designed by Peters and Fields. Now, with the exception of a few holding cells, the jail has moved out of the courthouse to a more modern facility.

Interviews conducted by the author: Elaine Smith, Ector County Library; Bobbie Klepper, Permian Historical Society; Terry G. Shultz, head of technical services, Dunagan Library.

Other resources: *Dallas Morning News, Texas Almanac, 1998–1999;* Tyler, Barnett, and Barkley, eds., *New Handbook of Texas,* vol. 2, 781; Kelsey and Dyal, *Courthouses of Texas.*

Edwards County (Rocksprings)

Edwards County land was the home of the Lipan Apaches until the mid-1800s, when white settlers began to move into the country. The county was created in 1858 and organized in 1883. It was named for Haden Edwards, an early leader and colonizer of Texas.

Understanding the sequence of county seats in Edwards County is not easy. When the county was first organized in 1883, the seat of government was Bullhead, but the name was later changed to Vance. In 1884, the county seat was moved to Leakey, where it remained until an 1891 election determined that the seat of government should be moved to Rocksprings. Leakey contested the results, but Judge James M. Hunter, along with a group of others, removed the county records to Rocksprings in the middle of the night. Not to be outdone, the citizens managed to have a new county, Real, taken out of

Edwards County jail, 1895–present, Rocksprings, Texas.
Built by contractors Davey and Schott.

Edwards County in 1913, and Leakey once again became a county seat—this time of Real County.

The original Edwards County jail was in Leakey and consisted of an iron cage in the center of a wooden building. When the county seat shifted to Rocksprings in 1891, the iron cage was moved and incorporated into the new lockup built in Rocksprings in 1895. That new facility was designed and built by Davey and Schott for $4,780. It is a beautiful, two-story building made of white limestone with sheriff's quarters on the first floor. Alamo Iron Works in San Antonio fabricated the original cages. In 1929, the jail was remodeled by Southern Prison Company at a cost of $6,740. It is still in use today and is certified by the Texas Commission on Jail Standards. The outside is unchanged from the day it was built and is a pleasant reminder of some of the local talent found in the Texas Hill Country.

Rocksprings has had its share of troubles from natural causes. In 1897, the attractive limestone courthouse burned, leaving only the rock shell. Undaunted, the citizens restored the building to its original perfection. Later on, in April 1927, Rocksprings was struck by a severe tornado that removed the roof from the courthouse and killed sixty-seven people.

Interviews conducted by the author: Neville G. Smart, county judge; Sarah McNealy, county and district clerk.

Other resources: Tyler, Barnett, and Barkley, eds., *New Handbook of Texas,* vol. 2, 802, vol. 4, 132, and vol. 5, 639, 469; Rocksprings Women's Club Historical Committee, *History of Edwards County;* Gray, *Pioneering in Southwest Texas;* Metz, *Roadside History of Texas.*

Ellis County (Waxahachie)

Ellis County was created in 1844 and named for Richard Ellis, president of the committee that declared Texas independent. The county was organized in 1850, and the town of Waxahachie, an Indian word meaning "buffalo," was named the county seat.

The Civil War years were agonizing for Ellis County citizens, whose agricultural life depended on slave labor. The white-to-black population ratio in 1860 was slightly more than one to four. Financial recovery came only with the mechanization of agriculture in the latter part of the nineteenth century.

The first jail in Ellis County was built in 1855 at a cost of $1,150. It was a two-story building of the dungeon type, 16′ square with double walls of hewn oak logs. There was no door to the first story; the only access was through a 2′ by 3′ trapdoor in the floor of the second story. Entry to the second level was by an outside stairway. The second jail was built of "hard stone" in July 1874 at a cost of $4,072.50. It measured 30′ by 22′ with 10′ between the floor and the ceiling. In December 1874, the court decided to add a second story for $2,500.

In 1887, Ellis County purchased still another lockup, using a sophisticated new concept in construction: a rotary cage that was on the cutting edge of prison

Ellis County jail, 1887–1929, Waxahachie, Texas. Equipped by Pauly Jail Manufacturing.

confinement. The cost of this building, on the corner of
Rogers and Water streets, was forty-four thousand dollars. It
was a stone-and-brick edifice with sheriff's quarters on the
first floor. The cells, on the second and third floors, were arranged as wedges in a circle around a central rotating vertical
axle. A stationary vestibule for the prisoner and the jailer
opened into one cell at a time at the wide end of the wedge
as the cell was rotated past it by hand crank. Two of these
jails were constructed in Texas: in Ellis County and Grayson
County. In addition, according to W. Robinson in *The People's
Architecture,* several were also built in the Midwest. The "death
cells" and the solitary confinement compartments were in the
basement. They were made of stone, 4½' square and 5' high,
with a single small barred window. Each one had a big iron
ring in the corner so prisoners could be chained inside. The
rare escape was not from the solitary confinement or the rotating cages but was accomplished by dislodging bricks and mortar from the walls. The building is still intact, but the rotary
mechanical parts have been removed.

In 1929, a fourth jail was built for Ellis County on the corner of Jackson and Franklin streets. It is a simple three-story
red brick structure bearing minimal decorative features. It
has now been replaced with a more modern detention center,
however, and the old building is used for county offices.

Interviews conducted by the author: Shannon Simpson, curator, Ellis
County Museum; Kirk Douglas.
Other resources: *Dallas Morning News, Texas Almanac, 1998–1999;*
W. Robinson, *People's Architecture.*

El Paso County (El Paso)

El Paso County was created in 1849 and organized in 1850.
Located in extreme West Texas, the county is home
to the oldest town in Texas, Ysleta, and the oldest jail, San
Elizario. In 1598, the Oñate expedition, after crossing the
Chihuahua Desert and surviving for four days without water,
found a river, El Río del Norte (Rio Grande), at a site near the
present town of San Elizario. The expedition gave thanks,

rested, and feasted for three days on local wild game, thereby establishing the claim of having celebrated the first Thanksgiving in North

El Paso County jail, 1917–1959 (in the courthouse), El Paso, Texas. Photo courtesy of El Paso Public Library, Southwest Collection.

America. During the next 250 years, the pass (El Paso) became the trade and travel route through the Franklin Mountains to New Mexico and California.

When El Paso County was organized in 1850, San Elizario was chosen as the county seat. An adobe building built in the 1820s as a residence was chosen to serve as courthouse and jail. The courthouse was known as the *jurado,* "place of judgment"; the jail was called the *carcel.* The two-room flat-top building, estimated to be 20′ by 50′, was fitted with two cells of wrought iron that are still in place today in the smaller south room. The larger space was used as a courtroom. In 1867, the county seat moved to Ysleta for one year and then shifted back to San Elizario. It moved again to Ysleta briefly, before finally shifting permanently to El Paso in 1883. A legend, never seriously disputed, says that Billy the Kid, posing as a Texas Ranger, broke into the jail at gunpoint, took the keys from the jailer, freed his friend Melguiades Segura, and rode off into Mexico.

The first penitentiary originally built as a county jail in El Paso was constructed in 1883 at 219 Campbell Street. It was used until 1917, when a new courthouse was built with a jail inside. The old county jail continued to be used as a city lockup for El Paso until 1959, when the building was razed.

Interviews conducted by the author: Terri M. Grant, Border Heritage Center; Sheldon Hall.

Other resources: *Dallas Morning News, Texas Almanac, 1998–1999;* Tyler, Barnett, and Barkley, eds., *New Handbook of Texas,* vol. 2, 849, vol. 4, 849, and vol. 5, 834; Horgan, *Great River;* Metz, *El Paso Chronicles;* Tyler and Tyler, *Texas Museums.*

Erath County (Stephenville)

Erath County was created in 1856 and named for George Erath, an early pioneer and surveyor. The county was organized that same year, and John Stephens donated land for a courthouse. The new county seat was named Stephenville for its benefactor. Indians and outlaws harassed the area until after the Civil War, when the overwhelming pressure of new settlers began to turn the tide.

The first jail, of indeterminate date, was a two-story board-and-batten building, twenty-four feet square, with the lockup on the second floor. The frail outside appearance of the structure is misleading; a similar building in Bee County had a double course of heavy timber under the board and batten and stands solid today. The second jail, built probably about 1880, was of quarried stone and had three stories with an interesting cupola on top. Sheriff's quarters were on the first floor, prisoners were kept on the second floor, and the jury room was on the third floor. It was said that the windows on the second floor, as well as in the third-floor jury room, were very narrow, only a few inches wide, allowing a minimum of light and air to pass. Nath Shands was sheriff around the turn of the century. When he decided to agitate for a new lockup, he began inviting visiting county citizens to spend the night in the jury room to get a sense of the smell of the prison. In 1904, the commissioners' court voted to spend $75,000 for a new facility.

Shands got his new jail in 1905, but by that time he was out of office. The new castlelike jail, built of brick and stone, had a front tower of four stories backed by a three-story main building. The structure was red brick trimmed with white stone arches over the windows. Crenellations along the ramparts and towers presented an image of strength. The building was to cost $28,000, although the voters had authorized

$75,000. The name of the architect is not known. Southern Structural Steel Company was the contractor for the building, which lasted until it was replaced in 1964. Both the 1880 and 1905 jails have been razed.

Interviews conducted by the author: C. Richard King; Pam Bethea, Erath County courthouse coordinator.

Other resources: *Dallas Morning News, Texas Almanac, 1998–1999;* Metz, *Roadside History of Texas;* Tyler, Barnett, and Barkley, eds., *New Handbook of Texas,* vol. 2, 880, and vol. 4, 970.

Falls County (Marlin)

The Texas legislature created Falls County in 1850. The county grew out of Robertson's colony community of Viesca, located at the falls of the Brazos River. It was a huge block of central Texas land that would eventually be divided into thirty counties. In 1834 Viesca became Fort Viesca and, in December 1835, was renamed Fort Milam in honor of Ben Milam, who was killed in the attack on San Antonio, a battle that temporarily secured San Antonio for the Texans as they began their fight for freedom.

In 1836, Fort Milam was abandoned in the Runaway Scrape as the Texans fled before the victorious Mexican army, which was advancing after taking the Alamo. After the battle of San Jacinto, people began to return to the area, but many of them relocated east of the river for better protection from hostile Indians. By request, the county seat was changed to Adams, and the name of the town was changed to Marlin.

The first jail in Falls County was built in 1852 and was a standard 14′ by 16′ dungeon with two stories of double-walled hand-hewn logs on the corner of Craik and Newton streets. It may have been good enough, but, for some reason, in July 1868 the court ordered that a contract be made to build a new keep on the same location, using some of the same materials. There is no picture or description of the 1868 jail.

In 1879, a new lockup was proposed for the same location, but protests by neighborhood citizens caused it to be placed on the west side of the courthouse square instead. It may have been that the prisoners endeared themselves to those on the outside by yelling unkind remarks at them as they passed by. At any rate, the new brick jail was said to consist of one and a half stories. The contractor was Edward Northcraft, and a tax was authorized to pay for the construction. The only known picture shows the jail near the 1878 courthouse.

On June 29, 1915, the commissioners' court opened bids for a proposed fourth detention center. The contract was awarded to the McKenzie Construction Company of San Antonio, even though their $23,425 bid was $2,425 more than the bid by Southern Structural Steel. The lockup was built on the same location as the previous one. The 1915 jail was demolished in 1946, when a new building was constructed elsewhere.

Interviews conducted by the author: Frances Braswell, Falls County clerk; Teresa Bailey; Jack Stem, Falls County Museum.

Other resources: *Dallas Morning News, Texas Almanac, 1998–1999;* Tyler, Barnett, and Barkley, eds., *New Handbook of Texas,* vol. 2, 942, and vol. 5, 514; Kelsey and Dyal, *Courthouses of Texas;* Eddins, ed., *History of Falls County, Texas.*

Fannin County (Bonham)

Fannin County was created in 1837 and organized in 1838. It was originally a gigantic area, reaching from East Texas into the Panhandle, a territory so large that it would ultimately be divided into twenty counties. Warren was the first county seat, but, in 1843, the community of Bois d'Arc, renamed Bonham in honor of William Butler Bonham, a Texas hero of the Alamo, was made the seat of government.

John Wesley Hardin, son of a Methodist minister, was born in Fannin County. By age sixteen, however, he was teaching school near Corsicana. During Reconstruction, his aunt's family was attacked by Northern occupation troops who killed the women and the son and burned down the house. From then on, it was "Wes" Hardin against the soldiers and the despised state police. By age twenty-one, Wes had killed thirty-nine men. He was finally arrested by Texas Rangers in Florida and sent to prison, where he studied and obtained a law degree. Paroled in 1894, he used his freedom in a restless practice of law. Within a year, he moved from Gonzales County to Karnes County to El Paso, where, in 1895, he was shot and killed by El Paso constable John Selman.

Fannin County has had four jails, all built at different times on the same lot. The first jail, constructed in 1857, cost $1,400. It was a typical dungeon, 18' by 18', with two-story triple oak walls that were eighteen inches thick. The second floor was 10' above the first, and a trapdoor in the center provided access to the first-floor prison. This jail burned in 1868, but it was replaced in 1870 with a two-room stone and brick building that cost $7,300.

The need for a larger, more modern facility was realized fifteen years later. In 1885, the county hired the architectural firm of Ritenour and Wood of Sherman to draw plans, and A. D. Chamberlain of Sherman was given the contract for construction. Champion Iron Fence Company built the cells and ironwork. The result was a modern two-story jail with sheriff's quarters and space for more than twenty-five prisoners.

Fannin County's fourth lockup was built in 1940. A yellow brick two-story building with a flat roof, it stands on the very same ground as the original 1857 jail and is still in use.

Interview conducted by the author: Tom Scott, Fannin County Museum of History.

Other resources: *Dallas Morning News, Texas Almanac, 1998–1999;* Tyler, Barnett, and Barkley, eds., *New Handbook of Texas,* vol. 1, 633, vol. 2, 945, and vol. 6, 827; Hodge, *History of Fannin County;* Cunningham, *Triggernometry.*

Fayette County (La Grange)

Named for the Marquis de Lafayette, the French nobleman who became an aide to George Washington during the American Revolution, Fayette County was created in 1837 and organized in 1838. La Grange, located on the Colorado River at the old La Bahía Road crossing, was designated as the county seat. Beginning in the eighteenth century and continu-

Fayette County jail, 1882–1985, La Grange, Texas. Designed by architects Andrewartha and Wahrenberger.

ing through the Mexican period, the La Bahía Road was an important trade and travel route between Mexico and the settlements of Goliad, Nacogdoches, and San Augustine, passing through the La Grange, Brenham, and Crockett areas.

The first jail cost $460 and was completed in July 1838. It was probably a wooden structure, and it was the custom to place prisoners in irons and chain them to a large stone or piece of timber inside the jail. After ten years of use, the keep was so dilapidated that it became necessary to pay selected citizens $3 per day to board and guard the prisoners. In 1852, some of the prisoners were lodged in Travis County or at Brenham or Bellville at "excessive expense."

In 1852 a new jail was proposed. The brick building was to be two stories high, 32' by 23', containing four rooms, one lined with "boiler iron." By 1854, the jail was finished and ready for use. Meanwhile, fiscal relief came to the counties in the form of legislation that allowed them to retain taxes, normally due to the state, if used to build or pay for jails or other public buildings.

The 1854 lockup was a good one and, with some remodeling in 1876, remained in service until the third jail was completed in 1882. In 1881, a committee of citizens accepted a bid by F. Schultze to build a jail designed by architects Andrewartha and Wahrenberger. The bid was $22,075, an amount

that would later be contested when construction was suspended. When the building was not completed in the appointed time, the county suspended Schultze and finished the
job but sued Schultze and his bondsmen for the difference in
costs. Notwithstanding the troubled contract, the jail is a striking Gothic-style building of cut stone that reminds one of
European cathedrals. It was used until 1985. Located on the
corner of South Main and West Crockett streets, the building
now serves as quarters for the Chamber of Commerce.

   Interview conducted by the author: Kathy Carter, director, Fayette
Heritage Museum and Archives.
   Other resources: *Dallas Morning News, Texas Almanac, 1998–1999;* Tyler,
Barnett, and Barkley, eds., *New Handbook of Texas,* vol. 2, 969, and vol. 3,
1179; Lotto, *Fayette County;* J. W. Williams and Kenneth F. Neighbours,
Old Texas Trails; Robinson and Webb, *Texas Public Buildings of the Nine-
teenth Century.*

Fisher County (Roby)

Fisher County was created along with many other Panhandle counties in 1876. It was named for Samuel R.
Fisher, secretary of the Texas Navy during the Republic. When
the county was organized in 1886, there was the usual contest
between towns to be named the county seat. Fisher and Roby
were the contenders. There were accusations of skullduggery,
but Roby
won the
vote by a
close mar-
gin. Later
it was deter-
mined that
one of the
"voters" by
the name
of Bill Purp
was actually
a dog

Fisher County jail, 1926–present, Roby, Texas.

owned by someone in Roby. The citizens of Fisher, of course, were howling mad.

After organization, the first commissioners' court met and, according to the minutes, "did not consider a jail needed." The court decided to make arrangements to board prisoners in the Nolan County jail—if and when the county should ever have a prisoner. In 1892, however, a stone jail was constructed in Fisher County and used for thirty-four years.

The second jail, built in 1926, was a three-story brick building with handsome Doric columns in front. Old-time Fisher County residents recall a case in 1927 when two young men stole a wagon load of cotton and took it to a gin to be processed. Everything was all right until someone remembered that the two did not own a farm. Where did they get the cotton? Checking around, it was learned that a farmer was missing a load of cotton. When Sheriff R. J. Smith went to arrest the thieves, one of them, Bill Smith, shot and killed him. After a stay in the Fisher County jail, Smith was sent to the penitentiary and executed in the electric chair.

As of 1996, the jail was clean and neat and is still certified by the State Commission for Jail Standards.

Interview conducted by the author: Violet Upshaw.
Other resources: Tyler, Barnett, and Barkley, eds., *New Handbook of Texas,* vol. 2, 1012, and vol. 5, 630; *Dallas Morning News, Texas Almanac, 1998–1999;* Sheffy, *West Texas Historical Association Yearbook.*

Floyd County (Floydada)

Floyd County was created in 1876 and organized in 1890. Until 1871, the Panhandle was the undisputed realm of the Comanche Indians and their Comanchero trading partners—some trade was legitimate and some was in stolen livestock. About 1871, the U.S. Army 4th Cavalry under Ranald S. Mackenzie began to penetrate the territory. In September of that year he chased the Comanches under Quanah Parker into Blanco Canyon, where some of his command were ambushed. Reinforcement by the rest of the troop, however, saved the day. On October 12, a strong blue norther struck, and the troops were withdrawn. The campaign continued through the years 1873 and 1874. Finally, Mackenzie surprised the Indians

Floyd County jail, 1925–present, Floydada, Texas (remodeled in 1971).

in Palo Duro Canyon. On September 28, 1874, he routed the warriors and killed all of their horses. On November 5 of that year, he fought one final battle near Lake Tahoka, twenty miles south of Lubbock. This, coupled with the slaughter of the buffalo by hunters, broke the back of Indian power and ended the Red River War. The late nineteenth century would see drought and grasshopper infestations, but recovery and prosperity returned.

Floyd County has no historic jail still standing. In June 1890, when the county commissioners organized, they ordered two cells and a safe from the Diebold agent, L. T. Noyes of Houston. The safe, of course, was for the county's records, and the cells were for the prisoners, although there was as yet no lockup. In the minutes of the commissioners' meeting of July 12, 1890, specifications for a 22' by 30' wood jail were recorded, and shortly afterward, construction bids were solicited. The commissioners received only one bid— and rejected it. The next day, perhaps with revisions, a price from J. N. Smith was accepted. The building was completed on February 15, 1891.

In 1925, Floyd County finished a more sophisticated jail, which was built by the Southern Structural Steel Company. The new lockup had three floors and a basement and contained residence quarters for the sheriff. There were bunks for forty-six prisoners, plus a section for women and a hospital ward. When the lockup was remodeled in 1971, the 1925 jail was completely incorporated into the new structure. The original building is not visible from the outside.

Interviews conducted by the author: Judge William D. Hardin; Carolyn Jackson, director of Floyd County Historical Museum; Nancy Marble.

Other resources: Tyler, Barnett, and Barkley, eds., *New Handbook of Texas,* vol. 1, 582, vol. 2, 246, 1042, and vol. 4, 416; Tyler and Tyler, *Texas Museums;* DeLorme Mapping, *Texas Atlas and Gazetteer.*

Foard County (Crowell)

Foard County was originally part of Hardeman County, whose county seat was the town of Margaret, about eight miles northeast of Crowell. When Foard County was created in 1891, it was named for Maj. Robert L. Foard of the Confederate Army. The county was organized that same year, and the newly laid out town of Crowell, on the property of George T. Crowell, became the county seat. An important natural feature in the county is the Pease River, where major settlements of Comanche Indians had been located before white settlers arrived.

In 1860, at the battle of the Pease, a group of Texas Rangers led by Frederick Sullivan ("Sul") Ross attacked a Comanche camp and captured Chief Peta Nocona's wife—the celebrated Cynthia Ann Parker. Nocona was killed; Cynthia Ann was repatriated and, against her will, brought back to the white community. She had been captured at the age of nine during a Comanche raid on Fort Parker in Limestone County in 1836. She never made

Foard County jail, 1931–present, Crowell, Texas. Designed by C. H. Leinbach.

the readjustment to civilization and died in 1871. Her son, Quanah Parker, became a famous Comanche warrior and chief.

The first jail in Hardeman/Foard County was built of locally fired brick from Pease River clay. It was constructed by the Pauly Jail Building and Manufacturing Company for $9,946 and was accepted in April 1886. It served as the county jail until the Foard County seat was moved to Crowell in 1891.

The first jail in Crowell was completed in 1896 and was built of locally quarried stone. It had two stories with the traditional crenellations and was used for thirty-five years. According to the commissioners' court minutes, the cells were built by the Southern Prison Company of San Antonio, which suggests that the keep was remodeled by that firm around 1927. In 1931 a new jail was built that is still in use today. The architect was C. H. Leinbach. It is a simple two-story, more or less rectangular brick building with sheriff's quarters on the first floor.

Interviews conducted by the author: Bettie Gafforb, Foard County Museum; Deputy Sheriff Eric Howard; Jackie Giggs, librarian; Clark Hitt, chair, Foard County Historical Commission.

Other resources: *Dallas Morning News, Texas Almanac, 1998–1999;* DeLorme Mapping, *Texas Atlas and Gazetteer;* Tyler, Barnett, and Barkley, eds., *New Handbook of Texas,* vol. 2, 1047; Sterling, *Trails and Trials of a Texas Ranger;* Tyler and Tyler, *Texas Museums.*

Fort Bend County (Richmond)

The area that is Fort Bend County was settled by some of Stephen Austin's Old Three Hundred in 1822. Austin's colonists sailed on the ship *Lively* from New Orleans and arrived at the mouth of the Brazos River in the fall of 1821. In the spring of 1822, a group walked inland along the river about one hundred miles to a large bend, where a high bluff overlooked the river. There they built a log structure that would come to be known as Fort Bend. During the Texas Revolution, Santa Anna was encamped with the main body of his army at Thompson's Ferry in the Fort Bend area. Learning that the officers of the rebel Texas government had gone to

Fort Bend County jail, 1897–1955, Richmond, Texas. Built by Diebold Safe and Lock Company.

Harrisburg, Santa Anna took a small detachment to pursue and capture the officials. He missed them at Harrisburg and again at Morgan's Point as they pulled away in boats headed for Galveston. He returned to his pursuit of Sam Houston and met him at San Jacinto.

The county was created in 1837, and Richmond was made the county seat in 1838. Before the Civil War, Fort Bend County enjoyed prosperity from the production of cotton, corn, and sugar cane, all of which were based on slave labor. After the war and the freeing of the slaves, the Jaybird-Woodpecker War took place, in which the northern Republicans (Jaybirds) and southern Democrats (Woodpeckers) had a shootout around the courthouse square on August 16, 1889. Gov. Sul Ross brought in the Texas Rangers and personally arbitrated a settlement, followed by the resignation of the sitting Republican government and its replacement by Democrats.

The first jail in Fort Bend County was put up before the courthouse was built in 1839. According to the *Confederate Museum Newsletter* (Apr. 1997), the lockup was described in the *Richmond Telescope and Literary Register* as "a safe and comfortable building." The second jail was built on the courthouse square for $4,550 and lasted until 1896. In that year, the county commissioners inspected the lockup and declared it insecure, overcrowded, and unhealthy. The result was a new jail in 1897 on property owned by Jane Long, dubbed the "Mother of Texas."

A contract was made with the Diebold Safe and Lock Company through their agent, L. T. Noyes, to build a jail for eighteen thousand dollars. The structure was a two-story red

brick building with a marble foundation. It included adequate
sheriff's quarters and a gallows that was used only twice but on
the same day in 1898, when Pete Autry and Emmanuel Morris
were hanged for murder. The facility served until 1955 and
even today is a classic example of the Romanesque Revival architecture popular in the 1890s. The jail has been renovated to
provide Richmond with a new police headquarters and to still
have extra space for a museum.

Interviews conducted by the author: Cheryl Vitek; Pete Shifflett.

Other resources: *Dallas Morning News, Texas Almanac, 1998–1999;* Tyler,
Barnett, and Barkley, eds., *New Handbook of Texas,* vol. 2, 1086, and vol. 6,
472; Metz, *Roadside History of Texas;* Sterling, *Trails and Trials of a Texas
Ranger; Confederate Museum Newsletter,* Nov. 5, 1997; *Preservation Texas Reporter,* April/May 1998.

Franklin County (Mount Vernon)

In 1875 Franklin County (originally Morgan County) was
created out of Titus County and named after Benjamin
Cromwell Franklin, the first appointed judge of the Brazoria
judicial district of the Republic of Texas. The county was organized in 1875, and Mount Vernon was voted the county seat.

Franklin County's first jail was built in 1875, probably in
response to the rampant crime that flourished after the Civil
War. Like so many first jails, it was wooden, built of two layers
of 2″ by 12″
planks and
covered by
a layer of
1″ by 12″
planking.
These
boards were
fastened
together
with nails
spaced 4″
apart, both

Franklin County jail, 1912–1993, Mount Vernon, Texas.
Designed by L. L. Thurmon.

vertically and horizontally. The building had two stories with an outside stairway to the second level; downstairs were two rooms, one for the county clerk and one for the sheriff. The structure was located on the site of the present courthouse and was built by John Brem for sixteen hundred dollars. The building still exists as a barn on private property and may be viewed on request.

The 1875 jail became the scene of a serious Wild West shootout in the spring of 1879. Court was in session, and the jail was bulging with criminals of all kinds. One day a youngster named Joe Morgan was temporarily guarding the prisoners while the sheriff ate supper. About seven friends and relatives of the prisoners chose that time to raid the lockup. With guns blazing and wielding a large sledge hammer for breaking down the door, they attacked. They killed Morgan first and then began shooting at anyone who showed up in the square. One man with a sledge hammer panicked and took off when the shooting began. Relentless pursuit by the sheriff and his deputies over the next year saw all but one of the raiders arrested or shot.

The second jail, also built of wood, was on the north side of the courthouse square. The third detention center, designed by L. L. Thurmon and built by L. R. Wright at a cost of $55,000, and a courthouse were built in 1912. The jail cages, of unknown manufacture, and some of the ironwork were moved from the second lockup into the new facility. This solidly built concrete building was used until 1993 and still stands north of the courthouse.

Interviews conducted by the author: Paul Lovier, justice of the peace; B. F. Hicks, president of the Franklin County Historical Society.

Other resources: *Dallas Morning News, Texas Almanac, 1998–1999;* Metz, *Roadside History of Texas;* Tyler, Barnett, and Barkley, eds., *New Handbook of Texas,* vol. 2, 1153, and vol. 4, 870; Hicks and Bolin, *Early Days in Franklin County.*

Freestone County (Fairfield)

Freestone County, named for an indigenous stone, was created in 1850 from Limestone County and organized in 1851. The area had been a part of the original Mexican land

grant of
1825 to
David G.
Burnet. In
October
1830, Bur-
net joined
his grant
with those
of Joseph
Vehlein and
Lorenzo de
Zavala to

Freestone County jail, 1857–1913 (remodeled in 1880),
Fairfield, Texas.

create the Galveston Bay and Texas Land Company for the purpose of colonizing their combined 3,743,163 acres of land in
East Texas. The company sold scrip to would-be colonists in
the East, allowing them to occupy land in the area. The change-
able Mexican laws created land title problems when shiploads
of colonists arrived at Galveston and were not allowed to settle
as planned. One ship, the schooner *Climax,* was wrecked near
Point Boliver, but the ten families aboard were saved.

    The county seat was originally called Prairie Mound but
was changed to Fairfield in 1851. The first log jail was built in
1852 at a cost of $600. It had a metal cage inside. A second jail
with a double wall, a 32″ outer wall, and an 18″ inner wall
of handmade brick was built in 1857 under contract to J. C.
Wallace and D. H. Love for $5,992. The floor of the second
level was made of thick oak planks on top of an iron subfloor.
The main prison was on the second floor, and the sheriff's
quarters were on the ground floor. The jail was remodeled in
1880. It is still standing and serves today as the Freestone
County Museum.

    In 1913 the third Freestone County jail was built of brick
on the courthouse square. It was a two-story square building
constructed in castle style with two towers and crenellations all
around. Southern Structural Steel Company built a nearly identical structure in 1913 in Leon County. The fourth Freestone
County jail, like its predecessor, had prison cells on the second
floor and sheriff's quarters on the first floor. It was razed in
1975, however, to build a modern prison in the same location.

Interviews conducted by the author: Sheriff James R. Sessions; Virginia Oliver, librarian.

Other resources: *Dallas Morning News, Texas Almanac, 1998–1999;* Metz, *Roadside History of Texas;* Tyler, Barnett, and Barkley, eds., *New Handbook of Texas,* vol. 2, 932, 1171, and vol. 3, 53; Tyler and Tyler, *Texas Museums;* Freestone County Historical Commission, *History of Freestone County Texas.*

Frio County (Pearsall)

Named for the Frio River, Frio County was created in 1858 from parts of Atascosa, Bexar, and Uvalde counties. Organized in 1871, the county was on the old Presidio Road connecting Mexico to Bexar and the Spanish East Texas colonies. Frio Town (originally Frio City), which had been laid out by A. L. Odin in 1871 where the Presidio Road crossed the Frio River, was named the county seat. Because of Indian troubles, settlement was slow until the late 1870s. The old Frio Town cemetery, where a grave marker states "Killed by Indians," calls to mind dangerous times on the Frio River. Nevertheless, the town grew and had a population of approximately 1,800 in 1880. The county population was 2,130 at the time.

The first jail was built in 1872 in Frio City from locally quarried sandstone. It had two stories and measured 20' by 24'. The foundation was set 3' in the ground, and the walls were 3' thick with an outside stairway. Folklore claims that several notorious prisoners stayed in the jail but does not say for how long. The escape record was so bad that, in January 1875, the district

Frio County jail, 1883–1967, Pearsall, Texas. Equipped by Pauly Jail Manufacturing.

judge ordered prisoner Joe Howell be transferred to "some other jail," and regularly thereafter prisoners were moved to the custody of the sheriff of Medina County. According to Allen A. Erwin in his book, *The Southwest of John Horton Slaughter,* the door had no lock and was held closed by means of a 20′ cypress log propped against it. This old lockup is on private property, and permission from the owner must be obtained in order to visit.

During 1881, the International and Great Northern Railroad laid tracks that passed sixteen miles south of Frio Town. Not surprisingly, Pearsall, a town on the railroad route, began to grow and attract people from Frio Town. In August 1883, a vote heavily supported a move of the county seat to Pearsall. The new county seat, of course, would need a new jail. J. J. Ligon of Palestine, Texas, representing the Pauly Company, offered to build one for eleven thousand dollars. The offer was accepted, and a two-story brick facility measuring 48′ by 28′ was built with an inside iron stairway to the second floor. With the benefit of electricity and a sanitary sewer system added later, the structure served for eighty-three years until 1967, when it was replaced by a new facility. The old jail now provides quarters for the Chamber of Commerce and a museum.

Interviews conducted by the author: Ruth A. Higdon; Robert Gorhum.
Other resources: *Dallas Morning News, Texas Almanac, 1998–1999;* Tyler, Barnett, and Barkley, eds., *New Handbook of Texas,* vol. 3, 5, 9; Frio County Centennial Corporation, *Historic Frio County;* Erwin, *Southwest of John Horton Slaughter;* Tyler and Tyler, *Texas Museums.*

Gaines County (Seminole)

Gaines County was formed in 1876 and named for James Gaines, signer of the Texas Declaration of Independence. It was organized in 1905 with Seminole as the county seat. This area had been the domain of the Comanche Indians until 1875, the year that marked the end of the Red River War. Cedar Lake, about twenty miles northeast of Seminole, was a campground used regularly by the Indians, and it is thought that Quanah Parker was born there. A brief skirmish with the Comanches was fought near Cedar Lake in 1875.

Gaines County jail, 1922–1994, on the third floor of the courthouse, Seminole, Texas. Designed by architects Sanguinet and Staats. Photo courtesy of Mary Thornbury, Gaines County Museum.

After the county was formed, ranching was the main enterprise until the turn of the century, when farming developed. Even then, progress was delayed because railroad service did not come until 1917, when the Midland and Northwestern finished a line to Seminole. For economic reasons the railroad service stopped in 1923.

Dan Cobb built the first jail in Seminole in 1907 for $240.50. It was a 12′ by 16′ wooden building with walls 9′ high. It was replaced in 1922, when a new courthouse was built with a jail on the third floor. Southern Steel Structural Company manufactured the cages and ironwork. The 1922 jail served the county until July 11, 1994, when prisoners began to be contracted out to other counties for incarceration because there were so few cases to be considered.

Interview conducted by the author: Mary Thornbury, Gaines County Museum.

Other resources: *Dallas Morning News, Texas Almanac, 1998–1999;* Tyler, Barnett, and Barkley, eds., *New Handbook of Texas,* vol. 3, 45, and vol. 5, 971; DeLorme Mapping, *Texas Atlas and Gazetteer;* Tyler and Tyler, *Texas Museums;* Newcomb, *Indians of Texas.*

Galveston County (Galveston)

Galveston County was created from Brazoria County in 1838. Its rich history dates back to that fateful day in November 1538, when Cabeza de Vaca and others washed ashore on or near Galveston Island. In 1785, the Spanish named the large bay north of the island Galveston Bay in honor of Count Bernardo de Gálvez, viceroy of Mexico. Early in the nineteenth century, Galveston was a haven for pirates, including Jean Lafitte, whose favorite prey was the slave ships en route to the East Coast. Lafitte left Galveston in 1821 under pressure from the United States. During the years immediately following, the island remained essentially unoccupied because the Mexican government, while accepting settlement in Texas by Anglo colonists, forbade occupation in coastal areas in order to restrict the colonists' trade to Mexico. As soon as Texas became an independent republic, the city of Galveston developed rapidly as a principal port.

Galveston probably takes the honors in terms of the number of jails the county has provided for its citizens. The first lockup was the conversion of the German brig *Elbe,* which had been stranded on the beach, victim of an 1837 hurricane. The hold of the ship, properly locked, served for three years until a proper wooden jail was built in 1840 on the southeast corner of Twentieth Street and Avenue E. The contractors were Lewis Minor and C. S. Johnson. Specifications detailed two lower rooms, one measuring 10′ by 20′ and a half-story single room. The walls, floor, and ceiling were lined with ⅛″ iron. The cost was four thousand dollars.

A third prison, constructed in 1847, was a jail and courthouse combination, solidly built of brick. The structure was a 50′ by 29′ rectangle of two stories that contained six cells. Later, additional compartments were added, and a 10′ brick wall was built around the building. The fourth lockup, built in 1878, was designed by a young Houston architect, Eugene Heiner, who won a competition to design the structure. The result was a sophisticated Second Empire brick building with a mansard roof, almost identical to the one he would design two years later for Harris County. At some time between 1889 and 1893, N. J. Clayton, prominent Galveston architect, made some drawings for modifications to the jail, but it is not known whether they were ever built.

In 1890, Heiner was called on once more to design a jail for Galveston. This facility, at 1628 Avenue A, was more Victorian in nature, brick with a pyramid roof but still retaining two small towers with crenellations. In 1913, a sixth jail with four floors and Romanesque design features was built on the corner of Seventeenth Street and Avenue A. None of these buildings are still in existence.

Interviews conducted by the author: David Bucek; Shelly Kelly; Edward Casey, Rosenberg Library.

Other resources: *Dallas Morning News, Texas Almanac, 1998–1999;* Tyler, Barnett, and Barkley, eds., *New Handbook of Texas,* vol. 1, 882, and vol. 3, 51, 56, 65, 73; Metz, *Roadside History of Texas;* Stuart, "The First Jails," *Galveston News,* December 16, 1906; Tyler and Tyler, *Texas Museums;* Scardino and Turner, *Clayton's Galveston.*

Garza County (Post)

Garza County was created in 1876 when the Texas legislature divided the western territories, including the Texas Panhandle, into counties. The county was not organized, however, until 1907, when it was named for the well-known Garza family of San Antonio, who owned a large ranch in Bexar County. Organization of this county, like many others, was delayed by Indian hostilities. Indeed, the last Indian raid in Garza County occurred on the large Curry Comb Ranch in 1883 in the northwestern part of the county.

The history of the area is intimately tied to the social and economic experiment initiated by C. W. Post, inventor of Post Toasties and founder of Post Breakfast Foods. Post's first product was Postum, a cereal product that was supposed to be a substitute for coffee and advertised as a cure for coffee nerves before the invention of decaffeinated coffee. C. W. Post (a bit of an eccentric who may have had bipolar disorder and experienced at least two nervous breakdowns) accumulated 250,000 acres of land to bring under agricultural management. His idea was to create a town site and to divide and fence plots of 160 acres in which to develop farms and raise livestock. The site of Post became the county seat in 1907, when the county was organized. Post was able to recruit about twelve hundred farmers with the promise of cheap land and imported fruit trees. He also tried a variety of crops with some success. In general, production went well until the crippling drought of the 1930s, the same years that the Great Depression seized the country, dealing yet another economic blow. Fortunately, the discovery of oil in 1925 mitigated some of the perversity of nature.

The first jail, of unknown date, in Garza County was a building of 2″ by 4″ pieces of lumber stacked flat on one another and nailed down, similar to the structure of the early jail in Dallam County. In 1911 the county bought a small cell block from Southern Structural Steel Company, and a structure measuring 16′ by 20′ was built around it to complete what became the second lockup.

In 1923 Guy A. Carlander of Amarillo designed a new courthouse that included a jail on its third floor. Two cells, including a walk-around, were purchased from Southern Steel Company for $5,635. Two or three years later, the old 1911 jail was moved to the north side of the courthouse and enclosed in a 22′ by 19′ brick building with 18″ thick walls. That facility served as a drunk tank for a number of years and is now used for storage.

In 1973 architects Stanford and Hall designed an annex, which became the fourth jail and law enforcement building. For one hundred thousand dollars, the Pharr Construction Company of Lubbock built that structure to the west of the courthouse.

Interviews conducted by the author: Sonny Gossett, county clerk; Linda Puckett, director of the Garza County Historical Museum.

Other resources: Tyler, Barnett, and Barkley, eds., *New Handbook of Texas,* vol. 3, 108, and vol. 5, 288; Metz, *Roadside History of Texas.*

Gillespie County (Fredericksburg)

Gillespie County was created in 1848 and named for Capt. R. A. Gillespie, a Texas Ranger under Jack Hayes in the Mexican War. The county was organized that same year. The town of Fredericksburg had been founded in 1846, when Baron John O. Meusebach brought 120 families west from New Braunfels to found the second of a series of Texas

Gillespie County jail, 1885–1939, Fredericksburg, Texas.

towns planned by the Adels-verein in Germany. In spite of a deadly cholera epidemic in 1846, Fredericksburg's population grew to one thousand during the first two years. This was made possible when Meusebach signed the Meusebach-Comanche Peace Treaty, which established a fairly peaceful environment for the German communities. Determined to remain German and disdaining the double layers of Anglo government (county and municipal), Fredericksburg, named for Prince Frederick of Prussia, was not incorporated until 1928.

The first jail in Gillespie County was built in 1852. It was a 14' by 14' stone building that soon proved to be too small. The second lockup was built by John Raegner and John Walch on the courthouse square and cost $413.50, to be paid over a two-year period. It was a 14' by 18' structure, a combination of stone and locally manufactured iron fittings. In January 1859, a third detention center was contracted to Ludwig Schmidt. This facility was an 18' by 30' building with four rooms and a cellar with thick stone walls. The $800 building was anything but escape proof, so a proposal was made to put a steel cage inside. The cost and excessive size of the cage, however, precluded that solution. By 1871, the escape rate was so great that county officials decided that a new jail was in order. The new prison was built in 1874 but burned in 1885, and an inmate died in the fire. Fredericksburg folk recall that one prisoner, held for some minor infraction, regularly broke out of jail at night. When daylight came, however, he would be in front of the jail, waiting for the sheriff to bring his breakfast.

In 1885, C. F. Priess and Brothers Builders built a two-story limestone jail in the 100 block of West San Antonio Street at a cost of $9,962. The ironwork, which seems to be of local manufacture, included four cells in the center of the second floor with a typical walk-around. The structure, although not used since 1939, still stands in good condition and has been renovated as a museum. In 1939, a new courthouse with a jail on the third floor was completed. This facility has since been replaced by a modern free-standing law enforcement building.

Interviews conducted by the author: Bill Wareing; Art Kowert; Sue Croon.

Other resources: *Dallas Morning News, Texas Almanac, 1998–1999;* Kelsey and Dyal, *Courthouses of Texas;* Tyler, Barnett, and Barkley, eds., *New Handbook of Texas,* vol. 2, 1014, 1160, and vol. 3, 166; Wilbarger, *Indian Depredations in Texas;* Tyler and Tyler, *Texas Museums.*

Glasscock County (Garden City)

Named for George W. Glasscock, who had been a flatboat partner of Abraham Lincoln in Illinois before he came to Texas in 1835, Glasscock County was created from Tom Green County in 1897. In the fall of 1835, Glasscock was involved in the siege of Bexar and participated in the "grass fight," one of the less familiar stories of the Texas Revolution. In late November 1835, about 150 Texians intercepted a Mexican pack train west of San Antonio. They thought the pack animals were carrying pay for the Mexican army, but after a sharp skirmish, with casualties on both sides, the packs were found to contain nothing but grass for the Mexican horses.

Glasscock County was organized in 1893, and in barely one month, the commissioners' court issued bonds and contracted with L. T. Noyes, the Diebold agent in Houston, to build a jail. The two-story limestone structure was completed in February 1894. The first floor was used for court sessions, and the jail was on the second floor. Later, when a new courthouse

Glasscock County jail, 1893–1980, Garden City, Texas. Built by Diebold Safe and Lock.

was finished in 1910, the jail was expanded to include both floors of the 1894 building.

In February 1893, the town of Garden City, named for a man named Gardner, was literally put on wheels and moved a mile and a half to a place with better water and higher ground, called New California. The name of the new location was then changed to Garden City, once again misspelling Gardner's name.

The original lockup served until 1980, when it was replaced by a new building. That reflected a note of optimistic necessity because the old jail is said to have gone for one seven-year period without admitting a single prisoner. Local lore has it that a tree grew up in front of the door, blocking the entrance. Today, however, the old jail is in fine shape on a beautifully manicured lawn.

Interviews conducted by the author: Susie Hilger, courthouse custodian; Helen Wilkerson, Glasscock County Historical Society.

Other resources: *Dallas Morning News, Texas Almanac, 1998–1999;* Tyler, Barnett, and Barkley, eds., *New Handbook of Texas,* vol. 3, 90, 182, 286.

Goliad County (Goliad)

Goliad County was created in 1836 around the existing Mexican municipality of Goliad as one of the original twenty-three Texas counties. The county was organized in 1837, and Goliad was chosen as county seat.

At this point, a word of explanation is justified. The reader must understand that, as the Spanish established missions across

Texas, each was accompanied by a presidio (fort) with its garrison, usually located a mile or two from the mission. The name of the mission established in this locality was La Bahía ("the bay"), referring to La Bahía Espíritu Santo, the Spanish name for Matagorda and Lavaca Bay. La Bahía, over a period of two hundred years, referred to three missions at three locations. The first site began with a presidio built in 1712 on the ruins of La Salle's ill-fated Fort St. Louis on Garcitas Creek, about twenty miles east of the present town of Victoria. It was named Presidio la Bahía del Espíritu Santo. Shortly after that, a mission called Mission la Bahía was established, fulfilling the format for colonization. For several reasons, the presidio and mission were moved, first to the south bank of the Guadalupe River (near present-day Mission, Texas) in 1726 and finally to the San Antonio River in 1749, near the present Goliad. The name of the community of La Bahía did not become Goliad until 1829, when it was so named in honor of Father Miguel Hidalgo y Costilla, who had been active in gaining Mexico's independence from Spain.

Goliad County has no standing historic county jail. In 1883, the county built a two-story stone lockup that was stuccoed possibly at a later date. It is remembered as a brown or buff-colored cube-shaped building surrounded by a high stone wall topped with broken glass bottles as was the custom. The facility was used until 1949, when it was replaced.

Interviews conducted by the author: Sheriff J. K. McMahan; Darwyn Duderstadt; Anne Welch, director, Goliad County; Rhonda Briones, librarian; Anne Bode; Patsy Light; Doris Freer, Goliad County Historical Commission.

Other resources: *Dallas Morning News, Texas Almanac, 1998–1999;* Tyler, Barnett, and Barkley, eds., *New Handbook of Texas,* vol. 3, 205, 214, 1179, vol. 4, 774, and vol. 5, 333; DeLorme Mapping, *Texas Atlas and Gazetteer;* Friedrichs, *History of Goliad.*

Gonzales County (Gonzales)

Gonzales County was one of the twenty-three original counties formed in 1836. It was organized in 1837, and Gonzales was designated as the county seat. Named for Rafael

Gonzales County jail, 1887–1975, Gonzales, Texas.
Designed by architect Eugene Heiner. Courtesy of
Hugh Shelton.

Gonzales, governor of Coahuila and Texas, the town of Gonzales was surveyed in 1825 as the capital of the Green Dewitt colony. By 1828, there were several cabins within a fort stockade. As the population grew, Gonzales gradually became the focal point for those who wanted to separate Texas from Coahuila. The conventions of 1832 and 1833, disapproved of by Mexico, created the background for the ultimate confrontation, and the first shot of the Texas Revolution was fired at the battle of Gonzales. The "come and take it" episode was in reality a minor skirmish, when the citizens of Gonzales successfully resisted the effort of soldiers from the Mexican garrison in San Antonio to repossess a cannon given to Gonzales pioneers for defense against Indians. During the battle of the Alamo in March 1836, men from Gonzales slipped through the Mexican forces into the Alamo to fight and die.

The first jail in Gonzales County was planned in 1852 and designed in detail by John Mooney. After much controversy, the facility was built in 1854 on block 4, the designated Market Square site. In October 1872, John Wesley Hardin was in the Gonzales jail. Hardin was a popular citizen of Gonzales County, and his friend Manning Clements slipped him a hacksaw blade. With the nonseeing eyes of the guards in his favor, Hardin sawed through the bars and, with the help of a horse, pulled himself through the window to freedom.

The second lockup was designed by Eugene Heiner of Houston and built adjacent to the courthouse by contractor Henry Kane in 1887. Snead and Company Iron Works, a local blacksmith, provided the cells. The building reflected a sophisticated design in the Victorian Italianate style with mansard roof and tower. Unfortunately, extensive renovations in 1905 by Southern Structural Steel Company of San Antonio removed the roof and tower. The original brick walls and floor plan remained, as well as many of the cells. The last prisoners were removed to a new jail in 1975. Since then, extensive renovations have been done on the old building to provide quarters for the chamber of commerce and the Old Jail Museum (414 St. Lawrence). The gallows were restored for museum purposes.

Interviews conducted by the author: Barbara Hand, Gonzales Chamber of Commerce; David Bucek; Stephen Fox.

Other resources: *Dallas Morning News, Texas Almanac, 1998–1999;* Tyler, Barnett, and Barkley, eds., *New Handbook of Texas,* vol. 2, 296, vol. 3, 230, and vol. 6, 238; J. T. Davis, *Historic Towns of Texas;* Cunningham, *Trigger-nometry;* W. Robinson, *People's Architecture.*

Gray County (Pampa)

Gray County, named after Peter W. Gray, member of the first Texas legislature, was created in 1876. When the area was organized in 1902, LeFors was selected as the county seat and remained so for twenty years. In 1929, however, the seat of government was moved to Pampa. *Pampa,* Spanish for "grassy plain," seems like a descriptive word for the Panhandle country in that day. Moving this county seat was a hard-fought campaign, requiring three elections between 1908 and 1928. It is said that the real story of the

Gray County jail, 1929–1991, on the fourth floor of the courthouse, Pampa, Texas. Designed by architect W. R. Kaufman. Photo by Stanley Gilbert. From the author's collection.

removal of the county records to Pampa is, to this day, a mystery.

Gray County's first jail was in LeFors and was a one-story stone building south of the courthouse. The second lockup was in Pampa after the county seat was moved. That jail was on the fourth floor of the new courthouse, which was designed by W. R. Kaufman and Son of Amarillo and completed in 1929. The courthouse was built in the Georgian style and cost $267,974. The fourth-floor jail accounted for $17,980 of that amount. The courthouse measured 120' by 85' and was constructed of steel and reinforced concrete with a tan brick veneer. The keep housed thirty-six prisoners and sheriff's quarters. In 1991, the jail was moved out of the courthouse and into a separate building.

Interviews conducted by the author: Richard Peet, Gray County judge; Wanda Carter, county clerk; Anna Davidson, curator, White Deer Land Museum; Darlene Birkes, Gray County Historical Commission.

Other resources: *Dallas Morning News, Texas Almanac, 1998–1999;* Tyler, Barnett, and Barkley, eds., *New Handbook of Texas,* vol. 1, 355, and vol. 3, 296; Metz, *Roadside History of Texas;* Kelsey and Dyal, *Courthouses of Texas;* Gray County History Book Committee, *Gray County Heritage.*

Grayson County (Sherman)

Grayson County was created in 1846 and named for Peter W. Grayson, attorney general of the Republic of Texas and a pro–Sam Houston Democrat. When Sherman became the county seat, the town site was moved three miles east of its original location to obtain better wood and water supplies.

About 1837, a river crossing on the Red River (near present-day Pottsboro) became a trading center known as Coffee's Trading Post, later called Preston. A steamboat with Sam Houston aboard rode up the Red River to Preston in 1840. A road was built from Preston to Austin and given the name Preston Road. The road met and joined the southern end of the Indian Nation Texas Road. The road and the river combined to make a thriving center of trade, augmented somewhat when it became a stop on the Butterfield Overland Mail route.

It is believed that the first jail was built in Sherman in 1847. It was a typical dungeon, made of hewn logs, two stories, with a trapdoor in the second floor to allow entrance of the prisoners to the doorless first level. It was 18' square, located on the northeast corner of Travis and Jones streets, and called the calaboose. That structure served until 1887, when a new jail was planned and built. In a politically charged and controversial atmosphere, the commissioners' court issued warrants for a new lockup and bought a lot in the 400 block between West Houston and West Lamar.

The 1887 facility utilized an innovative concept called a "rotary jail." That same year, Pauly Brothers of St. Louis sold a similar jail to the commissioners of Ellis County. The complicated mechanism cost one hundred thousand dollars but had cells for one hundred prisoners. The brick Victorian building was a beautiful bit of architecture and outlasted the jail cells by about twenty-four years. In 1912, it was decided that the rotary jail was impractical, so the cells were removed and replaced with stationary compartments. In 1928, the court decided that the jail had deteriorated, so plans were made to include a keep on the top floor of the new courthouse. The courthouse and jail were completed in 1936.

Interviews conducted by the author: Chris Baran, Red River Historical Museum; David Hawley, Grayson County Sheriff's Department.

Other resources: *Dallas Morning News, Texas Almanac, 1998–1999;* Tyler, Barnett, and Barkley, eds., *New Handbook of Texas,* vol. 3, 298, and vol. 5, 1021; J. W. Williams and Kenneth F. Neighbours, *Old Texas Trails;* Metz, *Roadside History of Texas;* Kelsey and Dyal, *Courthouses of Texas.*

Gregg County (Longview)

The area of Gregg County and surrounding counties was the historic land of the Caddo Indians. Their ancestral roots were in the Mississippi mound-building culture, which may have emerged as early as 700 A.D. Created in 1873 and organized that same year, Gregg County was named for Confederate Gen. John Gregg. Longview, the county seat, was founded in 1870 when the Texas Pacific Railroad laid tracks into Gregg County from Marshall, Texas.

Gregg County jail, 1932–1982, Longview, Texas. Built by Southern Prison Company of San Antonio.

The first jail in Gregg County was a two-story frame building built on the corner of Methvin and Court streets in September 1874. The people of Longview have no recollection of new jail construction between 1874 and 1932, when a new courthouse was built. A review of the Southern Prison Company Archives, however, reveals a photograph of a two-story brick jail with an out-building in a spacious lot, all enclosed by a wire-link fence about twelve feet tall. Labeled "Gregg County Jail, Longview, Texas," the picture does not fit any of the available descriptions of a Gregg County jail. The architectural style suggests a turn-of-the-century date, perhaps 1902 or thereabouts.

Production of cotton and corn was the basis of the economy of Gregg County until oil was discovered in 1931. The oil boom during the Depression had a significant impact in Longview. Within a few weeks the population grew from 16,000 to more than 100,000, and revenues surged as the economy changed from agriculture to petroleum production. As might be expected, the boom attracted a rowdy crowd of crooks and thieves to the tent cities of Gregg County and Kilgore. In February 1931, ten Texas Rangers descended at night on Kilgore and within two hours had three hundred suspects herded into the Baptist church, where they were "booked from the pulpit." Forty of them, including two wanted murderers and three bank robbers, were put in jail, while the rest were hustled out of town.

The 1932 courthouse in Longview, including a lockup on the fifth and sixth floors, was built at a cost of three hundred fifty thousand dollars. Southern Prison Company of San Anto-

nio provided the cells and ironwork. That facility was used
until 1982, when it was replaced by a prison that fulfilled the
requirements of the Texas Commission for Jail Standards.

Interviews conducted by the author: Nancy McWhorter, Gregg County
Historical Museum; Norman Black, Gregg County Historical Commission; Deputy Sheriff Robert Marshall.

Other resources: Tyler, Barnett, and Barkley, eds., *New Handbook of
Texas,* vol. 3, 329, and vol. 4, 284; *Dallas Morning News, Texas Almanac,
1998–1999;* Newcomb, *Indians of Texas;* Tyler and Tyler, *Texas Museums;*
Josephy, *500 Nations;* Centennial Book Committee, *Longview Texas Centennial, 1870–1970;* Sterling, *Trails and Trials of a Texas Ranger.*

Grimes County (Anderson)

Created and organized in 1846, Grimes County was
named for Jesse Grimes, a signer of the Texas Declaration of Independence. It is thought that the murder of Sieur
de La Salle by one of his own men in 1687 as he traveled east
from Matagorda in an effort to find the Mississippi River occurred near Navasota in Grimes County.

In 1833 Henry Fanthrope had bought one-fourth of the
land belonging to a man named Holland for twenty-five cents
per acre. He began farming, built a large barn, and finally constructed the Fanthrope Inn for stagecoach travelers. In 1846,
Fanthrope donated land for the county seat and established
Anderson, Texas, named after the last vice president of the Republic of Texas.

In the period before and after the Civil War, Anderson enjoyed a strong economy and at one time was the fourth largest
town in the state. It boasted six cotton gins, two sawmills, and
five hotels, but lack of transportation and roads finally caused
its decline. When the citizens denied a railroad to the Houston
and Texas Central line, the center of trade shifted to Navasota.

The first jail (1853) in Grimes County was a 15′ by 24′
wooden building. The facility apparently served its purposes
during the Civil War. Following that war, under the Republican regime in the South, the black population dominated the
political arena. In November 1900, the formation of the White
Man's Union Association brought about the defeat of the eight-

Grimes County jail, 1897–1956, Anderson, Texas. Built by Diebold Safe and Lock. Photo courtesy of Marcus H. Mallard.

term Republican sheriff, Garrett Scott, and resulted in a shootout on the courthouse square. Scott was wounded, and his brother and two others were killed, shifting political control to the Democrats.

The original jail burned in 1879 and was replaced with a new stone building that lasted for eighteen years. In 1897, a two-story brick Romanesque jail was designed and built by Diebold Safe and Lock Company. It was Diebold's custom to build the entire cage and cell complex, disassemble it, and ship it to its destination. Since Anderson had no railroad until 1903, such a shipment at that time seems a remarkable feat. The 1897 jail was used until 1956, when a new facility was built.

Interviews conducted by the author: Marcus Mallard, county commissioner; Elliott Goodwin.

Other resources: *Dallas Morning News, Texas Almanac, 1998–1999;* Grimes County Historical Commission, *History of Grimes County;* Tyler, Barnett, and Barkley, eds., *New Handbook of Texas,* vol. 1, 170, and vol. 5, 342; Metz, *Roadside History of Texas.*

Guadalupe County (Seguin)

Guadalupe County was created in 1842 by the Republic of Texas, but, after annexation, a new Guadalupe County was designated in 1846. An encampment by the Texas Rangers on the Guadalupe River had been laid out as a town site named Walnut Springs in 1838, but the name was changed to

Seguin in 1842, when it became the county seat. It was named in honor of Juan Seguín, Travis's messenger sent from the Alamo. Seguin

Guadalupe County jail, c. 1900–1936, Seguin, Texas. Photo courtesy of Nelda Kubala.

remained the seat of the new Guadalupe County created under the state government in 1846.

Initially, punishment in Seguin was pretty straightforward; citizens had a whipping post with a three-inch iron ring to hold a culprit while lashes were laid on. It was some time before the commissioners got around to building a jail. In late 1853, they advertised for bids, but there were no takers. Finally in 1854, a contract was let to A. Herron to build a jail for $2,950. This first jail in Guadalupe County was to be "of live oak blocks, two stories in height and in the eastern part of town."

During the nineteenth century, movement of prisoners between the jails at Gonzales, Seguin, and San Antonio was a chore for the sheriff or deputy. According to local information, there were several iron holding posts driven deep in the ground along the way to which a prisoner could be chained overnight to allow the law enforcement officer to rest. Families who lived along the way were also known to provide food and security for the weary lawmen.

The next Seguin jail—built in the late nineteenth or early twentieth century—was a two-story brick structure on Darnegan Street (originally Center Street). That building has been remodeled and now serves as the Health and Sanitation Building.

Interview conducted by the author: Nelda Kubala.
Other resources: *Dallas Morning News, Texas Almanac, 1998–1999;* Tyler, Barnett, and Barkley, eds., *New Handbook of Texas,* vol. 3, 360, and vol. 5,

967; McGuire, *Iwonski in Texas;* W. Robinson, *People's Architecture;* Weinert,
Authentic History of Guadalupe County.

Hale County (Plainview)

Created in 1876 and organized in 1888, Hale County was
named for J. C. Hale, who died at the Alamo. Plainview,
which had been established by Z. T. Maxwell in 1887, became
the county seat in 1888. The *New Handbook of Texas* reveals
that there have been six towns called Plainview in Texas, but
Hale County is the only one with a post office.

In the beginning, Plainview was isolated and supplied only
by freight wagons from Colorado City in Mitchell County,
150 miles away. The town flourished from the very beginning,
however, because of ranching. In 1881, the Cross L Ranch
operated twenty square miles of ranch land, which was later
sold to C. C. Slaughter. In a few years, it was discovered that
the land was on the vast underground Ogallala aquifer. In
time, the aquifer was producing water for perhaps 450,000
acres of irrigated farms. The discovery of oil in 1946 ensured
prosperity.

The first Hale County jail was a one-room sod hut built
about 1888 on a lot that would become the corner of Fifth
Street and Baltimore. The second lockup was built in 1890
and is said to have been a one-room building made of 2″ by 4″
planks stacked and nailed together. Since Diebold Safe and
Lock Company had a contract for this facility, it is presumed
that they manufactured a jail cell. The price was thirty-eight
hundred dollars, a part of which may been freight charges to
get the cage delivered without benefit of railroads.

Three detention centers were built in the twentieth century, all on the courthouse square. The first, built in 1908, was
part of a brick courthouse; the cost of the courthouse and jail
combined was seventy thousand dollars. In 1928, a freestanding jail was built on the northeast corner of the square. It had
three stories, with sheriff's quarters on the first floor. In the
1950s this structure was replaced by a new facility, which is
still in use on the courthouse square.

Interviews conducted by the author: Bill Hollers, county judge; John Sigwald, librarian; Pattie Guffee, Llano Estacado Museum.

Other resources: *Dallas Morning News, Texas Almanac, 1998–1999;* Metz, *Roadside History of Texas;* Tyler, Barnett, and Barkley, eds., *New Handbook of Texas,* vol. 3, 408, and vol. 5, 226; M. L. Cox, *History of Hale County, Texas.*

Hall County (Memphis)

Hall County was created in 1876 and organized in 1890. It was named for W. D. C. Hall, who was the secretary of war of the Republic of Texas. According to legend, the naming of the new town of Memphis was an accident. Two names had been submitted to postal authorities, but both had been rejected because other towns in Texas already had those names. While on a visit to Austin, J. W. Brice noticed a letter that had been addressed to Memphis, Texas, which could not be delivered since there was no town by that name in the state. Brice decided that Memphis should be the name of the new town. At the very worst, its citizens could expect to get at least one letter in the new post office.

Hall County has had three jails, counting the current one, which was built in 1981. The first was built in 1890 by Pauly Brothers on the corner of Fifth and Robertson streets. It was a two-story brick building that was used until 1915, when Pauly was once again asked to replace the old facility. The new building was used until 1981. Like the previous jail, it too was a red-brick, two-story rectangular structure and was built on the same site as the first lockup. The 1915 facility is now used as a Boy Scout meeting place under a ninety-nine-year lease with the county.

Hall County jail, 1915–1981, Memphis, Texas.

Interviews conducted by the author: Karen Crisman, librarian; Helen
Crisman, county judge, Kenneth Dale's office; David Wiggins; Jess R.
Mitchell.

Other resources: *Dallas Morning News, Texas Almanac, 1998–1999;* Tyler,
Barnett, and Barkley, eds., *New Handbook of Texas,* vol. 3, 417, and vol. 4,
611; Metz, *Roadside History of Texas.*

Hamilton County (Hamilton)

Hamilton County was created in 1842 by the Republic
of Texas and named for James Hamilton, the governor
of South Carolina who had supported Texas in its fight for independence. Hamilton had invested $218,000 in gold to help
the financially troubled new republic. It wasn't until 1858,
however, that Hamilton was designated a county by the State
of Texas and the town of Hamilton as the county seat.

James Rice, an early pioneer, established a store around
which a community formed in 1855; the area would eventually become the town of Hamilton. The period during and
after the Civil War was particularly difficult for Hamilton
County because of frequent Indian raids. During one such
incident in 1867, a group of Indians attacked a schoolhouse,
killed teacher Ann Whitney, and kidnapped one of the children. The kidnapped student, John Kuykendall, was a captive of the Indians in Oklahoma for two years before he was
released.

The first jail in Hamilton County was built in 1875 of wood
with 12″ thick cottonwood walls. A variation on the usual
structure, it was made of 1″ by 12″ rawhide planks stacked flat
and fastened to the boards below with a liberal use of nails.

The second lockup, built in 1877, was an attractive limestone building of Romanesque Revival design. Shortly after
this structure was finished, it held a prisoner by the name of
Garrison. Many of the citizens had lost horses to thieves, and
it eventually came to the public's attention that Garrison had
a lot of horses of uncertain origin. One night, a large group of
armed men came to town, supposedly to rescue Garrison, but,
after breaking him out of jail, they took him down to the large
oak tree in the cemetery, where he was hanged. No grand jury

action followed because no one could be found who had rec-ognized the men; everyone was certain that "they were from other counties."

A stone jail was built in 1894 but was replaced in 1938 by a brick building designed by Charles D. Weidner. It was con-structed during the Depression by the WPA on the same site that the 1894 jail had occupied.

Interviews conducted by the author: Kenneth Miller; Ruth Young.
Other resources: *Dallas Morning News, Texas Almanac, 1998–1999;* Tyler, Barnett, and Barkley, eds., *New Handbook of Texas,* vol. 3, 42, 431.

Hansford County (Spearman)

Named for John M. Hansford, a physician and controver-sial district judge in East Texas during the Regulator-Modulator War, Hansford County was created in 1876 and or-ganized in 1889. The Regulators were a group of law officers who dominated and oppressed the local citizens in the exercise of their official duties. When Judge Hansford did not accede to the Regulators' orders, they ambushed and assassinated him near his home. Finally, some of the more courageous members of the county, determined to oppose this abuse of power, formed a citizen's militia known as the Modulators.

Settlers did not come to the Panhandle in the first part of the nineteenth century because of the ferocity of the resident Indians, who subsisted mainly on buffalo. In the early 1870s, with the encouragement of the U.S. government, buffalo hunters came to the Panhandle to slaughter the animals for their hides, a valuable article of trade at the time. By 1877, the great herds of buffalo were gone, and the Indian presence was removed. Some of the hunters, however, stayed and became ranchers. Population growth was slow until the 1900s, when farmers, especially Scandinavians, began to move in.

In 1889, the town of Hansford, on the old Dodge City to Tascosa stagecoach road, was chosen as the county seat when the area was organized. As farming increased and the North Texas and Santa Fe Railroad bypassed Hansford, Spearman, founded in 1917, grew significantly and in 1929 was named the county seat. Older residents recall that there was no jail in Hansford. When it was necessary to retain a prisoner, he was chained or handcuffed to some sturdy structure in the courthouse basement.

Spearman was incorporated in 1921, and the city hall is said to have had a jail in it. The first Hansford County jail—of concrete with two cells, two windows, and one door—was built in the mid-1920s. It was used until 1960, when a jail annex to the 1931 courthouse was finished.

Interviews conducted by the author: Reba Hunter; County Judge Jim Brown; Mrs. J. D. Wilbanks.

Other resources: *Dallas Morning News, Texas Almanac, 1998–1999;* Haley, *Texas, An Album of History;* Tyler, Barnett, and Barkley, eds., *New Handbook of Texas,* vol. 3, 444; Hansford County Historical Commission, *Hansford County, Texas.*

Hardeman County (Quanah)

Hardeman County was created in 1858 from Fannin County and organized in 1884. It was named for Bailey Hardeman, coauthor of the Texas Constitution and secretary of state of the Republic of Texas in April 1836. He had moved to Texas with his extended family in 1835 and was soon involved in the independence movement. He obtained an eighteen-pounder cannon from the Lavaca River area and moved it to San Antonio for the Texan attack in December 1835. After the battle of San Jacinto, Hardeman, as acting secretary of state, negotiated two treaties with Santa Anna for the withdrawal of the Mexican soldiers from Texas.

The town of Margaret was designated as the first county seat in 1885, but when the Fort Worth and Denver City Railroad was put through north of the Pease River, the county seat was changed to Quanah in 1890. The name Quanah has an interesting derivation. During the battle of Pease River (twelve miles to the south) in 1860, Capt. Sul Ross, along with the Texas Rangers, attacked a Comanche encampment and, in the course of the fight, killed Chief Peta Nocona. Ross captured the chief's wife, who turned out to be the storied Cynthia

Ann Parker, and her infant daughter, Prairie Flower, her second child. Cynthia Ann's son, Quanah, however, remained with

Hardeman County jail, 1890–1973, Quanah, Texas. Photo by Stanley Gilbert. From the author's collection.

his tribe and became the famous Comanche warrior for whom the county seat of Hardeman County is named.

Pauly Jail Building Manufacturers built the Hardeman County lockup in 1890. The prison cells on the second floor are by Pauly Company, but there are also compartments manufactured by the Southern Structural Steel Company, which would indicate the jail was remodeled at some point, probably after 1914. The facility was used until 1973, when another lockup was built at a different location.

Interviews conducted by the author: Jerrie Meason; Clark Hitt.
Other resources: *Dallas Morning News, Texas Almanac, 1998–1999;* Tyler, Barnett, and Barkley, eds., *New Handbook of Texas,* vol. 3, 448, and vol. 5, 378; Metz, *Roadside History of Texas;* Sterling, *Trails and Trials of a Texas Ranger;* Quanah Chamber of Commerce, "Hardeman County."

Hardin County (Kountze)

Hardin County was created in 1858 from parts of Jefferson and Liberty counties. By specification of the legislature, it was named for William Hardin, a leader of the Texas Revolution. The town of Hardin, near the center of the county, was made the county seat. It is said that a log building in the town was used for a jail. Hardin remained the county seat until bypassed by the Sabine and East Texas Railroad in 1881.

The new town of Kountze, two miles from Hardin and on the railroad right-of-way, began to develop. In 1884, a vote

Hardin County jail, 1904–1958, Kountze, Texas. Photo courtesy of Hardin County Historical Commission.

to move the county seat to Kountze failed by a close count. In 1886, a fire, perhaps accidental, destroyed the courthouse in Hardin, and a new vote in 1887 was substantially in favor of moving the county seat. Because Kountze had no official courthouse building, court was held in various places until Herman and Augustus Kountze, founders of the town, donated land for a courthouse square in 1904. The domed courthouse was built in 1905.

That same year, a reinforced concrete block jail, the first in Kountze, was built by M. J. Lewman Company on the south side of the square at a cost of forty thousand dollars. It was a fortress-style structure with two stories, crenellated battlements, and a tower that housed a gallows. The sheriff's quarters were on the first floor, where Sheriff Miles D. Jordan (1932–1940) lived with his family. Mrs. Jordan, of course, cooked for her family and for the prisoners as well. Sheriff Jordan's son, Gene, recalls that one prisoner, a furniture maker named Schultz, made a desk for Mrs. Jordan. Gene Jordan still has the desk. The jail was used until 1958, when a new courthouse with a lockup was built.

Interviews conducted by the author: Dee Hatton, county clerk; Harold W. Willis, Hardin County Historical Commission; Gene Jordan, Hardin County historian.

Other resources: *Dallas Morning News, Texas Almanac, 1998–1999;* Tyler, Barnett, and Barkley, eds., *New Handbook of Texas,* vol. 3, 4456, 1159, and vol. 5, 1150.

Harris County (Houston)

Harris County was created in 1836 as one of the twenty-three original Texas counties. It was originally named Harrisburg County for John R. Harris, who had founded the municipality in 1824. During the Runaway Scrape in April 1836, Santa Anna had burned Harrisburg five days before the battle of San Jacinto. Houston, the county seat of Harris County, was laid out by August C. Allen and John Kirby Allen on Buffalo Bayou above Harrisburg very shortly after the victory at San Jacinto. To build a new city on Buffalo Bayou at its junction with White Oak Bayou, they had purchased property from a Mrs. Parrot, who had received title to the land after the death of her first husband, John Austin.

John K. Allen was a delegate to the governing body of the new republic, and the brothers' decision to name their new town Houston found support from the new Texas president, Sam Houston, for making their city the new nation's capital. The Allens also proposed building a structure for congress and a house for the president of the new republic.

Within a few months, Harrisburg County had its first jail (1837), located on the southeast corner of Congress Avenue and Fannin Street on the courthouse square. It was a simple box, 24′ by 24′ of heavy 12″ square hewn logs. The building was partitioned to make two cells, each 12′ square and a long room, 12′ × 24′. It was originally conceived as a single story, but for whatever reason, a second story was added before completion. The cells were

Harris County jail and courthouse, 1880–1895, at the corner of Preston and Caroline streets in Houston. Courtesy of Houston Public Library.

two dungeons in the simplest form, thus access to each was through a three-foot planked door, with an iron-grated door opening into the large room. Each cell had two small barred windows.

Citizens in the prestigious neighborhood that soon developed nearby despised the unpleasant presence of the jail and filed suit in the name of the city against the county. In 1838, the county lost the case in the 11th Judicial Court. Shortly afterward, the city of Houston built a combination city hall and jail on Congress Avenue. In an effort to appease the citizens, the county contracted with the city to keep county prisoners in the new city calaboose instead of in the jail on the courthouse square and also sent some prisoners to Galveston, thereby relieving the problem.

In May 1856, the county erected its second lockup on the northeast corner of Preston Avenue and Austin Street. Built by George Henry, the two-story brick building had six 10' by 12' cells and a 9½' high ceiling. Because the crime rate soon outpaced this facility, in 1877 plans were made to build a jail on the courthouse square. Having lost in court, however, the county bought another lot and commissioned a young Houston architect, Eugene Heiner, to design a new lockup to be placed on the southeast corner of Preston and Caroline. The result was an attractive, two-story brick-and-stone Second Empire structure with a mansard roof. The facility bore a striking resemblance to one built in Galveston by Eugene Heiner the previous year.

Crime increased along with the population in the fast-growing county, and in 1895 the commissioners called on Heiner again to build a much larger keep at the foot of Capitol Avenue and Bagby Street near Buffalo Bayou. The county had purchased four acres of land for the project. The new building contained not only a larger jail but also a criminal courts section. In 1910, however, the criminal courts were moved into a new civil courts building, and the vacated space in the 1891 jail was converted to housing for people with severe mental disorders.

In 1927, still another jail was completed by Bellows Construction Company at 624 Bagby, next to the former lockup.

It consisted of eight stories, including the basement, and cost $750,000. Designed by the Wyatt C. Hedrick firm of Fort Worth, it included criminal courts as well as four floors of prison cells. A women and children's area and a chapel were on the top floor. This jail was used until after World War II, when it was finally torn down to provide space for the Albert Thomas Convention Center.

Interviews conducted by the author: Deputy Sheriff Rand Clark; Stephen Bell; Judge Charles Bacarisse; Robert L. Dabney; Ray Miller; Paul Scott, Harris County Records Center; Thomas D. Anderson.

Other resources: *Dallas Morning News, Texas Almanac, 1998–1999;* Tyler, Barnett, and Barkley, eds., *New Handbook of Texas,* vol. 3, 479, 480, 721; *Telegraph and Texas Register,* Oct. 21, 1837; Robinson and Webb, *Texas Public Buildings of the Nineteenth Century;* McComb, *Houston;* Gurasich, *History of the Harris County Sheriff's Department, 1836–1983;* Work Projects Administration in the State of Texas, *Houston;* Houston Public Library–WPA/Maresh Collection.

Harrison County (Marshall)

Harrison County was created in 1839 and organized in 1842. It was named for James Harrison, advocate of the Texas Revolution and an early lawyer. The county was agricultural, dependent in many ways on slavery for the production of cotton. When the county was organized, land was donated for a county seat, and the town of Marshall was created and named for Texas Chief Justice John Marshall.

The Regulator-Moderator War, which began in Shelby County, marred the history of Harrison County. It lasted for about five years and originated as a result of land frauds and other irregular transactions involving the disputed area between Louisiana and Texas. Finally, after many killings, Pres. Sam Houston personally brought in the militia to end the fighting. After the dust settled, many members of the opposing factions fought side by side in the Mexican War ten years later.

In 1860, Harrison County, then with a population of fifteen thousand, had the third largest number of people of any county in Texas. In the last days of the Civil War, Marshall was twice chosen as the meeting place for planning the continued fighting of the Confederate armies west of the Mississippi. After the Civil War, Marshall was the base for occupying Union troops and also the center of the Freedman's Bureau. It was not until 1878 that the Citizens Party was able to regain control from the Reconstruction government.

Unfortunately, records of the Harrison County jails are gone. Ruth Briggs remembers the two-story red brick lockup on the corner of Wellington and Fannin streets. The facility was built in 1925 and, although dilapidated, was still in use in 1951.

According to a story about an incident following a performance in the Marshall Opera House in 1879, Maurice Barrymore, father of John, Ethel, and Lionel, was shot and wounded by a local tough, gunman Jim Currie. Barrymore, who had been national amateur boxing champion while at Oxford, confronted Currie, who shot Barrymore in the arm and then shot and killed Benjamin C. Porter, another member of the cast. According to Frank X. Tolbert, when Currie was tried and acquitted on grounds of temporary insanity, Barrymore compared the experience to a twin-bill performance: "We begin with a tragedy and end with a farce."

Interviews conducted by the author: Judge Ben Grant; Gail Beil; Martha Diesta; Hubert Bender, Marshall City Library; Ruth Briggs, volunteer, Harrison County Archives; Sue W. Moss.

Other resources: Tyler, Barnett, and Barkley, eds., *New Handbook of Texas*, vol. 3, 487, and vol. 5, 417; Metz, *Roadside History of Texas;* Sonnichsen, *I'll Die before I'll Run.*

Hartley County (Channing)

Hartley County was created in 1876 and organized in 1891, when the county population numbered 1,665. The county was named for Oliver Cromwell Hartley, an early Galveston lawyer and Texas legislator. The original county seat was Hartley. In 1903, however, it was moved to Channing— headquarters of the XIT Ranch—even though the Channing population at that time was only 250.

The XIT Ranch (about two hundred miles long, north to south, and thirty miles wide, east to west) occupied two-thirds of the county and was created when the Texas legislature traded three million acres of Panhandle land in payment for a new state capitol

Hartley County jail, 1906–present, Channing, Texas. Designed by architect O. G. Roquemore.

building. The syndicate that designed and built the capitol (which burned in November 1881) spent about $3.2 million on construction, which translates to about $1.07 per acre. The company began selling the ranch land in 1890, and within twenty years, it was three-fourths sold.

The first jail in Hartley County, built in 1892, was a two-story brick-and-sandstone structure. It now stands in a pleasant residential neighborhood of ranch-style homes with manicured lawns. The jail's useful life was brief, cut short by the change of the county seat to Channing, fifteen miles to the south. The facility is now in private hands, and plans are being developed to restore it.

The second lockup in Hartley County was built in Channing along with the adjacent courthouse designed by O. G. Roquemore. The two red-brick buildings rest on sandstone bases, complementing each other with arched windows and doors. Contractors Solon and Wickens completed the structures in 1906. The cube-shaped jail is still certified by the Texas Commission for Jail Standards. It has sheriff's quarters on the first floor and cells for seven inmates on the second floor. It has the typical lever-lock system popularized by Pauly Jail Building Company.

Interviews conducted by the author: Sheriff John Williams; Donna Bryant, jail owner; Pat Kirkenminde.

Other resources: *Dallas Morning News, Texas Almanac, 1998–1999;* Tyler, Barnett, and Barkley, eds., *New Handbook of Texas,* vol.3, 493, and vol. 6, 1101; Metz, *Roadside History of Texas.*

Haskell County (Haskell)

Haskell County was created in 1856 from Milam and Fannin counties. Native American hostilities were so bad that occupation progressed very slowly. The county was re-created in 1876 and organized in 1885. It was named for C. R. Haskell, one of the victims of the Goliad massacre. Cattle ranching began in the area in 1882, and W. R. Sandifer brought in the first sheep in the early 1880s.

On September 28, 1885, the commissioners' court took bids for the construction of the first county jail, which was to be made of brick and stone, 27′ by 37′ with walls 17′ high. Pauly Jail Builders and Manufacturers designed the facility. The keep served well enough, but by 1909, the increased population demanded a new detention center.

In 1909, the county contracted with Southern Structural Steel Company to design and build a new building. The new jail, at South First Street and Avenue D, was a three-story red-brick-and-stone Victorian structure similar to those built in Lubbock, Bellville, and Richmond. It had a tower on the northwest corner and faced west. The roofline was topped with crenulations and battlements, and the tower held a large water tank for the plumbing system. The first floor had quarters for the sheriff, whose wife cooked for the prisoners as well as for her own family. The jail was used until 1962, when it was demolished and replaced by a new building.

A familiar landmark was the old Haskell County jail, located at the southeast corner of the square.

Haskell County jail, 1909–1962, Haskell, Texas. Built by Southern Structural Steel. Photo courtesy of Johnson Kis Photo.

Giles M. Kemp was about six years old when he lived in the lockup while his father, Giles Kemp, was sheriff from 1934 to 1939. Kemp remembers Irene Jenkins, whose husband was a shoe cobbler; she herself was a sometime bootlegger. This occupation, of course, frequently led her to jail, which was a boon to the sheriff because Irene was a wonderful cook. The only people who could afford Irene's bootleg products were the town's well-to-do merchants and professionals. She used most of her bootleg-earned money to feed and clothe many in the black community during the Depression.

Bob Cousins served as sheriff from 1948 to 1954. When the lockup was full, Cousins would get Irene to come and help with the cooking. He remembers standing in the jail doorway at age five while his father, Al Cousins, who was sheriff from 1919 to 1921, turned away a lynch mob who wanted to abduct his prisoner.

Interviews conducted by the author: Sheriff John Mills; Wanda Hamm; Joan Strickland; Jack Jones.

Other resources: Tyler, Barnett, and Barkley, eds., *New Handbook of Texas,* vol. 3, 501; Metz, *Roadside History of Texas; Dallas Morning News, Texas Almanac, 1998–1999;* DeLorme Mapping, *Texas Atlas and Gazetteer.*

Hays County (San Marcos)

In 1831 Juan Martín Veramendi, mayor of San Antonio, and two others obtained a land grant from Mexico for the area that would become Hays County. Veramendi became vice governor and finally governor of Coahuila and Texas. In 1831 his daughter married Jim Bowie. Twenty years later, Edward Burleson, William Lindsey, and Eli Merriman bought the Veramendi grant and established the town of San Marcos on the San Marcos River. The county was established in 1848 with San Marcos as the county seat.

The first jail was built in 1873 at 170 Fredericksburg Street. Called the calaboose, it was a substantial building of brick and stucco and contained three cells. About a year after completion in June 1874, all twelve of its prisoners broke out and were pursued by horse and on foot until ten were recaptured. The

Hays County jail, 1885–1936, San Marcos, Texas. Designed by architect Edward Northcraft.

other two, it seems, were able to make good their escape. After a new facility was built in 1885, the old building became the lockup for black prisoners. During World War II, the 1873 jail was expanded with a frame addition and became the black USO; the structure now serves as an African American recreation center and museum.

In 1885 a second county jail was built next door facing Martin Luther King Street. Designed by Edward Northcraft, it was a two-story limestone structure in the Italianate style. It had a gallows that, although used twice, was later removed. Operated until 1936, the building shows faded elements of its original elegance but is still standing, though in poor condition.

Interviews conducted by the author: John Polanco, justice of the peace; Lila Knight Ethridge, Texas Historical Commission; Johnnie Armstead, African American Museum.

Other resources: *Dallas Morning News, Texas Almanac, 1998–1999;* Tyler, Barnett, and Barkley, eds., *New Handbook of Texas,* vol. 3, 520, vol. 5, 867, and vol. 6, 722; Metz, *Roadside History of Texas.*

Hemphill County (Canadian)

Hemphill County was created in 1876 along with other Texas Panhandle counties. It was organized in 1887 and named for John Hemphill, justice of the Republic of Texas. Development was fairly slow until the construction of the Southern Kansas Railroad in 1886 and the establishment of the towns of Canadian, Mendota, and Glazier. Canadian became the county seat.

The first jail was a modest wooden building that was replaced by a red-brick two-story lockup in 1890. The 1890 jail, designed by R. G.

Hemphill County jail, 1890–1982, Canadian, Texas. Designed by the architectural firm of R. G. Kirsch and Company.

Kirsch and Company, was the first permanent public building built in Hemphill County, predating even the courthouse. It served the community for ninety years until 1982—even through the riotous years of the 1930s' oil boom in nearby Borger, Texas.

In January 1897, prisoner Jim Harbolt, accused of murder, escaped from the Hemphill County jail by sawing through the window bars with a hacksaw blade and prying the bars loose with a crowbar. He let himself down to the ground with a rope made from bedding and was gone the next morning when Deputy Sheriff Dick Rathjen checked on his prisoner. Three days later, Harbolt was recaptured nearby, sick and showing much wear from his time out in the January Panhandle weather. He was sentenced to life in prison, and it was never determined who provided the tools for his escape.

In the summer of 1936, the old jail held the notorious bank robber and gunman Pete Traxler, age twenty-eight. Traxler was wanted in several Texas and Oklahoma counties for bank and highway robbery in addition to the murder of a deputy sheriff in Oklahoma. He was caught in a shootout with officers at a roadblock on the Canadian River bridge north of Canadian. Traxler spent some time under heavy guard in the hospital before being transferred to the jail in Canadian to await trial.

Interviews conducted by the author: Deputy Sheriff Joe Hoard; Libby Barker, Hemphill County Library.

Other resources: *Dallas Morning News, Texas Almanac, 1998–1999;* Tyler, Barnett, and Barkley, eds., *New Handbook of Texas,* vol. 3, 551; Hemphill County Preservation Committee, *Hemphill County History;* Stanley, *Rodeo Town.*

Henderson County (Athens)

Henderson County was created in April 1846 from Nacogdoches and Houston counties and was named for James Pickney Henderson, the first governor of the new state of Texas. In July 1839, the relentless pressure on the Cherokees by Mirabeau B. Lamar, president of the republic, had brought on the battle of the Neches in eastern Henderson County. The elderly chief Bowles, friend of Sam Houston, wearing a sword and sash given him by Houston, was shot from his horse while leading his warriors. The Texans prevailed in the battle, and the Cherokees retreated into Oklahoma, leaving their farms and villages behind.

Henderson's first county seat was in Buffalo, near a ferry crossing on the Trinity River. In 1848, the seat was first moved to Centerville and then to Athens in 1850, when the final perimeters of Henderson County were defined. By November 1850, Athens had a log courthouse that cost sixty-five dollars, and the following February, a water well was dug on the courthouse square. Repeated efforts to build a jail failed, for reasons not recorded in the commissioners' minutes. Finally, the original courthouse was sold, and the proceeds were used to build a lockup. The jail that was built in 1874 was

Henderson County jail, 1925–1991, Athens, Texas.

double walled and fashioned of 8″ square hewn-oak logs; it had two stories with an outside stairway to the second floor. In spite of its formidable construction, extensive repairs were begun on November 13, 1877, after all of the prisoners had escaped the previous night. In May 1883, a contract was made with J. J. Ligon of Palestine to remove the old Iron Bridge Company cages and replace them with four P. J. Pauly cells.

In 1897, the court planned a new lockup. Bids were received from three companies: Pauly, Diebold, and Doley and Komer. After voting, the court chose Diebold, represented by L. T. Noyes. On April 1, 1897, the new jail was accepted with praise lavished on Noyes for the quality of his work.

In September 1924, plans were submitted and accepted for a new detention center by H. A. Overbeck of Dallas, for which he was paid four hundred dollars. The contractor, L. R. Doughty of Dallas, completed the jail in June 1925. P. J. Pauly provided the cells and ironwork.

Interviews conducted by the author: Frank LaRue Jr., Henderson County Historical Commission; Joe Ed Young, juvenile probation officer.

Other resources: *Dallas Morning News, Texas Almanac, 1998–1999;* Tyler, Barnett, and Barkley, eds., *New Handbook of Texas,* vol. 1, 277, 810, vol. 3, 556, and vol. 4, 965; Henderson County Commissioners' Court Minutes.

Hidalgo County (Edinburgh)

Hidalgo County—named for Father Miguel Hidalgo y Costilla, a leader of Mexico's bid for independence from Spain—was created in 1852 from Cameron and Starr counties. During the nineteenth century, small villages developed along the Rio Grande. One of them, La Habitación, would become Edinburgh in 1852, when renamed by an emigrant from Scotland named John Young. The name of the town was changed to Hidalgo in 1885, however, when a U.S. post office was opened there. Hidalgo remained the county seat until 1908, when the seat of government was moved away from the flood-prone river to Chapin, about fifteen miles north and near the center of the county. Unfortunately, Dennis B. Chapin, a land developer for whom the town had been named, shot and killed a Texas Ranger in a saloon in San

Hidalgo County jail, 1886–1908, Hidalgo, Texas. Photo by Stanley Gilbert. From the author's collection.

Antonio. Although a jury acquitted Chapin, the citizens decided to change the name of their county seat to Edinburg.

The first county jail in Hidalgo County was built in 1886 of handmade brick on Esperanza Street in Hidalgo on the Rio Grande. The builder was S. W. Brooks, and the jail, still standing today in good condition, was used until the county seat moved to Edinburg in 1908. At that time, a bond election for seventy-five thousand dollars was passed to build a courthouse and lockup. The result was a handsome brick-and-stucco Spanish Revival–style jail with a red-tile roof designed by Atlee B. Ayres and H. I. Phelps of San Antonio. The keep contained sheriff's quarters on the first floor and a gallows that was used just once. A larger jail was built in 1922 and served the county well for fifty-six years until it was replaced in 1978. The 1908 Spanish Revival facility was used for various civic purposes after it was retired. It was subsequently restored and made into the attractive Hidalgo County Historical Museum.

Interview conducted by the author: David McCue, Hidalgo County Historical Museum.

Other resources: *Dallas Morning News, Texas Almanac, 1998–1999;* Tyler, Barnett, and Barkley, eds., *New Handbook of Texas,* vol. 2, 786, and vol. 3, 589; DeLorme Mapping, *Texas Atlas and Gazetteer;* McAllen, "Jewel of the Rio Grande"; Fowler, "Jailhouse Museums."

Hill County (Hillsboro)

Hill County was created in 1853 from Navarro County and named for George Washington Hill, Sam Houston's secretary of war. The area was in the Mexican land grant

given to
Sterling C.
Robertson
located
immediately
north of
the Stephen
Austin
grant. As
one might
suspect,
some dis-
agreement

Hill County jail, 1893–1984, Hillsboro, Texas. Photo by
Mavis Kelsey Sr.

arose between Robertson and Austin about the boundary, but
since Robertson was unable to fulfill his colonization obligation, the grant was transferred to Austin.

Hillsboro was located on 220 acres of land donated by
Thomas M. Steiner near the center of the county. It was not
incorporated until 1881, but the first jail was built in 1857.
That structure was of heavy log construction in two parts, separated by a stone partition. Originally located on North Waco
Street about a block from the courthouse, it was moved to the
northwest corner of the courthouse square in 1870. The original cost was $1,793, but the facility lasted until 1876, when it
was replaced by a larger building that included quarters for the
sheriff. According to Helen Brady Cox, the second jail, built
in 1876, burned in 1893.

W. C. Dodson of Waco designed the third jail, built in
1893, at 120 North Waco Street. It is an imposing brick two-
story blend of Victorian and medieval styles, including crenellations around the entire roofline. The facility contained quarters for the sheriff and one deputy. The cells for the prisoners
were in the large back portion of the building. It is said that
Elvis Presley spent a night there as a guest during the 1950s
while stationed at Fort Hood.

After killing a man named Baker, who was the owner of
a jewelry store in Hillsboro, the dangerous Raymond Hamilton, a renegade of the 1930s, was put in the jail. He escaped
by overpowering the jailer, running out of the building, and
stealing a car being fueled across the street. The sheriff fol-

lowed a trail of spilled gasoline and caught the fugitive. Hamilton had taken a gun from the sheriff's office, but the gun fortunately had a faulty firing pin and would not shoot. Hamilton was sent to Huntsville prison, where he killed a guard before being executed in the electric chair. After ninety-one years of service, the jail was replaced in 1984. With some refurbishing, it became the Hill County Cellblock Museum.

Interviews conducted by the author: Helen Cox Bandy; Ellen Beasley; Sheriff Brent Button.

Other resources: *Dallas Morning News, Texas Almanac, 1998–1999;* Tyler, Barnett, and Barkley, eds., *New Handbook of Texas,* vol. 3, 619, 623, and vol. 5, 620, 623; Pool, Triggs, and Wren, *Historical Atlas of Texas;* Kirkpatrick, *Early Settlers' Life in Texas and the Organization of Hill County.*

Hockley County (Levelland)

Although Hockley County was created in 1876 along with the other Panhandle counties, it was not organized until 1921. The early economy of the area was based on ranching. During the late 1920s, however, the large tracts began to be sold off into smaller parcels to farmers. Oil production began in 1937, and by 1950 there were more than three thousand producing oil wells.

The county seat, Levelland, was surveyed and platted in 1912 by C. W. Post, the breakfast cereal magnate, and named Hockley City. Development did not take place until 1921, however, when the name was changed to Levelland. The story is that the first commissioners' court meeting was held in 1921 in a Cadillac automobile on the very site selected for the courthouse. The courthouse, however, was not built until 1927. Meanwhile, the first lockup was built of lumber and used until the permanent courthouse was completed with a detention center inside. Only the more benign prisoners were kept in the wooden jail, while the more hostile ones were sent to Lubbock for safekeeping.

In 1927, E. C. Clicknor won a contract to build a courthouse. It was described as a three-story edifice with "a floor above the third floor" for the jail. The prison area was accessed by means of a spiral staircase from the third floor. Sheriff Donald Caldell recalls the troubles in getting recalcitrant prisoners up to the six cells on the jail level.

The third lockup, a large two-story brick building, was built on the northwest corner of the courthouse square in 1938. It contained thirteen cells manufactured by the Southern Prison Company of San Antonio and had sheriff's quarters on the first floor. All of the cages were on the second floor, but there were no facilities for women. The structure was used until 1984, when a new facility was built.

Interviews conducted by the author: Jo Beth Parks, county treasurer; Murray Stewart; Sheriff Donald Caldell.

Other resources: Tyler, Barnett, and Barkley, eds., *New Handbook of Texas,* vol. 3, 645; Metz, *Roadside History of Texas;* DeLorme Mapping, *Texas Atlas and Gazetteer.*

Hood County (Granbury)

Hood County was created by the Texas legislature in 1866 and named for Civil War hero Gen. John Bell Hood. The county seat was located on a spring-fed creek and named Granbury in honor of Gen. Hiram B. Granbury of Waco. In 1875, however, citizens in the southern part of the county successfully petitioned to sever the southern portion to create a new county, which was named Somervell. Economic differences were the basis for this change. Hood County's economy was based on cattle production and not on slave labor; the East Texas counties were largely cotton plantations, which required slave labor. A few slaves came to Hood County with their former masters as freed people, and a few came independently. In 1900, for example, only three percent of the population was black.

The first jail in Hood County was a log building on the bank of the Brazos River near the edge of what is now Lake Granbury. There was a legal hanging in the county in 1875 before the second jail was built, but the story is that the sheriff used a convenient oak tree about three-quarters of a mile northeast of the jail.

The second lockup (located at 208 North Crockett Street and built in 1885) was a two-story white limestone building

Hood County jail, 1885–1983, Granbury, Texas.
Photo courtesy of Vircenoy Baker Macatee.

with a commanding tower on the corner. The commissioners' court authorized construction for $10,000. J. N. Haney of Granbury contracted to build the lockup for $9,500. He put up the limestone structure and contracted the cells and ironwork to the P. J. Pauly Company. The jail included living quarters for the sheriff's family, and Haney built a separate room for a kitchen behind the building. The tower on the corner was for a gallows, which was never completed and never used. On New Year's Eve, after the new jail was finished, it is said that one of the stonemasons, in his jubilation, celebrated too much and became the very first prisoner to spend the night. The jail was used for its intended purpose for almost a hundred years before retirement. The building has now been carefully restored by the citizens and serves as a museum.

Interviews conducted by the author: Vircenoy B. Macatee; John Bohon; Sally Bohon.

Other resources: Tyler, Barnett, and Barkley, eds., *New Handbook of Texas*, vol. 3, 275, 687; Metz, *Roadside History of Texas*; Hood County Museum Committee, "The Jail, A Self-Guided Tour"; J. C. Campbell, *Scenes of Granbury and Hood County*.

Hopkins County (Sulphur Springs)

Hopkins County was created in 1846 and named for the David Hopkins family, early pioneers in the area. Tarrant, the county seat, proved subject to frequent flooding, so the seat of government was moved five miles south to Sulphur Springs.

The first jail was in Tarrant, where a typical dungeon was built in 1852. It was 18' square, double walled, and crafted of hewn-oak timbers. The structure had two barred windows, each 8" square. To prevent prisoners from escaping by sawing their way out, the walls and floors were studded with ten- or twenty-penny nails, four inches apart. The jail was paid for by the sale of confiscated cattle. A man named Pleasance brought some cattle into Texas from Louisiana to graze. An obscure law on the books forbade anyone from out of state from letting cattle graze in Texas, so the wheels of justice naturally ground away, and Pleasance's fines paid for the jail. One horse thief managed to escape when his visiting sister smuggled in an extra bonnet and smock, which the prisoner donned and was then allowed to pass by the guard, who later commented that the girl "sure did have big feet."

The county seat was moved to Sulphur Springs in 1871, and the second jail was built that year. The 18' square log building stood on Jefferson Street (now Broadway). Half of the structure served as a jail, and the other half served as quarters for the sheriff's family. The logs were specified to be 10" by 12", dovetailed, and spiked at the corners. Access to the keep was by a stairway between the jail and the sheriff's quarters.

In 1882, a new courthouse was built on the east side of the square. In addition, a brick building was constructed behind the courthouse to serve as a jail. Both of these structures burned in 1894, but the cages were saved and covered over with a shelter to be used until a new prison could be built. Within weeks, new plans were ready, and bids were solicited in the *Houston Post* and the *Dallas News.* Sonnefield and Emmons of Dallas won the bid and built the granite and Pecos sandstone courthouse that still stands today. Shortly after, a marvelous brick and stone jail, the fourth, was completed for $13,000. In 1926, the thirty-two-year-old jail was replaced by a fifth structure designed by Smith and Praeger and built by T. D. Masters and Company. The first floor provided living quarters for the sheriff. The Pauly Company furnished the cells and ironwork for $14,088.25.

Interview conducted by the author: Juanita Ridgell, Hopkins County Genealogical Society.

Other resources: *Dallas Morning News, Texas Almanac, 1998–1999;* Tyler, Barnett, and Barkley, eds., *New Handbook of Texas,* vol. 2, 62, vol. 3, 694, and vol. 6, 145, 206; Metz, *Roadside History of Texas;* St. Clair, *History of Hopkins County, Texas; Hopkins County Pictorial History,* vol. 1, 247; Orren, "History of Hopkins County."

Houston County (Crockett)

Houston County was created in 1837 and named for Sam Houston, hero of the battle of San Jacinto. Early farming carried on the traditions of the Southern states, producing cotton with slave labor. The county seat was designated in 1837 as well and named for Davy Crockett, one of the heroes of the Alamo and a friend of the founder.

The first courthouse was a log building that also served as a fortress against Indian raids, which continued as late as the 1850s. The record of the county jails is obscure, possibly because two of the five courthouses burned. A brick courthouse, built in 1851, burned in 1865; the next courthouse, built in 1869, burned in 1882. The first jail of record was begun in 1871 but burned before completion. Courthouse fires in early Texas were common, but Houston County seems to have had an inordinate number of fires in the years immediately following the Civil War.

Ned Patton, retired county attorney, recalls a stucco jail of uncertain vintage on West Goliad Street, which was used until about 1918. It was replaced by a two-story red-brick lockup on Clay Street (now South Third Street) near the Fannin Street corner. After retirement, the Goliad Street building became a hotel. The red-brick facility on Clay Street was used until 1938, when a new courthouse was built with a lockup on the third floor. In 1975, the courthouse was remodeled, and the jail was moved to a new building.

While there were several escapes from the early jails, one prisoner, Earl Joiner, dug out some bricks in 1934 and gained his freedom. The jailer was indicted for aiding in the prisoner's escape, but a jury found him not guilty.

Interviews conducted by the author: Eliza Bishop, Houston County Historical Commission; Ned Patton; R. C. von Doenhoff.

Other resources: *Dallas Morning News, Texas Almanac, 1998–1999;* Tyler, Barnett, and Barkley, eds., *New Handbook of Texas,* vol. 3, 728; Metz, *Roadside History of Texas.*

Howard County (Big Spring)

Howard County, named for Volney E. Howard, U.S. congressman from Texas in the 1850s, was created from Bexar County in 1878 and organized in 1882. The big spring, which gave the county seat its name, is now dry as a result of the widespread use of irrigation wells in the Texas Panhandle north of Howard County. By the time the Central Texas and Pacific Railroad came to Big Spring in 1881, the ranching industry was already established—most notably the giant C. C. Slaughter Long S Ranch, second in size only to the XIT. Big Spring became a shipping hub for farm and ranch products for a vast area.

After the county's organization, it was necessary to send prisoners to the newly finished jail in Mitchell County. The expense for their transportation, board, and extra guards was substantial. Indeed, in August 1882, a judge was authorized to arrange plans, materials, and a contractor to build a calaboose, but nothing came of it.

In December 1882, the Texas and Pacific Railroad offered to give a whole city block to Big Spring to build a courthouse and jail. The city quickly accepted the offer, and plans were solicited through advertisements in the *Galveston News* and the *Dallas Herald.* Within two months, J. H. Millikin and Company in Weatherford was awarded a contract to build the structures for $33,700. The courthouse-with-jail building was completed in 1884. The lockup was a double-iron cage with two-inch bars and an iron floor. There were two more iron-lined cells with barred windows and grated doors. Since no jail manufacturing company is recorded, the ironwork may be of local manufacture. The location of the cells within the courthouse is not included in any recorded description.

By 1905, anxiety regarding the stability of the courthouse

occasioned the employment of an engineer from Abilene, who determined that the south wing was dangerous and should be condemned. His advice was taken, and, in 1907, bonds were passed. Plans for a new courthouse by M. M. Rocke of Big Spring were accepted. The new courthouse, like the former, contained a jail. This building was of pink sandstone and lasted for forty-five years until replaced by a new facility in 1958.

Interviews conducted by the author: Lonnie Smith, Big Spring Police Department; Sheriff Bill Jennings.

Other resources: Tyler, Barnett, and Barkley, eds., *New Handbook of Texas,* vol. 1, 537, and vol. 3, 748; Metz, *Roadside History of Texas;* Tyler and Tyler, *Texas Museums;* Hutto, *Howard County in the Making;* Pickle, *Getting Started.*

Hudspeth County (Sierra Blanca)

Hudspeth County was created out of El Paso County in 1917. It comprises 4,571 square miles—about three million acres. It has one hundred miles of Rio Grande frontage, sharing its southern border with Old Mexico and its northern border with New Mexico. Its elevation varies from 3,500 to 7,400 feet. Rainfall is but ten inches annually. When created, the county was named for Claude Benton Hudspeth, state senator from El Paso. Sierra Blanca, the county seat, is named for the nearby mountain range.

In the late 1870s, the area was the scene of the Salt War, a bloody politician-versus-populist fight over salt-mining rights. According to historian Walter Prescott Webb, the trouble began in 1869, when two factions in El Paso tried to commercialize the deposits. The conflict lasted until 1877, when a mob of local and northern Mexicans laid siege to the Texas Ranger camp at San Elizario. San Elizario, the center of all of this trouble, was looted by the mob. Local citizens and Texas Rangers, including Maj. John B. Jones, finally retook San Elizario, and the mob disappeared into Mexico.

In 1881, Collis P. Huntington's Southern Pacific Railroad, which was building eastward from the Pacific, and Jay Gould's

Texas and Pacific Railroad, building westward from central Texas, met at Sierra Blanca. Gould drove in the silver spike, completing the second transcontinental railway—and the town of Sierra Blanca was born.

The courthouse, with jail included, was built and finished in 1921. The structure represents the only adobe courthouse in Texas. Buetell and Hardie of El Paso were engaged to design and supervise the construction, and the result was a Spanish-style building with a red-tile roof. The jail occupied the second floor of the west wing of the courthouse and had space for seven prisoners. The Pauly Jail Building Company manufactured the cells and ironwork. It was not entirely surprising that two prisoners, using spoons, managed to escape by digging out through the adobe bricks. The jail was used for prisoners until 1983. The building is now used for record storage.

Interviews conducted by the author: Patricia Bramblett, county and district clerk; William D. Boyd of Boyd and Associates, architects.

Other resources: *Dallas Morning News, Texas Almanac, 1998–1999;* Tyler, Barnett, and Barkley, eds., *New Handbook of Texas,* vol. 3,763, and vol. 5, 781, 783; DeLorme Mapping, *Texas Atlas and Gazetteer;* W. P. Webb, *Texas Rangers.*

Hunt County (Greenville)

Hunt County was created and organized in 1846. It was named for Memucan Hunt, secretary of the Texas Navy from 1838 to 1839. He worked on the United States–Texas Boundary Commission and also served one term in the Texas legislature. Greenville, the county seat, was incorporated in 1852 and named for Gen. Thomas Jefferson Green, Texas soldier and legislator.

Soon after the Civil War, the county was troubled by the Lee-Peacock feud, a conflict that matched the Union League, an organization of Northern carpetbaggers and scalawags, against a group of proud ex-Confederate soldiers led by Bob Lee, a former captain in Gen. Nathan Bedford Forrest's cavalry. The feud went on for more than four years and resulted in more than a dozen murders, mostly from ambush.

The first jail in Hunt County was on the northeast corner of the courthouse square. Built of logs, the structure was 14' by 17' with two rooms. In the traditional manner, access to the prison was solely by a trapdoor in the floor of the second story, which was reached by an outside stairway. The jail was built by A. J. Hefner, who came to Hunt County in 1851. In 1870, a second lockup was built, once again with two stories. The second floor contained iron cages for about ten prisoners with a walk-around so the prisoners could exercise. The manufacturer of the cells is not known.

In 1929, a new courthouse was built with a jail on the fifth and sixth floors. The building was an attractive combination of brick and stone designed by C. H. Page Jr. and Brother. The Southern Prison Company manufactured the cells and ironwork.

Local execution of prisoners by hanging, usually from a scaffold in the jail yard, was not uncommon before 1923. According to Harrison's *History of Greenville and Hunt County, Texas,* Greenville had a great many public hangings.

Interviews conducted by the author: Carol Taylor, librarian in charge of genealogy and local history, and Mary Ann Kerstetter, reference department, W. W. Harrison Library, Greenville.

Other resources: *Dallas Morning News, Texas Almanac, 1998–1999;* Tyler, Barnett, and Barkley, eds., *New Handbook of Texas,* vol. 3, 320, 784; Sonnichsen, *I'll Die before I'll Run;* Kelsey and Dyal, *Courthouses of Texas;* Ramsdell, *Reconstruction in Texas;* Harrison, *History of Greenville and Hunt County, Texas;* Ingmire, *Archives and Pioneers of Hunt County, Texas,* vol. 1.

Hutchinson County (Stinnett)

Although established in 1876, Hutchinson County was not organized until 1901. It was named for Judge Anderson Hutchinson, a pioneer jurist and writer. When Judge Hutchinson was holding court in San Antonio in 1842, Mexican troops under Gen. Adrián Woll occupied the city, took the judge and jurors prisoner, marched them back to Mexico, and put them in Perote Prison in Vera Cruz. Six months later, they were released at the request of the United States.

The first county seat of Hutchinson County was Plemons, about ten miles east of present-day Stinnett. It remained the seat of government until 1926, even though the branch line of the Rock Island Railroad, which ran through Stinnett, had by-passed it.

Central Hutchinson County was the scene of two famous Indian fights at a place called Adobe Walls near the Canadian River. On November 26, 1864, Col. Kit Carson with the U.S. Cavalry was ambushed by a large group of Comanche and Kiowa Indians near Adobe Walls, an abandoned trading post. With the aid of two howitzers, Carson and his men were able to fight their way to safety. The second battle of Adobe Walls occurred in June 1874 about one mile from the old adobe ru-ins where several buildings had been put up. At dawn, 600–700 Indians attacked a group of twenty-eight buffalo hunters, including one woman. The first attack was driven off, but two of the defenders were killed; later skirmishes claimed two more, one by his own weapon. The siege lasted four days. On the second day, William ("Billy") Dixon made his famous one-mile shot (actually 1,538 yards) with his new .50-caliber Sharp's rifle. His random shot at a group of Cheyenne warriors at that distance knocked one of them off his horse, according to author Mildred P. Mayhall. The Indian was stunned by the spent bullet but not killed.

When the county was organized in 1901, Billy Dixon was made sheriff. The town grew slowly and by 1905 had only fifteen families. When the county seat moved to Stinnett in 1926, a new courthouse-and-jail combination was planned and then completed in 1928. The brick-and-concrete Texas Renaissance–style building was designed by William C. Townes and built by C. S. Lambie of Amarillo. The jail and sheriff's quarters were on the top floor. Folger Adams Company of Joliet, Illinois, manufactured the cells and ironwork. The facility was used until 1982; in that year, the courthouse was remodeled, and the jail was moved.

Interviews conducted by the author: Judge Jack Worsham; Edward Benz, director, Hutchinson County Museum.

Other resources: *Dallas Morning News, Texas Almanac, 1998–1999;* Tyler, Barnett, and Barkley, eds., *New Handbook of Texas,* vol. 1, 34, 993, vol. 3, 804, vol. 5, 240, and vol. 6, 104; DeLorme Mapping, *Texas Atlas and Gazetteer;* Kelsey and Dyal, *Courthouses of Texas;* Mayhall, *Indian Wars of Texas.*

Irion County (Mertzon)

Irion County was created from Tom Green County in 1889. It was named for Robert Anderson Irion, a physician and secretary of state of the Republic of Texas. The original county seat, Sherwood, named for an original settler, Granville Sherwood, had been founded in 1886 and was virtually the only population center in the county.

In January 1865, when the territory was still part of Bexar County, the battle of Dove Creek was fought near present-day Mertzon at the junction of Dove Creek and Spring Creek. A force of 360 Texas militia and 160 Confederates attacked about 1,400 Kickapoo Indians—women, children, and 400 warriors. The generally peaceful Kickapoo were leaving Texas, migrating into Mexico. At the end of the day, the battle-worn Texans retreated in disarray in a freezing rain. The result of the battle was eleven Indians and thirty-six Texans dead. The Indians finally reached Mexico, where they were given sanctuary.

When Irion County was organized in 1889, the town of Sherwood built a courthouse with a lockup inside. It was used for eleven years, until a larger adjacent courthouse was built in 1901. The original courthouse then became a full-time jail. The architectural and contracting firm of Martin and Moodie built both courthouses. In 1892, an unknown person, thought to have been a woman, shot a prisoner, James Wilson, to death. Wilson had tried to force his attentions on the woman, whose husband was often away from home.

Irion County jail and courthouse, 1889–1937, Sherwood, Texas. Photo ca. 1905. Courtesy of Joyce Gray.

The prisoner even spread uncomplimentary stories about her. The county clerk at that time said that someone passed his desk in the courthouse about the time of the murder. No one could identify the person or even say for certain whether it was a man or a woman, so there was no indictment. In 1942, the 1890 jail and courthouse in Sherwood were torn down to salvage the iron from the jail for the World War II war effort.

The town of Mertz, later changed to Mertzon, was laid out in 1908. In 1911, the Kansas City, Mexico, and Orient Railway, of which M. L. Mertz was a director, bypassed Sherwood and went to Mertzon. The county seat eventually followed, and in 1937 Mertzon became the seat of government. In that year, a new courthouse, including a jail on the third floor, was constructed. It was designed by David S. Castle of Abilene, for which he was paid $800. Balfanz Construction Company of Abilene won the construction contract for $62,000, and Southern Prison Company provided the cells and ironwork for $6,300. The third-floor jail in the courthouse is no longer used for prisoners since it would have been too costly to modernize to comply with the 1984 standards mandated by the Texas Commission on Jail Standards.

Interview conducted by the author: Joyce Gray, Irion County Clerk Office.

Other resources: *Dallas Morning News, Texas Almanac, 1998–1999;* Tyler, Barnett, and Barkley, eds., *New Handbook of Texas,* vol. 2, 690, vol. 3, 868, vol. 4, 638, and vol. 6, 525; DeLorme Mapping, *Texas Atlas and Gazetteer;* Crawford, *History of Irion County.*

Jack County (Jacksboro)

Members of the Peters colony populated the area now known as Jack County as early as 1855. The county was created by the Texas legislature in 1856 and was quickly organized in 1857. It was named for P. C. Jack and W. H. Jack, early advocates of the Texas independence movement. A community on Lost Creek was renamed Jacksboro when selected as the county seat in 1858. In 1868, Fort Richardson was built a half mile to the south, and, to pacify the country, for

Jack County jail, 1877–1940, Jacksboro, Texas. Designed by J. E. Flanders. Photo from Southwest Collection and Special Collections, University of Texas Tech Library, Lubbock, Texas.

the next ten years it served as the northern fulcrum of the war for U.S. troops.

The infamous Warren Wagon Train Raid occurred about twenty-five miles from Fort Richardson while Gen. William T. Sherman was there on a fact-finding tour to determine whether the Indian problem had been exaggerated. Indeed, General Sherman's party passed unmolested while the Indians waited for an easier target to appear. The Indians then attacked the wagon train, killing many, but a few escaped and fled to the government office at the reservation to report the disaster. Sherman was finally convinced that the Indian threat was real and personally arrested Chief Satanta and Chief Big Tree, the leaders of the raid, when they returned to the reservation.

The first jail was built in Jacksboro in 1860 and is said to have been made of wooden planks. It cost $1,590 but was generally considered a poor product. Jack County financed a "red stone" jail in 1877. In 1885, J. E. Flanders designed a new courthouse and a third jail. The contracting firm of Strain, Risley, and Swinburn finished the project in 1886. Built about one block from the courthouse, the stone facility was two stories tall and measured 23′ by 30′ with walls twenty-four inches thick. Two rooms were designated as the jailer's quarters. The cells were provided by a less well-known manufacturer, Thomas Patent. The building was used until 1940.

Jack County's fourth jail was on the fourth floor of a new courthouse completed in 1940. Architects Voelcker and Dixon designed the building, and the contractors were Templeton and Cannon of San Angelo. The courthouse and lockup are still in good condition and certified by the state commission. The $200,000 project was partially financed by a $90,000 grant from the Work Projects Administration of the Depression era.

Interviews conducted by the author: Juanita Damron and Delyn Lewis, G. T. Ritchie Public Library; Judge Mitchell Davenport; Deubrella Horton; Kyra Osborne, Texas Tech Southwest Collection.

Other resources: *Dallas Morning News, Texas Almanac, 1998–1999;* Tyler, Barnett, and Barkley, eds., *New Handbook of Texas,* vol. 2, 1015, and vol. 3, 890, 891; Huckabay, *Ninety-four Years in Jack County, 1854–1948;* Kelsey and Dyal, *Courthouses of Texas;* Mayhall, *Indian Wars of Texas.*

Jackson County (Edna)

Jackson County was part of Stephen F. Austin's colony, and six of the original three hundred families settled in the area in the 1820s. After the battle of San Jacinto, Jackson County was one of the original twenty-three counties created by the new Republic of Texas. The community of Texana was made the county seat. Texana, originally called Santa Anna, was a small enclave at the junction of the Navidad and Lavaca rivers. It slowly grew into a shipping point and military training area for the Republic of Texas. By 1840, there was regular steamboat service from Texana to Matagorda Bay. In 1881, the New York, Texas, and Mexican Railroad requested thirty thousand dollars from the people of Texana to bring the railroad to their town, but the appeal was denied. The train went to Edna instead, and by 1882 the county seat and the people had moved to Edna. The early town of Texana is now buried under Lake Texana, which was built on the Navidad River in 1979.

It is said that there was no crime in Jackson County until the murder of John Conrey in 1835, according to John Menefee in I. T. Taylor's *Cavalcade of Jackson County.* The murderer was tried by a jury and sentenced to be hanged. A struggling lawyer, however, appealed his case to the provisional Texas government, and a new trial was ordered. Unfortunately, the Mexican invasion, followed by the Runaway Scrape, caused the release of the prisoner, who disappeared and was never brought to justice. Determined to prevent such a travesty in the future, the citizens, on their return to Texana after the battle of San Jacinto, built the first jail in Jackson County.

Details are not available, but it must have been a reasonably good facility because, in June 1883, Edna paid nine hundred dollars to have it moved to the new county seat. The second jail was built in Edna about 1886. It was a two-story rectangular brick building with a tower on one corner. It served until 1921, when it was razed to make room for a new jail in 1922. The new lockup had a gallows and sheriff's quarters. Southern Structural Steel Company provided the cages and ironwork. The building was used until 1982, when a new facility was built. The 1922 jail was remodeled as a children's museum.

Interview conducted by the author: Virginia Lawrence.

Other resources: *Dallas Morning News, Texas Almanac, 1998–1999;* Tyler, Barnett, and Barkley, eds., *New Handbook of Texas,* vol. 3, 897, and vol. 6, 267; I. T. Taylor, *Cavalcade of Jackson County.*

Jasper County (Jasper)

In 1835 Jasper County was a Mexican municipality. After Texas independence in 1836, it became one of the first twenty-three counties created by the Texas Republic. The county was organized in 1837 and named for Sgt. William Jasper, a hero of the American Revolution. The community of Jasper developed from an early settlement by John Bevil on the Angelina River in 1824. There was a jail on the town square in "Bevil's Settlement" as early as 1828. Later the town was named Jasper and in 1844 became the county seat.

The original 1828 jail and adjacent courthouse burned in 1849 but were replaced by new structures shortly afterward. The second lockup, although hardly escape proof, lasted until 1902. In 1904, a third jail, with a built-in gallows, came to be known as the "gallows jail" because more than a few legal hangings occurred there. The gallows jail was followed in 1935 by a WPA detention center, a product of the Depression years. The barred windows from the 1904 jail were recycled into the new keep by the cost-conscious builder. Designed by W. C.

Meador and located on the courthouse square, the structure
had three floors. The ground level had a unique drive-through
arrangement: A prisoner could be brought in and unloaded
behind locked gates. The Southern Prison Company provided
the cells and ironwork for $6,508.19. The kitchen and storage
area were on the ground floor; the sheriff's office and the
women's cells were on the second floor; and the third floor
housed the main prison. The facility was used until replaced
in 1988. Although the cellblocks are still in place, the building
is now used to store the county's archives.

Interview conducted by the author: Linda Primrose, Jasper County Historical Commission.

Other resources: *Dallas Morning News, Texas Almanac, 1998–1999;* Tyler,
Barnett, and Barkley, eds., *New Handbook of Texas,* vol. 3, 914, 915; Mar-
shall and Eurich, *Once upon a Time; Jasper News-boy,* Feb. 13, 1936, and
Mar. 19, 1936.

Jeff Davis County (Fort Davis)

Jeff Davis County is part of that vast West Texas territory
known as the Big Bend, encircled almost 180 degrees
by the Rio Grande as it flows between Texas and Mexico.
Originally, Jeff Davis County, Brewster County, and Presidio
County were all part of Presidio County, with Fort Davis as
the county seat.

In 1885, the people of Marfa decided to become the
county seat of Presidio County. The vote that year carried,
and the seat of government moved to Marfa. Since the new
counties were not yet organized, the people of Alpine and Fort
Davis petitioned to divide the territory of Presidio County
into three counties: Brewster, with the county seat in Alpine;
Jeff Davis County, with the seat of government at Fort Davis;
and the remainder of Presidio County, with Marfa as the
county seat.

In 1880, when Fort Davis was the county seat of the un-
divided Presidio County, William Jenkins contracted to build
a courthouse and jail for $2,400. The adobe courthouse had
offices and a large courtroom. The jail—a typical dungeon

except that it was underground—was under the sheriff's office, accessed only by a trapdoor in the floor of the office. The walls were lined with stones, some of which had iron rings set into them so prisoners could be chained to the walls. There were two or three small openings at the top of the walls to admit air and light. When Jeff Davis County was organized in 1887, Fort Davis was made the county seat. In 1910 a new courthouse-and-jail combination was designed by L. L. Thurmon and Company of Dallas, and bids were taken for construction. The Falls City Construction Company won the contract for $47,000. The original lighting was by carbide gas, but those fixtures were replaced by electric lights in 1920. Southern Structural Steel Company provided the jail, new cells, and ironwork.

Interviews conducted by the author: Sheriff Steve Bailey; Peggy Robertson, county clerk; Mildred Nored.

Other resources: *Dallas Morning News, Texas Almanac, 1998–1999;* Tyler, Barnett, and Barkley, eds., *New Handbook of Texas,* vol. 1, 728, and vol. 3, 921; DeLorme Mapping, *Texas Atlas and Gazetteer;* Scobee, *Fort Davis, Texas 1583–1960.*

Jefferson County (Beaumont)

Jefferson County was one of the original twenty-three counties created by the Republic of Texas in 1836. Organized in 1837, the county was named for Thomas Jefferson. The town of Beaumont began in 1824 as a community known as Tevis Bluff on the Neches River. Henry Millard and others bought land from Noah Tevis Survey and laid out a town. In 1835, the name of the town was changed to Beaumont, the maiden name of Millard's wife.

The biggest event in local history was the signal day, January 10, 1901, when the Spindletop oil gusher blew in, marking the beginning of the twentieth century and its great achievements, many of which were fueled by the new petroleum industry. Within one year, nearly five hundred oil companies, including Texaco, Exxon, Magnolia, and Gulf Oil, had been chartered there, and their products would transform the transportation industry. Equestrian and pedestrian speed records

would soon
fall before
those of the
internal
combustion
engine.

The first
jail in Jeffer-
son County
is described
in the 1838
court min-
utes. It was

Jefferson County jail, 1892–1932, Beaumont, Texas. Photo
courtesy of Tyrrell Historical Library, Beaumont.

two stories, 16′ by 20′. Its double walls consisted of 10″ timbers separated by a 10″ space filled with 9″ square timbers set
upright. There were two 2′ square windows with double iron
grating. The doors were to be double, each 6″ thick, and both
sides lined with iron. Prisoners were to be kept in the lower
floor.

Another jail of unknown date is described in an interview
by the *Beaumont Enterprise* in 1905. Capt. George W. O'Brian,
age seventy-two, recalled, "It was a two-story log structure
with a trapdoor with a padlock underneath and in the center."
Prisoners were kept in the upper story, and the guards lived
on the first floor.

In 1892 architect Eugene Heiner designed a courthouse
and jail for Jefferson County. His creation was a beautiful
brick-and-stone Italianate courthouse flanked by a massive two-
story stone fortress with crenellations. In 1932, a new courthouse, including a lockup, was built on the site of the 1892
jail. The fourteen-story building contained a detention center
on the eighth and ninth floors. Fred C. Stone and A. Babin
designed it in Art Deco style. The jail was moved soon after
the end of World War II in order to comply with jail standards.

Interviews conducted by the author: Judy Linsley and Penny Clark,
Terrell Historical Library; William Seale.
Other resources: Tyler, Barnett, and Barkley, eds., *New Handbook of
Texas,* vol. 1, 447, vol. 3, 925, and vol. 6, 29; *Dallas Morning News, Texas
Almanac, 1998–1999;* Haley, *Texas from the Frontier to Spindletop;* Metz, *Road-
side History of Texas; Beaumont Enterprise,* Apr. 16, 1905; Jefferson County

Board of Commissioners' Minutes, 1838, 1–3; Landry, *Outlaws in the Big Thicket;* Linsley and Rienstra, *Beaumont;* W. Robinson, *People's Architecture.*

Jim Hogg County (Hebronville)

Jim Hogg County—named for Texas Gov. James S. Hogg (1851–1906)—was created from Brooks and Duval counties in 1913. Jim Hogg County was organized within weeks of its creation, and Hebronville was designated the county seat.

Immediately setting about building a courthouse and jail, the county commissioners chose H. T. Phillips of San Antonio as the architect. Phillips designed a neoclassic-style courthouse with an adjacent two-story jail of concrete and stucco. The Ewing and McGee Construction Company completed the buildings in May 1914 at a cost of $9,219, including $3,000 for the jail cells. The cages were manufactured by the Southern Structural Steel Company. The lockup was arranged with sheriff's quarters on the ground floor. On the second floor were the cells and a room for the jailer. This structure was used until 1981, when a new facility was built; the old jail has not been used since.

Interviews conducted by the author: Richard Blansit, county clerk's office; Gloria Diana Rodriquez, county and district clerk.

Other resources: *Dallas Morning News, Texas Almanac, 1998–1999;* Tyler, Barnett, and Barkley, eds., *New Handbook of Texas,* vol. 3, 94.

Jim Wells County (Alice)

After Texas independence, San Patricio County, including present Jim Wells County, was one of the original counties created by the new republic. It represented all of the country south of Bexar County and west of the Nueces River to the Rio Grande. Nueces County was created out of San Patricio County in 1846 after Texas became a state. Jim Wells County, in turn, was created in 1911 from Nueces County and organized in 1912. It was named for J. B. Wells Jr., a contemporary developer.

THE COUNTY JAILS OF TEXAS

The first county jail in the future Jim Wells County was the 1877 facility for Nueces County. After Jim Wells County was organized in 1912, the new county used the prison facilities at Corpus Christi.

The future county seat, Alice, originated as a depot on the San Antonio and Aransas Pass Railroad. The town, built in 1888, was originally called Bandana, then Kleberg, and finally Alice, for Alice King Kleberg. The county prospered, first as a cattle delivery point and later as a result of oil production after 1931. In June 1904 Alice was incorporated, and in 1912 a two-room frame city jail was built. After Jim Wells County was organized in 1912, with Alice as the county seat, county prisoners continued to be sent to Nueces County for safekeeping. The 1912 city jail no doubt then served as a holding cell until prisoners could be moved. In 1926 a two-story brick county jail, the first for Jim Wells County, was built, and the small frame structure was razed. The lockup was expanded and renovated in 1961 and continues in use today.

For years, Jim Wells County was part of the political fiefdom of Archer Parr and his son George. The darker side of county history has to do with the Democratic senatorial primary of 1948, in which Lyndon Baines Johnson was running slightly behind Gov. Coke Stevenson. Miraculously, the ballot box of precinct 13 in Alice was "adjusted," and 203 votes were added, putting Johnson ahead. Although the election was contested, the ballots from that particular box were lost or stolen, and on appeal Johnson won in the federal courts.

Interviews conducted by the author: Catherine Parker, South Texas Museum; Eunice Wells, Texas Historical Commission and South Texas Museum.

Other resources: *Dallas Morning News, Texas Almanac, 1998–1999;* Metz, *Roadside History of Texas;* Tyler, Barnett, and Barkley, eds., *New Handbook of Texas,* vol. 3, 943, and vol. 6, 69.

Johnson County (Cleburne)

Johnson County, named after Col. M. T. Johnson, who served in the Mexican War, was created and organized in 1854 and had three seats of government in rapid succession:

Wardville, Buchanan, and Cleburne. When Camp Henderson, a temporary Confederate military station, was made the county seat in 1868, it was renamed Cleburne for Confederate Gen. Pat Cleburne.

The first courthouse was built in Wardville in 1854, but the village proved to be a bad site because of periodic flooding, poor water supply, and its noncentral location. After the county seat moved to Buchanan in 1856, the first jail was built and completed in 1858. John W. Westbrook cut the logs in his nearby mill and erected the jail for $795. The building was described as a double-log structure with rocks and stones placed between the logs. When the county seat moved to Cleburne in 1867, the jail was also moved and erected on Chambers Street. The lockup, while of sound construction, was nevertheless subject to frequent escapes. One trick was for a prisoner's friends to tie a rope to the logs and, with the aid of a couple of horses, pull the corner of the jail down.

In 1872, J. W. Anderson constructed a new jail at 100 E. Chambers Street. It had two 16' square stories with inside walls of eight-inch logs. Later, because of escapes, an outside wall of stone was added. Nevertheless, even after a twelve-hundred-pound iron door was added, escapes still occurred. According to one humorist, the upper story had a trapdoor "through which the prisoner went in and out when they didn't go through the stone wall." Another jail was built of brick and stone in 1874. This one, also two stories tall, measured 24' by 32'. Still a fourth jail was built in 1884 at 116 South Mills Street. This red-brick building seems to have been satisfactory for fifty-three years. It was replaced by a new lockup designed by the architectural firm of W. G. Clarkson and Co. in 1938 and built by contractor L. L. Smith.

Interview conducted by the author: Dan Leach, Texas Historical Commission.

Other resources: *Dallas Morning News, Texas Almanac, 1998–1999;* Kelsey and Dyal, *Courthouses of Texas;* Metz, *Roadside History of Texas;* Tyler, Barnett, and Barkley, eds., *New Handbook of Texas,* vol. 1, 799, vol. 3, 966, and vol. 6, 823; Tyler and Tyler, *Texas Museums;* Block, *History of Johnson County and Surrounding Areas.*

Jones County (Anson)

Jones County was created in 1858 and named for Anson
Jones, the last president of the Republic of Texas. Jones
took office in 1844, negotiated the annexation of Texas into
the United States in 1845, drew up the state constitution, and
swore in James Pinckney Henderson as the first governor of
the State of Texas. Jones County was re-created in 1876 and
organized in 1881. In that year, Phantom Hill, near the abandoned Fort Phantom Hill, was named temporary county seat,
but Jones City, sited on a proposed railroad route that never
materialized, became the permanent county seat and was renamed Anson in November 1881.

One of the early frontier forts, Fort Phantom Hill was built
on the Clear Fork of the Brazos River in 1851. The site was
poorly chosen in view of the fact that it lacked both a dependable water supply and adequate timber for building. After
much hardship, the fort was deserted in 1854. In June 1856,
however, Col. Robert E. Lee and his infantry camped on the
site en route to Fort Chadbourne in Coke County. In 1858,
the site was used again as Station Number 54 for the Butterfield Overland Mail, established to provide a southern route to
the California gold fields. During the 1870s, Phantom Hill was
again occupied, this time by buffalo hunters. By 1880, it had a
population of more than five hundred and in 1881 was chosen
as the temporary county seat prior to the move to Anson.
After systematically decimating the buffalo herds, the buffalo
hunters departed, and by 1892 Phantom Hill was described in
the *San Antonio Express* as having "one hotel, one saloon, one
blacksmith shop and 10,000 prairie dogs."

In Anson in 1882, a frame courthouse measuring 24' by 32'
was constructed with a jail inside. In 1886, a red-brick courthouse was built with a jail in the basement, but it was short
lived because of faulty construction. In 1909, an attractive new
courthouse, which is still standing, was designed by Elmer
George Withers and completed in 1910. At the same time,
a freestanding red-brick lockup was erected half a block from
the courthouse square.

In 1941, a reinforced concrete jail replaced the 1910 facility on the same lot. This was a new concept in jail construction, using the Art Deco style, wherein the ornamentation was molded directly into the concrete as it was poured. The Southern Steel Company provided cages and doors. The building is still in use today as the sheriff's office, although it has been renovated for its present usage.

Interviews conducted by the author: Maxie Kohout, Texas Historical Commission; Dave Reeves, retired sheriff.

Other resources: *Dallas Morning News, Texas Almanac, 1998–1999;* Metz, *Roadside History of Texas;* Tyler, Barnett, and Barkley, eds., *New Handbook of Texas,* vol. 2, 1113, and vol. 3, 994; Kelsey and Dyal, *Courthouses of Texas;* DeLorme Mapping, *Texas Atlas and Gazetteer;* W. Robinson, *People's Architecture.*

Karnes County (Karnes City)

Karnes County was created and organized in 1852 at the behest of two merchants at a trading post called Alamita on the La Bahía Road between Goliad and San Antonio. The county was named for Henry W. Karnes, soldier and scout for the Texas Army. Alamita was designated the county seat, but the name was later changed to Helena. Helena remained the county seat until bypassed by the San Antonio and Aransas Pass Railroad in 1892. In 1894, an election was held, and Karnes City, with its railroad right-of-way, was made the new county seat. In the dark of night, the county records in Helena were spirited away to Karnes City even though the citizens of Helena had posted an armed guard to keep an eye on the books. When wagons came from Karnes City, a guard climbed aboard and rode back to Karnes City. He later explained that he had kept an eye on the records and that no one had said anything about shooting anyone.

The first jail in Karnes County was in Helena; it was an iron cell, 10′ by 10′, built by Z. King and Son Company of Cleveland, Ohio. Completed in January 1876, the structure cost twenty-two hundred dollars. Before that facility was available, the sheriff routinely took prisoners to the blacksmith

to be fitted with irons that allowed them to be fastened for
safekeeping.

When the county seat moved to Karnes City in February 1894, the cells from the Helena jail were also moved at
a cost of $350. Shortly after, the Diebold Safe and Lock Com-
pany was employed to build a jail using the cages salvaged
from Helena. The Karnes City lockup was completed in
June 1894. Even before the new structure was finished, a gallows was constructed on the Karnes City courthouse square
for the hanging of a train robber-turned-murderer. He was
captured and put in the Helena jail by Sheriff J. J. Seale. He
was tried in Helena, convicted, and sentenced to be hanged.
He was then moved to the new county seat of Karnes City,
where the scaffold was awaiting his execution on May 25,
1894. In 1957 a new jail was built on the courthouse square
in Karnes City.

Other resources: *Dallas Morning News, Texas Almanac, 1998–1999;* Tyler,
Barnett, and Barkley, eds., *New Handbook of Texas,* vol. 3, 544, 1034;
Commissioners' Court Records compiled by Herbert Puckett; Thonhoff,
"Historic Helena" and "Karnes County Courthouse Centennial Tribute";
Didear, *History of Karnes County and Old Helena.*

Kaufman County (Kaufman)

Settlement in Kaufman County, created and organized
in 1848 and named for D. S. Kaufman, soldier, lawyer,
and member of the U.S. congress, began in the 1840s. The
county's first jail was a house of large, neatly hewn logs purchased in 1856. One prisoner, known as "Spanish Jack," bored
several holes in one of the floor logs, removed them, and
made good his escape. In 1871, James Brown, a local carpenter, erected a second jail, a two-story frame structure with two
rooms below and two above. One of the upper rooms contained a strong iron cage. The second lockup was used until
a substantial stone building with a metal roof was put up in
1884. J. E. Flanders, who was paid the grand sum of $50 for
the plans, designed the 1884 jail. Building the structure, however, cost $25,200 — a very large sum for that time. P. J. Pauly

Brothers received $12,700 for the cells and ironwork. Facing on Washington Street, the jail contained spacious living quarters for the sheriff on the ground floor. It was torn down in 1953.

Kaufman County had an unusual arrangement with other towns in the county. An agreement allowed for the maintenance of a calaboose in Terrell, and later a similar contract was made with Forney, Crandall, Kemp, and Elmo. In the case of Terrell, the county actually purchased the jail building and lot in 1877 but expected the city to pay for the incarceration of prisoners, who were, of course, a city obligation. From time to time, the jail in Terrell is referred to as a "branch jail" in court minutes. Terrell's failure to pay the appropriate fees to the county caused the sheriff of Kaufman County to "take full control of the county jail," and we may presume that meant also that city prisoners could not be lodged there. Indeed, the sheriff was authorized to move the jail since it was county property. Articles in the Galveston paper indicate that Terrell then built its own lockup.

In many instances, it was not unusual for towns near the county seat to have so-called holding cells to house county prisoners who were pending transfer to the county jail. Kaufman County seems to have formalized this arrangement more so than most.

Interviews conducted by the author: Horace P. Flatt, Texas Historical Commission; Justin Sanders.

Other resources: *Dallas Morning News, Texas Almanac, 1998–1999;* Tyler, Barnett, and Barkley, eds., *New Handbook of Texas,* vol. 3, 1039–40; Tyler and Tyler, *Texas Museums;* Cave, *Kaufman, a Pictorial History; Kaufman Sun,* Apr. 8, 1884.

Kendall County (Boerne)

Kendall County was formed from Kerr County and Blanco County in 1862 and organized that same year. German immigrants had settled much of the Hill Country in the 1840s, including the area of Kendall County. The famous Meusebach-Comanche treaty with Native Americans created a fairly peaceful, if not perfect, period of coexistence for settlers. In 1862, the county was named for George W. Kendall, pioneer journalist, humorist, and member of the Santa Fe expedition.

Kendall County jail, 1884–1989, Boerne, Texas. Photo from San Antonio Light Collection, Institute of Texas Cultures, University of Texas–San Antonio.

The creation of Kendall County coincided with the outbreak of the Civil War, an event that led to the infamous battle of the Nueces. The German communities were in general antislavery and pro-Union. While en route to Mexico to avoid Confederate service, a group of about sixty-eight Unionist German Texans, camping on the Nueces River, were attacked by the Confederate cavalry. Nineteen of them were killed, and nine who had been wounded were executed. Two months later, eight of those who escaped the battle scene were killed while trying to cross the Rio Grande into Mexico.

It is believed that, before 1884, Kendall County prisoners were held in neighboring Kerr or Blanco county jails. The first lockup in Kendall County was built of limestone in Boerne in 1884. The Pauly Jail Building and Manufacturing Company designed the three-story rectangular building, which was used as a detention center until 1989, when a new keep was built near the Boerne city limits. The 1884 facility still stands today.

Interview conducted by the author: Henry Dell, Kendall County Public Library.

Other resources: *Dallas Morning News, Texas Almanac, 1998–1999;* Tyler, Barnett, and Barkley, eds., *New Handbook of Texas,* vol. 3, 1060, 1062, and vol. 4, 1054; W. Robinson, *People's Architecture.*

Kenedy County (Sarita)

Kenedy County—one of the last counties to be originated in Texas—was created and organized in 1921. It was named for Capt. Mifflin Kenedy, an early cattleman and steamboat captain. At age sixteen, Kenedy taught school briefly before shipping out as a cabin boy on a voyage to Calcutta, India. At eighteen, he taught school again and by age twenty-four was a riverboat captain. During the Mexican War he served as captain of the *Corvette* in the Gulf of Mexico. In 1860, he joined in partnership with Capt. Richard King in the ranching and cattle business.

Kenedy County was sparsely settled until the nineteenth century, when Spanish and Mexican land grants began to encourage ranching. After the Mexican War, Americans began to move into the disputed territory south of the Nueces River in spite of hostile Indians. During the Civil War, Kenedy and King operated twenty-six boats, trading along the Rio Grande, selling cotton, delivering munitions and guns to the Confederacy, and accumulating cattle and ranch land. In 1882 Kenedy bought four hundred thousand acres of land that would become the base of his operations in Kenedy County.

In 1903, the St. Louis, Brownsville, and Mexico Railroad built into South Texas, and John G. Kenedy, son of Mifflin, platted a town on the route. He named it Sarita after his daughter. Sarita served as county seat of Willacy County from 1911 until 1921; then, when Kenedy County was formed in 1921 from part of Willacy and Hidalgo counties, Sarita became the county seat.

The Kenedy County courthouse with a jail on the third floor was completed in 1921 and continues to serve today. The architect was H. S. Phelps of San Antonio, and the cells and ironwork are by the Southern Structural Steel Company.

Interview conducted by the author: Kenedy County Sheriff Rafael Cuellar.

Other resources: *Dallas Morning News, Texas Almanac, 1998–1999;* Tyler, Barnett, and Barkley, eds., *New Handbook of Texas,* vol. 3, 1067, and vol. 5, 897; Metz, *Roadside History of Texas.*

Kent County (Jayton)

Kent County was created in 1876 but was not organized
until 1892. It was named for Andrew Kent, who died
defending the Alamo. Kent was one of the thirty-two volunteers from Gonzales who marched through the Mexican forces
to aid the besieged Alamo. The area that was to become Kent
County was for centuries dominated by the Comanche Indians. In 1872, Ranald Mackenzie fought an engagement with
the Indians at Treasure Butte near the site where the town of
Clairemont would be founded in 1888.

When Kent County was organized, Clairemont became
the county seat and remained so until 1954. In 1909, however,
the Stamford and Northeastern Railroad was built across the
northeastern corner of Kent County, missing Clairemont. As a
result, the town slowly declined. The new town of Jayton, on
the railroad route, began to grow, and in 1954 the county seat
was moved to Jayton.

In 1895 the first jail in Kent County was built of red sandstone blocks in Clairemont. It was a simple one-story rectangular building, 24′ by 18′, and plumbing was not one of its
features. The jail is pretty much intact today, with the iron
cages in place, hoping perhaps for a comeback or recollecting
the more exciting days of 1930, when the county population
was 1,831. The old red sandstone courthouse nearby, west
of Highway
208, once
had two
stories, but
fire elimi-
nated the
second story
years ago.
The jail was
abandoned
in 1953,
and both
buildings

Kent County jail, 1895–1954, Clairemont, Texas.

are relics of an earlier age. Clairemont is now a ghost town, home to only two families.

Interview conducted by the author: Cornelia Cheyne, county district clerk.

Other resources: *Dallas Morning News, Texas Almanac, 1998–1999;* Tyler, Barnett, and Barkley, eds., *New Handbook of Texas,* vol. 2, 127, and vol. 3, 1073; Wallace, *Ranald S. Mackenzie on the Texas Frontier.*

Kerr County (Kerrville)

Kerr County was created in 1856 from Bexar County. It was named for James Kerr, soldier, surveyor, politician, physician, and member of Austin's Old Three Hundred. He received his league of land in the area later named Jackson County. Kerr County is dominated by the headwaters of the Guadalupe River. It was first settled by Joshua D. Brown on the river at the present site of Kerrville. Indian depredations caused Brown's settlement to be temporarily abandoned, but in 1856 the establishment of Camp Verde, at one time the site of the U.S. Army's experimental use of camels as pack animals, provided the necessary protection for development of the new county. In 1858, Charles Schreiner, a young German immigrant, bought the Williams Store adjacent to Camp Verde. Creating the foundation for an entrepreneurial legend, Schreiner provided liquor to the troops and wood and beef to the fort.

Kerrville, originally called Brownsborough, became the county seat in 1856, but because of the Indian raids, the seat was moved to Comfort in 1860. In 1862, Comfort found itself in Kendall County when that county was formed, and once again Kerrville became the county seat.

The county built a two-story stone courthouse-and-jail combination on the corner of the Kerrville courthouse square in 1862. In 1876, a new three-story courthouse was built on the square, and the former facility became the jail. The 1876 courthouse burned in 1925 and was replaced with a new building with a lockup on the third floor designed by Adams and Adams. When an annex was added in 1976, the jail was moved to the second floor.

Interviews conducted by the author: Robert A. Denson, county judge; Herbert A. Peterson, Butt-Holdsworth Memorial Library.

Other resources: *Dallas Morning News, Texas Almanac, 1998–1999;* Tyler, Barnett, and Barkley, eds., *New Handbook of Texas,* vol. 1, 948, and vol. 3, 1076, 1077; DeLorme Mapping, *Texas Atlas and Gazetteer;* R. Bennett, *Kerr County, Texas, 1856–1956.*

Kimble County (Junction)

Although created from Bexar County in 1858, Kimble County remained dominated by Comanche and Kiowa Indians until the 1870s. The county was organized in 1876 and named for George C. Kimble, one of the volunteers from Gonzales who went to the aid of those in the Alamo. The rugged mountains and brush of the North and South Llano River valleys provided a perfect hiding place for every kind of thief and murderer until the county was organized. Once that took place, District Judge W. A. Blackburn recognized the critical situation and called for help from the Texas Rangers.

In the spring of 1877, Maj. John B. Jones sent four parties of six or seven Rangers out to make a sweep of the hills and valleys and pick up anyone of uncertain occupation and bring them to Junction. According to Texas Ranger James B. Gillett, the parties came

Kimble County jail, 1892–present, Junction, Texas. Remodeled in 1904 by the Southern Structural Steel Company, San Antonio.

together at Junction with fifty or sixty prisoners; the net included two escaped convicts, several murderers, and a number of horse and cattle thieves.

The first county seat was in Kimbleville, about a mile and a half northeast of the present site of Junction. Incarceration there meant being chained to a tree until the court got around to hearing the case. The first real jail in Kimble County was constructed about the time of the Rangers' foray. It was a log-and-cedar-post structure erected in 1877, probably completed just in time for those caught in Major Jones's dragnet. O. C. Fisher's book says that the prisoners were "confined in shackles in a place called 'the bull pen.'"

Aside from dealing with Major Jones's prisoners, the jail and courts must have been busy because about a dozen murders around town were recorded before the second lockup was built in 1892. That new facility consisted of two stories of local limestone with walls two feet thick. It has lasted until today and is still certified by the Texas Commission for Jail Standards. In 1904, the jail was modernized by installing new cells manufactured by the Southern Structural Steel Company. The structure can accommodate nineteen prisoners. In its day, the lockup held notables such as members of the Dalton Gang in February 1896 and, in that same year, Gip Hardin, brother of John Wesley Hardin. The jail is at 415 Pecan Street.

Interview conducted by the author: Yvonne Smith, Kimble County Sheriff's Department.

Other resources: *Dallas Morning News, Texas Almanac, 1998–1999;* Tyler, Barnett, and Barkley, eds., *New Handbook of Texas,* vol. 3, 1100; Metz, *Roadside History of Texas;* Gillett and Quaife, *Six Years with the Texas Rangers, 1875–1881;* Fisher, *It Occurred in Kimble.*

King County (Guthrie)

King County was created in 1876 and organized in 1891. It was named for William P. King, one of the thirty-two volunteers from Gonzales who went to help the defenders of the Alamo and died at the hands of Santa Anna. The

county seat,
Guthrie,
was named
for W. H.
Guthrie, a
stockholder
of the
Louisville
Land and
Cattle
Company,
which held
large tracts

King County jail, 1894–present, Guthrie, Texas. Photo by
Stanley Gilbert. From the author's collection.

of land in the area when the county was organized. In 1900,
Samuel Burke Burnett bought the land of the Louisville Land
and Cattle Company, and his property is still operating as part
of the 6666 (Four Sixes) Ranch. Guthrie is now the center for
the vast 6666 Ranch as well as for the 168,000-acre Pitchfork
Ranch, thirteen miles west.

Built in 1894, the jail in King County was a two-story
structure of local red sandstone. In 1917 the building was remodeled, and the second story was removed. The lockup is no
longer used to hold prisoners; they are instead transferred to
Dickens County. According to Leon Metz, the facility was
called the "Friday Night Jail" in the early days because many
cowboys ended up there on Friday nights.

William F. Ballard has told a story about a gunfight in
1916. According to Ballard, a tough by the name of Henry
Upton would come to the saloon to drink, an activity that
caused him to become hostile. He and Sheriff White Moore
were not the best of friends. One day, Upton and narrator
Ballard went out the back door of the saloon about the same
time. Sheriff Moore, always keeping an eye on Upton, went
out the front door. As Upton reached the street, he saw the
sheriff and pulled his gun. The sheriff was quick on the draw
and shot Upton square in the chest. Upton fell dead next to
Ballard. Ballard's comment on the event was this: "It was a
hard and tough life in those days."

Interview conducted by the author: Sheriff Jim Waller.

Other resources: *Dallas Morning News, Texas Almanac, 1998–1999;* Tyler, Barnett, and Barkley, eds., *New Handbook of Texas,* vol. 2, 1138, vol. 3, 110, 1392, and vol. 5, 220; Metz, *Roadside History of Texas;* King County Historical Society, *King County.*

Kinney County (Brackettville)

Kinney County was created from Bexar County in 1850. It was organized in 1874 and named for N. L. Kinney, the founder of Corpus Christi. Legend has it that, in 1688, Spanish officer Alonso de León, on his third trip into Texas in search of La Salle's Fort Saint Louis, encountered a Frenchman called Jean Jarry, who was living as a "king" among the Indians. It is believed that the encounter between them was in the vicinity of Kinney County and that the Indian village was in the Anacacho Mountains. Because of Jarry's propensity for prevarication, however, his story was not believed and was never confirmed, but he may have been a deserter or survivor from La Salle's expedition.

Fort Clark was founded in 1852 at Las Moras Springs as a base for a campaign against the Kickapoo and Lipan Apache Indians in Mexico. The post was abandoned by the United States during the Civil War but re-opened in 1873. The Indians were making raids into Texas and then withdrawing into Mexico for protection. After the

Kinney County jail, 1896–1974, Brackettville, Texas. Photo courtesy of William F. Haenn, Zack Davis Collection, Brackettville, Texas.

Civil War, the punitive expeditions penetrated as far as seventy miles into Mexico to destroy the Indian villages. Fort Clark became famous for the use of black Seminole scouts (the offspring of Seminoles and free blacks or runaway slaves) in its campaign. The army found them to be excellent scouts and prized their service during the Indian wars.

Brackettville began as a stop on the San Antonio to El Paso stage route in 1852. Oscar B. Brackett, who operated a freight wagon service between San Antonio and Mexico, established a trading post called Brackett near Fort Davis. He opened a post office in 1873 and named it Brackettville. Brackettville was made the county seat of Kinney County in 1876, but the county jail was not built until 1896. Constructed with the local limestone, it was two stories tall and had two tiers of cells, plus special cells for women. The jail was used until 1974 but has now been remodeled as a civic center, and the second story has been removed.

Interviews conducted by the author: Sheriff Leland Burgess; Deputy Sheriff Warren Outlaw; Sarah Terrezas, librarian.

Other resources: *Dallas Morning News, Texas Almanac, 1998–1999;* Tyler, Barnett, and Barkley, eds., *New Handbook of Texas,* vol. 1, 691, 692, and vol. 3, 1118; Metz, *Roadside History of Texas;* Weddle, *Wilderness Manhunt;* Manney, *Kinney County;* DeLorme Mapping, *Texas Atlas and Gazetteer.*

Kleberg County (Kingsville)

Kleberg and nearby counties were the scene of a little-known drama in North American history. In 1568, English privateer John Hawkins suffered grave damage to his fleet in a raid on a Spanish coastal town in Central America. One of his ships sank, and the others were so badly damaged that there was not room aboard for the entire crew to make the trip back to England. The ever-resourceful Hawkins put 114 sailors ashore just south of the mouth of the Rio Grande. Most of the castaways were lost to history, but David Ingram, Richard Brown, and Richard Twide walked first to Canada and then to the Atlantic coast, where they were picked up in October 1569 by a French ship and returned to England.

Kleberg County was created from Nueces County in 1913 and organized that same year. It was named for Robert Justice Kleberg, an 1880 graduate of the University of Virginia, lawyer, friend of Capt. Richard King, and founder of the 825,000-acre King Ranch. After King's death in 1885, his widow, Henrietta King, asked Robert Kleberg to help run the ranch for her. Kleberg married Alice Gertrudis King, youngest daughter of Henrietta and Richard King. Their son, Robert Justice Kleberg Jr., managed the ranch after his father's death in 1933 until his own death in 1974.

The town of Kingsville was really the creation of Henrietta King. Anticipating a railroad to Brownsville, just after the turn of the century she designated a large piece of the ranch near the headquarters as incentive for rail construction. In 1903, when the St. Louis, Brownsville, and Mexico Railroad was built along that line, the town of Kingsville was surveyed and laid out by the King Ranch surveyor. Lots were sold, and eventually the town became a cattle-shipping point, railroad repair facility, and university town.

Kingsville was incorporated in 1911, and in 1913 Kleberg County was formed from Nueces County. The first order of business was to vote a bond issue of $125,000 for construction of a courthouse and jail. Atlee B. Ayres designed a Texas Renaissance building with the jail on the third floor. The courthouse has weathered well through the years, but in 1997, the jail was moved to a new facility out of town.

Interviews conducted by the author: Sheriff Tony Gonzales; Cecilia Ares Hunter, Texas A&M–Kingsville.

Other resources: *Dallas Morning News, Texas Almanac, 1998–1999;* Tyler, Barnett, and Barkley, eds., *New Handbook of Texas,* vol. 1, 105, and vol. 3, 1106, 1107, 1115, 1136–39; Kelsey and Dyal, *Courthouses of Texas;* Syers, *Texas;* Kleberg County Historical Commission, *Kleberg County, Texas.*

Knox County (Benjamin)

Knox County was created from Bexar and Young counties in 1858. It was named for Henry Knox, U.S. secretary of war in George Washington's first cabinet. The area that was to become Knox County was prime buffalo country before the arrival of white explorers and settlers. Since buffalo were the principal food staple for the Indians, the Native American menace to area pioneers was substantial. In 1856, the United States deployed elements of the 2nd Cavalry under Col. Albert Sidney Johnston and Col. Robert E. Lee to help protect the frontier forts and settlers. U.S. forces were withdrawn, however, during the Civil War.

Knox County jail, 1888–1953, Benjamin, Texas. Photo by Stanley Gilbert. From the author's collection.

After that conflict, the county was re-created in 1876 and then organized in 1886 with Benjamin as the county seat. Benjamin was named for the founder of the town, Benjamin Bedford, who was the son of Hilary H. Bedford, president of the Wichita and Brazos Stock Company.

After organization, a two-room wooden building served as a courthouse until 1888, when a large brown sandstone facility was built. One block to the west, the county constructed a substantial two-story jail of similar sandstone. The old jail is an elaborate structure with carved stone cornices and quoins. Commodious sheriff's quarters were on the first floor, and the prison and a gallows were on the second floor. The jail was used until the early 1950s, when the county built a new structure. The old prison stands today, very much in its original configuration, except for slight modifications to make it into a residence. Wyman Meinzer, the owner, a widely known nature photographer, has done much of the conversion and restoration.

Interviews conducted by the author: Wyman Meinzer; Mary Jane
Young, Texas Historical Commission.

Other resources: *Dallas Morning News, Texas Almanac, 1998–1999;* Tyler,
Barnett, and Barkley, eds., *New Handbook of Texas,* vol. 1, 490, vol. 3, 990,
1149, and vol. 4, 142; Knox County History Committee, *Knox County
History;* W. Robinson, *People's Architecture;* Fowler, "Jailhouse Museums."

Lamar County (Paris)

Lamar County was created from Red River County in
1840 and named for the second president of the Republic
of Texas. The area lay between the Sulfur River on the south
and the Red River on the north. When the county was first
organized in 1841, the county seat was in Lafayette, several
miles northwest of present-day Paris, Texas. It was moved to
Paris, however, when George W. Wright donated fifty acres
to create the seat of government.

Before 1874, a jail of unknown description stood on South
Main Street near Kaufman Street. In 1874, however, a two-
story stone lockup, designed by W. A. McGinnis in the shape
of a "T" and measuring 24' by 40', was built facing east on
North Main Street. The cells consisted of two tiers of steel
cages provided by Pauly Jail Building and Manufacturing; the
cells and ironwork cost sixty-six hundred dollars. The front
part of the building was brick and contained the jailer's residence. The facility had a metal roof topped by multiple lightning rods, and a 12' high board fence surrounded the building.
The jail was destroyed by fire in 1916.

The great Paris fire of March 21, 1916, destroyed fourteen
hundred buildings in a path from southwest to northeast, including the 1897 courthouse and the 1874 jail. The commissioners decided that a new jail should be integrated into a new
courthouse. Architects Sanguinet and Messer drew plans for
a four-story granite building with a basement and a fourth-
floor jail. The facility was erected on the site of the previous
courthouse and has been described by Willard B. Robinson
as Richardsonian Romanesque.

A contract was made with the Pauly Jail Building and
Manufacturing Company to supply the cages and ironwork.

The lockup had separate areas for white and nonwhite prisoners. Each apartment had nine cells that could accommodate four prisoners each. Every cage had a separate sewer and shower connection. There was a separate area for women that was arranged in wards rather than cells. Finally, there was also a hospital ward. The jailer's office was situated in the center. The costs of maintaining certification by the Texas Commission on Jail Standards, however, prompted the county to complete a new facility on Brown Street in April 1993.

Interviews conducted by the author: Skipper Steely; Butch Williams; Ron Brothers, Texas Historical Commission.

Other resources: *Dallas Morning News, Texas Almanac, 1998–1999;* Metz, *Roadside History of Texas;* Tyler, Barnett, and Barkley, eds., *New Handbook of Texas,* vol. 4, 39, and vol. 5, 53; Neville, *Backward Glances.*

Lamb County (Littlefield)

Lamb County was created in 1876 but not organized until 1908; the town of Olton was chosen as the county seat. The area was named for George A. Lamb, one of the nine Texans killed at the battle of San Jacinto. Lamb was twenty-two years old and a member of Sidney Sherman's 2nd Cavalry. The town of Olton was named for the son of A. B. Powell, who had the first post office in that town.

In the early days, the giant XIT ranch dominated the county, but in 1901, George Littlefield bought three hundred thousand acres from XIT. When the Santa Fe Railroad planned a route from Lubbock to Clovis, New Mexico, Littlefield encouraged a right-of-way through his ranch and founded a town that would become Littlefield. Over a period of years, several attempts were made to move the seat of government to that community. Finally, in 1946, the vote was in favor of making Littlefield the county seat.

In 1908, Olton, the first seat of government, built a nine-room wooden courthouse, mostly with donated citizen labor. A separate wooden structure served as a jail. The courthouse burned in 1922. By 1923, a new brick-and-concrete courthouse with a jail inside was completed and used until the county seat was moved to Littlefield in 1946. The Olton courthouse and jail were empty for a while, but in 1949 the building was remodeled and became the Olton Memorial Hospital. The hospital, however, closed in 1959, and the building was razed in 1964.

Interviews conducted by the author: Jo Ann Austin, Lamb County Library; Linda Roper, Olton Sand Crawl Museum and Library.

Other resources: *Dallas Morning News, Texas Almanac, 1998–1999;* Tyler, Barnett, and Barkley, eds., *New Handbook of Texas,* vol. 4, 43, 44; Kelsey and Dyal, *Courthouses of Texas.*

Lampasas County (Lampasas)

Lampasas County was created in 1856. Its name derives from the Spanish word for the native lilies found in nearby streams. The town of Lampasas, originally called Burleson, was in the 1,280-acre tract of land given to John Burleson for his service during the Texas Revolution. When the county was organized in 1856, the town's name was changed to Lampasas, and the community was made the county seat. Early white settlers discovered the medicinal benefits of the nearby mineral springs.

After the Civil War, buffalo hunting and later the capture and breaking of wild mustangs became important enterprises. Lawlessness was rampant, and the years between 1873 and 1877 were punctuated by the shots fired during the Horrell-Higgins feud, much of which took place in downtown Lampasas. The county records suf-

Lampasas County jail, 1883–1970, Lampasas, Texas. Photo courtesy of Lampasas County Historical Commission.

fered losses, first in the courthouse fire of December 1871 and again in the flood of September 1873.

Between 1856 and 1940, there were three jails in Lampasas County. The first is thought to have been a picket- or palisade-type enclosure, replaced later by a dungeon with the prison below ground and a log building at ground level.

William Perkins, a physician, had occasion to visit a patient in the Lampasas jail in October 1871. Afterward he wrote the following to the *Lampasas Dispatch:* "In an apartment (well nigh air tight) and of dimensions length 9 ft., breadth 8 ft., height 7 ft. were confined five prisoners. In this dungeon were five men compelled to breathe this 500 ft. of air (not half allowance for one). . . . Such punishment is enforced and sustained in such a manner as to bring up ideas of the black hole of Calcutta." It took twelve years for the commissioners to respond to Perkins's complaint.

In 1883, a new courthouse and a separate jail were erected. The new lockup was two stories of masonry construction and occupied the same general site as the previous jails. The architect and builder are unknown. In 1970, the facility was replaced by a modern jail on the same ground.

Interviews conducted by the author: Jeff Jackson; Shirley Blake.

Other resources: Tyler, Barnett, and Barkley, eds., *New Handbook of Texas,* vol. 4, 49; Metz, *Roadside History of Texas;* Sonnichsen, *I'll Die before I'll Run;* Kelsey and Dyal, *Courthouses of Texas; Lampasas Dispatch,* Oct. 25, 1871.

La Salle County (Cotulla)

La Salle County was created from Bexar County in 1858. Located on the edge of the Nueces River, the area was subject to the depredations of outlaws and Indians, typical events in the disputed territory between the Nueces River and the Rio Grande.

The county was organized in 1880, and the settlement of Cotulla, near the abandoned Fort Ewell, was designated the county seat. The minutes of the first commissioners' court meeting on January 3, 1881, authorized Sheriff J. M. Buck to buy two pairs of handcuffs and one pair of leg irons. Sheriff Buck, elected in November 1880, resigned in May 1881. Sheriff W. O. Tompkins was appointed in June 1881, but the office became unaccountably vacant in January 1883. The third sheriff, C. B. McKinney, served for four years before he was shot and killed.

J. W. Hargus, a physician who practiced in the area, later recalled that "more than once I was led blindfolded into a thicket to doctor a wounded outlaw. I have treated gunshot wounds of 259 men and have seen 108 men with bullet holes in them that did not need treating." He neglected to say whether the latter were beyond treatment.

Meanwhile, the town of La Salle had been founded on the International and Great Northern Railroad right-of-way "across the tracks from Cotulla." In 1882 La Salle was designated the temporary county seat pending a vote; the vote in 1883, however, favored Cotulla by a two-to-one count, even though La Salle had already built a courthouse and the first La Salle County jail.

Once Cotulla became the county seat, citizens completed a courthouse with an adjacent jail in 1884. This second La Salle County lockup had two stories and was built of "Cotulla bricks." It held two sections of three cages each, separated by a 4' corridor. Each cage was 5' by 7' by 7'. The jail outlasted three courthouses, two of which were destroyed by fire in 1896 and 1904. In 1931, a new Art Deco courthouse containing a jail on the top floor, designed by Henry T. Phelps of San Antonio, was built. The 1931 jail is not in use today because, since World War II, prisoners have been sent to nearby Pearsall for safekeeping.

Interview conducted by the author: Sheriff Luis Rene Benavides.

Other resources: *Dallas Morning News, Texas Almanac, 1998–1999;* Metz, *Roadside History of Texas;* Tyler, Barnett, and Barkley, eds., *New Handbook of Texas,* vol. 2, 1100, vol. 3, 367, and vol. 4, 83; Casto, *Settlement of the Cibolo-Nueces Strip;* Ludeman, *La Salle;* Tise, *Texas County Sheriffs;* DeLorme Mapping, *Texas Atlas and Gazetteer.*

Lavaca County (Hallettsville)

Lavaca County was created in 1846 and organized in 1852 with Petersburg, a settlement about six miles southeast of Hallettsville, as the county seat. The county is named for

the Lavaca
River,
which flows
through it.
After orga-
nization, an
election was
held in 1852
that favored
moving the
seat of gov-
ernment to

Lavaca County jail, 1885–present, Hallettsville, Texas.

Hallettsville. A single building in Petersburg had served as
church, courthouse, sheriff's office, and school. Prisoners were
locked in a barn or boarded in private residences. Until 1861
an open-air cage served as a jail.

The election of 1852 to move the county seat was vigor-
ously contested; the litigation that followed lasted until 1860.
The removal of county records to Hallettsville in 1852 was accomplished by a group of armed citizens from that community. Petersburg has now disappeared but was located near the
end of Texas Highway 2616, southeast of Hallettsville.

Lavaca County played a role in the famous Sutton-Taylor
feud of the 1870s. It seems that a posse of the state police, including Bill Sutton, "arrested" William and Henry Kelly from
DeWitt County. Although charged with only minor offenses
in Lavaca County, the posse shot and killed the unarmed prisoners while en route to Hallettsville, supposedly for trying
to escape. The Kellys were members of the Taylor family, who
had already lost relatives to Capt. Jack Helm's hated state police. This marked the beginning of the Sutton-Taylor feud.

Before 1885, Halletsville had a cell in a wooden courthouse
for holding prisoners. The first real lockup in Lavaca County
was built in 1885 and is still in use as a jail today. This makes
the facility the second oldest lockup in continuous use in
Texas. The oldest is in San Saba County and was built in 1884.
Architect J. E. Deitz designed the Lavaca County jail, and
contractors Pickett and Mead built it for $12,111. Provision
was made for four cages to be provided by Pauly Brothers for
$4,000. The jail contained no gallows, but two executions by

hanging were carried out by constructing temporary gallows on the courthouse square.

Interviews conducted by the author: Darlene Stacy; Sgt. W. O. Williamson, deputy sheriff; Sam Tise.

Other resources: *Dallas Morning News, Texas Almanac, 1998–1999;* Metz, *Roadside History of Texas;* Tyler, Barnett, and Barkley, eds., *New Handbook of Texas,* vol. 3, 419, vol. 4, 106, and vol. 5, 167; Sonnichsen, *I'll Die before I'll Run;* Kelsey and Dyal, *Courthouses of Texas.*

Lee County (Giddings)

Lee County was formed in 1874 as a result of an 1873 conference between representatives from nearby Burleson, Washington, Fayette, and Bastrop counties. A petition was sent to the legislature, and the county was formed and organized in 1874.

Giddings was founded in 1871 on the route of the Houston and Central Texas Railroad. Originally, the town was in Washington County but moved to Lee. When it came time to choose a county seat, a contest arose between Giddings and Lexington, but Giddings won because of its location on the railroad.

The first jail in Lee County was built before the county was organized. It was a so-called calaboose on the Houston and Central Texas Railroad track. It is said to have been a two-story frame building, but there is no written record of its existence.

The new county commissioners proposed the first official lockup in

Lee County jail, 1915–1974, Giddings, Texas. Built by Southern Structural Steel.

March 1875, and a contract was given to Edward Northcraft and George W. Donelson of Hays County that same month. The jail, 22' by 28', was built on block 146. It was a two-story brick edifice on a stone foundation and contained sheriff's quarters. On the first floor was a special high-security dungeon made of steel plate.

The next jail in Lee County was built in 1915. It was also on block 146, constructed next door to the older 1875 jail before that building was torn down. Located one block from the courthouse, the modest two-story solid concrete-and-stucco building was T-shaped. The contractor was the Southern Structural Steel Company. In 1974 a modern detention center was built on the corner of the same block 146, and the 1875 jail was remodeled and used as an office for the sheriff.

Interviews conducted by the author: Sheriff Joe Goodson; Lydia Siegmund.

Other resources: *Dallas Morning News, Texas Almanac, 1998–1999;* Tyler, Barnett, and Barkley, eds., *New Handbook of Texas,* vol. 1, 744, vol. 3, 154, and vol. 4, 144; Kelsey and Dyal, *Courthouses of Texas;* W. Robinson, *People's Architecture.*

Leon County (Centerville)

Leon County was created in 1846, and although the origin of the name is controversial, the consensus is that it comes from an area called Leon Prairie. When the county was organized in 1846, the legislature suggested that the county seat be called Leona. Leona remained the seat until 1850, when it was moved to Centerville, a more central location.

During and after the Civil War, the previously expanding economy was severely crippled until the arrival of the International–Great Northern Railroad, which reduced the county's earlier reliance on Trinity River boats for market access.

There were at least three jails in Leon County before 1940. The first, date unknown, was probably a log building that was replaced in 1887 by a two-story brick lockup with unusual architectural features. The architect is unnamed, but the build-

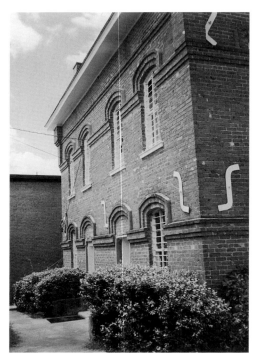

Leon County jail, 1887–1913, Centerville, Texas.

ing has stilted arches over the windows, pilasters, and string-courses accenting its otherwise simple design. The contractor was Robb and Wilson Company, who built it at a cost of $3,850. Other interesting features are the S-shaped metal plates on the outside walls at the second-floor level, reinforcing the floor and wall union. This building is now used as a tax office.

The old jail was the scene of a 1910 breakout. Frank Bates and his son, who were being held for murder, attacked Deputy Sheriff Jeff St. John and shot him in the face with a .41-caliber Colt pistol. The prisoners had been charged with the murder of B. T. Moon in an argument over some hogs. After shooting the deputy, the prisoners ran out of the jail and continued hightailing it down the road toward the town of Buffalo, followed by a dozen armed citizens. The pursuit resulted in the father's being mortally wounded and the son slightly hurt. Both were returned to the prison, where the elder Bates died the next day. Deputy Sheriff St. John miraculously made a full recovery.

In 1912, the county built a new jail, once again two stories of brick. It was designed and built by the Southern Structural Steel Company. This castle-style keep features two towers with crenellations and battlements. It was used until a new facility was built in 1969.

Interviews conducted by the author: Brenda Greer, Leon County Genealogical Society; Ruby R. Johnson, Texas Historical Commission.

Other resources: *Dallas Morning News, Texas Almanac, 1998–1999;*
Tyler, Barnett, and Barkley, eds., *New Handbook of Texas,* vol. 4, 159, 164;
W. Robinson, *People's Architecture;* Cowden, *Historical Texas County Jails;*
Leon County Heritage Society, *Leon County History;* Gates, *History of Leon
County;* Leathers, *Through the Years.*

Liberty County (Liberty)

Liberty County, one of the original twenty-three Texas
counties, was created in 1836. The town of Liberty was
founded in 1818 near the old Trinity River crossing (the ancestral home of the Orcoquisac or Atakapan Indians) and was
chosen as the governmental seat when the county was organized. Liberty was incorporated in 1837 and shortly thereafter
became a shipping point for cotton and cattle. Sam Houston
owned two plantations in the area.

The jail history in Liberty is a bit sketchy. In 1838 Liberty
advertised for bids to build a two-story lockup to be constructed of double crib 12″ hewn logs with vertical 12″ logs
between the cribs. The description in the advertisement was
the dungeon pattern, which characterized Texas jail construction for the next thirty years.

In 1876 Asa Abshier was paid fifty dollars to construct a
calaboose, but details of the building were not specified since
it was as-
sumed that
everyone
knew what
a calaboose
was. Around
1887, a
brick facility
was built,
known for
years as
"the old red
brick jail."
The date of
construction

Liberty County jail, 1931–present, Liberty, Texas. Photo
courtesy of Watson Neyland Collection, Sam Houston
Regional Library and Research Center, Liberty, Texas.

is not specified anywhere, but the architecture is characterized by stilted arches over the windows and stringcourses at first- and second-floor levels, which was typical of that time. Another lockup is thought to have been built in 1931. It was a three-story brick square with the usual crenellations on top and sheriff's quarters on the ground floor. The structure appears in the Southern Structural Steel Company's catalogue, so that firm is likely to have provided the steel cages and perhaps even built the jail.

Interviews conducted by the author: Darlene Mott, Sam Houston Regional Library; Judge Lloyd Kirkham.

Other resources: *Dallas Morning News, Texas Almanac, 1998–1999;* Tyler, Barnett, and Barkley, eds., *New Handbook of Texas,* vol. 1, 274, and vol. 4, 18, 188; Newcomb, *Indians of Texas;* Robinson and Webb, *Public Buildings of the Nineteenth Century;* Partlow, *Liberty, Liberty County, and the Atascocito District.*

Limestone County (Groesbeck)

Limestone County was created from Robertson County in 1846 and organized that same year. It was the original home of the Tehuacana (or Tawakoni) and Waco Indians, who were, generally speaking, an agricultural society.

The first county seat was Springfield. After the Houston and Central Texas Railroad bypassed Springfield in 1873, the county seat was moved to Groesbeck, a small town on the rail line. Groesbeck was named for Abram Groesbeck, a director of the railroad. Springfield had built a 20' by 25' two-story wooden jail on a brick foundation. The frugal citizens moved the structure, including the bricks for the foundation, to Groesbeck, making the keep the first public building in town.

In 1880, a new facility was built for $7,648. By 1909, however, the 1880 jail was inadequate, so the commissioners' court ordered that lockup to be torn down and a larger one built on the same foundation, using more or less the same plan. C. J. Kauhl was given the contract for $3,720. The result was a three-story structure with the sheriff's quarters occupying part of the ground floor. There were six two-person cells on the remainder of the ground floor, and the second and third floors each had fifteen two-person cells. This building served until 1987, when the mandates of the Commission for Jail Standards mandated new jail construction.

The story of the Indian raid on Fort Parker on May 19, 1836, by 500–700 Kiowa and Comanche Indians is a legend uniquely associated with Limestone County. Many Texans are familiar with the kidnapping of nine-year-old Cynthia Ann Parker and her six-year-old brother John by the attacking Comanche Indians. The two children and two adult women were taken prisoner, and eight men and women were killed. Cynthia Ann lived with the Comanche Indians until repatriated against her will after the battle of Pease River in 1860. Her husband, Chief Nocona, was killed in that battle, but her son, Quanah, escaped with the Indians, later to become a famous Comanche chief. Cynthia Ann never readjusted to the white lifestyle, however. She died sometime after 1870. John grew to maturity among the Indians and declined an offer to return to civilization. Sometime later, he developed smallpox and was abandoned by the Indians, according to custom. Folklore has it that a Mexican girl, Donna Juanita, nursed him to recovery and that the two returned to Mexico, became ranchers, and raised a family.

Interviews conducted by the author: C. B. Willard, retired Groesbeck chief of police; Eleanor F. Holmes, Limestone county judge.

Other resources: Tyler, Barnett, and Barkley, eds., *New Handbook of Texas,* vol. 3, 349, vol. 4, 198, and vol. 5, 60; DeLorme Mapping, *Texas Atlas and Gazetteer; Dallas Morning News, Texas Almanac, 1998–1999;* Newcomb, *Indians of Texas;* Welch, *Historic Sites of Texas;* Walter, *History of Limestone County;* Ferguson, *And the Clock Struck Ten; Groesbeck Journal,* archived at the Maffett Memorial Library, Groesbeck, Tex.

Lipscomb County (Lipscomb)

Lipscomb County was created in 1876 and named for Abner S. Lipscomb, who was secretary of state for the Republic of Texas in Mirabeau B. Lamar's administration. The area that would become Lipscomb County is in the extreme northeastern tip of the Texas Panhandle, one of the last hold-

Lipscomb County jail. 1916–1971, Lipscomb, Texas. Photo by Stanley Gilbert. From the author's collection.

outs of the Kiowa and Comanche Indians, ending with their defeat in the Red River War of the mid-1870s.

The county was organized in June 1887, and the town of Lipscomb, less than a year old, was made the county seat. Lipscomb is a rare example of a community that was able to remain the county seat even after a branch of the Panhandle and Santa Fe Railroad bypassed it in favor of another town—Higgins, in this case. Higgins was built on the railroad line and today has ten times the population of Lipscomb, but Lipscomb remains the seat of government.

In order to justify themselves as worthy of having the county seat, the citizens of Lipscomb built a frame courthouse and a one-story stone jail, both completed before the year of 1887 was out. The jail was of local manufacture and strong enough for its time. A second jail was built in 1916, when the new Classic Revival courthouse designed by W. M. Rice was constructed. The jail, made of concrete blocks in an 18′ by 20′ rectangle, contained two cells with steel ceilings and floors manufactured by the Pauly Jail Manufacturing Company. Three walls of each cage were made of steel plate, and the front side was made of flat steel bars, two inches wide and held together by rivets. There is a record of one escape—when a prisoner sawed through the steel bars of the jail door.

Interviews conducted by the author: Coweta Sperry, county clerk; Mildred Berkere, Texas State Historical Commission; Sheriff James Robertson.

Other resources: *Dallas Morning News, Texas Almanac, 1998–1991;* Tyler, Barnett, and Barkley, eds., *New Handbook of Texas,* vol. 4, 214, 225; DeLorme Mapping, *Texas Atlas and Gazetteer.*

Live Oak County (George West)

When the Spanish arrived, Coahuiltecan Indians, a
hunter-gatherer group that included subgroups such
as the Karankawas, Payayas, Aranamas, and Tamiques, occupied most of coastal and southern Texas. They were the inhabitants of what would become Live Oak County.

Early settlement by Anglos began about 1828, when James
McMullen and John McGloin brought in two hundred Irish
Catholic families. Many settled in Corpus Christi, but some
stayed along the Nueces, Atascosa, and Frio rivers. Live Oak
County was created in 1856 from San Patricio and Nueces
counties and organized that same year. Oakville, the first
county seat, began as a stage stop on the San Antonio to Corpus Christi route. After the Civil War, widespread lawlessness,
cattle rustling, and murder were rampant. In 1875, at the end
of Reconstruction, Capt. L. H. McNelly and the Texas Rangers arrived and restored order.

Joseph Bartlett built the first courthouse and jail in Oakville in 1857. In 1885, a two-story stone keep went up. It
had walls eighteen inches thick and double-iron grates on the
cells. The structure cost seven thousand dollars and had sheriff's quarters on the first floor. After the county seat moved,
the lockup was used as a residence for a time. The building
still stands—empty but symbolic of the early days of Texas law
enforcement.

George West was named for rancher George Washington
West, who
settled and
started
ranching in
the area in
1861. With
a hundred–
thousand-
dollar
incentive,
West per-
suaded the

Live Oak County jail, 1885–1918, Oakville, Texas.

San Antonio, Uvalde, and Gulf Railroad to build its route
through his town on the west bank of the Nueces River. When
the county seat moved to George West in 1918, the old jail
was left behind, but the rest of the town gradually followed. In
George West, a new courthouse, designed by Alfred Giles, was
built and completed in 1919. The building had a jail on the
third floor and a gallows—never used—with the usual trapdoor and a ring in the ceiling for the rope. The jail served until 1962, when a new facility was completed outside of the
courthouse.

Interviews conducted by the author: Sheriff Sam Huff, retired; Sheriff
Larry Busby; Deputy Sheriff Glen Thompson.

Other resources: *Dallas Morning News, Texas Almanac, 1998–1999;* Newcomb, *Indians of Texas;* Metz, *Roadside History of Texas;* Tyler, Barnett,
and Barkley, eds., *New Handbook of Texas,* vol. 4, 242, 1094; W. Robinson,
People's Architecture; Live Oak County Centennial Association, *Live Oak
County Centennial.*

Llano County (Llano)

Llano (Spanish for "plains") County was created and organized in 1856. The area was settled by Anglos as early
as 1840 and by Germans after John O. Meusebach negotiated
a treaty with the Comanches in Gillespie County in 1847.
One group, composed of university intellectuals and liberals,
founded Bettina, a socialist colony, north of the Llano River
near Castell. Although a year's crop was successfully harvested,
within a year the group broke up over disagreement about
who should do the work.

The Comanches were troublesome until well after the
Civil War. When two five-member families were killed in separate incidents in 1874, eight men under Capt. James R. Moss
trailed and surprised a large group of raiders on Packsaddle
Mountain, thirteen miles southeast of Llano, and defeated
them, ending the depredations.

The court minutes of 1881 refer to a jail with an iron roof
built about 1873 after legislation had been passed in Austin to
allow Llano County to retain certain taxes for 1873 and 1874
to build a lockup. Plans were made to build a new facility

in 1881, but
the com-
missioners
were dis-
appointed
when only
one bid was
submitted.
In 1882
the firm
of Martin,
Byrnes, and
Johnson of-

Llano County jail, 1895–1995, Llano, Texas.

fered to build a keep on the southeast corner of the square for
seventy-six hundred dollars. The offer was accepted.

When finished, the jail had two levels: The lower one was
below ground and had an iron cell, while the second level
contained the sheriff's quarters. Curiously, no sanitation arrangements were provided, and not until 1890 was a sewer line
installed leading to a nearby ravine that emptied into the Llano
River. This, plus the stockyard adjacent to the jail, must have
discouraged loitering about the calaboose. Finally, the city
of Llano sued the county to remove the jail and the adjacent
mess. The county lost first in local court and then in appellate
court.

In 1895, the commissioners' court made a contract with
Pauly Jail Building and Manufacturing Company to build
a lockup designed by F. B. and W. S. Hull. The result was an
impressive four-story Romanesque Revival building constructed of gray granite. This facility now serves as a museum
operated by the local chapter of the Daughters of the Republic
of Texas.

Interview conducted by the author: Mrs. William R. Miller, Daughters
of the Republic of Texas.

Other resources: *Dallas Morning News, Texas Almanac, 1998–1999;*
Tyler, Barnett, and Barkley, eds., *New Handbook of Texas,* vol. 1, 512, and
vol. 4, 248, 249; Metz, *Roadside History of Texas;* DeLorme Mapping, *Texas
Atlas and Gazetteer;* Almond and Franklin, *Cobwebs and Cornerstones;*
Oatman, *Llano, Gem of the Hill Country;* Fry, "History of Llano County,
Texas."

Loving County (Mentone)

Loving County encompasses 673.1 square miles with a total population of sixty-four in 2004 — the least populated county in the United States. Created in 1887, it was first organized in 1893, but after the failure of an irrigation venture, it was abandoned and declared disorganized until 1931. It was then reorganized, making it the youngest county in Texas. The town of Mentone was founded in 1925 by oil prospectors. Oil production began in 1925 and caused a brief period of activity, resulting in a population that peaked at 600 in 1935.

The county was named for Oliver Loving, famous early cattleman and partner of Charles Goodnight, founder of the Goodnight-Loving Trail. In June 1867 Loving was seriously wounded in an Indian ambush on a trail drive with Goodnight. After several days without food or shelter, he managed to get to Sumner in New Mexico, where he died of complications from the amputation of his arm. Goodnight had Loving buried in Sumner but returned after finishing the trail drive and transferred his body to Weatherford, Texas, for final burial.

After reorganization in 1931, the county built a courthouse and jail in 1935. The building was two stories of yellow brick, approximately 60′ square with a 14′ by 20′ cage on the second floor. Within the cage was a single 6′ by 7′ cell containing two bunks. There was no kitchen, so food had to be brought in when prisoners were there. According to Judge Donald C. Creager, however, both crime and prisoners were rare. He told of one incident many years ago, before air-conditioning, about a man who was inclined to tipple a bit and was a hazard to the citizens when he drove his car. In spite of many warnings and promises on his part, he always reverted to his old habits. Finally he was arrested and sentenced to three days in jail in the middle of July. After his summer experience, he said he intended never to be locked up there again — and he kept the promise and gave up the bottle.

Interviews conducted by the author: Donald C. Creager, Loving County judge; Crystal Bryant, Texas and Southwestern Cattle Raisers Association.

Other resources: *Dallas Morning News, Texas Almanac, 1998–1999;* Tyler, Barnett, and Barkley, eds., *New Handbook of Texas,* vol. 4, 310, 311; De-Lorme Mapping, *Texas Atlas and Gazetteer;* Metz, *Roadside History of Texas;* J. E. Haley, *Charles Goodnight;* J. M. Hunter, *Trail Drivers of Texas.*

Lubbock County (Lubbock)

Lubbock County was created in 1876 and organized in 1891. It was named for Col. Tom Lubbock, a Texas Ranger and an officer in the Civil War. It is thought that the Lubbock area is the site of the oldest human habitation in Texas. Artifacts on twelve-thousand-year-old campsites, including prehistoric animal skeletons, have been found along Yellow House Canyon, which runs northwest to southeast through the Lubbock city limits. In 1849 Capt. Randolph Marcy of the U.S. Army declared the area a desert that was unable to support animals or humans. In 1877 Yellow House Canyon (near present-day Lubbock Lake) was the site of a battle between buffalo hunters and Indians from the reservation in Indian Territory (Oklahoma). The Indians inflicted three casualties on the group of hunters, including one dead, but withdrew to the reservation.

Today agribusiness has become the mainstay of the economy. The first courthouse and jail were built in 1891, shortly after the town of Lubbock was established, as a compromise between two settlements promoted by competing developers. The jail provided a space for a variety of community activities: Not only did it serve as the first school-house, but the Metho-

Lubbock County jail, 1931–present, Lubbock, Texas.

dist, Baptist, and Quaker churches also held services there. Seldom have prisoners had such a good opportunity for reha- bilitation. From 1891 to 1910, the population grew from 33 to 3,624, so the need for a full-time jail was evident. In 1910 the Southern Structural Steel Company was commissioned to build a three-story brick lockup very similar to the ones con- structed in Haskell County in 1909 and McCulloch County in 1910. That facility was used until 1931.

By 1930 the population of Lubbock County had grown to 39,104. In 1931 a three-story, poured-concrete Art Deco jail was built, and provision was made for later additions. The ar- chitect was S. B. Haynes, and the contractor was H. H. Shell, both of Lubbock. The building cost $113,992. The original 1931 jail, with additions, is still in use.

Interview conducted by the author: Sally Abbe, Lubbock City Histori- cal Preservation Office.

Other resources: *Dallas Morning News, Texas Almanac, 1998–1999;* Metz, *Roadside History of Texas;* Tyler, Barnett, and Barkley, eds., *New Handbook of Texas,* vol. 4, 321, 322, and vol. 6, 1116; DeLorme Mapping, *Texas Atlas and Gazetteer;* W. Robinson, *People's Architecture.*

Lynn County (Tahoka)

Lynn County, like many other Panhandle counties, was created in 1876. It was not organized, however, until 1903. The county was named for G. W. Lynn, one of the de- fenders of the Alamo. Tahoka was named for a nearby lake that was a traditional Indian campground. The county is mostly above the escarpment that forms the caprock, one of the geo- logical features of the Texas Panhandle, thereby placing the area in the part of Texas known as the High Plains. The for- mation known as the caprock is not technically a rock but rather an impervious layer below the topsoil. Other character- istics of the High Plains are the numerous playas, which are shallow lakes formed by the collection of surface water. They vary in size from a few acres to several hundred acres but may go dry in a dry season. For centuries, the plains above and be- low the caprock were frequented by vast herds of buffalo.

After the county's organization, the population slowly increased, and in 1916 the county built its second courthouse, which included a jail on the fourth floor. W. R. Rice designed the courthouse, a four-story concrete-and-brick structure in the Classical Revival style. The building is now listed on the National Register. The cells and ironwork were provided by the Pauly Jail Building Company and were said to be of "tool-proof Bessemer steel." A gallows-type trapdoor was located inside the jail, but there is no record of its use. The keep remained in operation until 1960, when a new free-standing jail was built behind the courthouse.

Interviews conducted by the author: Sheriff Charles R. Smith; J. F. Brandon, county judge.

Other resources: *Dallas Morning News, Texas Almanac, 1998–1999;* Tyler, Barnett, and Barkley, eds., *New Handbook of Texas,* vol. 1, 969, and vol. 4, 351; Texas Department of Transportation, "Texas Official Travel Map."

Madison County (Madisonville)

Named for James Madison, the fourth president of the United States, Madison County occupies territory between the Trinity and the Navasota rivers. In prehistoric times, the Caddo Indians and the Bidai, a subgroup of the Atakapans, lived along the Trinity and the Brazos rivers. In 1845 a German scientist, Ferdinand Roemer, visited a Caddo village of grass-covered conical huts resembling haystacks about fifteen feet tall. He described the Caddos' peaceful and friendly nature. They cultivated corn in small patches and supplemented this diet with buffalo meat. Roemer declined an invitation to sleep in one of the huts, however, because of the "ever-present pesky little insects."

The future Madison County would rest at the crossroads of two of the early highways of Texas—the trails that became known as the Old San Antonio Road and the La Bahía Road, both of which crossed the county. Madison County was formed from Leon, Walker, and Grimes counties in January 1853 and organized eighteen months later.

In 1856 Madison County built its first jail in the standard

configuration for the time. It was a two-story log building with no windows or doors on the lower floor. Prisoners were lowered into the dark airless prison by a ladder through a trapdoor in the floor of the second level. In his 1971 thesis, Judge Cecil N. Neely quotes pioneer Joel N. Jenkins, who described the courthouse square in 1857 as having a few small stores, two saloons, and a jail.

Because of courthouse fires, information on jails in Madisonville in the latter half of the nineteenth century is only conjecture. Madison County has had six courthouses, three of which were destroyed by fire in 1858, 1867, and 1873.

In 1896, a two-story brick lockup was located near the courthouse on South Elm Street adjacent to the Baptist Church. That facility was used until 1970, when a new courthouse was built with a jail in the basement. The church bought the old jail property.

Interviews conducted by the author: Lynda Breeding, Madison County Library; Cecil N. Neely, county judge; Roger Knight Jr., Texas Historical Commission; Joyce Coleman, county clerk.

Other resources: *Dallas Morning News, Texas Almanac, 1998–1999;* Tyler, Barnett, and Barkley, eds., *New Handbook of Texas,* vol. 1, 456, and vol. 4, 454, 456; Kelsey and Dyal, *Courthouses of Texas;* Newcomb, *Indians of Texas;* Roemer, *Texas;* Williams and Neighbours, *Old Texas Trails.*

Marion County (Jefferson)

Marion County was created in 1860 and named for Gen. Francis Marion (the "Swamp Fox") of American Revolutionary fame. The county seat, Jefferson, was founded about 1842 and named for Thomas Jefferson. Big Cypress Bayou and Caddo Lake, so important in Jefferson's future development, were the result of a seventy-five-mile logjam, the Red River raft above Shreveport, Louisiana, which caused the water to back up in the bayou. As early as the 1830s, the United States began, with some success, to clear a pass for commerce through the obstruction. Meanwhile, Jefferson enjoyed a period as a shipping center for riverboats from Texas to Shreveport and New Orleans.

By 1870, Jefferson was second only to Galveston as a Texas port for the shipment of cotton and cattle, and one-fourth of Texas' trade goods passed through her streets. She was also pioneering the new age of artificially manufactured ice (invented in France in 1859) for the shipment of beef. In 1874, however, the U.S. Corps of Engineers, using newly invented nitroglycerine, cleared the logjam, and gradually the water level dropped by eight feet, ending Jefferson's days as a port.

There are no standing historic jails in Marion County, and only minimal traces remain of those that once stood there. A review of the commissioners' court records shows that Lieutenant Allamon of the U.S. Army of Occupation offered the sheriff of Marion County the services of his soldiers to guard prisoners. For this purpose, the county erected a temporary jail near the fort at Four Mile Branch, for which they paid $170.66. News clippings indicate that a lockup was built in Jefferson, but prisoners were often sent to the Harrison County jail in Marshall. Organized law and order was in total disarray for about thirty years after the Civil War.

Interviews conducted by the author: Rosanne Bumgartner, Texas Heritage Archives and Library; Jesse M. DeWare III; Phil Hewitt, Texas Heritage Archives; Marcia Thomas, Vintage Theater.

Other resources: *Dallas Morning News, Texas Almanac, 1998–1999;* Tyler, Barnett, and Barkley, eds., *New Handbook of Texas,* vol. 3, 924, and vol. 5, 491; Metz, *Roadside History of Texas;* J. T. Davis, *Historic Towns of Texas;* Tarpley, *Jefferson;* Bullard, *Marion County Texas, 1860–1870;* McKay and Spellings, *History of Jefferson, Marion County, Texas.*

Martin County (Stanton)

Martin County was created in 1876 and organized in 1884. The county was named for Wylie Martin, an early pioneer and one of Stephen Austin's first settlers. Stanton was originally called Grelton when it was established in 1881 as a section station on the Texas and Pacific Railroad. German Catholic immigrants later changed the name to Mariensfield. Finally in 1890, surprisingly enough, the name was changed to Stanton in honor of President Lincoln's secretary of war. The

Martin County jail, 1908–1975, Stanton, Texas.

railroad, in an effort to promote the area, developed an experimental farm and separately sold land to farmers for as little as $1.50 per acre.

The original jail in Martin County was in the southeast corner of the 1885 courthouse. It consisted of a cell block whose plaque read "Patd. P. J. Pauly and Bros. Sept. 15, 1874 of St. Louis, Missouri." When the new jail was built in 1908, the complete cell block was moved to a new location on the northwest corner of the square, and the red sandstone jail was built around it. The result was a slightly different arrangement, with the sheriff's quarters on the second floor and the jail and prisoners on the ground floor. One room on the first floor was used variously as bedroom, kitchen, and sheriff's office. The prison area consisted of two compartments, one containing four bunks and the other, three. The prisoners shared a common washbasin and commode, but there was no bath.

The old jail was used until 1975. Since then it has served as a museum, a library, and quarters for the chamber of commerce. The preservation and restoration of the old lockup is a tribute to many Martin County citizens and to the Martin County Historical Commission.

Interview conducted by the author: Angie Brown, Martin County Historical Commission.

Other resources: *Dallas Morning News, Texas Almanac, 1998–1999;* Tyler, Barnett, and Barkley, eds., *New Handbook of Texas,* vol. 1, 532; Williams, "Old Jail Has Worn Many Hats," *Stanton Reporter,* Nov. 20, 1983; Kelsey and Dyal, *Courthouses of Texas;* Tyler and Tyler, *Texas Museums.*

Mason County (Mason)

Mason County was created in 1858 and organized in 1861. The town of Mason, in the shadow of Fort Mason, was chosen as the county seat. Fort Mason, probably named for Gen. Richard Barnes Mason, was established in 1851 by the United States to protect the frontier. Some notable officers stationed there include Albert Sidney Johnson, Earl Van Doren, Edwin Kirby Smith, Robert E. Lee, John Bell Hood, and John P. Hatch. Apache, Kiowa, and Comanche Indians were especially aggressive in the area.

Before the Civil War, Mason County did not need a jail. For the rare prisoner, the sheriff used the guardhouse at Fort Mason. The fort was closed during the Civil War, at which time thieves and cattle rustlers, in addition to hostile Indians, increased their depredations at an alarming rate. The fort was reopened in December 1866 but closed again about 1870.

The courthouse and the first jail were built in Mason in 1869. The lockup was on the northeast corner of the square. It was unusual in that the stone walls were lined with post oak timbers to protect the soft mortar. The jail played a role in the early part of the Mason County War, when Sheriff John Clark arrested and jailed nine men for stealing cattle. When four of the prisoners broke out, one was shot, and three were hanged on the spot. The Mason County War had begun. For the next few years, prisoners moved in and out of the jail pretty much at will, often with outside help.

By 1875 the ever-increasing cattle theft and murder rates were completely out of hand.

Mason County jail, 1898–present, Mason, Texas.

The Civil War had been a major influence in aligning the American-born secessionists against the German immigrant settlers, who had been antisecessionists. These two groups in the Mason County War would cost the county a dozen deaths by lynching or ambush. Ultimately a call for forty Texas Rangers under Maj. John B. Jones was required to restore the peace. Pacification was not achieved until 1877.

Finally, after the Mason County War had been brought under control, a two-story red sandstone jail was built in 1898. The contract was awarded to L. T. Noyes of Houston, general contractor for the Diebold Safe and Lock Company. The price was eighty-five hundred dollars, money well spent because the jail is still in use today. It has living quarters for the sheriff on the ground floor, and the prison occupies the second floor.

Interviews conducted by the author: Sheriff Melvin Metzher; Jane Hoerster, Mason County Historical Commission.

Other resources: *Dallas Morning News, Texas Almanac, 1998–1999;* Metz, *Roadside History of Texas;* Tyler, Barnett, and Barkley, eds., *New Handbook of Texas,* vol. 2, 1110, and vol. 4, 142, 544, 545; Sterling, *Trails and Trials of a Texas Ranger;* Sonnichsen, *I'll Die before I'll Run;* Gillett and Quaife, *Six Years with the Texas Rangers, 1875–1991;* W. P. Webb, *Texas Rangers;* Cowden, "Historical Texas County Jails"; Jordan, *Yesterday in Texas Hill Country;* Lemburg and Hoerster, *Mason County Jail;* Hadeler, "Mason County Hoodoo Wars," http://www.texfiles.com/texashistory/hoodoowar.htm.

Matagorda County (Bay City)

Matagorda County was part of Stephen Austin's colony. Fifty-two families began arriving as early as 1822. At Austin's request, the town of Matagorda—with the blessing of the Mexican government—was founded in 1827 as a military establishment. By 1832 there were fourteen hundred residents, and the town became the center of the Mexican Matagorda Municipality.

After Texas won her independence from Mexico at San Jacinto, Matagorda County became one of the original twenty-three counties of the new republic. The county was organized in 1837, and the town of Matagorda (Spanish for "brush") was the natural selection for the county seat.

The first jail was ordered by the commissioners' court on May 16, 1853, but it was not completed and accepted until November 1853. In 1870 a new

Matagorda County jail, 1931–1983, Bay City, Texas. Photo courtesy of Mary Belle Ingram, Matagorda County Museum.

wooden jail was built. In October 1881 the commissioners ordered a third wooden jail. William Dunbar was paid $500 in $20 gold pieces to build it. The jail, about 20' by 20', built of heavy lumber, and with a hip roof, had barred windows and a double plank door. The keep was used until 1894, when the county seat was moved to Bay City. The building still exists today, moved only a short distance from its original location. It was purchased by George Culver and converted into a residence.

In 1894 Bay City became the county seat. The commissioners' court made a contract with L. T. Noyes, agent for the Diebold Safe and Lock Company, to build a two-story brick facility and provide all of the materials and labor for $8,475. R. A. Mathis was appointed the supervising architect. In December 1895 the jail was completed. In 1909 the P. J. Pauly Company was asked to submit plans for a new lockup. The county took no action on the plans, however, and W. L. Boney was authorized to make repairs to the 1895 jail, so a new facility was evidently not built.

In April 1931 the county approved plans by Harry D. Payne of Houston for a fifth jail, and warrants for eighty thousand dollars for the construction were approved. The jail, a three-story Art Deco edifice made of brick, was completed in 1932. It was used for more than fifty years before its retirement.

Interviews conducted by the author: Mary Belle Ingram, Texas Historical Commission; Phyllis Culver.

Other resources: *Dallas Morning News, Texas Almanac, 1998–1999;* Tyler, Barnett, and Barkley, eds., *New Handbook of Texas,* vol. 1, 421, and vol. 4, 555, 556; Matagorda County Commissioners' Court Minutes; Brown, *Episcopal Church in Texas;* Metz, *Roadside History of Texas.*

Maverick County (Eagle Pass)

Maverick County was created in 1855 from Kinney County but was not organized until 1871. It was named for Sam Maverick, a native of South Carolina and an 1825 Yale graduate who moved to Texas in 1835. He took part in the siege of Bexar in December 1835 but soon afterward came down with chills and fever. He went home to recover but returned to Texas in 1838. Maverick, who had become a judge, was captured in San Antonio during Gen. Adrián Woll's invasion of Texas in 1842 and taken to the Perote Prison in the Castle of San Carlos in Vera Cruz. After release, he developed a cattle operation on Matagorda Peninsula, where his stock ranged freely, unbranded. Eventually, according to folklore, any and all unbranded cattle came to be known as mavericks.

Located two miles upstream from the historic smugglers' crossing of the Rio Grande, Eagle Pass, the county seat, is named for the eagles that roosted in the trees nearby. Fort Duncan, near Eagle Pass, was established in 1849. Before 1871, Maverick County business was conducted in San Antonio by horseback, a long, hard, and risky trip. There was no jail at the time, and the justice of the peace was the only law. Prisoners were chained to a tree or placed in the Fort Duncan stockade to await the arrival of the sheriff, who then had to escort them to San Antonio.

In 1875 a jail was built with 18″ stone walls lined with 5″ live oak timbers. As Eagle Pass continued to grow, the decision was made to stop renting space for the court and to build a courthouse with an adjacent lockup. In 1885 San Antonio architects Wahrenberger and Beckman designed a Romanesque Revival courthouse and an adjacent two-story jail resembling a fort on the corner of North Jefferson and Quarry streets. The walls were 17″ thick masonry with a plastered surface.

Unfortu-
nately, in
1946 the
sixty-year-
old jail was
torn down
to make
room for
a modern
structure.
The beauti-
ful court-
house
has been
preserved.

Maverick County courthouse and jail, 1885–1946, Eagle
Pass, Texas. Photo courtesy of Al Kinsall, Fort Duncan
Museum Collection, Eagle Pass.

   In a famous case in 1889, Dick Duncan was tried for the
murder of four members of a San Saba family. Detective work
by the Texas Rangers connected Duncan to the four bodies
found in the Rio Grande. After conviction and appeal, he was
hanged in September 1891.

   Interviews conducted by the author: Al Kinsall, *Eagle Pass News;*
Romelia Cardona, Maverick County Human Resources Department.
   Other resources: *Dallas Morning News, Texas Almanac, 1998–1999;* Metz,
Roadside History of Texas; Tyler, Barnett, and Barkley, eds., *New Handbook
of Texas,* vol. 2, 751, vol. 4, 54, 575, and vol. 5, 156; W. Robinson, *People's
Architecture;* Kelsey and Dyal, *Courthouses of Texas;* Dorothy Ostrom
Worrell, *Eagle Pass News Guide,* Eagle Pass, Tex., June 16, 1949; Ben E.
Pingenot, *Eagle Pass News Guide,* Eagle Pass, Tex., Sept. 17, 1971.

McCulloch County (Brady)

In 1831 Jim Bowie and his brother Rezin explored the San
Saba River valley, looking for silver mines. They found
no silver but encountered plenty of Indians. The story goes
that they fought a large group of Tawakonis on Calf Creek in
southwestern McCulloch County for nine days before making
their escape. The number of Indians varies from 100 to 200,
depending on who is relating the tale, but no one ever accused
Jim Bowie of underestimation in telling a story. The town of

McCulloch County jail, 1910–1974, Brady, Texas.

Camp San Saba on the San Saba River in southern McCulloch County is in the vicinity of an early Texas Ranger camp and near the spot where John Meusebach, founder of Fredericksburg, met and negotiated a peace treaty with the Comanche chiefs in 1847.

McCulloch County was created in 1856, but hostile Comanche Indians delayed settlement until after 1870. When the county was organized in 1876, Brady City, named for nearby Brady Creek, was chosen as the county seat. Its name was later shortened to Brady.

In 1877 the court advertised for bids to build a courthouse and a jail. Only one bid—by John McDonald of Austin—was submitted. It was accepted, and the job was completed by January 1878. Rapid growth, widespread lawlessness, or both began to tax the jail's capacity within a few months. In 1885 it was necessary to remove prisoners to Mason or San Saba counties for safekeeping. In 1886 eighty-nine hundred dollars for construction was approved, but procrastination ruled while the commissioners studied the problem. Pressure for a new lockup mounted, and in 1909 the old jail and lot were sold, and a new site was purchased one block away on block 21 (original city survey block number).

The Southern Structural Steel Company built the new facility. By April 1910 an imposing Romanesque Revival facility in red brick was finished. It included the usual gallows arrangement, extensive jailer's quarters on the first floor, and cells for the prisoners on the second and third floors. The cost was $13,950. The lockup was used until 1974 before replace-

ment. The Heart of Texas Historical Museum inherited the
building and now maintains an excellent museum within.

Interviews conducted by the author: Wayne Spiller; Murle Hendley,
Heart of Texas Museum; Beverly Striegler, secretary, Heart of Texas
Museum.

Other resources: *Dallas Morning News, Texas Almanac, 1998–1999;* Tyler,
Barnett, and Barkley, eds., *New Handbook of Texas,* vol. 1, 697, 898, 946,
and vol. 4, 3887; Metz, *Roadside History of Texas;* DeLorme Mapping,
Texas Atlas and Gazetteer; Barfoot, "History of McCulloch County, Texas";
W. Robinson, *People's Architecture.*

McLennan County (Waco)

Named for settler Neil McLennan, McLennan County
was created from Milam County and organized in 1850.
The area was the traditional home of the Tonkawa, Waco, and
Wichita Indian tribes, who camped on the banks of the Brazos
River near several springs. After they were displaced by Anglos,
the area around Waco Spring was conveyed to the commissioners of the new county and reserved as a public square and
land for schools and churches. The community became Waco
when incorporated in 1856. Waco's economy was cotton based
until after the Civil War, when the cattle drives to Kansas and
the Midwest expanded. Hoping to eventually capitalize on the
cattle drives, the city officials hired a New York civil engineer,
Thomas M. Griffith, to supervise the construction of a toll
bridge for cows, wagons, and people across the 475-foot-wide
Brazos River. The bridge was completed in 1869 and served
until 1971.

Taking advantage of favorable legislation, McLennan
County decided to devote its entire share of the state tax in-
come for the years 1854 and 1855 toward building a county
jail. The facility was completed in October 1855 on the northeast corner of Franklin and Third streets. Although the adjacent courthouse site was sold and the courthouse moved, the
lockup remained in place until June 1874, when a second jail
and a third courthouse were planned. The architect for the
new project was W. C. Dodson of Waco. Apparently in July

The historic old jail house, another view.

McLennan County jail, 1903–1953, Waco, Texas. Photo courtesy of the Texas Collection, Baylor University, Waco.

of that year the prisoners, eschewing the prospect of moving into a comfortable new slammer, attempted a jailbreak. Additional guards arrived to squelch the escape, and the ungrateful prisoners soon found themselves secured in the new jail described only as having a tin mansard roof.

McLennan County's third detention center was proposed, and bonds were passed by a vote of two to one for a new courthouse complex in April 1900. W. C. Dodson was again employed as the supervising architect, while J. Riely Gordon of Dallas provided complete drawings and specifications. P. H. Harris of Waco built and completed the new structure in December 1903. It served until 1952.

McLennan County perhaps holds the record in Texas for the last legal execution by hanging on July 30, 1923. On that day Roy Mitchell, a black man convicted of rape and serial murder, was hanged on a scaffold built on the county courthouse lawn.

Interviews conducted by the author: E. L. Henson; Kendra Trachta, Institute of Texan Cultures at San Antonio; Kay Elliott, deputy county clerk; Kent Keeth, Baylor University Library, Texas Collection; Bill Buckner, McLennan County Library.

Other resources: *Dallas Morning News, Texas Almanac, 1998–1999;* Tyler, Barnett, and Barkley, eds., *New Handbook of Texas,* vol. 4, 430, and vol. 6, 776; McLennan Commissioners' Court Minutes, Dec. 10, 1903; Metz, *Roadside History of Texas;* W. Robinson, *People's Architecture;* Reading, *Arrows over Texas.*

McMullen County (Tilden)

McMullen County was created in 1858 and organized in 1862. It was named for Irish entrepreneur John McMullen, founder of San Patricio, Texas. Because of uncontrolled Indian attacks and widespread lawlessness in the Nueces Strip, especially during the Civil War, the county was abandoned. In 1877, however, it was reorganized, and Dog Town was chosen as the county seat.

Dog Town was a small community that formed on the banks of the Frio River around 1858. At that time it was called Rio Frio and consisted of about thirty people huddled together for protection. Sometime after 1860 the name was changed to Dog Town, supposedly because the citizens awakened one morning to find fifteen dogs dead on the street after a cowboy shooting spree. The name stuck and was accepted until the town was selected and surveyed in 1877 to be the county seat. Discretion prevailed, and the name was changed to Tilden in honor of Samuel J. Tilden, unsuccessful Democratic candidate for president in 1876. (Tilden won the popular vote but lost in the electoral college.)

Shortly after organization in 1880, the county built its first and only jail at a cost of twenty-eight hundred dollars. Built of native limestone blocks, it was a single-story rectangular structure located about fifty feet east of the courthouse. It was used until a new courthouse annex, including a jail complex on the first floor, was built in 1967. After being abandoned as a lockup, the 1880

McMullen County jail, 1880–1969, Tilden, Texas. Photo by Stanley Gilbert. From the author's collection.

building became a grocery store. Later Maude Holland and Pearl Holland used it as a café and beer hall called the Jail House Café. After that it became the office of the Soil and Water Conservation District #353. Even the jail cell in the courthouse annex is no longer used—prisoners are now sent to George West in Live Oak County.

Interviews conducted by the author: Judge Elaine Franklin; Judge Linda Lee Henry; Larry D. Coffman, soil conservation officer.

Other resources: *Dallas Morning News, Texas Almanac, 1998–1999;* Tyler, Barnett, and Barkley, eds., *New Handbook of Texas,* vol. 4, 437, and vol. 6, 497; Kelsey and Dyal, *Courthouses of Texas.*

Medina County (Hondo)

Named for the river that flows through the area, Medina County was created from Bexar County in 1894 and organized in that same year. The river, in turn, was named for an early Spanish engineer, Pedro Medina.

Henri Castro, for whom Castroville is named, was a French-man from Paris who obtained two land grants from the Republic of Texas in 1842. One of his grants was four miles west of the Medina River. He then purchased sixteen leagues of land (about 70,848 acres) located between the Medina River and his grant, giving him the water necessary for his colony. Castro proceeded to recruit farmers from Alsace-Lorraine and arranged ships and transportation to bring them to Texas to settle along the Medina River and lands west. Many of the original cot-

Medina County jail, 1893–1946, Hondo, Texas.

tages, built in the Alsace tradition, stand today and are occupied by descendants of Castroville's colonists.

When Medina County was organized, Castroville was
made the county seat. The Southern Pacific Railroad, however, building westward in 1880, asked the Castroville citizens
for a bonus to bring the tracks to them. When the bonus was
denied, the tracks went south of town. As expected, within
ten years the people voted to move the county seat to Hondo,
where the Galveston, Harrisburg, and San Antonio Railroad
had built a town and sold lots in 1881.

The first jail in Hondo was built in 1893. The two-story
native limestone building with a prominent tower in front had
sheriff's quarters and a gallows, which is said to have been used
only once. The facility was constructed by Martin, Byrnes,
and Johnson on the northeast corner of the courthouse square
and was used until 1946. In that year a new jail was built next
door, and the old jail was made into full-time sheriff's quarters.

Interviews conducted by the author: Judge David F. Montgomery;
Oliver Reinhart.

Other resources: *Dallas Morning News, Texas Almanac, 1998–1999;* Metz,
Roadside History of Texas; Tyler, Barnett, and Barkley, eds., *New Handbook
of Texas,* vol. 1, 1424, vol. 3, 681, and vol. 4, 602; Kelsey and Dyal, *Courthouses of Texas.*

Menard County (Menard)

Menard County was created from Bexar County in
1858 and organized in 1871. Both the county and
the county seat were named for the founder of Galveston,
Michel B. Menard. Menard County's history as a Spanish territory began in the San Saba River valley. The pleasant and
fertile valley, long the domain of Apaches and Comanches,
beckoned as a place to set up a mission to convert the Indians
to Christianity. In 1737 priests and colonists set about constructing Mission Santa Cruz de San Saba and its protective
presidio on the banks of the San Saba River near present-day
Menard. In March 1758 hundreds of Wichita and Comanche
Indians swarmed out of the surrounding hills and overran

Menard County jail, 1871–1886, Menard, Texas.

and burned the log mission. The presidio, with some of the soldiers and mission members, weathered the attack. In August 1759 the Spanish launched a punitive expedition against the Indians but were defeated in the battle of Spanish Fort on the Red River. The presidio got a new commander and garrison, but after eleven years of deprivation and adversity, the soldiers were withdrawn as the Spanish frontier retreated.

One hundred years later, as Anglos began to move in, the Indians were no less dangerous. Sudden attacks and killings were frequent. In 1871 the first jail in Menard County was built just west of the later Lukenbach Hardware Building. The first floor had a store in front with the jail at the back. The second floor, accessed only by an outside stairway on the west wall, was the courtroom. Behind the courtroom was the entrance—through a trapdoor and down a ladder—to the dungeon-type cell below. Ida Mae Davis's father, a friend of the sheriff, told her about one prisoner who jumped over the trapdoor each time they tried to put him down the ladder, so the sheriff finally picked him up by the feet and dropped him through the door head first. Recently the jail was purchased and restored as a private residence.

The second jail, completed in June 1886, was a freestanding, two-story limestone cube. It had castled turrets on each corner and crenellations on all four sides. Vickery and Haynes Company of Kimble County built it at a cost of $12,500. The facility was used for forty-five years until 1931, when a new courthouse with a jail on the top floor was completed.

Interviews conducted by the author: Tommye Phillips, librarian; Ida Mae Davis.

Other resources: *Dallas Morning News, Texas Almanac, 1998–1999;* De-Lorme Mapping, *Texas Atlas and Gazetteer;* Tyler, Barnett, and Barkley, eds., *New Handbook of Texas,* vol. 2, 1111, vol. 4, 614, and vol. 5, 878; Menard County Historical Society, *Menard County History.*

Midland County (Midland)

The Texas legislature created Midland County from Tom Green County in 1885. In the pioneer years Indian raids were a continual threat. The annual rainfall in the area averages a little less than fourteen inches. It is thought, however, that about twenty-two thousand years ago the Midland area was cool and wet, and fossil remains of "Midland Man" indicate that human precursors lived in the area then. The partial skull from the Folsom Culture (9,000–8,000 B.C.) found there is that of a woman. The big event in Midland's modern history was the discovery of oil in Midland County and nearby counties in 1923. The vast reservoir of the Permian Basin would build a remarkable city within a few years in that unpretentious landscape.

In August 1885 the Midland Town Company donated $3,000 to build a jail and courthouse. The commissioners accepted the grant and solicited bids for an adobe structure. In September of that year the only bid was rejected, so a frame courthouse was constructed instead and later a brick building with a soli-

Midland County jail, 1930–present, Midland, Texas. Courtesy of Southern Steel Company.

tary jail cell with two bunks. The cost was $3,000, and the lockup was used until 1905. Surprisingly, crime was not a big problem. The first person arrested was brought to court for the use of "loud and abusive language." Actually, during that time, about the only other thing that could bring about a fine was gambling. However, since almost everyone gambled a little, fines were rarely imposed.

About 1909, the court contracted with the Southern Structural Steel Company to build a jail. The finished product turned out to be similar to the 1909 Haskell County jail and the 1910 McCulloch County jail. The facility was a three-story brick Victorian design with white marble arches over the windows and commodious sheriff's quarters on the first floor. This building was used until 1930.

The third courthouse in Midland was built in 1930 with a jail on the fourth floor. The cells and ironwork were provided by Southern Prison Company. The Art Deco building, designed by Voelcker and Dixon, was extensively remodeled in 1974. The original style was completely erased by handsome Greek Revival changes designed by Dixon and Staley. A fifth floor was added to the courthouse, and the jail was moved to a separate location.

Interviews conducted by the author: Sgt. Robert Crowley, Midland County Sheriff's Department; Kathee Forrest, Southern Steel Company; Nancy R. McKinley, president, Midland Historical Society.

Other resources: *Dallas Morning News, Texas Almanac, 1998–1999;* Tyler, Barnett, and Barkley, eds., *New Handbook of Texas,* vol. 4, 706, 708; Griffin, *Land of the High Sky;* Tyler and Tyler, *Texas Museums;* Metz, *Roadside History of Texas;* Kelsey and Dyal, *Courthouses of Texas.*

Milam County (Cameron)

Milam County was created in 1836 as one of the original twenty-three counties of the Republic of Texas. In 1846 the town of Cameron was founded and named for Ewing Cameron, a Texas soldier and casualty of the ill-fated Mier expedition. When Burleson County was created out of Milam County, Cameron became the new county seat for the latter.

In 1845
Robert H.
Flanniken,
sheriff from
Febru-
ary 1845 to
July 1846,
said the first
jail "was
built of logs,
hewn square
and fitted
one on the

Milam County jail, 1895–1974, Cameron, Texas.

other," whereas another source says there was no jail in Milam
County. The consensus is that there was a double-walled log
dungeon with a single trapdoor in the top through which prisoners were admitted by ladder. Milam County sent some prisoners to the Burleson County jail in Caldwell, a situation that
lasted until about 1875, when a new lockup became available.

In 1874 the commissioners began planning another jail and
a new courthouse. There was a temporary delay, however,
while the choice between Rockdale and Cameron as the seat
of government was resolved. After the vote favored Cameron,
the commissioners chose architects Larmour and Klerke to design the new jail, and a contract was awarded to Jackson and
Arnold in 1875 for construction. Cells and iron doors were
ordered from the Pauly Jail Manufacturing Company. In
July 1875 the two-story brick jail, on the corner across from
the courthouse, was complete. It was now possible to separate
prisoners with minor offenses from the more violent element,
a new concept in prison management at that time.

By 1893, the 1875 jail had deteriorated, and the commissioners decided to build a new structure. This time, the
county contracted with Pauly Jail Manufacturing to both design and build the jail. Pauly was capable of planning the
whole project, prefabricating the cells and ironwork, shipping
the components to Texas, and assembling the structure on site.
In 1895 the jail was completed. (This facility most resembled
an 1896 lockup in Austin County.) The jail had sheriff's quar-

ters (consisting of seven rooms) on the first floor. There were eleven prison cells on the first floor, four on the second, and two on the third. The gallows was never used, but in 1907 a prisoner was taken from the building by a mob and hanged from the limb of a tree on the courthouse square. The old red jail was used until 1974.

The notorious bank robber Whitey Walker was held in the Milam County jail in the 1930s. He managed to escape but left a note for Sheriff L. L. Blalock saying, "I hate to do this to you, Mr. Blalock, you've been so kind to me—but I'll be back." He was correct. He was soon recaptured in Arkansas and returned to the Milam County jail.

Interview conducted by the author: Charles D. King, Milam County Historical Museum.

Other resources: *Dallas Morning News, Texas Almanac, 1998–1999;* Tyler, Barnett, and Barkley, eds., *New Handbook of Texas,* vol. 1, 917, and vol. 4, 119; Batte, *History of Milam County, Texas;* Werner, *History of the Buildings and the People of Old Town Cameron;* Neely, "Jail for Milam County"; W. Robinson, *People's Architecture.*

Mills County (Goldthwaite)

Mills County was created in 1887 from surrounding Brown, Comanche, Hamilton, and Lampasas counties. It was named for John Mills, an early pioneer in the area. In 1885 the town of Goldthwaite had been founded by the Gulf, Colorado, and Santa Fe Railroad and named for railroad agent Joe E. Goldthwaite. When Mills County was formed, Goldthwaite became the county seat.

Before the Civil War, the population was sparse due to violent raids by the Apache and Comanche Indians, who preyed on each other as well as on the white settlers. After the war, the failure of law enforcement in the frontier counties allowed an influx of horse thieves, rustlers, and gunmen. As might be expected, vigilantism developed, and, in turn, a countervigilante group formed, all of which resulted in a further degeneration of law and order. A good jail was needed, but even when present, it was not always used. The vigilante groups, known

as mobs,
were in re-
ality secret
organiza-
tions for
both good
and bad.
In 1897
the Texas
Rangers
were called
in. Over
time and

Mills County jail, 1888–1950, Goldthwaite, Texas.

with some difficulty, they restored order by arresting some of
the self-appointed agents of justice.

The first jail in Goldthwaite was a building constructed of
2″ by 12″ lumber with a flat roof, built on the south side of
the courthouse square. It was a much-needed calaboose that
would serve until a more permanent structure could be finished. In 1888 the first masonry jail was completed, two years
before the courthouse was finished, giving some idea of the
priorities of the desperate citizens. Designed by J. B. Dumas
and built by Green and Nichols of Lampasas, the two-story
native limestone building is still in excellent condition today.
L. T. Noyes, agent for the Diebold Safe and Lock Company,
contracted to provide the cells and ironwork for $4,300, while
the original cost of the building was $4,550. The first floor
contained generous sheriff's quarters, and the prisoners were
kept on the second floor. There was a fire in the jail in 1911,
but the facility was restored to its original condition. The
structure continued to serve its intended purpose until the
1950s. The first-floor sheriff's quarters are now used by
the chamber of commerce.

Interviews conducted by the author: Normajo Reynolds, Goldthwaite
Chamber of Commerce; Beulah Roberts, county clerk.

Other resources: *Dallas Morning News, Texas Almanac, 1998–1999;* Tyler,
Barnett, and Barkley, eds., *New Handbook of Texas,* vol. 3, 203, and vol. 4,
752; Bowles, *No-man's Land Becomes a County;* Sonnichsen, *I'll Die before
I'll Run.*

Mitchell County (Colorado City)

Named for Asa and Eli Mitchell, brothers who were at the battle of Gonzales and soldiers at the battle of San Jacinto, Mitchell County was created in 1876, along with numerous other Panhandle counties, and organized in 1881. Colorado City began as a Ranger camp in 1877, and after the Texas and Pacific Railroad made a station there, it became a shipping point for cattle.

At first the county had no jail, and prisoners were simply chained to a convenient mesquite tree. The first jail bonds were passed in February 1881, and a simple two-story cube fortress of native limestone was built with a tower on one corner. There were crenellations on all four sides of the roof. The architect and builder are unknown.

In January 1881 a popular, successful, and proud cattleman, P. Patterson, ran for sheriff of the new county. Before the election Patterson was inclined to drink too much and had been arrested by the Texas Rangers three times and chained to a mesquite tree until sober. When defeated in the election, he blamed the Rangers for the loss. On May 16, 1881, near the Nip and Tuck Saloon, Patterson cursed three Texas Rangers, J. M. Sedberry, Jeff Davis Milton, and L. B. Wells. When asked to give up his gun, Patterson refused, and an effort to disarm him followed. Patterson drew his gun and shot at Sedberry, missing, but Milton and Wells both drew, and Patterson was killed. The Rangers turned themselves in to Sheriff Dick Ware, who arrested them.

Mitchell County jail, 1915–?, Colorado City, Texas. Photo courtesy of the Heart of West Texas Museum, Colorado City.

In a change of venue, they were tried in Taylor County and acquitted.

Dick Ware, who had won the election, was famous as the Texas Ranger who killed Sam Bass on July 18, 1878. The story is that Ware was in a barbershop in Round Rock getting a shave and haircut when Sam Bass and Seaborn Barnes came into town to rob the bank. Hearing a commotion, Ware jumped from the barber's chair and ran into the street, where he shot Barnes and wounded Bass. Later, Ware said he knew he had hit Bass because he saw the dust puff out of his clothes when he was shot. Before he died of his wound, Bass said that the man who shot him had shaving lather all over his face. Ware served as sheriff of Mitchell County from February 9, 1881, to November 15, 1892.

In 1915 another jail was built by contractor Ray Mayo for seventy-five hundred dollars. Southern Structural Steel of San Antonio designed the structure and provided the cells and ironwork. Dick Gregory was the sheriff from 1922 until 1941. During that time there was little to do in the small West Texas town, and a number of the young boys were getting into trouble. Sheriff Gregory bought baseballs and bats and required the youngsters to come to the jail yard and play baseball every weekday afternoon. In 1936 an annex was added, and the sheriff's quarters were moved there so that the whole 1915 building could serve as the jail. The facility was used until 1952, when a new structure designed by Batter Brasher was built.

Interviews conducted by the author: Dorothy Forbs, Heart of West Texas Museum; Sheriff Patrick Toombs.

Other resources: *Dallas Morning News, Texas Almanac, 1998–1999;* Tyler, Barnett, and Barkley, eds., *New Handbook of Texas,* vol. 2, 223, and vol. 4, 752; W. Robinson, *People's Architecture.*

Montague County (Montague)

Montague County, named for Daniel Montague, early pioneer and land surveyor, was created in 1857 from Cooke County and organized the following year. Montague

Montague County jail, 1927–1980, Montague, Texas.

was the foreman of the jury in 1862 that was responsible for the "great hanging" in Gainesville, in which forty men, so-called Union sympathizers, were hanged for treason against the Confederacy. It is generally felt that most of the men were innocent. After the Civil War, Montague fled to Mexico and was the only member of that jury that avoided prosecution during Reconstruction.

Montague County is bordered by the Red River on the north. One mile south of the river is the town of Spanish Fort, near the sites of two historic Taovaya Indian villages. (The Taovayas were a subgroup of the Wichitas, who were allies of the Comanches.) In 1759 the Spanish, under Col. Diego Ortiz Parilla, conducted a punitive expedition against the Indians for their devastating raid against the San Saba mission in Menard County the previous year. They found the villages well fortified with stockade and moat and under French influence. After four hours of battle, during which the Spanish were never able to breach the fortifications, the attackers fled, leaving two cannons and much equipment.

Little is recorded of the first jail in Montague County. The second lockup was on the third floor of the courthouse, which was designed by George Burnett in 1912. The Pauly Jail Manufacturing Company provided the cells and ironwork. The facility was used until a third—and separate—detention center was built on the corner of the courthouse square in 1927. The Southern Prison Company built the two-story 1927 jail of brown brick. It had quarters for the sheriff on the first floor and a sixteen-bed cellblock on the second floor. The jail was used until 1980, when it was replaced with a modern facility.

Interviews conducted by the author: Melvin Fenoglio, Texas Historical Commission; Judge Cleve E. Steed.

Other resources: *Dallas Morning News, Texas Almanac, 1998–1999;* Tyler, Barnett, and Barkley, eds., *New Handbook of Texas,* vol. 3, 47, 309, vol. 4, 794, 795, and vol. 6, 3, 4; Newcomb, *Indians of Texas.*

Montgomery County (Conroe)

Montgomery County was created in 1837 from Washington County and was named for Andrew Jackson Montgomery, a cousin of Gen. Richard Montgomery, veteran of the American Revolution. Andrew Montgomery entered Texas at age eighteen as a scout with the James Long expedition and was befriended by the Bidai Indians, thus avoiding expulsion by the Spanish after the expedition was defeated. He founded a trading post that would later become the town of Montgomery.

Montgomery was selected as the first county seat in 1837. In March 1838, a house was rented to serve as the courthouse, and in April the court addressed the problem of a jail. A log keep was built; in 1842 a two-story frame courthouse was constructed. As the town thrived, that structure was replaced in 1855 by a large brick building.

Conroe began as a sawmill site, and eventually, driven by the new lumber industry, the population reached three hundred. The Santa Fe Railroad soon extended its tracks to the sawmill. In 1889 an election was held, and the county seat was moved to Conroe.

In 1891 Houston architect Eugene Heiner designed a courthouse and a separate jail for the new county seat. Both buildings were built of steel and locally manufactured brick. The contractors were Moody and Ellis of Greenville, Texas, who completed the project in the fall of 1891 at a cost of $25,295. The jail burned in 1931, and in 1936 a new courthouse with a lockup on the top floor, designed by Joseph Finger, was constructed. In 1965 the courthouse was extensively remodeled, and the jail was moved.

Interviews conducted by the author: Terri Strozier, secretary for Judge Alan Sadler; Gertie Spencer, Heritage Museum of Montgomery County.

Other resources: *Dallas Morning News, Texas Almanac, 1998–1999;* Tyler, Barnett, and Barkley, eds., *New Handbook of Texas,* vol. 1, 278, vol. 4, 801, 803, and vol. 6, 998; Gandy, "History of Montgomery County, Texas"; Montgomery, *History of Montgomery County.*

Moore County (Dumas)

Moore County, in the extreme northern Texas Panhandle, was created along with other Panhandle counties in 1876, when the territory was wrested from the Comanche Indians at the end of the Red River War. The Indians of the Panhandle probably arrived in strength in Texas in the late seventeenth century. By the time Anglo settlers arrived in the nineteenth century, the Comanche were dominant. After the Red River War of the 1870s, the Panhandle settlers were free of the Indian threat, and ranching and later farming slowly developed.

The county was organized in 1892 and named for Commodore Edwin Ward Moore, commander of the navy of the Republic of Texas. The county seat of Dumas was named for Lewis Dumas, president of the Panhandle Townsite Company, which bought railroad easements and laid out the town. Dumas had a difficult beginning. Since there was no railroad, everything had to be hauled by wagon from Amarillo. In 1931 the North Plains and Santa Fe Railway Company extended a line into Dumas. In 1926 oil production had begun in Moore County and other adjacent counties, and the railroad followed the development. It is interesting to note that two-thirds of the helium produced in the United States is extracted from the natural gas wells in Moore County.

In the summer of 1927 Capt. William Sterling's Rangers arrested "Shine" Popejoy and broke up the large still that he had located in a Moore County canyon. When they took Popejoy to Dumas, they were surprised to learn that there was no jail. That was corrected when the second courthouse in Moore County, designed by Berry and Hatch, was built in 1930 with a county lockup on the top floor. The facility included sheriff's quarters and was used until 1979, when a separate jail was built next to the courthouse.

Interviews conducted by the author: Sheriff H. T. Montgomery; Deputy Sheriff Troy L. Walker.

Other resources: *Dallas Morning News, Texas Almanac, 1998–1999;* Tyler, Barnett, and Barkley, eds., *New Handbook of Texas,* vol. 1, 475, 650, vol. 2, 723, and vol. 4, 826; Metz, *Roadside History of Texas;* DeLorme Mapping, *Texas Atlas and Gazetteer;* Newcomb, *Indians of Texas;* Mike Cox, *Texas Ranger Tales;* Sterling, *Trails and Trials of a Texas Ranger.*

Morris County (Daingerfield)

Morris County in East Texas is one of the smallest counties in the state. It is heavily wooded and, before 1800, was for centuries the home of the Caddo Indians. The county is named for W. W. Morris, an early judge and legislator. The county seat, Daingerfield, is named for Capt. London Daingerfield who, with about one hundred men, fought a lengthy and bloody engagement with the Indians in 1830 over the use of a spring near the present site of Daingerfield. Daingerfield was killed in the battle, but a town with his name began to develop there near the spring.

Morris County did not exist until it was created from Titus County in 1877. Daingerfield became the county seat. Around that time, the Louisiana, Arkansas, and Texas Railroad laid track but missed Daingerfield by about half a mile. Naturally, a new town developed near the track, and so "New Town" was used to distinguish the new part from "Old Town."

The first jail in Morris County was built in Old Town in 1881. Although made of wood, it was used until 1896, when a two-story brick lockup was constructed on Jefferson Street in

Morris County jail, 1896–1971, Daingerfield, Texas.

New Town. The 1896 jail had sixteen bunks in a single large room on the second floor. In the center of the room, an iron ball and chain were fixed to the floor to accommodate unruly or troublesome prisoners. That facility was used for seventy-five years.

Interviews conducted by the author: Sheriff C. R. Blackburn; Kathy Kimberly; William R. Porter, district judge; Doris McNatt.

Other resources: *Dallas Morning News, Texas Almanac, 1998–1999;* Tyler, Barnett, and Barkley, eds., *New Handbook of Texas,* vol. 2, 472, and vol. 4, 846; Tyler and Tyler, *Texas Museums;* Kelsey and Dyal, *Courthouses of Texas;* McKellar, *History of Daingerfield, Texas.*

Motley County (Matador)

Motley County, along with other Panhandle counties, was created in 1876 after the vast herds of buffalo had nearly been exterminated and the Indians had been removed to reservations. It was organized in 1891 and named for J. W. Mottley, signer of the Texas Declaration of Independence. Unfortunately, the spelling of his name was a little damaged in the process.

In 1879 a cattle company was formed by retired buffalo hunter Henry Campbell and banker A. M. Britton. Campbell bought land on the Pease River. He then bought cattle and occupied an abandoned dugout at Ballard Springs, named for a fellow buffalo hunter he had known. Campbell and Britton named their company the Matador Cattle Company. Additional financing was needed, so Britton went to Dundee, Scotland,

Motley County jail, 1891–1979, Matador, Texas.

and found investors. The firm's name was changed to the
Matador Land and Cattle Company. Soon the company controlled 1,500,000 acres and owned fifty thousand head of
cattle.

The Motley County jail was built in 1891 because citizens
and cowboys grew tired of taking turns guarding prisoners.
Judging from the long list of escapees, the sievelike structure
seems to have held only the most apathetic of detainees. The
very first prisoner, convicted of murder, escaped twice before
being sent in desperation to the penitentiary in Huntsville.

The 1891 jail, built by J. F. Aiken and J. T. Cornett, was
a simple cube of locally quarried limestone. It had two stories
with cells for the prisoners on the top floor and jailer's quarters
on the ground floor. There was a gallows with a trapdoor at
the top of the stairs to the second floor, but it was never used.

At the turn of the century, one convicted murderer, named
Danby, was a first-class water witcher. In that arid country,
water-well witching was a valuable skill, so the ranchers would
get Danby out of jail so that he could come and help. Danby
always came back, but on the day before his scheduled hanging, he did not return and was never heard from again. Locals
said his execution would have been a waste of a rare talent.

Interviews conducted by the author: Ardyth Bagwell, Armstrong
County historian; Lucretia Campbell, county and district clerk; Suzanne
Abbott, librarian.

Other resources: *Dallas Morning News, Texas Almanac, 1998–1999;* Tyler,
Barnett, and Barkley, eds., *New Handbook of Texas,* vol. 4, 553, 857; Metz,
Roadside History of Texas; Brown, *Motley County's Gallows.*

Nacogdoches County (Nacogdoches)

Nacogdoches County was named for the Nacogdoches
tribe of Indians, one of the large Caddo group that occupied the area. The town of Nacogdoches, like the city of
Bexar (later San Antonio), has played a long and important
role in Texas history. Early European explorers in the area
included Sieur de La Salle in 1685 and Alonso de León from
Mexico in 1689. In 1716 Domingo Ramón founded six mis-

Nacogdoches County jail, 1779–1868, Nacogdoches, Texas.
Photo from McDonald, *Old Stone Fort*. East Texas Research
Center, photo #P67A5 and Texas Tides Grant Project,
http://sfasu.edu.

sions in East Texas. One of these, Our Lady of the Guadalupe, was at the present site of Nacogdoches. The mission was on the traditional east–west Indian trading route, a trail that eventually became the route of the Old San Antonio Road (present-day state highway 21) between San Antonio and Nacogdoches. The viceroy in Mexico withdrew the colonists and the priests from the missions in 1772. By 1779, however, Antonio Gil Ibarvo returned to Nacogdoches, possibly with his eye on the smugglers' trade, and rebuilt the town. He also built a two-story stone building measuring 70′ by 20′ and 20′ tall; this edifice would later be known as the "Old Stone Fort." Over the next 125 years it would serve as general store, jail, trading post, fort, saloon, hotel, and fulcrum of conspiracy until torn down in 1902.

No one seems to doubt that the stone fort probably served as an early jail during the days of the republic. There are no verifiable records of early jail construction. After the Civil War, however, R. D. Orton was elected sheriff in 1867 and served until 1873. The Orton house reputedly had a "strong room" that was used to hold prisoners until their sentence was determined. Long jail sentences were not in vogue at the time. Trials were quick, justice swift, and either the accused was not guilty or punishment was meted out.

In 1912 Nacogdoches County built a new courthouse and constructed a two-story lockup on the southeast corner of the courthouse square at Main and North streets. Both buildings were used until 1958, when a new one-story courthouse, including a jail, was erected on the same corner.

Interviews conducted by the author: Bryan Holt Davis; Al Cage, Stephen F. Austin University; Campbell Cox; Carolyn Erickson; Sheriff Joe Evans; Tammy Gibson, City of Nacogdoches; Jere Jackson, Texas Historical Commission; John Lightfoot, retired sheriff; Mrs. Adlai Mast, Historical Association boards in Nacogdoches and Virginia, Texas; Diana Walker.

Other resources: *Dallas Morning News, Texas Almanac, 1998–1999;* Tyler, Barnett, and Barkley, eds., *New Handbook of Texas,* vol. 4, 686, 923, 925, 1140; Weddle, *Wilderness Manhunt;* Kelsey and Dyal, *Courthouses of Texas;* McDonald, *Old Stone Fort;* Nacogdoches Jaycees, *Bicentennial Commemorative History of Nacogdoches;* Nacogdoches Historical Society, *Nacogdoches Texas Centennial, 1716–1936.*

Navarro County (Corsicana)

Navarro County, fifty miles south of Dallas, was the home of the Comanche and Kickapoo Indian tribes in the early nineteenth century. Early settlers were John and Silas Parker, who came in 1833. They built a fort near the Navasota River, now in Limestone County about six miles north of Groesbeck. The fort, later known as Fort Parker, was the site of the famous Comanche Indian raid in 1836 in which Cynthia Ann Parker and others were kidnapped.

Navarro County was named for José Antonio Navarro, one of three Mexicans who signed the Texas Declaration of Independence. When the county was organized in 1846, Navarro was allowed to name the county seat. He named it Corsicana for Corsica, his parents' birthplace.

In 1894 oil and natural gas were discovered during a drilling for artesian water. This was the first major discovery west of the Mississippi River. J. S. Cullinan and Company built the first oil refinery in Texas in 1898. This established Corsicana as "the premier city of the Texas oil industry." (The company eventually passed through many hands and finally ended up with Exxon. As of this writing, production has been shut down.)

The first jail in Navarro County was a double-walled, single-room log building, probably a dungeon type. It is uncertain how long the log structure was used, but in 1876 the county built a new lockup and yet another in 1892. The location of these facilities is uncertain, and few photographs exist.

In 1884 the county bought 976 acres of land for a "poor farm." They built two houses, one for paupers and one for convicts—only slight distinction was made between the two. Two years later, three additional houses were built, one for the superintendent, one for people with severe mental disorders, and a "pesthouse" for those with smallpox. The convicts who were trusties were hired out to nearby farmers, and their pay for this work (one dollar per day) was applied to their fines. In 1906 a two-story brick jail, designed by architect W. B. Lockhead, was built on the poor farm. That same year, ten two-room cottages were built for the paupers. The poor farm was abolished in 1944.

In 1928 a new jail, at least partially built by Southern Prison Company of San Antonio, was completed. It was used until 1983 and finally torn down in 1996.

Interview conducted by the author: Bobbie Young, Navarro County Historical Society.

Other resources: *Dallas Morning News, Texas Almanac, 1998–1999;* Tyler, Barnett, and Barkley, eds., *New Handbook of Texas,* vol. 2, 339, 1113, and vol. 4, 954, 955; Metz, *Roadside History of Texas;* Navarro County Historical Society, *Navarro County History,* vol. 5; Rundell, *Early Texas Oil.*

Newton County (Newton)

Newton County was created in 1846 and was named for John Newton, a soldier of the American Revolution. The county is bordered on the east by the Sabine River and Louisiana and on the west by Jasper County. In some places, the county is less than eight miles wide. It has the highest annual rainfall, fifty-four inches, of any county in the state.

The prehistoric Indians of the area, the Atakapan (meaning "man-eaters" in the Choctaw language) were related to the Karankawa Indians and lived along the Sabine River and west to the Trinity River. Discussion of the Karankawa Indians inevitably brings up the question of cannibalism. After returning

to civiliza-
tion in 1721,
François
Simars de
Bellisle
wrote the
following
about the
Atakapans:
"When they
returned,
they threw
this Indian

Newton County jail, 1903–1936, Newton, Texas.

on the prairie. One of them cut his head off and another one
cut his arms off while they skinned him at the same time. Several of them ate the yellow fat which was still raw and finally
they devoured him completely." (In 1719 the captain of the
French ship *Maréchal d'Estrée* put Simars de Bellisle and four
others ashore on Galveston Island to fill water casks. Inexplica-
bly, he did not stay to pick the men up. All of them died except Bellisle, who remained a captive of the Indians until 1721,
when he made his escape with help from the Hasini Caddos.)

Newton County was cut out of Jasper County and organized in 1846. Burkeville was made the county seat in 1848,
but the seat of government was moved to Newton in 1853.
At that time, a wooden courthouse and jail were built on the
courthouse square. Following the Civil War, however, there
was no lockup. Verval Brown Cates tells about her grandfather, who was sheriff of Newton County from 1873 to 1884.
He kept the prisoners at home in a cabin he had built for that
purpose. Each prisoner had a ball and chain and was allowed
out during the daytime but locked in the cabin at night.

Interim details are unclear, but in 1903 a new courthouse
was built on the square with a separate jail on the southeast
corner. The architects were Martin and Moore of Comanche,
Texas. One person recalls that, around 1910, when he was
a child, a black man was convicted of murder and held in the
old jail. As the day of execution approached, the child and his
cousin would peep into the jail in anticipation of the awful

event and see the intended rope stretched up on the gallows, holding a sandbag to remove any elasticity.

In 1936 the old jail was torn down, and a new structure was built attached to the south side of the courthouse The architect was W. C. Meador, who had designed a lockup for nearby Jasper County. The Works Progress Administration did the construction, and the Southern Prison Company was the contractor for the cells and ironwork at a cost of $6,508.19. This facility was used until 1981.

Interviews conducted by the author: Mrs. Earl Hines, Texas Historical Commission; Bonnie Smith, Newton County Historical Commission.

Other resources: *Dallas Morning News, Texas Almanac, 1998–1999;* Tyler, Barnett, and Barkley, eds., *New Handbook of Texas,* vol. 4, 1003, 1005, and vol. 6, 1147; Newcomb, *Indians of Texas;* Bolton, *Texas in the Middle Eighteenth Century; Jasper News-boy,* Feb. 13, 1936, and Mar. 19, 1936; Newton County Historical Commission, *Glimpses of Newton County History;* Hines, *Newton County Nuggets.*

Nolan County (Sweetwater)

Nolan County was created in 1876 and organized in 1881. It was named for Phillip Nolan, the first of a long line of unauthorized adventurers who came to Texas. Nolan was a protégé of Gen. James Wilkinson, whose dubious career saw him in and out of the army, swearing allegiance to the Spanish governor in New Orleans and even scheming with Aaron Burr and later turning against him. Nolan made five forays into Texas between 1794 and 1800, supposedly to trade and catch wild horses. On his last trip he ventured as far north as the Brazos River near Waco, where he was intercepted and killed by Spanish troops.

Sweetwater, named for a nearby creek, was designated the county seat when the county was organized. Before the first jail was built, prisoners were either boarded under guard in a private home or chained to a convenient tree. In the spring of 1882 Martin, Byrnes, and Johnson completed the first jail, a two-story stone building. In 1884, the Sweetwater lockup was disinfected, and privies were added. Heating came in 1885.

By 1904 a concrete floor had been added, and the Southern Structural Steel Company had completed renovations that included steel cages.

Nolan County jail, 1912–1927, Sweetwater, Texas. Photo courtesy of Travis Monday.

In 1912 Nolan County's second jail, a three-story red brick building on the corner of Third and Locust streets, was built for fifteen thousand dollars. Southern Structural Steel Company was once again the contractor, including the cells and ironwork.

By 1927 the commissioners again considered building a new lockup and first consulted Page Brothers, Austin architects. After some discussion, however, the county officials decided to remodel the top floor of the three-story courthouse, which had been built in 1917. The third floor had never been fully utilized and seemed appropriate for use as a detention center. The contractor for the work was Myers and Johnson, and Pauly Jail and Manufacturing Company received the contract to provide the cells and ironwork. The cost was $39,214. The old red brick jail was sold and razed in 1928. On October 27, 1927, a few days before the new facility was to be occupied, six prisoners made their escape from the old lockup. One of the escapees was recaptured, however, and became the first resident of the new jail in November. Two attempted escapes from the new structure were frustrated in December and the following March. The building was used for fifty years until a new courthouse with a jail was built in 1977.

Interviews conducted by the author: Frances Cupp, Nolan County Pioneer Museum; Donnie Rennefeld, Nolan County sheriff; Carlos Morris; Travis Monday.

Other resources: *Dallas Morning News, Texas Almanac, 1998–1999;* Tyler, Barnett, and Barkley, eds., *New Handbook of Texas,* vol. 4, 1026, and vol. 6, 973; W. Robinson, *People's Architecture; Sweetwater Weekly Reporter,* Nov. 12, 2000; *Nolan County News,* Oct. 27, 1927; *Sweetwater Daily Reporter,* Nov. 18, 1927.

Nueces County (Corpus Christi)

Nueces County was formed from San Patricio County in 1846 and included all of the territory south of Bexar County to the Rio Grande and east to the Nueces River. San Patricio County had been one of the original twenty-three counties formed by the Republic of Texas in 1836. Nueces County was organized in 1846 under the state government, and Corpus Christi was incorporated that same year and became the county seat.

Corpus Christi began as a trading post that was founded in 1836 by Henry Lawrence Kinney and William P. Aubrey on the west coast of Corpus Christi Bay. By 1846 the settlement, originally called Kinney's Stockade, was flourishing and beginning to be known as Corpus Christi, the Spanish name of the bay on which it was located. Contemporary visitors described it as "a half-dozen stores and a grog shop" with about fifty resident families. In July 1845, Zachary Taylor and a small army camped near Kinney's Stockade and stayed for nine months while Washington officials negotiated unsuccessfully with the Mexican government to avoid war over the pending annexation of Texas to the United States.

In 1857 Nueces County bought three lots from Henry Kinney for three hundred dollars and built a second courthouse to replace the temporary 1846 building. In time, two additional courthouses would be built on these lots, one in 1876 and another in 1914. In 1892 a two-story brick jail was built on one of the lots next to the older courthouses. The architect was J. Riely Gordon and Laub. The Reid and Sutherland Company constructed the facility. This lockup was used for twenty-three years.

In 1915 the old courthouses were torn down, and a reinforced concrete-and-brick Classical Revival building, designed by Harvey L. Page of San Antonio, was built on the three lots at Mesquite and Belden streets. The contractor was Gordon Jones Construction Company of San Antonio. The first four floors held the courtrooms and offices. The new county jail, with cells and ironwork provided by the Southern Structural Steel Company, occupied the top two floors and was separated from the lower floors by an air space for noise control. The jail section included jailer's quarters and law enforcement offices. The courthouse and jail were remodeled in 1930, 1965, and 1970. The 1915 jail was used until 1977.

Interviews conducted by the author: Faryce Goode-Macon, Corpus Christi City Planning; Margaret Walberg; Patrick McGloin, restoration architect.

Other resources: *Dallas Morning News, Texas Almanac, 1998–1999;* Tyler, Barnett, and Barkley, eds., *New Handbook of Texas,* vol. 2, 332, vol. 4, 1054, and vol. 5, 872; J. C. Martin and R. S. Martin, *Maps of Texas and the Southwest, 1513–1900;* Syers, *Texas;* Kelsey and Dyal, *Courthouses of Texas;* Fehrenbach, *Lone Star.*

Ochiltree County (Perryton)

Ochiltree County is in the extreme northern Texas Panhandle and shares its northern border with Oklahoma. It was created in 1876 and organized in 1889. At the end of the Red River War in 1875, the U.S. Army forced the Indians onto reservations in Oklahoma, opening the country for settlement. The county and original county seat were named for William Beck Ochiltree, who served the Republic of Texas as a judge and secretary of the treasury and was an officer in the Confederate army.

During the early years the owners of Cresswell Ranch controlled most of the area within the county, but ranching gradually yielded to increased wheat farming. Growers, however, faced the problem of access to a railroad to move their products to market. By 1915 Ochiltree had a courthouse, a school, several churches, and a new jail. The lockup was apparently built of 2″ by 4″ lumber, stacked flat and nailed down. It had a concrete floor and half-inch iron bars over the windows. This jail was moved in 1919 to the new county seat of Perryton and placed on the courthouse square.

In 1919 the North Texas and Santa Fe Railroad built tracks from Oklahoma to Spearman in Hansford County, passing eight miles north of Ochiltree and eight miles south of Gary, Oklahoma. The two towns merged to form Perryton, named for County Judge George M. Perry. When the railroad gave lots to the citizens to move, the residents voted to relocate the county seat, their houses, and their businesses to Perryton. When the Ochiltree post office closed, the village became a ghost town.

By 1924 Perryton had a quality concrete-and-brick jail with up-to-date cells of unknown manufacture. It was not long, however, before a prisoner tore a stool from the concrete floor and chipped a hole large enough for him to escape. Mabel McLarty recalls that, when she worked in the courthouse, there was a prisoner serving time in the old Main Street jail who would slip out and leave a beautifully handwritten note saying when he would be back—and he always kept his word.

Interviews conducted by the author: Julie Williams and Mike Blank, Museum of the Plains; Mabel McLarty; Deputy Sheriff Bobby Kyle.

Other resources: *Dallas Morning News, Texas Almanac, 1998–1999;* Tyler, Barnett, and Barkley, eds., *New Handbook of Texas,* vol. 4, 1103.

Oldham County (Vega)

Oldham County was created from Bexar County in 1876. It was organized in 1880 and named for W. S. Oldham, a one-time Confederate senator. When the Indians in Texas were moved to reservations in Indian Territory, the Texas Panhandle was opened to settlement and ranching. Spanish sheepmen *(pastores)* from New Mexico settled as early as 1870. The main geographic feature of the Oldham County landscape is the Canadian River (a center for Pueblo Indian culture in prehistoric times), which traverses the midriff of the county west to east, much of it bounded by high bluffs and notorious areas of quicksand.

The first settlement was on the north side of the Canadian River at a rare spot that was a good ford for sheep and cattle to cross. Although the community was first called Atascosa (Spanish for "boggy"), the name soon became shortened to Tascosa, and when the county was organized in 1881, Tascosa was chosen as the county seat. It was not long before Tascosa had all the markings of a small booming cow town; it was three hundred miles west of the frontier, but somehow whiskey and women found it. That was undoubtedly influenced by the fact that it was on the route of the cattle drives to the Kansas market. Charles Goodnight came through there in 1879 en route to the Palo Duro. Later visitors included Temple Houston, attorney and son of Sam Houston, Billy the Kid, and his friend John B. ("Catfish") Gough.

In 1882 the state of Texas made a deal to trade public land for a new capitol building, a fire having destroyed the previous one in November 1881. Three million acres of public land in ten western counties were drawn off, thus creating the famous XIT Ranch. Oldham County was largely included in the XIT, except for a small part in the southeast corner.

The first jail and courthouse were built in Tascosa in 1884. The courthouse still stands and is used as a museum. The jail was dismantled, and in 1915 its two cells were moved to the lockup in Vega, the new county seat. The jail in Vega was razed many years ago. No pictures remain.

Interviews conducted by the author: Sheriff David Medlin; Carolyn Richardson, Texas Historical Commission.

Other resources: *Dallas Morning News, Texas Almanac, 1998–1999;* Tyler, Barnett, and Barkley, eds., *New Handbook of Texas,* vol. 1, 991, and vol. 4, 209, 1135; L. M. Hunter, *Book of Years;* Browder, *Donley County;* J. E. Haley, *Charles Goodnight.*

Orange County (Orange)

Orange County was created from Jefferson County in 1852 and was possibly named for an orange grove planted by early settlers near the mouth of the Sabine River. The Neches River bounds the county on the west; the Sabine

Orange County jail, 1897–1924, 1924–1952, Orange,
Texas. Photo courtesy of Orange County Historical Society.

River and Louisiana form the eastern boundary. The two rivers combine to form Sabine Lake, which in turn flows through Sabine Pass to the Gulf of Mexico. Indian artifacts such as Clovis points have been found, showing that the area has been occupied for more than ten thousand years. It was home to the Atakapa Indians, the last half dozen or so, who were identified in the area at the turn of the century.

Orange was called Green's Bluff in 1830, then Madison, and finally Orange when it became the county seat in 1852. During the Civil War, a major battle took place at Sabine Pass (Jefferson County) when a Union force, some four thousand strong, attempted a landing to dominate the river and railroad traffic. The Confederates had built a fortification, Fort Griffin, with six heavy artillery pieces to defend the pass. Two of four Union gunboats were destroyed before the assault was called off. Richard ("Dick") Dowling, a young lieutenant, was given much of the credit for the accurate cannonade and defense.

The first jail in Orange County was built in 1861, a 16′ by 16′ two-story log building, probably a dungeon, which was typical of the period. It was undoubtedly destroyed by the severe hurricane that struck Orange in 1867. Some time after the hurricane, a board shack was built on pilings over the Sabine River on Front Street at Fourth Street and used as a jail. For its time, it was a practical, if not environmentally perfect, solution to incarceration. The location solved the sanitation problem, and the river was no doubt a deterrent to escape. Getaways were rare, according to the local newspaper, because

prisoners often stayed only one night before being hanged
from a nearby oak. At first, city and county prisoners were
kept together in the calaboose. In 1892 the city government
of Orange converted the first floor of the old fire station into
a jail to replace the dilapidated riverside lockup. In 1897 the
county built a two-story red brick facility for prisoners. The
structure was used until 1924, when it was replaced by a three-
story brick jail built by Southern Structural Steel Company of
San Antonio. The 1924 jail was used until 1952.

    Interview conducted by the author conducted by the author:
Howard C. Williams, Orange County Historical Commission.
    Other resources: *Dallas Morning News, Texas Almanac, 1998–1999;* Tyler,
Barnett, and Barkley, eds., *New Handbook of Texas,* vol. 2, 1102, vol. 4,
1161, and vol. 5, 745; Delorme Mapping, *Texas Atlas and Gazetteer;* Metz,
Roadside History of Texas.

Palo Pinto County (Palo Pinto)

Palo Pinto County was created from Bosque and Navarro
counties in 1856 and organized in 1857. Mineral Wells
is the largest town in the county, but Palo Pinto, with a population of 411, has managed to remain the county seat. The
Brazos River crosses the county from northwest to southeast
in an exaggerated serpentine course and provides the water for
the 15,588-acre Possum Kingdom Lake.

    The county was named for Palo Pinto Creek. The town,
surveyed in 1857, was originally called Golconda by order
of the legislature, but good judgment prevailed, and the name
was changed to Palo Pinto when the town was chosen as the
county seat in 1858. That same year, a frame courthouse and
adjacent log jail were constructed. Before that time, prisoners
were kept in the Weatherford jail for a fee.

    The specifications of the 1858 lockup called for it to be
two stories, 16′ square, and made of 8″ timbers. The log structure served until 1880, when a substantial two-story sandstone
jail was built across the street from the courthouse square.
The architect and builders were Martin, Byrnes, and Johnson.
When first completed, the ground floor of the jail was used

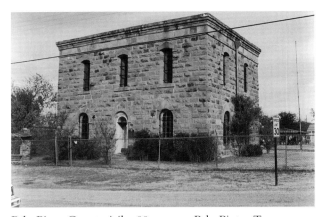

Palo Pinto County jail, 1880–1941, Palo Pinto, Texas.

for county offices while the second courthouse was being completed. After the courthouse was finished, the lockup provided space for a jailer's residence on the first floor with the sheriff's office and the prisoners' cells on the second floor. In 1907 the Pauly Jail Building Company extensively remodeled the structure, adding a steel trapdoor for the administration of the death penalty. During its history, only two prisoners escaped, one of them by digging his way out through the soft sandstone.

The jail was used until 1941, when the Works Progress Administration completed the new courthouse with a lockup on the top floor. The 1880 structure is the oldest building in the county and is now used as the Palo Pinto County Pioneer Museum.

Interviews conducted by the author: Jean Price; Sandra Bunson, office of the county clerk.

Other resources: *Dallas Morning News, Texas Almanac, 1998–1999;* Tyler, Barnett, and Barkley, eds., *New Handbook of Texas,* vol. 1, 29, 31; Palo Pinto County Historical Commission, *History of Palo Pinto County;* Biffle, "Texana—The Wrong Man Hanged for 1880 Murder," *Dallas Morning News,* Dec. 7, 1997; W. Robinson, *People's Architecture;* Clarke, *Palo Pinto Story;* Fowler, "Old Jailhouse Museums."

Panola County (Carthage)

Panola County was created in 1846 and given the name of the Indian word for "cotton," *panola.* The town of Pulaski was made the temporary county seat, but an 1848 elec-

tion desig-
nated an
uninhabited
spot near
the center
of the
county as
the perma-
nent center
of govern-
ment. The
spot was on
land owned

Panola County jail, 1891–1953, Carthage, Texas. Photo by
Stanley Gilbert. From the author's collection.

by Jonathan Andrews, who gave one hundred acres for the
new town. Spearman Holland (a state legislator and Civil War
veteran) suggested naming the new community Carthage after
the town in Mississippi. Proceeds from the sale of lots around
the public square were used to fund the first public buildings,
a courthouse, and a log jail.

The first permanent lockup was designed by J. N. Carnes
and built in 1891. It was a two-story red brick building with
a T-shaped footprint. The contractors were Baker and Mc-
Daniel, who finished the building for $4,250. Of special inter-
est was the ornamental work of the brick mason, showing
round and stilted arches over the doors and windows and an
elaborate brick design at the cornices. A well-defined string-
course ran below the second floor, and the corners and en-
trances were enhanced by distinctive pilasters. F. J. Meyers
Manufacturing Company of Covington, Kentucky, manufactured the ironwork and prison cells for $2,915. The design of
the cell bars is unusual, and indeed this is the only jail in Texas
found to have been contracted by that company.

The county used the old keep until 1953, when it was sold
to the city of Carthage and used until 1965. The combined
efforts of the Panola County Heritage Society, the Panola
County Historical Commission, the Panola County Historical
and Genealogical Association, and the City of Carthage have
restored the jail to pristine condition to serve as a museum.
The building is on the National Register of Historic Places.

Interviews conducted by the author: Leila Belle LaGrone; Andy Anderson; Oliphant and Louise Wooley, museum docents.

Other resources: *Dallas Morning News, Texas Almanac, 1998–1999;* Tyler, Barnett, and Barkley, eds., *New Handbook of Texas,* vol. 1, 1003; W. Robinson and Webb, *Texas Public Buildings of the Nineteenth Century.*

Parker County (Weatherford)

Parker County was created from Bosque and Navarro counties in 1855. It was named for Isaac Parker, early pioneer, Texas Ranger, and state legislator. Isaac was an uncle of Cynthia Ann Parker, who was kidnapped from Fort Parker by Comanche Indians in May 1836. An election selected Weatherford to be the county seat; the town was named for Jefferson Weatherford, a member of the Texas senate. Frequent raids by Kiowa and Comanche Indians troubled the early days of Parker County, especially during the Civil War. These were not checked until 1870.

The first jail in Parker County was attached to the new brick courthouse in 1858 and cost four thousand dollars. Although the courthouse burned in 1874, probably a victim of arson, the jail was spared and used until 1880. A third courthouse also burned in 1884.

In 1880 a new stone lockup of locally quarried rock was built on Palo Pinto Street. It was three stories tall with the sheriff's quarters on the ground floor. As was often the custom at that time, the kitchen was a separate building on the north side, a precaution against fire danger. In 1904 the jail was remodeled, and the third story was removed for unknown reasons. It is known, however, that the stone salvaged from the third floor was used to rearrange the quarters to the west side of the building. The jail was used until 1958, when it was replaced by a modern building on Trinity Avenue.

Interviews conducted by the author: Francis Skiles, Texas Historical Commission; Kelley McCauley.

Other resources: *Dallas Morning News, Texas Almanac, 1998–1999;* Tyler, Barnett, and Barkley, eds., *New Handbook of Texas,* vol. 5, 63, and vol. 6, 858; *Weatherford Exponent,* Apr. 25, 1880; *Weatherford Democrat,* Jan. 9, 1958, and Aug. 14, 1958; Smythe, *Historical Sketch of Parker County and Weather-*

ford, Texas; Parker County Historical Commission, *Pictorial History of Parker County.*

Parmer County (Farwell)

The Texas legislature created Parmer County in 1876 and named it for Martin Parmer, one of the participants in the Fredonian Rebellion and a signer of the Texas Declaration of Independence. The county was not organized until 1906. Its isolation on the extreme western edge of the Texas Panhandle was a deterrent to traffic, even after the creation of the XIT Ranch.

In 1882, after the capitol building in Austin burned, the Texas legislature traded three million acres of public land for a replacement. The Texas Land Capitol Syndicate was formed, and the acreage, scattered over seven Panhandle counties, was made into the giant XIT Ranch. Almost all of Parmer County lay within the XIT Ranch property.

The town of Farwell was surveyed in 1905 and became the shipping point for XIT cattle. Enough cowboys were mobilized to vote in the town as the new county seat. Dissidents called it a "dirty laundry" election because it was claimed that a cowboy was a citizen of whatever place his laundry was done at any given time and so was eligible to vote there.

The first jail in Parmer County was a wooden structure made by stacking 2" by 4" boards flat on top of each other and nailing them down with large spikes. That building was used for ten years before it was sold to Bailey County for one hundred dollars. In 1917 Parmer County built a new brick courthouse and a one-story brick jail, both designed by C. Risser. Attractive Roman arches decorated the Texas Renaissance courthouse in front, with the cube-shaped jail erected behind it. The need to provide a more secure facility, however, became apparent after a multiple murder in 1926. The prisoner who was arrested admitted to having killed thirteen people—two women and their eleven children—in California and Texas. Found guilty, he was sent to Huntsville, where he died in the electric chair in 1928. In that same year, due to the fear of losing such a prisoner to a lynch mob, an additional story was added to the jail. The Southern Structural Steel Company of San Antonio contracted the ironwork and jail cells for the second floor. In 1973 a new law enforcement center was built, using the cells from the 1928 addition.

Interviews conducted by the author: Colleen Stover, office of the county clerk; Hugh Mosele, Parmer County Historical Commission; Gary Blair, sheriff of Parmer County.

Other resources: *Dallas Morning News, Texas Almanac, 1998–1999;* Tyler, Barnett, and Barkley, eds., *New Handbook of Texas,* vol. 2, 67, and vol. 5, 963; Kelsey and Dyal, *Courthouses of Texas.*

Pecos County (Fort Stockton)

Pecos County was created from Presidio County in 1871 and organized in 1872. Activity by Anglos began as early as 1858, when the U.S. government established Camp Stockton at Comanche Springs, a giant spring of fresh water that had been an Indian encampment and stopping place for centuries. It was also a rest stop for the Butterfield Overland Mail (which operated from 1858 to 1861) and for travelers on the San Antonio to El Paso road. In 1859 Camp Stockton became a U.S. Army outpost for the defense of travelers and freighters. It was abandoned, however, during the Civil War. In 1867 the army returned and built a new facility that they again named Fort Stockton. The army, however, neither bought nor rented the property. Most of the buildings were adobe, but one of the new buildings was a stone guardhouse. In 1868 Peter Gallagher of San Antonio bought a large tract of land in the area, including the military establishment and Comanche Springs and surveyed a town site of 160 acres. He called it Saint Gall. When Pecos County was organized in 1875, Saint Gall was named the county seat. Citizens were generally unhappy with that name, however, and changed it to Fort Stockton in 1881.

In the early days of a county, it was not unheard of for the guardhouse of a nearby fort to be used to hold civil prisoners, especially immediately after the Civil War. A Pecos County courthouse and jail were built, however, in 1883. Thomas B.

Robertson contracted the jail. Originally conceived as a one-story building, it was later altered to two stories at a cost of $1,725. Liv-

Pecos County jail, 1913–1975, Fort Stockton, Texas.

ing quarters for the sheriff were on the ground floor, and the prisoners were kept on the second story.

In 1913 the jail was torn down, and the Falls City Construction Company of Louisville, Kentucky, built a new lockup designed by Jack Richardson on the same site. The copious living quarters for the sheriff were on the ground floor, and prisoners were kept on the second floor.

As a child, Ann Brissman resided in the jail in the 1930s when her father, Sheriff William Patrick Rooney, lived there. The Rooney children would sometimes have a party in the evening and dance on the front porch. She also remembered climbing a tree near the jail and playing cards through the window with the prisoners. Sheriff Bruce Wilson also lived in the quarters, although the prisoners were moved out of the building in 1975 into the new law enforcement center.

Interviews conducted by the author: Ann Rooney Brissman; Jackie Johnson, Annie Riggs Museum; Sheriff Bruce Wilson.

Other resources: *Dallas Morning News, Texas Almanac, 1998–1999;* Tyler, Barnett, and Barkley, eds., *New Handbook of Texas,* vol. 2, 245, 1119, and vol. 5, 120; C. W. Williams and Wallace, *Texas' Last Frontier;* Daggett, ed., *Pecos County History,* vol. 1.

Polk County (Livingston)

Polk County was created and organized in 1846. It was named for Pres. James K. Polk, who was president of the United States when Texas was admitted as a state in 1845.

Livingston, originally called Springfield, was made the county seat in 1846. It was named for the Kentucky hometown of Moses F. Choates after he donated one hundred acres to the town. By 1860, the population was eighty-three hundred, of which approximately half were slaves.

The first jail in Livingston was a one-room log cabin built in 1846. Details are unclear, but in the last part of the 1880s, a two-story red brick jail was built on the corner of Abby and Washington streets. According to Onyda Kimball Laird, who lived there when her father, L. D. Kimball, was sheriff from 1937 to 1948, the structure had sheriff's quarters on the first floor. The family and the prisoners entered the building through the same door. The detainees were directed up the stairs to the second floor, where the cells awaited them. The living quarters were on one side, and an "evidence storage room" was on the other. She remembers that, in one case, bootleggers were caught and the evidence (booze) was properly stored. It seems that one of her brothers got into the evidence, and, when the case came to trial, the liquor was gone. The sheriff quickly provided more evidence so the trial could proceed.

The next jail was finished in 1940, and the Kimball family moved into the five-room sheriff's quarters on the first floor. The architect was Emory S. White of Livingston, and the structural engineer was Walter P. Moore of Houston. The Yarborough Construction Company of Austin erected the building at a cost of thirty-one thousand dollars. The story would not be complete without Onyda Kimball Laird's recollection of the time her brother found a teargas grenade in his father's desk drawer. The youngster pulled the pin, and, when it began to spew forth its contents, he dropped it and ran. Laird says that they managed to evacuate the family as well as the prisoners.

Interviews conducted by the author: Wanda Bobinger, Murphy Memorial Museum; Onyda Kimball Laird.

Other resources: *Dallas Morning News, Texas Almanac, 1998–1999;* Tyler, Barnett, and Barkley, eds., *New Handbook of Texas,* vol.4, 248, and vol. 5, 257; Kelsey and Dyal, *Courthouses of Texas.*

Potter County (Amarillo)

Potter County was created in 1876, organized in 1887, and named for Robert Potter, a soldier at the battle of San Jacinto, signer of the Texas Declaration of Independence, secretary of the Texas Navy, and commander of the Port of Galveston.

In the 1870s Amarillo began as a camp for buffalo hunters and bone collectors around a place called Playa Amarillo (*amarillo* is Spanish for "yellow"), so named because of the yellow soil in the area. At first called Rag City because of the tents pitched on the prairie, the town was platted in 1887 by J. T. Berry of Abilene in anticipation of the arrival of tracks for the Fort Worth and Denver City Railroad. The name was changed to Amarillo when the settlement was chosen as the county seat.

After the seemingly inexhaustible underground water of the Ogallala Reservoir was discovered in 1883, wheat and grain production rapidly expanded. During the 1870s, three ranches—the LIT, the LX, and the Frying Pan—were the main enterprises. When the Fort Worth and Denver City Railroad arrived in 1887, everything came together. The cattle from North Texas, Oklahoma, and New Mexico, the feedlots, wheat, and the railroads all merged to make Amarillo the shipping center of the Panhandle. Natural gas with rare helium content was discovered in 1918.

In 1888 the county commissioners advertised in the *Fort Worth Gazette* for bids to build a courthouse and jail. Martin, Byrnes, and Johnson won the bidding process and completed the buildings in May 1889 for twenty-three thousand dollars. Unhappily, torrential rains arrived about the time of completion, and within two years "Old Town" Amarillo was abandoned in favor of higher ground one mile east of the original flood-prone site, in the Glidden and Sanborn addition, "New Town." The courthouse and jail soon stood alone one mile from the business district, requiring clerks to walk the distance to the 1889 building. In 1896 the courthouse in Old Town was dismantled and reconstructed in New Town, but the lockup was left behind.

In 1906 a new stone courthouse and a two-story jail were completed on higher ground at 501 South Taylor in New Town. The architects were Townes, Lightfoot, and Funk of Amarillo, and the Southern Structural Steel Company manufactured the cells and ironwork. The 1906 jail was replaced in 1932 upon the completion of an eight-story concrete-and-terra-cotta courthouse with a lockup on the top floor. This facility served Potter County until 1988.

Interviews conducted by the author: Sergeant Olivares, Potter County Sheriff's Department; Robert Forrester, Texas Historical Commission; Lueise Tyson; Dulciena Almager; Betty Bustos, Panhandle-Plains Historical Museum, Canyon, Texas.

Other resources: *Dallas Morning News, Texas Almanac, 1998–1999;* Tyler, Barnett, and Barkley, eds., *New Handbook of Texas,* vol. 1, 140, and vol. 5, 299; Key, *In the Cattle Country;* Kelsey and Dyal, *Courthouses of Texas.*

Presidio County (Marfa)

Presidio County, named for an old Mexican town on the Rio Grande, was created from Bexar County in 1850. Serious exploration by the Spanish began after Cabeza de Vaca made his incredible return to civilization in 1536. The town of Presidio, on the Rio Grande where the Concho River joins it out of Mexico, has a history of occupation and agricultural usage by the Jumano Indians dating to 1500 B.C.

Fort Davis was established by the U.S. Army in 1854, abandoned during the Civil War, and then reopened in 1867. When Presidio County was reorganized in 1871, the town of Fort Davis was voted to be the county seat. The reorganization was not finalized until 1875, but by that time, the voting records had been lost in a fire, probably set by someone who wanted to move the county seat to Marfa.

In 1880 an adobe courthouse was built in Fort Davis. The new facility had a jail that was a stone-lined cellar under the sheriff's office, accessed by a trapdoor in the floor of the office. Generously, the sheriff ventilated the dungeon by putting two small holes in the trapdoor.

The
pressure
was still
on to move
the county
seat to
Marfa. J. M.
Dean, an
El Paso
attorney,
owned land
in the Marfa

Presidio County jail, 1886–1994, Marfa, Texas.

area, which might have influenced the call for a new election.
The next election used ballots that required voters to write
out "For remaining at Fort Davis" if that was their wish, but
of course, most people in that day could not write. The vote
was 392 to 302 to move—and the county seat shifted to Marfa
in 1885.

In 1886 San Antonio architect Alfred Giles designed a
county jail for the new seat of government. The two-story,
freestanding structure was built of brick at a cost of twenty-six
thousand dollars. It had large sheriff's quarters on the ground
floor. In the same year, a courthouse, complete with a statue
of "Lady Justice" on top, was built a short distance away from
the lockup. A favorite story is told about a young cowboy
who claimed that he had been jailed unfairly. When released,
he shot the scales out of the hand of Lady Justice with the
comment, "There is no justice in this county." Sheriffs and
their families lived in the jail until 1972. Afterward the building continued in use until 1994. That year, a new detention
center was completed nearby, and the old jail was renovated
for record storage.

Interviews conducted by the author: Deputy Sheriff Rusty Taylor;
Ramona Lara, county and district clerk; Barbara Wood, Chamber of
Commerce.

Other resources: *Dallas Morning News, Texas Almanac, 1998–1999;* Tyler,
Barnett, and Barkley, eds., *New Handbook of Texas,* vol. 4, 503, and vol. 5,
330; Metz, *Roadside History of Texas.*

Rains County (Emory)

Named for Emory Rains, a senator in the congress of the Texas Republic and later in the state legislature, Rains County was created in 1870 mostly from Wood County. In establishing the area, the legislature said that the seat should be called Emory. The town of Springville, a centrally located community, was chosen as the county seat, and its name was changed to Emory. Emory prospered through the 1920s, but the Great Depression and low farm prices depleted its population. Even after World War II, recovery was slow. Today a major feature is Lake Tawakoni, a popular recreational spot that attracts tourists.

Any record of early jails has disappeared after a series of courthouse fires. In 1872 a wooden courthouse was built, but fire destroyed it in 1879 along with the county records. In 1884 a brick courthouse was constructed. In 1908 it too burned, although this time the records were salvaged. A new courthouse was completed in 1909.

In the mid-1880s, a freestanding brick jail was erected on the courthouse square. That facility remained in place until 1962, when an annex and a lockup were added to the back of the courthouse. Much of the original 1880s' ironwork and the prison cells were moved into the new structure. During the 1962 construction, there was a prisoner in the jail, and one of the workers left a cutting torch unattended on the floor near the prisoner's cell. By the time the worker returned, the prisoner had almost finished cutting his way to freedom.

Rains County courthouse, 1909–present, Emory, Texas. Jail was annexed in 1962. Photo courtesy of Bob Fisk.

Interviews conducted by the author: Virginia Northcutt, Rains County Public Library; Bob Sisk, county judge.

Other resources: *Dallas Morning News, Texas Almanac, 1998–1999;* Tyler, Barnett, and Barkley, eds., *New Handbook of Texas,* vol. 2, 873, and vol. 5, 417, 418; Kelsey and Dyal, *Courthouses of Texas.*

Randall County (Canyon)

Randall County, in the northern Panhandle, was created in 1876 about the time that the Comanche Indian threat was diminishing. The county was not organized, however, until 1889, due in part to delays by the interests of the large ranches. When organized, the town of Canyon City, which had originally been laid out by Lincoln G. Conner as headquarters of the T Anchor Ranch, was chosen as the county seat. The name was later shortened to Canyon. In 1876 Charles Goodnight founded the first headquarters of the JA Ranch in Palo Duro Canyon. Ranching remained the major enterprise until the turn of the century, when increased wheat farming began to dominate.

The county was named for Horace Randal, a Confederate brigadier general in the Civil War. Randal was generously given an extra "l" to his name when the county was named, and the error was never corrected. In 1849 Randal and another man were the first Texans to be accepted by the U.S. Military Academy at West Point, but because of problems with mathematics and English grammar, Randal took five years to graduate. He served in the Indian Territory, as well as Fort Davis, Texas, but resigned his commission in 1861 and joined the Confederate army. During the Civil War, he moved up from first lieutenant to brigadier general but was killed at the battle of Jenkins Ferry, Arkansas, in April 1864.

There is no standing historic jail in Randall County. According to retired deputy sheriff Ray Tinsley, in 1940 the county population was barely seven hundred, and there was no lockup. After World War II, the county obtained a war surplus navy "tank" (a cell), which was installed in a small building across from the courthouse square. This became the first jail of record, a tiny one-cell building on Sixteenth Street. Later, in 1956, a lockup was built on the courthouse square.

Interviews conducted by the author: Ted Wood, Randall County judge; Leroy Hutton, Randall County clerk; Betty Bustos, Panhandle Plains Museum; Ray Tinsley, retired deputy sheriff.

Other resources: *Dallas Morning News, Texas Almanac, 1998–1999;* Tyler, Barnett, and Barkley, eds., *New Handbook of Texas,* vol. 1, 964, and vol. 5, 406, 407; Delorme Mapping, *Texas Atlas and Gazetteer;* Metz, *Roadside History of Texas.*

Reagan County (Big Lake)

Until the mid-1870s, the area that was to become Reagan County was Indian territory. Reagan County was created from Tom Green County in 1903 and was named for John H. Reagan, a veteran of the Cherokee War and later a captain in the militia at Nacogdoches. During the Civil War, he was postmaster general of the Confederacy, after which he was imprisoned by the United States on an island in Boston harbor. He was granted amnesty in 1876 and later became the first chair of the Texas Railroad Commission.

When Reagan County was organized, the only town in the county, Stiles, was made the county seat. It was named for Gordon Stiles, donor of the land for the town. Stiles flourished, and by 1911 it had a school, a post office, a newspaper, and a stone courthouse, but when the Kansas City, Mexico, and Orient Railroad planned to come to town, a local rancher would not let them cross his ranch. The result was that the railroad went

Reagan County courthouse and jail, 1925–1999, Big Lake, Texas.

south to Big Lake, a small town named for a nearby shallow depression that sometimes had water in it. In 1923 oil was discovered near Big Lake when the Santa Rita #1 came in on University of Texas land. By 1925 the county seat had moved to Big Lake, and by 1928 the population had grown to 2,000. In Stiles, the post office closed in 1939, and by 1990 the population there was only 16.

Henry Jepson was the first sheriff of Reagan County. Years later, Lanzo Stidham told Sheriff Jepson's grandson, Jepson Petit, how Sheriff Jepson, in the absence of a jail, had chained him to a horse hitching post overnight for safekeeping. The first jail was not built in Stiles until 1904 and was made of 2″ by 4″ planks stacked and nailed to each other, a similar method of construction of early jails in other counties. The structure was about 6′ by 8′ with two small windows for ventilation. It was used until 1911, when a stone courthouse with a jail on the top floor, designed by Oscar Ruffini of San Angelo, was completed. When the county seat moved to Big Lake in 1925, the cages were moved out of the Stiles courthouse and incorporated into the top floor of the new courthouse in Big Lake. That facility was used until 1999, when a new freestanding lockup was built.

Interview conducted by the author: James Weatherby.
Other resources: *Dallas Morning News, Texas Almanac, 1998–1999;* Delorme Mapping, *Texas Atlas and Gazetteer;* Tyler, Barnett, and Barkley, eds., *New Handbook of Texas,* vol. 1, 508, 533, vol. 4, 452, and vol. 5, 464, 467; Metz, *Roadside History of Texas.*

Real County (Leakey)

Apache, Tonkawa, and Comanche Indians occupied this Hill Country land in prehistoric times. Real County lies mostly between the headwaters of the Nueces and the Frio rivers, both of which run in a southerly direction through the county, the Nueces along its western border and the Frio through the eastern part. Real County was formed from Edwards County in 1913 and named for Julius Real, the sole Republican in an otherwise Democratic legislature at that

Real County jail, 1918–1978, Leakey, Texas. Courtesy of
Real County Historical Commission.

time. The town of Leakey was named for John Leakey, who arrived in 1856 and established a settlement near a spring that bears his name. A post office opened in 1883, and Leakey became the Edwards County seat in 1884, supplanting the earlier county seat of Bullhead. The Leakey County courthouse burned in 1888, however, and in 1891 the county seat was moved to Rocksprings. When Real County was organized in 1913, Leakey became the county seat.

During the time Leakey was the seat of government for all of Edwards County, there was no road from Leakey to Camp Wood, twenty miles west. Prisoners from the Camp Wood area were chained to a post set in the ground. The sheriff would make the trip on horseback from Leakey to Uvalde, then to Camp Wood, and retrace his steps to Leakey, a round-trip of 160 miles. Later, a small concrete building served as a holding jail in Camp Wood. A road from Leakey to Camp Wood was not completed until 1953.

When Leakey was the county seat, a wooden jail with a single iron cage in it served as a detention center. When the seat of government moved to Rocksprings, the compartment went also. In 1913, when Leakey became the county seat of the new Real County, a new courthouse and jail were thus necessities. In 1918 a two-story courthouse was built with a lockup on the first floor between the sheriff's office and the county clerk's office. There were two cells, measuring 7' by 5' and 7' tall, purchased from the Southern Structural Steel Company for one thousand dollars. Two privies sat outside to the south. Indoor plumbing did not come until 1945. This jail was used until 1978.

Interview conducted by the author: Marjorie Kellner, county and district clerk, retired.

Other resources: *Dallas Morning News, Texas Almanac, 1998–1999;* Commissioners' Court Record, Mar. 21, 1917; Tyler, Barnett, and Barkley, eds., *New Handbook of Texas,* vol. 4, 132, vol. 5, 469, and vol. 6, 698; Kellner, *Wagons, Ho!*

Red River County (Clarksville)

Until the eighteenth century, the Caddo Indians occupied the area that became Red River County. Incursions by the French along the Spanish frontier in Texas made the Spanish nervous and led to their efforts to establish a presence in the area around Nacogdoches.

Since the drainage of the Red River was part of the Mississippi watershed as claimed by La Salle in 1682, France claimed the area in Texas south of the river; Spain, however, claimed it as part of New Spain. In 1763 France, anticipating the loss of the French and Indian War, ceded Louisiana to Spain, frustrating possible British claims to the territory. This relieved the border tensions between France and Spain. France later reclaimed Louisiana but sold the entire territory to the United States in 1801. Suddenly the United States' neighbor to the south was Spain.

After Red River County was organized and Clarks-

Red River County jail, 1889–1983, Clarksville, Texas. Designed by William H. Wilson.

ville became the county seat, a small wooden jail was built, followed shortly by a log jail, probably a double-crypt dungeon, commonly used at that time. The log jail burned, and in 1850 a 20′ by 30′ brick jail with an 18′ ceiling was built on the bank of Delaware Creek, probably near West Broadway.

The fourth jail, built in 1887, was an elaborate three-story stone building one block from the square. William H. Wilson designed it in Renaissance Revival style, similar to the design of the nearby courthouse he had done three years before. Pauly Brothers of St. Louis provided the cells and ironwork. Though substantial in every way, the jail lacked amenities, such as indoor plumbing for the jailers' quarters as well as for the cellblocks on the top floor. A wood stove provided heat. The bars on the windows were so soft that they could be filed with a fingernail file. Escapes became routine, and repair bills for the window bars became unacceptably large. In 1983, the 1887 jail was replaced by a modern structure, and the old facility is now being converted into a museum.

Interviews conducted by the author: Mary Hausler, retired county clerk; Mavis P. Kelsey Sr.

Other resources: Tyler, Barnett, and Barkley, eds., *New Handbook of Texas,* vol. 1, 11, vol. 2, 142, and vol. 5, 495; Cowden, "Historical Texas County Jails"; Stroud, *Gateway to Texas;* W. Robinson, *People's Architecture;* Ambrose, *Undaunted Courage;* Kelsey and Dyal, *Courthouses of Texas.*

Reeves County (Pecos)

Reeves County in far West Texas was created from part of Pecos County in 1883 and organized in 1884. The Pecos River, which flows east and then southeast to the Rio Grande, defines the eastern edge. Traveling along this river, Spanish explorer Antonio de Espejo encountered the Jumano Indians, who had small farms that they irrigated for raising corn and vegetables.

The county was named for Confederate Gen. George R. Reeves, who served in the Texas legislature before and after the Civil War. Pecos, the county seat, began in 1881 as a station on the Texas and Pacific Railroad as it built its way across Texas. One of the most famous inhabitants of Pecos was Rob-

ert Clay Allison, said to have been the most dangerous gunman in Texas. In 1866, after the Civil War, Allison worked as
a cowboy for Oliver Loving and Charles Goodnight when
they made their famous cattle drive to New Mexico and later
to Denver. Allison had a reputation for lightning speed with
his gun and proved it, to the sorrow of several men. This
tough Texan played by the rules, however, and did not spend
time in jail. He died from a fall from his wagon while hauling
supplies to his ranch.

Martin, Byrnes, and Johnson built the first Reeves County
jail in 1886. It was a two-story brick cube with limestone lintels over the windows and doors. The sheriff's quarters were
on the first floor; the second floor contained prison cells made
by an unknown manufacturer. The second lockup was built
in 1912 on the southeast corner of the courthouse square. The
three-story jail had two corner towers, typical of the castle
style popular at the turn of the century. White stone arches
over the openings and three stringcourses marking the three
floors highlighted the otherwise austere building. The architect and builder are unknown, but the design is similar to that
of buildings by Southern Structural Steel of San Antonio. In
1935 a new courthouse with a jail inside was authorized to be
built at a cost not to exceed $144,000. The building was fin-
ished in 1937, "an interesting mixture of Classical Revival and
Mediterranean," according to Kelsey and Dyal in *Courthouses
of Texas*. The jail was moved out of the courthouse in 1974.

Interviews conducted by the author: Sheriff Arnulfo Andy Gomez;
Dorinda Millan, West of the Pecos Museum.

Other resources: *Dallas Morning News, Texas Almanac, 1998–1999;* Newcomb, *Indians of Texas;* Kelsey and Dyal, *Courthouses of Texas;* Tyler, Barnett, and Barkley, eds., *New Handbook of Texas,* vol. 1, 123, and vol. 5, 119,
123, 508, 509; W. Robinson, *People's Architecture;* Metz, *Roadside History of
Texas.*

Refugio County (Refugio)

Refugio County was one of the original twenty-three
counties created by the new Republic of Texas in 1836.
It was organized in 1837 and named for the Spanish mission

Nuestra Señora del Refugio (Our Lady of Refuge). Various disappointments caused the mission to be abandoned in 1830.

Mexico allowed Anglo settlement beginning in 1822; Mexican law, however, forbade these communities within ten leagues (about thirty miles) of the coast. A special concession was given in 1828 to Col. James Power and fellow Irishman James Hewetson, who agreed to settle Catholics from Ireland in the area.

During the Goliad debacle, the battle of Refugio in March 1836 consisted of several skirmishes with the Mexican army by elements of James Fannin's army. Against Gen. Sam Houston's orders, some of the Texans left La Bahía to rescue families at Refugio, only to fall into the hands of Mexican Gen. José de Urrea. Most were taken back to La Bahía and executed in the Goliad massacre.

After San Jacinto, in an effort to organize the penniless county, the commissioners used the mission in Refugio as a courthouse, one room of which served as a jail. In 1856 they built a frame courthouse with one room dedicated as a lockup. The Civil War and then Reconstruction lasted until 1874. In 1868 Judge W. L. Rea, then a child, arrived in Refugio with his parents. He later wrote, "There was no jail. Prisoners were chained up in one of the rooms of the courthouse."

The loss of manpower as a result of the Goliad massacre demoralized the government. There were not enough citizens to fill the county commissioners' jobs. In 1869 the county seat was moved to St. Mary's on Copano Bay and in 1871 shifted to Rockport. The court met there only one time before Aransas County was created from Refugio County and Rockport became its county seat.

In 1871 Refugio again became the seat of government, and a new courthouse was built. In 1879 it became the victim of arson, so a fourth courthouse was constructed in 1880. About this time, a single-room wooden jail, measuring 10' by 20', was built with two small barred windows. This keep was used until a new courthouse, a three-story brick building with a jail on the third floor, was finished in 1919. The contract for the cells and ironwork went to the Pauly Jail Building Company. In 1955 the jail was moved into a new annex of the courthouse.

Interviews conducted by the author: Melba Lenhart; Tom Shelton, Institute of Texan Cultures, San Antonio.

Other resources: *Dallas Morning News, Texas Almanac, 1998–1999;* Metz, *Roadside History of Texas;* Tyler, Barnett, and Barkley, eds., *New Handbook of Texas,* vol. 4, 440, 1070, and vol. 5, 306, 512, 513; Delorme Mapping, *Texas Atlas and Gazetteer;* Huson, *Refugio.*

Roberts County (Miami)

Roberts County was created in 1876 and named for not one but two notable Texans: John S. Roberts, soldier of the Fredonian Revolution and signer of the Texas Declaration of Independence, and Gov. O. M. Roberts, chief justice of the Texas Supreme Court, two-term governor, and a founder of the Texas State Historical Association.

In 1879 the overland stage from Mobeetie to Las Vegas, New Mexico, needed a stop in the area that would become Roberts County. Marion Armstrong built a dugout shelter on Red Deer Creek for the stage, and when the Southern Kansas Railroad (later called the Panhandle and Santa Fe) built into the county in 1887, the town of Miami was platted at the site of the old coach stop. When the county was organized, Oran won out over Parnell to become the county seat. In 1898, however, a new electorate chose Miami as the seat of government. Parnell has now disappeared into the surrounding ranch land, and Miami is the only town in the whole of Roberts County. Some of its citizens moved to Miami in 1898, but many left for other Panhandle towns.

No one seems to remember what was used for a courthouse after the records were moved from Parnell to Miami, but a brick jail was built on the northeast corner of the courthouse square. The building was about 20′ wide and 30′ long and included three locally manufactured cell blocks and an end room that was used to store county maintenance equipment. The original cellblock was constructed with three cells surrounded by a walk-around.

Elmer George Withers designed the plans for a courthouse that was built in 1913. Remodeled in 1960, the Classical Revival building is still used today. In that year, the old brick jail was demolished, and the sheriff's office and the venerable cells were moved into new offices downtown.

Interviews conducted by the author: Vernon Cook, justice of the peace; Fannye Greenhouse; Robert Howard; Sheriff Dana Miller; Cecil Gill, Texas Historical Commission.

Other resources: *Dallas Morning News, Texas Almanac, 1998–1999;* Tyler, Barnett, and Barkley, eds., *New Handbook of Texas,* vol. 4, 702, and vol. 5, 69, 611, 613; Kelsey and Dyal, *Courthouses of Texas.*

Robertson County (Franklin)

Robertson County was created in 1837 by the legislature and was organized in 1838. It was named for Sterling Clack Robertson, a plantation owner and veteran of the battle of New Orleans. The southern boundary of Robertson's colony was the San Antonio Road, common with the northern boundary of Austin's colony. The original area of Robertson's colony would ultimately be divided into thirty Texas counties. By 1847 Robertson had settled six hundred families in his and Austin's colonies.

When Robertson County was organized in 1838, Franklin, now referred to as Old Franklin, became the county seat and retained the designation until 1850. The first jail and courthouse were contracted in Old Franklin in 1837 and completed in 1839. The county seat was moved to Wheelock in 1850 and once again to Owensville in 1856. After the Civil War, the Houston and Texas Central Railroad built into the new town of Calvert.

In 1870 Reconstruction Judge I. B. Ellison

Robertson County jail, 1882–1988, Franklin, Texas.

moved the county seat to Calvert. A courthouse was never built, but Calvert did build an imposing jail, which was completed in 1875. The structure was red brick, built in the style of a castle, with crenulations all around. It stands today, a reminder of the days when cotton was king and Calvert was a booming agricultural and trade center. This impressive building was used as a lockup until 1880. In spite of its prosperity, Calvert had its share of troubles: In 1873 a yellow fever epidemic took many lives; later, in 1891, a blazing fire razed the business district; and in 1899 a devastating flood washed away much of the rebuilt business district.

In 1879 the citizens voted to move the county seat to Morgan, later renamed Franklin for the original county seat. In 1882 the citizens, pleased with the new county seat, built a courthouse and jail designed by F. E. Ruffini of Austin. The structure was well designed in typical Ruffini Italianate style, but careless additions through the years have distorted the original attractive appearance. The original cost was $11,185, and the builder was James B. Smith. The jail, by virtue of remodeling and additions, was able to continue in use until 1988.

Interviews conducted by the author: Judy Limmer, deputy county clerk; Cooper Wiese.

Other resources: *Dallas Morning News, Texas Almanac, 1998–1999;* Tyler, Barnett, and Barkley, eds., *New Handbook of Texas,* vol. 1, 911, vol. 2, 1153, vol. 4, 1133, vol. 5, 620, 621, 623, and vol. 6, 920, 992; Harris, *Dictionary of Architecture and Construction;* W. Robinson, *People's Architecture;* Kelsey and Dyal, *Courthouses of Texas;* Cowden, *Historical Texas County Jails.*

Rockwall County (Rockwall)

Rockwall County is Texas' smallest county. It was created from Kaufman County in 1873 and organized the same year. Named for a natural geological formation that, for many years, prehistoric Indians were thought to have made, Rockwall County is now dominated by the Ray Hubbard Lake, which was formed by damming the East Fork of the Trinity River. The lake covers 13.5 percent of the county's surface. The county seat, Rockwall, was incorporated in 1873. The old

National Highway of Texas passed through Rockwall in 1844 as it made its way from Red River County to Dallas and ultimately to Austin. That road and the Preston Road from Coffee's Trading Post on the Red River to Dallas were two of the earliest roads built by the new state of Texas.

Rockwall County has had three courthouses, each including a jail within its walls. The second lockup, built in 1892, had steel loops in the ceiling for restraining prisoners by chaining. That jail was used for forty-eight years, until the Works Progress Administration built a new courthouse and jail in 1940. The 1940 jail was on the top floor of the new courthouse and was used until 1987.

Sheriff E. W. Hall served from 1920 until 1935. He told his grandson, Congressman Ralph Hall, a story about a young woman whose husband traveled out of town from time to time. One time her husband came home early, and she claimed molestation by an unknown person. She picked a black man from a lineup as the culprit. Sheriff Hall knew the man and proceeded to lock him up. Confident of the man's innocence, the sheriff told the prisoner that he was going to leave the cell door unlocked and the back door open and when the 9:15 P.M. train left, the man was supposed to be on it. Once assured that the sheriff was not going to shoot him, the prisoner said, "Sheriff, I'll catch that train even if it has already left."

Other resources: *Dallas Morning News, Texas Almanac, 1998–1999;* Tyler, Barnett, and Barkley, eds., *New Handbook of Texas,* vol. 5, 640; Kelsey and Dyal, *Courthouses of Texas;* Tise, *Texas County Sheriffs;* J. W. Williams and Neighbours, *Old Texas Trails.*

Runnels County (Ballinger)

Runnels County was created in 1858 and organized that same year. It was named for H. G. Runnels, a one-time Mississippi governor who moved to Texas in 1842 after wounding Volney E. Howard, a congressman and newspaper editor, in a duel. Runnels became a planter in Brazoria County and represented that area at the 1845 convention.

In 1852 the 8th U.S. Infantry built a camp, later to become Fort Chadbourne, in the future northern Runnels County. The first

Runnels County jail, 1925–present, Ballinger, Texas.

county seat was Runnels City on Elm Creek, about five miles north of present Ballinger. In 1886, however, the Gulf Coast and Santa Fe Railroad built a line into the county and created the town of Ballinger. In 1888 Ballinger became the seat of government; the old rock jail at Runnels, complete with gallows, was dismantled, and the stone was hauled to Ballinger for construction of a lockup on Sixth Street and Strong Avenue.

Jim Flynt was elected sheriff in November 1907. During his first term in office, the bank at Rowena, ten miles southwest of Ballinger, was robbed. Within three hours, Sheriff Flynt had the robbers in jail. John Perkins became sheriff in 1914. In 1919 the Newton gang robbed the bank in Winters, Texas, but with Flynt's help, Perkins trailed and captured two of the culprits and killed the third in the town of Buffalo Gap, twelve miles south of Abilene. The two apprehended robbers managed to escape by burning a hole in the ceiling and roof of the jail but were caught again.

In 1925, after thirty-seven years, the old jail was retired, and a new facility was completed on the Ballinger courthouse square for forty-nine thousand dollars. Sheriff Earl McWilliams and his family soon occupied the quarters. Ella McWilliams, with the help of her two daughters, cooked for the inmates as well as for her own family. The lockup is still in use today.

Interviews conducted by the author: Jeannette Findley, Texas Historical Commission; Neuman Smith, Runnels County Historical Commission.

Other resources: *Dallas Morning News, Texas Almanac, 1998–1999;* Tyler, Barnett, and Barkley, eds., *New Handbook of Texas,* vol. 3, 746, and vol. 5, 716; *Ballinger Ledger,* Thursday, June 29, 1961; Delorme Mapping, *Texas Atlas and Gazetteer;* Newcombe, *Indians of Texas;* Tise, *Texas County Sheriffs.*

Rusk County (Henderson)

The congress of the Republic of Texas created Rusk County from Nacogdoches County in 1843. The county was named for Thomas J. Rusk, lawyer, soldier, and signer of the Texas Declaration of Independence. He also assisted in removing Pres. David Burnet from Harrisburg before the battle of San Jacinto and served with distinction in that conflict. In 1838 he defeated the Córdoba Rebellion, a conspiracy of Mexican agents allied with the Cherokee Indians in the Nacogdoches area. Later, in 1839, he defeated the Cherokees in the battle of Neches. The county seat was named for James P. Henderson, first governor of the state Texas.

Settlers began moving into the area as early as 1829. They were mostly farmers, many with slaves. The first jail in Rusk County in 1848 was wooden, typical of the dungeons of that time. By 1860, on the eve of the Civil War, the population was 15,803, of which 6,132 were slaves. The property value of the slaves represented one-half of the total property value in the county.

Recovery from the Civil War was slow and difficult for whites and blacks alike. The county remained agricultural, and former slaves became tenant farmers, sharing the harvest on a one-third or one-half basis. In 1878 a heavy all-iron jail was built. It was one story tall, located half a block north of the 1878 courthouse, where the Baptist church now stands. F. E. Ruffini was the architect for this structure.

A turning point came with the discovery of oil, a saving grace during the depression of the 1930s. The petroleum industry had its dark side, however, as demonstrated by the disastrous explosion of natural gas (methane) in the heating system of the New London School in March 1937. Two hundred ninety-seven people, including teachers and children, were killed. This disaster prompted the gas industry to add a chemical, mercaptan, to the otherwise odorless, colorless natural gas to give it a distinctive smell that would alert people to its presence.

In 1930 a new courts and office building with a jail on the top floor was built, replacing the 1878 Ruffini metal structure. The 1930 facility, however, was removed in 1991 from the courts building to a new free-standing law enforcement building.

Interviews conducted by the author: Carol Wingo, deputy county clerk; Virginia Knapp, Rusk County Historical Commission; Carol Farrell, Rusk County Chamber of Commerce.

Other resources: *Dallas Morning News, Texas Almanac, 1998–1999;* Metz, *Roadside History of Texas;* Tyler, Barnett, and Barkley, eds., *New Handbook of Texas,* vol. 2, 324, vol. 5, 556, and vol. 6, 729.

Sabine County (Hemphill)

Named for the Sabine River, Sabine County was one of the original twenty-three counties created in 1836. The first seat of government was Milam, but a new town, Hemphill, was destined to become the county seat in 1858. The town was named for John Hemphill, a Pennsylvania native who came to Texas in 1838, practiced law in Washington-on-the-Brazos, became a judge in the Fourth Judicial District, and served in both the Seminole War and the congress of the Confederacy.

The eastern terminus of the Old San Antonio Road passed through northern Sabine County and crossed the Sabine River near the site of Gaines Ferry. In 1716 José Domingo Ramón made a road from the Presidio San Juan Bautista on the Rio Grande to Natchitoches, Louisiana. The purpose was to block French incursions into East Texas by the establishment of missions in the Nacogdoches area.

Although an 1875 fire destroyed the county records, local wisdom describes the first jail there as a log building of unknown type. Later, a frame building was used as a temporary lockup until a two-story brick structure was built on the square in 1903. This Victorian-style keep had decorative brickwork

Sabine County jail, 1903–1984, Hemphill, Texas.

and orna-
mental
string-
courses with
a prominent
gallows
tower on
one corner.
The original
cost was
eighty-eight
hundred
dollars,
but after several escapes were made by prisoners, Judge Will
Davidson called on the Southern Steel Company to install
steel cages, which had been left out in 1903. Since then, only
one prisoner has escaped: a very small man who crawled out
through a vent pipe and climbed down the back of the jail
to freedom. In 1909 there was a public hanging on an outdoor
scaffold built for that purpose; the indoor gallows was used
only once—in 1922. With the benefit of the new cells, the
1903 jail was used until 1983. The facility has now been made
into a museum with many historic artifacts. The cells and gallows are intact, including the dangling rope from the ring in
the tower ceiling.

Interviews conducted by the author: Robert Cecil McDaniel; Edward M.
Farrell; Ray Groff, Sabine County Jail Museum.

Other resources: *Dallas Morning News, Texas Almanac, 1998–1999;* Tyler,
Barnett, and Barkley, eds., *New Handbook of Texas,* vol. 3, 550, vol. 4, 292,
and vol. 5, 742; Kelsey and Dyal, *Courthouses of Texas;* J. W. Williams and
Neighbours, *Old Texas Trails.*

San Augustine County (San Augustine)

San Augustine was one of the first counties created by the
new Republic of Texas in 1836. It was named for the
Mexican municipality that governed the area before the battle
of San Jacinto. In the late eighteenth century, Spain sought

to build missions in East Texas to offset the influence of French traders among the Native Americans.

The Louisiana Purchase in

San Augustine County jail, 1919, San Augustine, Texas.

1803 caused great uneasiness in Spain about American ambitions in Texas. In fact, for much of the century, discord and violence abounded. There was disagreement between Spain and the United States about the eastern boundary of Spanish Texas at that time. The two countries agreed on a neutral ground to avoid an armed confrontation, but the territory became a catchall for horse thieves and fugitives from both nations. (The neutral ground was bounded by the Gulf of Mexico on the south, the 32nd parallel on the north, the Arroyo Hondo on the east, and the Sabine River on the west.) In 1810 and 1812 both countries sent military expeditions into the area to capture brigands. The boundary was finally set in 1821 by the Adams-Onis Treaty. Still, in 1827 the Fredonian Revolution broke out and was followed in 1832 by the battle of Nacogdoches. A number of mercenaries came from the area to participate in the Texas Revolution. A disgruntled alcalde, Vincent Córdoba, led an insurrection against the Texas Republic in 1838. A few years afterward, the Regulator-Moderator War, which lasted from 1840 to 1844, broke out in the same area.

The first jail in San Augustine County was a log building, the description of which has been lost. In 1858, according to Harry P. Noble Jr., the second lockup was a two-story building of 12″ hewn oak logs and a 12″ thick birch wall around the perimeter. The building was 20′ by 32′. After the Civil War, Reconstruction began. Hundreds of armed, displaced, unemployed, disenfranchised, and angry young men from both

North and South made a volatile and dangerous mix until late in the century. Many disagreements were settled with powder and ball.

The third jail in San Augustine, built in 1883 and still standing, is a two-story red brick rectangle of Victorian design. The fourth lockup, built in 1919, is still in use but is scheduled for retirement very soon. It is a two-story square brick-and-concrete edifice with white plaster covering. The walls are 14″ thick and, according to retired sheriff Nathan Tindall, has resisted all attempts by prisoners to escape.

Interviews conducted by the author: Nathan Tindall; Curt Goetz, county judge.

Other resources: *Dallas Morning News, Texas Almanac, 1998–1999;* Tyler, Barnett, and Barkley, eds., *New Handbook of Texas,* vol. 4, 517, 817, 818, and vol. 4, 983; Noble, *As Noble as It Gets.*

San Jacinto County (Coldspring)

San Jacinto County was created in 1869 and organized the following year. The area had been the home of the Atakapan Indians, whose numerous artifacts are found along the county's abundant spring-fed creeks.

In the 1820s pioneers trickled up the Trinity River, many obtaining Mexican land grants in San Jacinto County. The first post office, established in 1847, was called Coonskin. Some sophisticate, however, changed the name to Cold Spring in 1850; finally, in 1894, the spelling was changed to Coldspring. The name is descriptive enough. There are many springs still flowing in the little valley of the original community, about one-quarter mile north of the present town.

The first jail, a wooden building built around 1870, seemed to satisfy the community's needs for a time, but in 1887 a more substantial lockup was built of locally fired red brick. L. T. Noyes of Houston, a representative of the Diebold Company, was the builder. The structure was remodeled and expanded by the Southern Structural Steel Company in 1911. New cells and a hangman's trapdoor were installed at that time. The gallows was never used for an official execution, but one episode occurred when vigilantes broke into the building and forced the jailer to give them the prisoner, whom they promptly hanged.

The courthouse and several other buildings in the valley

San Jacinto County jail, 1887–1980, Coldspring, Texas.

burned in a devastating night fire in 1915; fortunately, the red brick jail escaped the conflagration. Natives like to tell about the prisoner who was awaiting execution when the fire broke out. Since nearby buildings were burning, threatening the jail, the jailer released the prisoners, including the condemned man, who pitched in to fight the blaze. Showing its appreciation in a moment of benevolence, the court changed the prisoner's sentence to life in prison. Some say that the inmate enjoyed some freedom and lived unofficially in the community at large for many years.

After the fire, the courthouse was rebuilt up the hill to the south, but the old red brick jail remained in place at the original town site and was used until 1980. Today the building serves as a museum of Coldspring memorabilia.

Interviews conducted by the author: Jane Guisinger and Billie Trapp, Old Jail Museum docents.

Other resources: *Dallas Morning News, Texas Almanac, 1998–1999;* DeLorme Mapping, *Texas Atlas and Gazetteer;* Tyler, Barnett, and Barkley, eds., *New Handbook of Texas,* vol. 2, 196, and vol. 5, 857; Kelsey and Dyal, *Courthouses of Texas.*

San Patricio County (Sinton)

The Republic of Texas formed San Patricio County as one of the original twenty-three counties. The area had been called San Patricio municipality as part of Mexico, and the

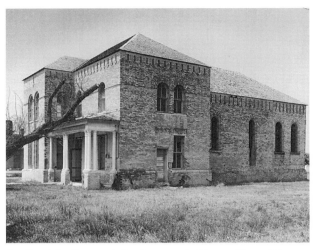

San Patricio County jail, 1894–1928, Sinton, Texas. Photo courtesy of Helen Hunt Johnson.

name was passed on to the new county of the Republic of Texas. The county covered a large area from the Nueces River to the Rio Grande and would in time be subdivided into fifteen counties, reaching its present size in 1855. The town of San Patricio was named the county seat.

Anglo settlement began in 1829, when John McMullen and James McGloin settled two hundred families of newly arrived Irish immigrants recruited from New York. In 1830 these settlers established a community on the left bank of the Nueces River, known as San Patricio de Hibernia. The previous year, James Power and James Hewetson had recruited Irish Catholics from Ireland and settled them in Refugio.

In 1872 the court commissioned Viggo Kohlert to build a two-story frame courthouse with a large courtroom upstairs. One of the downstairs rooms was to be built of heavy timber to serve as a jail. The lockup was to have a large mesquite stump set deep in the ground below the floor and a ring fixed securely to it to which a prisoner could be chained.

In 1894 the county seat was moved to Sinton, where a new courthouse and separate jail were built. The yellow brick keep had two stories and included a large sheriff's quarters. The prison cells were in the back wing on the first floor. To access the cells, one had to enter through the front door and go down a hallway that passed through the sheriff's residence. An iron door separated the living quarters from the jail. The bedrooms of the sheriff's living space were also on the second floor but had a separate door and stairway. Helen Hunt Johnson lived in the jail when her father, Samuel Frank Hunt, was sheriff from 1922 to 1940. She says that her father was a "hound dog man" and was very proud of his dogs. She relates that he loved to take pictures of the children, but she realizes that the children were always holding the dogs' leashes, and she suspects that the children were there to hold the dogs for the photographer.

The 1894 jail was used until 1928, when a new courthouse with a jail on the top floor was completed. The architect for that building was Henry T. Phelps, and the contractor was H. N. Jones. The Southern Prison Company provided the cells on the top floor for $15,274. The structure was used until 1982.

Interviews conducted by the author: Kay Watley, secretary to County Judge Josephine Miller; Helen Hunt Johnson.

Other resources: *Dallas Morning News, Texas Almanac, 1998–1999;* Tyler, Barnett, and Barkley, eds., *New Handbook of Texas,* vol. 3, 954, and vol. 5, 872; Kelsey and Dyal, *Courthouses of Texas;* DeLorme Mapping, *Texas Atlas and Gazetteer;* Tise, *Texas County Sheriffs;* "Early History of San Patricio County," *San Patricio County News,* 1934; *San Patricio County News,* July 15, 1973.

San Saba County (San Saba)

San Saba County was created in 1856 from Bexar County and named for the San Saba River, which flows east through the county and empties into the Colorado River. The latter river defines the entire northeastern border of San Saba County. The San Saba River arises some seventy-five miles southwest as the crow flies, from the town of Menard in Menard County. The name was originally taken from the Santa Cruz de San Sabá mission, founded in 1757 by the Franciscan fathers near present-day Menard, Texas.

After San Saba County was created and organized, a site for the county seat was chosen near the San Saba River. The town was named San Saba. Although farming and ranching were successful, production was insufficient to justify railroad service until 1911. San Saba County was the last county in the state to have paved roads.

San Saba County jail, 1884–present, San Saba, Texas.

The decades of the 1880s and 1890s were troubled times in the area. Law and order completely disappeared and were replaced by vigilante rule. San Saba, as well as Llano, Mills, and Lampasas counties were hostage to large bands of thieves and rustlers, referred to as the "mob." Several wealthy ranchers organized a counter force to seek justice, which was not available in courts. They were known as the "Mob," although neither group had a name and both denied their existence. The counter force, augmented by hired gunmen, seemed connected to mysterious murders and lynchings. Both sides were eventually taken over by armed men who engaged in open warfare. By 1896, more than fifty people had been killed, but all of the trials resulted in hung juries or acquittal.

Finally, Capt. Bill McDonald and four Texas Rangers, including W. J. L. Sullivan, were summoned, but a quick solution was not forthcoming. The Texas Rangers had tried earlier to pacify the county, but this time a fearless young attorney, W. C. Linden, had recently been elected district attorney. Linden was also known to be handy with his pearl-handled Colt .45, which he always wore. In a landmark trial in April 1897, Linden won a conviction of two of the mob. Soon trial convictions in other counties followed, and the mobs began to break up.

San Saba County has the oldest jail in continuous use in Texas. Built in 1884, it is a fine example of nineteenth-century jail construction. It is a two-story cube with a central tower on the front. Constructed of rusticated limestone, the building

has a flat roof with bracketed cornices and stilted arches that
accent the openings.

Other resources: *Dallas Morning News, Texas Almanac, 1998–1999;* Metz,
Roadside History of Texas; DeLorme Mapping, *Texas Atlas and Gazetteer;*
Tyler, Barnett, and Barkley, eds., *New Handbook of Texas,* vol. 5, 87, 884;
Newcomb, *Indians of Texas;* Reading, *Arrows over Texas;* Dabney, "The Rule
of Law vs. Mr. Colt"; Sonnichsen, *I'll Die before I'll Run.*

Schleicher County (Eldorado)

Schleicher County was part of a three-million-acre land
grant to Henry Francis Fisher in 1842. The area lay generally between the Llano River and the Colorado River. Fisher
and Burchard Miller sold their interest in the company and
their rights to the land grant to the Adelsverein. Because of
hostile Indians, however, most of the immigrants settled in
Comal and Gillespie counties. Schleicher County was cut out
of Crockett County in 1887 and named for Gustav Schleicher,
one of the Adelsverein immigrants. He was a trained engineer,
and among his various works was a bridge he built over the
Guadalupe River on the road between San Antonio and New
Braunfels.

The town of Eldorado began in 1859 as a ranch headquarters, but when the county was organized in 1901, it was
made the county seat. In 1905 the county decided to build
a jail; T. S.
Hodges
agreed to
undertake
the project
for the sum
of $8,750.
The two-
story build-
ing he con-
structed is
of rusticated

Schleicher County jail, 1905–1963, Eldorado, Texas.

limestone and has decorative Roman arches over the front entrance and second-floor windows. There was a gallows, but it was never used. The first floor provided the sheriff's quarters, and the second floor contained the jail cells. Originally, the prison part was one big room on the second floor, but in the 1920s the Southern Structural Steel Company installed a cellblock with two-person cages on the second floor.

According to retired sheriff Orville Edmiston, who lived with his family in the jail quarters for twenty-five years, there was only one escape from the lockup. A Mexican national requested an opportunity to take a bath and was allowed into the open area around the cages. Instead of bathing, he knocked a hole in the ceiling and crawled to a place where he could let himself down into the hallway; from there, he slipped out and disappeared into the mesquite brush without leaving a forwarding address.

Interviews conducted by the author: Orville Edmiston; Jerri Whitten, librarian, Schleicher County Library; Dorothy Evans.

Other resources: *Dallas Morning News, Texas Almanac, 1998–1999;* Tyler, Barnett, and Barkley, eds., *New Handbook of Texas,* vol. 1, 512, 1017, vol. 2, 1014, and vol. 5, 918, 919; Schleicher County Historical Society, *History of Schleicher County.*

Scurry County (Snyder)

Like other Panhandle counties, Scurry County was created in 1876 from Bexar County. It was organized in 1884 and named for W. R. Scurry of the Confederate Army. General Scurry and Maj. Gen. John Magruder were instrumental in the recapture of Galveston from Union forces on January 1, 1863. The Confederates launched a land and sea attack, using mounted artillery on river steamers with cotton bales as redoubts, the so-called cottonclads.

Snyder was named for William H. Snyder, who opened a trading post in 1877 to supply buffalo hunters. Soon there was a community of dugouts and tents around his store.

Scurry County had three early jails, the first in 1884, built by Sheriff W. W. Nelson on the northeast corner of the courthouse square. It was described as 8′ wide, 10′ long, and 8′ high, made of 2″ by 4″ boards laid flat and nailed down. After two years, it was replaced by a new lockup,

Scurry County jail, 1912–1978, Snyder, Texas. Photo courtesy of Aline Parks, Scurry County Museum.

which was joined to a new courthouse by a corridor. Both were made of locally fired brick.

The third jail, which is still standing, was built in 1912. The three-story red brick structure has two front corner towers and is accented by light-colored brick arches and stringcourses. The lockup contained sheriff's quarters on the ground floor, prison cells on the second floor, and a hospital on the third floor. The building was in use until 1978, when it was replaced by a modern facility.

Interviews conducted by the author: Dee Wilson, Noah Project; Aline Parks, Scurry County Museum.

Other resources: *Dallas Morning News, Texas Almanac, 1998–1999;* Tyler, Barnett, and Barkley, eds., *New Handbook of Texas,* vol. 2, 245, vol. 3, 51, and vol. 5, 946, 1129; Catton and McPherson, *American Heritage New History of the Civil War;* Metz, *Roadside History of Texas.*

Shackelford County (Albany)

Shackelford County was created from Bosque County in 1858 and organized in 1874. The area was named for Jack Shackelford, surgeon and veteran of the Texas Revolution and survivor of the Goliad massacre.

Shackelford County jail, 1927–present, Albany, Texas.

Fort Griffin, originally called Camp Wilson, was one of the U.S. Army forts that were established to protect settlers from Indian and outlaw depredations. It served briefly as the county seat. Camp Wilson, built on the floodplain of the Clear Fork of the Brazos River in 1867, was moved to high ground on a nearby one-hundred-foot bluff, and the name was changed to Fort Griffin. (There were two Fort Griffins, one in Shackelford County and one in Jefferson County, built by the Confederacy to guard Sabine Pass.) Buffalo hunters, gamblers, camp followers, and others soon established the town of Fort Griffin on "the flat" near the fort. The town is said to have had five legitimate businesses and ten saloons, testimony to the dryness of the climate. Trail driving is dry work, especially when one realizes that, in one year, 1871, a total of five hundred thousand head of cattle passed through on the dusty drives to Kansas.

Before Shackelford County was organized, Fort Griffin was the law, and the army stockade held those who threatened the peace. With the prospects of the army's departure, Henry Jacobs, the first sheriff, donated land that was to become the site of Albany and later the county seat. Jacobs served as sheriff until February 1876, when John Larn was elected sheriff, possibly because he had a track record of six victorious gunfights. In 1877 killings in the name of law and order were frequent. In June 1878 nervous local ranchers arrested Larn and put him under heavy guard in a picket house one block south of the square since the new 1878 stone jail was still unfinished. A few days later, nine masked men overpowered the jailer and, with Winchesters, terminated Sheriff Larn's term in office.

In 1878 the two-story limestone jail was finally completed, becoming the first permanent building in the county. A Fort Worth architect, John Thomas of Thomas and Werner, designed and built the lockup; Gerard B. Allen of St. Louis provided the cells and ironwork. Sheriff's quarters were on the first floor, and a large room was on the second floor, where two cells were placed, surrounded by the usual walk-around. The windows had no panes, only shutters, so the place was well ventilated both summer and winter. Since there was very little money on hand for wages, as the stonemason laid each stone, he carefully carved his name or sign into it, so that when money became available, he could be paid. The cost of the jail was nine thousand dollars. The keep was used until 1927.

In 1926 the county contracted to build a new jail designed by the Pauly Brothers Jail Manufacturing Company. Bailey, Burns, and Fitzpatrick, contractors, won the bid and completed the facility in May 1927 for $39,500. The building is still in use as a jail.

Interviews conducted by the author: Shirley W. Caldwell, Texas Historical Commission; Diana Wilsong, Old Jail Museum; Drew Gomber, Hubbard Museum of the American West; Joan Farmer.

Other resources: *Dallas Morning News, Texas Almanac, 1998–1999;* Tyler, Barnett, and Barkley, eds., *New Handbook of Texas,* vol. 1, 93, vol. 2, 205, 1102, and vol. 5, 983, 984; Fowler, "Jailhouse Museums"; Hart, *Old Forts of the Southwest;* West Texas Historical Association, *West Texas Historical Association Quarterly* 20.

Shelby County (Center)

Shelby County was one of the original counties created by the new Republic of Texas and was organized in 1837. It was named for Isaac Shelby, a soldier of the American Revolutionary War. Shelbyville was the original county seat of Shelby County, but a contested 1866 election favored Center. The records were moved to Center under cover of darkness.

Shelby County was on the western edge of the "neutral ground" between Spain and the United States. The area was never precisely defined, although the Sabine River was generally considered to be the western boundary of Louisiana.

Shelby County jail, 1883–1915, Center, Texas. Designed by John Joseph Emmett Gibson.

The neutral ground, the result of an 1806 agreement between Spain and the United States, provided that the area would remain unregulated. It became a lawless haven for desperate renegades who no doubt became some of the citizens of several counties in eastern Texas. In 1821 the Adams-Onis Treaty finally settled the boundary between Louisiana and Spain.

The jail in Shelbyville, when it was the county seat, is thought to have been a small wooden building located on the courthouse square. Inside there were iron rings to which prisoners were chained while awaiting their day in court. Punishment for serious crimes was usually swift and final, while lesser offenses might call for flogging or fines. There was little provision for costly long-term incarceration.

After the county seat was moved to Center, the first jail was a wooden building with an iron compartment built by R. B. Wilson, who was a blacksmith as well as a gunsmith. The lockup was located on Shelbyville Street about half a mile from town.

In 1883 Shelby County employed Irishman John Joseph Emmett Gibson to design a courthouse and jail. The result was a strikingly compatible pair of buildings resembling Irish castles. The lockup was a two-story red brick rectangle with a steeply pitched roof. In 1915 J. W. Smith of Shelby County designed a new detention center. It was a two-story cement-block masonry building that served as the county keep until 1974. The 1883 jail building has been used for the chamber of commerce for some time and has recently undergone major renovations.

Interviews conducted by the author: Mattie Dellinger; Sheriff James Moore.

Other resources: *Dallas Morning News, Texas Almanac, 1998–1999;* Tyler, Barnett, and Barkley, eds., *New Handbook of Texas,* vol. 1, 1009, 1011, vol. 4, 983, vol. 5, 13, and vol. 6, 252; DeLorme Mapping, *Texas Atlas and Gazetteer;* Metz, *Roadside History of Texas;* Kelsey and Dyal, *Courthouses of Texas.*

Sherman County (Stratford)

Sherman County was created in 1876 and organized in 1889 after Comanches had been removed to the Indian Territory. The county was named for Gen. Sidney Sherman of Kentucky, who arrived with a full contingent of cavalry to fight in the battle of San Jacinto. The area was surveyed by the Chicago, Rock Island, and Gulf railroad in 1874. For this service, the railroad was paid in sections of land, arranged in checkerboard fashion, with Texas retaining the alternate sections for future settlement. When the county was organized, the small town of Coldwater on Coldwater Creek was made the county seat. In 1901, although a stone courthouse and a jail had been built in Coldwater, the citizens voted to move the seat of government to Stratford, which had been named for Stratford, Virginia, the boyhood home of Robert E. Lee.

The threat of an injunction by dissidents of the move to Stratford prompted the court to meet promptly at 1:00 A.M. on May 6, 1901, to canvas the votes. Although the injunction did arrive by horseman, it was too late to halt the vote. The actual move was still highly contested, and in desperation the county records were removed in the dark of night to Stratford, where the only "courthouse" was a tent. The Texas Rangers were summoned to make sure things remained calm. A wooden courthouse and jail were soon built, and shiny Diebold cells from Coldwater were brought to the new jail. These two cells were 6′ by 8′ and had four bunks each. They were installed in the 1901 Stratford jail, where they remained until the courthouse burned in 1922.

After the 1922 fire, a new concrete courthouse with brick veneer, designed by Parker and Rittenberry in the Renaissance style, was built in Stratford. The original Coldwater Diebold jail cells, which had been contracted by L. T. Noyes, were moved into the third floor of the new courthouse to begin their third life. The cells remained in use until 1972. Since the old jail cells could not meet the new requirements set by the Committee for Jail Standards, a new free-standing lockup was built. The courthouse still stands.

Interviews conducted by the author: Karl Dretske; Sheriff Jack Hale.
Other resources: *Dallas Morning News, Texas Almanac, 1998–1999;* DeLorme Mapping, *Texas Atlas and Gazetteer;* Tyler, Barnett, and Barkley, eds., *New Handbook of Texas,* vol. 2, 1997, vol. 5, 1023, and vol. 6, 119; Kelsey and Dyal, *Courthouses of Texas.*

Smith County (Tyler)

Smith County was created in 1846 and named for Gen. James Smith, veteran of the battle of New Orleans and a friend of Col. Sam Houston in the Tennessee militia. In 1836 Smith brought one hundred well-equipped troops from Tennessee to Texas to aid in the Texas Revolution, arriving on April 22. In 1844 Smith was sent by Sam Houston to East Texas to stop the Regulator-Modulator War.

Smith County was organized in 1846, and Tyler was made the county seat. The two-day battle of the Neches River was fought in July 1839 near present-day Tyler. Chief Bowles, friend of Sam Houston and wearing a sword given him by Houston,

Smith County jail, 1881–1916, Tyler, Texas.

was shot from his horse and died in the battle, resulting in the expulsion of the Cherokee Indians from East Texas. Many of them fled across the Red River into Indian Territory in Oklahoma, accomplishing the aim of Mirabeau Lamar, president of the Texas Republic.

Altogether, Smith County has had many jails. In 1849 the first one was built of hewn pine logs. The second one, on East Jefferson Street, was perhaps the same structure, dismantled and moved to the new site. In August 1856 the court recommended advertising for proposals to build a new lockup. Specifications required it to be of brick, wood, and iron with two prison rooms, one with an iron cage, jailer's quarters, kitchen, and sheriff's office. This jail was built and served until after the Civil War.

In August 1881 Eugene Heiner designed an Italian Renaissance building with stilted arches and quoins. In its original configuration, the jail had two stories in front and one story for the prison cells in the rear. The King Iron Bridge Company provided the cells and ironwork for $4,950. In 1894 the Diebold Safe and Lock Company renovated and expanded the building to double the number of cages by adding a second floor to the rear. The Southern Structural Steel Company renovated the structure again in 1905. The jail was used until 1916.

Architects Sanguinet and Staats designed Smith County's fifth jail on South Spring Street at Erwin in 1915; it was built by E. L. Twing Company, general contractors, of San Antonio. The Pauly Jail Building Company provided the cells and ironwork. This keep was used until a new courthouse was built in 1954, with a jail on the top floor—the sixth jail for Smith County.

Interview conducted by the author: Mary Jane McNamara, Smith County Historical Society.

Other resources: *Dallas Morning News, Texas Almanac, 1998–1999;* Tyler, Barnett, and Barkley, eds., *New Handbook of Texas,* vol. 4, 965, 967, vol. 5, 1102, 1113, and vol. 6, 967; Metz, *Roadside History of Texas;* W. Robinson, *People's Architecture;* Newcomb, *Indians of Texas;* Gilbert, "Jails of Smith County."

Somervell County (Glen Rose)

Somervell County was created from Hood and Bosque
counties in 1875. A town with the unlikely name of Glen
Rose was made the county seat. Glen Rose is on the left bank
of the Paluxy River a short distance before it enters the Brazos
River. T. C. Jordan bought an established grist mill, Barnard's
Mill, from its founder, Charles Barnard, in 1871. Jordan's wife,
a native of Scotland, suggested the name Glen Rose in recog-
nition of the lovely wild roses growing in the area.

Somervell County was named for Gen. Alexander Somervell, participant in the siege of Bexar in October 1835 and
the battle of San Jacinto in April 1836. In October 1842 Sam
Houston ordered Somervell to lead a punitive expedition into
Mexico as reprisal for the Mexicans' three invasions into
Texas. This became known as the Somervell expedition. The
mission aborted in mid-December; half of the volunteers then
defied orders to return to Texas and continued on to the ill-
fated Mier expedition.

Somervell County is second only to Rockwall County as
the smallest county in Texas. Its first jail, built in 1884, was
based on a plan by J. J. Liggon, agent for the Pauly Jail Manufacturing Company. The lockup was constructed of concrete,
rocks, and locally quarried stone. It was a Spartan affair, one
story in height, with unglazed, barred windows and a dirt
floor. All of the ironwork and the cells were provided by Pauly.

A wood
stove was
made avail-
able to take
the chill
from the
inhospitable
room. This
jail was used
until 1934,
when it was
demolished

Somervell County jail, 1934–1979, Glen Rose, Texas.

to make room for a new stone-and-concrete structure built by the Works Project Administration during the Depression era.

The 1934 jail had two stories, with sheriff's quarters on the ground floor and the old Pauly compartments recycled and put on the second floor. The windows had glass panes. It was later necessary to put screens in the windows to prevent the prisoners from making weapons by breaking the glass. The usual wood stove provided heat. Later, one of the prisoners managed to hit the sheriff with a stick of stove wood, take the keys, and escape. The wood stove was subsequently replaced with a gas stove.

Interview conducted by the author: Betty Gosdin, Somervell County Heritage Center.

Other resources: *Dallas Morning News, Texas Almanac, 1998–1999;* Tyler, Barnett, and Barkley, eds., *New Handbook of Texas,* vol. 3, 190, and vol. 5, 1144, 1145.

Starr County (Rio Grande City)

Starr County was created from Nueces County and organized in 1848 after the Treaty of Guadalupe Hidalgo was signed in 1846, ending the U.S.-Mexican War. The county was named for James Harper Starr, a physician and secretary of the treasury of the Republic of Texas. Historically, the Coahuiltican Indians occupied the area along the Rio Grande and no doubt were the first Indians encountered by the Spanish as they began to explore the Rio Grande valley in the sixteenth century. The Coahuilticans willingly joined the Spanish missions and accepted Christianity. After a while, however, many of them began to die of the white man's diseases, while many others were absorbed into the Spanish population.

In 1847 Henry Clay Davis established Rio Grande City on his ranch at a spot on the river called Davis's Landing. In an effort to protect citizens from Mexican and Indian depredations, the U.S. Army established Camp Ringgold on land leased from Davis in 1848. The camp became Fort Ringgold and after the Civil War took on a more permanent nature. The fort remained in use until 1944, but the Rio Grande City Consolidated School District is now the custodian of the grounds.

In 1854 Mifflin Kenedy, partner of Capt. Richard King, built a warehouse for use in their riverboat trade in Rio Grande City. The storehouse was later used as a courthouse and jail, complete with a hanging tree on the patio. During renovations in 1915, two skeletons, allegedly found in the patio, were believed to be victims of the hangman's noose.

In 1886 Samuel Wallace Brooks, a contractor from Brownsville, built a new courthouse and jail on the north end of Bratton Avenue. These buildings were used until 1935, when the county constructed a new courthouse designed by Stanley W. Bliss. The lockup was in the basement and was in use until a freestanding jail was built in 1993.

Interviews conducted by the author: Sam Ramos, Texas Historical Commission; Juan Guerra, sheriff, Starr County.

Other resources: *Dallas Morning News, Texas Almanac, 1998–1999;* Metz, *Roadside History of Texas;* Tyler, Barnett, and Barkley, eds., *New Handbook of Texas,* vol. 2, 1116, vol. 3, 1064, vol. 5, 584, and vol. 6, 66, 67; DeLorme Mapping, *Texas Atlas and Gazetteer;* Reading, *Arrows over Texas;* Newcomb, *Indians of Texas;* Greene, *When Rio Grande City Was Young.*

Stephens County (Breckenridge)

Stephens County was created in 1858 and originally named Buchanan County for Pres. James Buchanan. In 1861, however, since the president was no longer in favor, the name was changed to Stephens County in honor of Alexander H. Stephens, vice president of the Confederate States of America. Breckenridge (not to be confused with Breckinridge, a suburb of Dallas) was originally called Picketville and became the county seat in 1876, when the county was organized. It was named for John C. Breckinridge, U.S. senator from Kentucky and later vice president of the United States.

In 1877, apparently growing tired of paying $1.50 per day to hire men to guard prisoners, the commissioners' court decided to build a jail. J. Sphar of Weatherford drew the plans and specifications, and A. Miller of Breckenridge contracted to build the jail for four thousand dollars. The building was to be made of stone, 22' wide by 28' long, and two stories high. The foundation was

Stephens County jail, 1877–1927, Breckenridge, Texas. Photo courtesy of Swenson Memorial Museum.

to be dug 18" below grade and was to measure 18" high and 24" wide. The jail was completed in the fall of 1877. There is evidence that extensive work was done in 1910. "Historical Sketches of Stephens County" reports that George Bingham remembers working on the jail in 1910, when he was a boy. Pictorial evidence, however, indicates that the work would have been a major repair or reconstruction of the interior and not the construction of a new structure.

The old courthouse burned in 1925, and, when a new courthouse was built in 1926, a jail was included on the top floor. That building is still used today.

Interviews conducted by the author: Sheriff James D. Reeves; Freda M. Mitchell, Swenson Memorial Museum.

Other resources: *Dallas Morning News, Texas Almanac, 1998–1999;* Metz, *Roadside History of Texas;* Kelsey and Dyal, *Courthouses of Texas;* Breckenridge Bicentennial Committee, "Historical Sketches of Stephens County"; Hartsfield, "History of Stephens County, Texas"; Tyler, Barnett, and Barkley, eds., *New Handbook of Texas,* vol. 1, 718, 719, and vol. 6, 88.

Sterling County (Sterling City)

Sterling County was created from Tom Green County and organized in 1891. It was named for buffalo hunter W. S. Sterling, who settled in the area and lived there for more than twenty years. The North Concho River, which runs west to

Sterling County jail, 1912–present, Sterling City, Texas.

east through the county, was the hunting ground of the Comanche, Lipan, and Kiowa Indians until after the Civil War. Pearls from clams in the Concho River were highly prized by the Indians and may explain the inspiration for a local legend: the "cache of Spanish pearls."

There is a story about a desperate battle between Indians and U.S. troopers on "Tower Hill," five miles south of Sterling City. The date and circumstances of the battle have been lost in time, and only the relics, accidentally found, are left to reconstruct the story. The buried remains of an Indian in full headdress, a chief with a bullet hole in his skull, constitute the evidence of the conflict. Several rifles, probably of 1824–1850 vintage, some military-type brass buttons, and a sterling silver cup with an inscription dated 1844 were buried with the Indian. It is left to the reader to fill in the drama.

As the army pushed the Indians from the area, settlement slowly began. In the early years, the area was open range; then homestead laws encouraged the arrival of new ranchers, some of whom purchased up to seven sections of land. As the homesteaders and small ranchers began fencing their property, fence cutting followed. This was a widespread problem at first, but vigorous action by the Texas Rangers soon discouraged the practice. The legislature made fence cutting a felony, and by 1890 the offense was mostly under control.

There was no formal jail in the early days of Sterling County, but in 1912 the Southern Structural Steel Company was called upon to design and build a lockup. The result was a two-story limestone cube with sheriff's quarters on the first floor and seven cells for prisoners on the second floor. In 1960 the jail was expanded to its present size. It is still used and is approved by the Texas Commission for Jail Standards, but long-term incarceration is usually delegated to one of the surrounding counties.

Interviews conducted by the author: Dan Glass, Texas Historical Commission; Pinky Humble, Sterling City Library; Vera Allen; Jim Davis.

Other resources: *Dallas Morning News, Texas Almanac, 1998–1999;* Metz, *Roadside History of Texas;* Tyler, Barnett, and Barkley, eds., *New Handbook of Texas,* vol. 6, 93; W. P. Webb, *Texas Rangers; San Angelo Morning Times,* Aug. 26, 1931; *Sterling City News-Records,* Oct. 5, 1934.

Stonewall County (Aspermont)

Stonewall County was created along with fifty-four other Panhandle counties by the fifteenth Texas legislature in 1876. It was named for Gen. Stonewall Jackson of the Confederate Army, hero of the battle of First Manassas. The county was organized in 1888, and the town of Rayner was made the county seat. In 1898 the seat of government was moved to Aspermont, eight miles to the west, but a protest delayed movement of the public buildings until 1900. Aspermont was the creation of A. L. Rhomberg, who platted the town in 1889 and named it with the Latin words meaning "rough mountain."

The first jail was completed in Rayner in November 1890, even before the courthouse was finished. The lockup contained cages and ironwork by Pauly Jail Building and Manufacturing. Once the

Stonewall County jail, 1910–1953, Aspermont, Texas. Photo by Stanley Gilbert. From the author's collection.

county seat was officially moved, the businesses began to move also, and the town of Rayner, except for the stone courthouse, essentially vanished.

In 1901 the court ordered the Pauly cages moved to Aspermont and directed that a "house," measuring 18′ by 24′, be built over the cages. The structure was to have 10′ walls, three windows, and one door; it would serve as the county jail for nine years. It was not until 1910 that a new two-story stone lockup was built, still utilizing the original Pauly cells. Additional cages were ordered, and the final version had eight compartments of unknown capacity on the second floor. William Bailey Bingham, father of Mrs. E. Dean Scroggins, was the popular sheriff from 1920 to 1937 and was known for enforcing the law without carrying a gun. Mrs. Scroggins remembers living in the jail when she was a child and says that the lockup filled up on weekends with drunks, all of whom were fined and released on Sunday. Scroggins's mother cooked for her family and for the prisoners as well. Remnants of the 1910 stone jail are still there, although the second floor has been removed. The jail was used until 1953.

Interviews conducted by the author: Sheriff Bill Mullen; Mrs. E. Dean Scroggins.

Other resources: *Dallas Morning News, Texas Almanac, 1998–1999;* Kelsey and Dyal, *Courthouses of Texas;* Tyler, Barnett, and Barkley, eds., *New Handbook of Texas,* vol. 1, 268, vol. 5, 461, and vol. 6, 113.

Sutton County (Sonora)

Sutton County—named for John S. Sutton, veteran of the Army of the Republic of Texas, a Texas Ranger, and a Confederate officer at the battle of Val Verde in New Mexico—was created from Crockett County in 1887 and organized in 1890. Sutton County is in arid country devoid of surface water. In 1884 A. J. Winkler drilled a successful water well, and a community, Winkler's Well, formed. When the county was organized in 1890, the town of Sonora, two miles north and founded in 1887, had sufficient population to be voted the county seat. That town was named for Sonora,

Mexico, the home and name of one of the family servants of Charles G. Adams, one of the three organizers of the town.

In July 1890, on the

Sutton County jail, 1892–1980, Sonora, Texas.

day the county was organized, the commissioners ordered one pair of handcuffs, one single handcuff with a lock, and two pairs of leg irons. In 1891 J. Q. Adams, one of the founders of Sonora, shot and killed another pioneer, Isaac Miers, in an argument over whose turn it was to water his sheep at the town well. The need for a jail was evident. The local blacksmith happened to also be the justice of the peace. In one case, he had to chain a wrongdoer to a post and finish shoeing a horse before he could hold a trial.

In February 1891 a contract was let for Sutton County's first jail. Oscar Ruffini of San Angelo designed a lockup and a courthouse in Second Empire style, using native limestone for both. Pauly Jail Building and Manufacturing contracted to provide the cells and ironwork for $11,700. The building contractor was Z. D. Gifford. The sheriff's quarters were on the first floor, and the cells on the second. The commissioners accepted the jail in September 1891.

The jail, rated for fourteen prisoners, was 41′ by 29′ in outside dimension. The ceilings of both the first and second levels were made of steel. The second floor contained two steel cells separated by a corridor, and there were two iron cells for female prisoners or detainees with serious mental disorders. There was no electricity. The prison units, installed by Pauly, came fully equipped with toilets and washbasins, but there was no sanitary system to which they could be attached. Water pressure from the well was zero, so the conveniences

would not work anyway. The sheriff's family used the out-
house, located twenty feet away, and the prisoners had chamber pots. The jailer was paid six dollars per month to haul water from the well. In 1896 the water system was moved to the
top of the hill, and at last there was enough pressure to run
a sanitary system.

Today the old jail has been replaced by a new structure that
was finished in 1980. The 1891 jail, however, continues to
serve the community as a museum. The building is still sound,
testimony to the skills of Oscar Ruffini and the craftspeople of
more than one hundred years ago.

Interviews conducted by the author: Jo Ann Palmer, Sutton County
Historical Society; Sheriff Joe Fincher.

Other resources: *Dallas Morning News, Texas Almanac 1998–1999;* Metz,
Roadside History of Texas; Kelsey and Dyal, *Courthouses of Texas;* Tyler,
Barnett, and Barkley, eds., *New Handbook of Texas,* vol. 1, 159; Eaton,
"Sutton County Jail."

Swisher County (Tulia)

Swisher County was created in 1876 and organized in
1890. It was named for J. G. Swisher, veteran of the Texas
Revolution. The dominant topographical feature is Tule
Creek, which flows from west to east into the Prairie Dog
Town Fork of the Red River. During the Red River War
against the Plains Indians, after years of frustrated searching,
Col. Ranald S. Mackenzie discovered the Indians' hiding place
in nearby Palo Duro Canyon. In a dawn attack in 1874,
Mackenzie's troopers won a decisive victory over the Kiowa,
Cheyenne, and Comanche Indians. Although many Indians
were killed, the fact that Mackenzie killed all of the horses
meant the end of the Indians' ability to survive. This victory
broke the back of Indian power in the Texas Panhandle.

In 1883 Charles Goodnight bought the Tule Ranch, 170,000
acres of land in the eastern part of the future Swisher County,
adding to the already large holdings of the JA Ranch. His
headquarters were located twelve miles east of present-day
Tulia in Palo Duro Canyon. There Goodnight and his wife

built a house and other necessary adjuncts to the large ranching operation, such as a bunkhouse, mess hall, dairy, poultry yard, blacksmith shop, and tin shop. His partner was John George Adair, English owner of a large Irish estate and a brokerage firm in New York. Upon the death of Adair, Goodnight received 140,000 acres of land and twenty thousand cattle for his one-third interest. He did not get the headquarters property, where he had lavished so much effort in organizing one of the outstanding ranches in the West. The annual profit, 72 percent, was impressive, but more important still is the record Goodnight gave it as an institution of goodwill and fair dealing.

These principals still live in legend. Before there were jails in this part of the world, Goodnight organized the cattle ranchers and their cowboys to apprehend rustlers and other lawbreakers and then to pass them along from ranch to ranch until they could be turned over to jails that existed in Colorado.

The present jail for Swisher County is on the site of the original lockup built in Tulia in 1890. Billy Sue Gayler, whose husband was Sheriff John Gayler, says that the jail has been remodeled at least three times and is still certified by the Commission for Jail Standards. Originally the jail was two stories built of brick with limestone trim. The sheriff's quarters were on the first floor, and two cells for prisoners were on the second floor.

Interview conducted by the author: Billie Sue Gayler, Swisher County Museum.

Other resources: *Dallas Morning News, Texas Almanac, 1998–1999;* Tyler, Barnett, and Barkley, eds., *New Handbook of Texas,* vol. 4, 416, vol. 5, 28, and vol. 6, 181, 585; J. E. Haley, *Charles Goodnight;* Flores, *Caprock Canyonlands;* Tise, *Texas County Sheriffs;* DeLorme Mapping, *Texas Atlas and Gazetteer.*

Tarrant County (Fort Worth)

Tarrant County was created in 1849. It was one of twenty-eight counties created from the area of the Peters colony. (In 1843 Peters and Company had contracted with the Repub-

Tarrant County jail, 1917–present, Fort Worth, Texas.

lic of Texas to bring in 250 families per year to Texas.) When the county was created, Birdville, previously called Bird's Fort, was designated the county seat. Bird's Fort had been established in 1840 by Col. Jonathan Bird and was located about nine miles east of where Fort Worth would be built in June 1849 on the south bank of the Trinity River at its junction with the Clear Fork. The post served until abandoned in September 1853.

In 1860, when the time came to hold an election for the county seat, the Fort Worth crowd was ready. Both Birdville and Fort Worth offered open barrels of whiskey at their respective polls, but the Fort Worth advocates had slipped over in the dark of election eve and siphoned the Birdville whiskey into their own barrels to augment their influence on the voters. They managed to bring fifteen citizens of Wise County to vote for Fort Worth, and Fort Worth won by seven votes.

In 1876 the Texas and Pacific Railroad arrived, providing a way to move cattle to northern and eastern markets. As the stockyards expanded, the Missouri, Kansas, and Texas Railroad arrived to assist in the burgeoning cattle market.

Between 1849 and 1856, two courthouses and one jail had been built in Birdville. The lockup is described as a two-story building, 40′ by 18′, but other details, including the date of construction, are unknown. After the county seat moved to Fort Worth in 1860, the Civil War and Reconstruction obscured the story of jail construction. In 1877, however, a local firm, Thomas and Werner, built a jail, but to the commissioners' great embarrassment, locks were not included. This circumstance resulted in the escape of six criminals, including murderers, horse thieves, and highwaymen.

In 1884 Houston architect Eugene Heiner designed a new jail for Fort Worth. The building was north of the old courthouse and cost sixty thousand dollars. It was used until 1917, when a new criminal courts building, including a lockup, was built on the site of the original 1849 military Fort Worth. Fort Worth architects Sanguinet and Staats designed the Classical Revival–style building. It contained the criminal court rooms and offices for the sheriff and the district attorney. The jail, including the gallows, occupied the top four floors. The jail continues in use today.

Interviews conducted by the author: Chief Deputy Sheriff Hank Pope; Sarah Biles, North Fort Worth Historical Society; David Bucek, architectural historian.

Other resources: *Dallas Morning News, Texas Almanac, 1998–1999;* Tyler, Barnett, and Barkley, eds., *New Handbook of Texas,* vol. 1, 559, vol. 2, 1122, and vol. 6, 206, 207, 751; Metz, *Roadside History of Texas;* Knight, *Fort Worth;* W. Robinson, *People's Architecture;* W. Robinson, *Gone from Texas;* DeLorme Mapping, *Texas Atlas and Gazetteer.*

Taylor County (Abilene)

Named for three brothers, Edward, James, and George Taylor, who died defending the Alamo, Taylor County was created in 1854 and organized in 1878. Buffalo Gap was named the county seat. Abilene was created in 1880, when local landowners enticed the Texas and Pacific Railroad to route the tracks north of Buffalo Gap to the site of Abilene. The Hashknife Ranch donated much of the acreage for Abilene, which was named after Abilene, Kansas, a shipping point for many of the early Texas cattle drives.

Buffalo Gap, the first county seat of Taylor County, was established in 1857. It lay on a very distinct typographical feature of the county, the Callahan Divide, which runs more or less east and west across the midriff of the county. It is an elevated escarpment that drains to the Brazos River on the north and the Colorado River on the south. There is a gap in this high

Taylor County jail and courthouse, 1879–1883, Buffalo Gap, Texas.

ground through which flows Elm Creek, a historic watering place for the great buffalo herds as they migrated to the southern wintering grounds.

Buffalo Gap was a natural choice for the first county seat in 1874, and by 1879, a substantial building had been completed for a courthouse and jail. Designed and built by Martin, Byrnes, and Johnson, the brown sandstone edifice was 36′ by 34′ and two stories high. It contained offices on the first floor and a jail cage on the second floor. The gallows, conspicuously displayed at the head of the stairs to the jail, was reportedly never used. An interesting feature of the construction was the use of Civil War cannonballs inserted between the building stones to add stability and to prevent the displacement of stones by a prisoner intent on escape.

After the railroad arrived in Abilene, agitation soon began to move the county seat. The vote in October 1883 was final, but there was a serious armed confrontation on the outskirts of Buffalo Gap. Eventually cooler heads prevailed, and the dispute was settled by arbitration. Abilene already had a board-and-batten building that had served as a holding jail. In 1896 Pauly Jail Building and Manufacturing built a three-story rusticated stone lockup with a prominent central tower on Pecan Street

In 1931 a modern five-story prison replaced the old jail. David Castle and G. F. Campbell designed the Art Deco structure with stylized scenes in relief around the top. Suggs Construction Company erected the building, and the Southern Prison Company of San Antonio provided the cells and ironwork. After World War II, a new jail, the Taylor County Detention Center, was built on South 27th Street.

Interviews conducted by the author: Larry Abrigg, Texas Historical Commission; Jack Holden; Mildred Cornelius; John Anderson, Abilene Public Library.

Other resources: *Dallas Morning News, Texas Almanac, 1998–1999;* Tyler, Barnett, and Barkley, eds., *New Handbook of Texas,* vol. 1, 8, 813, and vol. 6, 223; DeLorme Mapping, *Texas Atlas and Gazetteer;* Zachary, *History of Rural Taylor County.*

Terrell County (Sanderson)

Terrell County was created in 1905 and organized that same year. It was named for Alexander Watkins Terrell, district judge, Confederate general, representative to the Texas State House, and minister to the Ottoman Empire. Sanderson began in 1882 as a town site platted by Cyrus ("Charlie") Wilson on the proposed route of the Galveston, Harrisburg, and San Antonio Railroad. He originally called the town Strawbridge but later changed the name to Sanderson for a railroad engineer.

Terrell County has evidence of prehistoric Indian occupation, especially along the Rio Grande and adjacent canyons, where middens and artifacts are numerous. In the area of Dryden, the only other town in the county, there are rock shelters with pictographs and blackened walls from ancient campfires.

The railroad tracks through the rough and remote country between Del Rio and Sanderson were irresistible to train robbers. In the early 1900s "Black Jack" Ketchum robbed a Southern Pacific train but missed ninety thousand dollars. In 1912 Ben Kilpatrick, formerly of the Butch Cassidy gang, attempted, with his companion "Ole Buck," to rob a Southern Pacific train east of Sanderson. D. A. Trousdale, the express messenger, killed Kilpatrick with a blow to the head with an ice mallet and then shot Ole Buck in the head when Buck peeked through the door to find out what was going on.

The first jail in Sanderson was a double-walled adobe building built before the turn of the century. It was on the corner of Oak and Second streets. The structure had one room with a ceiling of split cedar posts and two feet of earth piled on top. It is claimed that no escape occurred from this primitive calaboose. The jail was torn down after being heavily damaged by a flood in 1905. Sanderson was at the end of the railroad tracks, an oasis, so to speak, for thirsty cowboys. It was noted for its accumulation of hard cases and gunmen. The need for a larger jail was soon apparent, and a three-story brick lockup was built in 1907, when the courthouse was constructed. It was located on the courthouse square and had sheriff's quarters on the first floor. The jail was used until 1930, when the courthouse was remodeled and a jail added to the top floor. This facility was used until 1984.

Interview conducted by the author: Terry ("Tex") Tolar.
Other resources: *Dallas Morning News, Texas Almanac, 1998–1999;* Tyler, Barnett, and Barkley, eds., *New Handbook of Texas,* vol. 5, 830, and vol. 6, 258, 262; Metz, *Roadside History of Texas;* Downie, *Terrell County Texas;* Wilson, *Southern Pacific Lines.*

Terry County (Brownfield)

Terry County, whose center is forty miles southwest of Lubbock, was created in 1876. It was named for Benjamin Franklin Terry, who moved to Texas with his mother in 1833, when he was twelve years old. In 1861 he organized Terry's Texas Rangers, later known as the Confederate Texas 8th Cavalry. Unfortunately, Colonel Terry was killed in the very first action of his unit in Kentucky during the Civil War. Before that time, Terry had developed a successful sugar plantation and, with William J. Kyle, had contracted to build the first railroad in Texas, the Buffalo Bayou, Brazos, and Colorado Railway from Harrisburg to Richmond in 1851. By 1856, the tracks had reached only as far as the Brazos River, but Harrisburg was already enjoying a commercial bonanza. Houston, sniffing a good thing, arranged financing for a rail line to connect to the track ten miles west of Harrisburg. Terry and Kyle built the new railroad, which soon became known as the Houston Tap.

Brownfield was platted in 1903 by W. G. Hardin and A. F. Small on land purchased from A. M. Brownfield. When the county was organized in 1904, Brownfield was chosen as

county seat
in a close
election.
Movement
into the
county had
been slow
until 1890,
when the
state began
making ten-
year leases
of school

Terry County jail, 1916–1926, Brownfield, Texas. Photo by
Stanley Gilbert. From the author's collection.

land to settlers. In addition, in 1901 large blocks of railroad
land began being sold to farmers, who expanded cotton and
corn production.

The first jail in Terry County was a 1916 wooden building
on the southeast corner of the courthouse square. Its one
room contained two steel cells. In 1925 a new lockup was built
on the second floor of a new courthouse. After retirement,
the little wooden jail was given to the Terry County Heritage
Museum.

Betty Hamilton recollects election day around the courthouse during her school days. Prisoners would call down to
the children and throw money for them to go purchase ciga-
rettes for them. In 1951 the courthouse was remodeled and
expanded. The 1925 jail in the courthouse is still in use.

Other resources: *Dallas Morning News, Texas Almanac, 1998–1999;* Metz,
Roadside History of Texas; Tyler, Barnett, and Barkley, eds., *New Handbook of
Texas,* vol. 1, 772, and vol. 6, 265, 266.

Throckmorton County (Throckmorton)

Throckmorton County was created in 1854 and named
for William E. Throckmorton, a physician. Occupying
the edge of civilization on the Texas frontier, the area, not surprisingly, was not organized until 1879. The first option for

Throckmorton County jail, 1893–1986, Throckmorton, Texas.

a county seat was Williamsburg, but when the county was organized, Throckmorton was chosen to be the seat of government.

Throckmorton was at the crossroads of trails leading west. Capt. Randolph B. Marcy, after serving with Zachary Taylor at Palo Alto and Resaca de la Palma in the Mexican War, returned to Texas. In 1849, directed by the advice of Manuel, a Comanche guide, Throckmorton blazed the route known as Marcy's Trail from Santa Fe, New Mexico, to Fort Smith, Arkansas. That same trail in 1871, just west of Fort Belknap, would be the scene of the Warren Wagon Train Massacre.

Throckmorton County and adjacent Young County were the first to try the idea of placing Native Americans on a reservation. Two areas were to be provided, one on the clear fork of the Brazos in extreme southeastern Throckmorton County for the Comanche, and another, known as the Brazos Reservation on the Brazos River, for the Cherokee, Choctaw, Waco, Tonkawa, Wichita, Caddo, and Tehuacanas. The Brazos Reservation, finally expanded to 36,000 acres, was in the area south of present-day Graham, Texas. Keeping the Indians on the reservation turned out to be difficult; the Comanche, especially, slipped off and raided settlers, then returned immediately to the sanctuary of the reservation. The settlers, in ever-increasing numbers, coveted the prime farmland of the Brazos Reservation and finally would not be denied. After four years, both reservations were abandoned, and the Indians were removed to Indian Territory in Oklahoma.

The first jail in Throckmorton County in the 1880s was a plank calaboose, 14′ by 14′ and made of 2″ by 6″ boards laid flat and nailed down to the planks below. This type of construction was frequently used pending construction of a more durable prison. In 1893 the bid of the Pauly Jail Building and Manufacturing Company was accepted for a second jail for $10,250. It was a substantial two-story sandstone building that still stands today as a testimony to its builder. The old jail was used until 1986. The 1893 lockup has now been made into the Throckmorton County Museum, and the Pauly cells are still in the old jail as originally built.

Interview conducted by the author: Mattie Barrington, Throckmorton County Museum.

Other resources: *Dallas Morning News, Texas Almanac, 1998–1999;* Metz, *Roadside History of Texas;* Tyler, Barnett, and Barkley, eds., *New Handbook of Texas,* vol. 1, 714, 932, vol. 4, 504, and vol. 6, 487; DeLorme Mapping, *Texas Atlas and Gazetteer;* Newcomb, *Indians of Texas;* J. W. Williams and Neighbours, *Old Texas Trails;* Merriman, *Once upon a Time in Throckmorton,* vol. 2.

Titus County (Mount Pleasant)

Titus County was created from Red River and Bowie counties in 1846 and was named for Andrew Jackson Titus, who fought as a young soldier in the Mexican War and served one term in the Texas legislature from 1851 to 1852 before his premature death at age thirty-two.

When Titus County was formed in 1846, Mount Pleasant was named the county seat. Not surprisingly in fertile East Texas, Titus County was an agricultural community dependent on slave labor. At the end of the Civil War, the loss of capital in terms of freed slaves was more than one million dollars, not counting the devaluation of the land now dispossessed of labor to produce crops. The Reconstruction government enforced laws unevenly, and many men were arrested on flimsy charges and confined to the large military stockade near Jefferson. Newly freed slaves roamed about, and many became surly. This was the background that developed outlaws such as Cole Younger and the Dalton gang.

Titus County is complicated by its bad luck with five courthouses. The second courthouse, built in 1851, is said to

Titus County jail, 1917–1985, Mount Pleasant, Texas.

have fallen down in 1867. The fourth was destroyed by fire in 1894 with the loss of all records. The 1895 courthouse has been extensively remodeled twice, so that none of its original character is now evident.

The first jail in Titus County, date unknown, was on the courthouse square. It was two stories, built of huge 10″ square hewn logs, carefully notched and fitted together. It was lined on the inside with large slabs of heart pine and fastened with nails so close together that sawing into the wood would have been difficult. The first-floor jail had two tiny barred windows, high up, allowing minimal light and essentially no communication with the outside. Access to the first floor was through a trapdoor in typical dungeon fashion.

In 1917 a red brick jail on the corner of West Second and North Van Buren streets was built. The three-story building contained prison cells on the third floor and a gallows that was never used. There was a jury room on the second floor, and quarters for the sheriff were located on the first floor. C. W. Vaughn built the jail, and F. J. Meyers Manufacturing Company of Covington, Kentucky, provided the cages and ironwork. After sixty-three years, the 1917 jail was replaced by a new building in the mid-1980s.

Interviews conducted by the author: John Moss, retired sheriff; Jeanette McCoy, Mount Pleasant Public Library; Claude Alexander, Texas Historical Commission.

Other resources: *Dallas Morning News, Texas Almanac, 1998–1999;* Tyler, Barnett, and Barkley, eds., *New Handbook of Texas,* vol. 4, 868, and vol. 6, 507; Kelsey and Dyal, *Courthouses of Texas;* Jurney, *History of Titus County;* Russell, *Story of Titus County, Texas.*

Tom Green County (San Angelo)

Tom Green County was created in 1874 and was named for Gen. Thomas Green, veteran of three Texas wars as well as the Somervell expedition. He helped operate the two cannon known as the "Twin Sisters" at the battle of San Jacinto, fought at the battle of Monterey in the Mexican War, and participated in the battle of Galveston early in the Civil War and later in the Red River Campaign, where he was killed.

Tom Green County was organized in 1875 with Ben Ficklin as the county seat. In the beginning, the county was a large area from which eleven additional counties would be carved. Ben Ficklin remained the county seat until 1882, when a tremendous flood washed the town away with substantial loss of life. The seat of government was moved shortly afterward to San Angelo. Originally called Santa Angela, San Angelo was founded as a trading post across the Concho River from Fort Concho, which was established in 1867. As with all frontier towns, San Angelo's early days were characterized by saloons, brothels, and gambling houses, but the location on good water and the surrounding farm and ranch land positioned it well for cattle business. San Angelo has evolved into a diversified business, farming, and ranching community with a state university, a retirement community, and exceptional medical facilities.

The first jail was in Ben Ficklin and is said

Tom Green County jail, 1882–1884, San Angelo, Texas. Courtesy of Tom Green County Historical Society Collection, West Texas Collection, Angelo State University, San Angelo.

to have been a log cabin with a dirt floor. It was mostly for the confinement of drunks. Soldier prisoners from Fort Concho set this hoosegow afire, but they almost suffocated before they could be released. The jail was washed away in the big 1882 Concho River flood.

The second county lockup, this time in San Angelo, was not much of an improvement in that it was a log picket-style building of conservative dimensions. In 1884 the commissioners employed a local architect, Oscar Ruffini, brother of Frederick Ruffini of Austin, to design a more imposing facility. This turned out to be a three-story castle, a limestone structure with a central tower and crenellations. In 1912 Ruffini designed an addition to the west side that more than doubled the prison space. The sheriff's quarters and the gallows were in the original structure, and the cells were in the new building. Another renovation was done in 1957, but the old jail was finally replaced with a modern facility in 1977, and the handsome old building was torn down.

Interviews conducted by the author: Ann Campbell and Tanya Morris, Porter Henderson Library, Angelo State University; Evelyn Lemons, Fort Concho Historic Landmark; Ross McSwain; Ralph Chase.

Other resources: *Dallas Morning News, Texas Almanac, 1998–1999;* Tyler, Barnett, and Barkley, eds., *New Handbook of Texas,* vol. 3, 316, vol. 5, 792, and vol. 6, 522; Newcomb, *Indians of Texas;* Bess Nasworthy Collection, Angelo State College; Tom Green County Historical Society, *Historical Montage of Tom Green County;* W. Robinson, *Gone from Texas* and *People's Architecture.*

Travis County (Austin)

Travis County, named for the hero and defender of the Alamo, Col. William Barret Travis, was created in 1840 from Bastrop County and organized in 1843. It is not easy to separate the history of Travis County from that of Austin, Texas, the capital.

After the Republic of Texas won its independence from Mexico, Columbia, now West Columbia, was made the first seat of government. Gen. Sam Houston was elected the first president of the new republic. After three months, the town

of Houston,
newly cre-
ated by
the Allen
Brothers on
the muddy
banks of
Buffalo
Bayou, was
selected as
a temporary
capital. But
in Decem-

Travis County jail, 1876–1931, Austin, Texas. Photo
C00610, Austin History Center, Austin Public Library.

ber 1836 President Houston ordered the government moved
to Houston. Mirabeau B. Lamar, perhaps anticipating his turn
as president, had proposed two spots on the Colorado River
as potential sites for the capital, but Houston vetoed a bill to
move his chosen capital to La Grange.

Lamar got his way, however, when he was inaugurated as
the second president of the Republic of Texas. In January 1839
a little colony called Waterloo on the Colorado River, upstream from La Grange, changed its name to Austin and became the capital. The first few years in Austin were troubled
by Comanche raids, horse theft, and the usual gunfights in
saloons. Adding insult to injury, the Mexicans invaded three
times and finally captured San Antonio in March 1842. Sam
Houston, once again president of Texas, ordered the public
records moved to Houston for safekeeping. When the citizens
of Austin refused, Sam Houston sent armed men for the documents, resulting in the "Archives War." The records were
never transferred, and when the constitutional convention for
annexation was held in 1845, Texans made Austin the permanent capital.

The construction of a jail in Austin was discussed at a commissioners' court meeting in 1840, but not until 1847 were
plans actually drawn and eighteen hundred dollars set aside for
the first jail. That structure is believed to have been a typical
dungeon located on the courthouse block on West Fourth
Street and built by Thomas H. Jones. The building was lost

to fire in 1855. That same year, a tax was set aside to build the first permanent courthouse and lockup.

The new courthouse was located on the old courthouse block bounded by Guadalupe and San Antonio streets and West Third and West Fourth streets. The building measured 70' by 50' and stood 28' high. Within the brick walls of the structure were a jail and a dungeon that was 16' by 16' with 4' thick stone walls. The 8' walls of the keep were covered by an arched stone ceiling 4' thick at the base and tapered to 2' at the center. The jail was moved in 1876, but the old building was not razed until 1906.

During the Civil War, not much was done about a jail. During Reconstruction, arrests of citizens on spurious charges were so numerous that a palisade prison was built of 12' timbers planted in the ground. Called the Bull Pen, it was patrolled by armed troops on an elevated walkway.

In 1868 a seven and one-half cent tax was imposed to finance a courthouse and jail. The result in 1876 was a prison with twin towers on Eleventh Street between Congress and Brazos streets. The architectural firm of Larmour and Klerke designed the edifice. The towers and the walls were crenulated castle-style all around. At one time the jail held a young bank clerk, William Sidney Porter, who was mistakenly convicted of bank embezzlement as a result of a clerical error. Porter would later become famous as a writer of short stories under the nom de plume O. Henry. There was no gallows in the jail but rather a courtyard in which a gallows could be constructed when needed.

Next door, west of the jail, was the seven-room sheriff's residence. The proximity of the sheriff came in handy shortly after the completion of the lockup. One morning, one of the prisoners was visited by his brother. At an opportune moment, the visitor threw red pepper into the deputy's eyes, and the two brothers bolted for the door. Hearing the commotion, Sheriff George B. Zimpelmann quickly mounted his horse and, after a two-block pursuit, corralled the sprinters. He found an extra space in the prison for the brother.

In 1931 Travis County built a modern courthouse designed by Page Brothers, architects, with the sixth and seventh floors

dedicated for use as a new jail. The limestone building was located on the square at Eleventh and Guadalupe streets. Additions and renovations were made in 1959 and 1962, and the jail
was used until 1990.

Interviews conducted by the author: Susan K. Soy, Austin History Center; Donna Woods, Austin History Center; John Anderson, Lorenzo de
Zavala State Archives and Library; Margo Frasier, sheriff, and Jim Sylvester,
deputy sheriff, Travis County.

Other resources: *Dallas Morning News, Texas Almanac, 1998–1999;* Tyler,
Barnett, and Barkley, eds., *New Handbook of Texas,* vol. 1, 299, 965, and
vol. 4, 553, 843; Kelsey and Dyal, *Courthouses of Texas;* Weems, *Austin
1839–1889;* Humphrey, *Austin;* Barkley, *History of Travis County and Austin,
1839–1999;* Travis County Commissioners' Court Record, Mar. 1855;
F. Brown, *Annals of Travis County;* Bateman and Hart, *Waterloo Scrapbook;
Austin Statesman,* Feb. 27, 1893, and June 5, 1938.

Trinity County (Groveton)

Trinity County lies between the Neches River on the east
and the Trinity River on the west. Under the Mexican
government, the area that is now in Trinity County was part
of the Nacogdoches municipality. In 1850 the Texas legislature
established Trinity County, obviously named for the river. The
town of Sumpter, named for Sumpter County, Alabama, was
made the temporary county seat. Sumpter was voted the permanent seat of government in 1854, and a courthouse and jail
were built there that same year.

The first Trinity County jail was a typical dungeon, two
stories tall and built of logs hewn to 10″ for the floors and walls.
The walls were double, with a 6″ space between the 10″ logs
for both the first- and second-story floors. That space was
filled with 6″ poles placed vertically from top to bottom so
that, if a prisoner sawed through the horizontal log, the vertical one would drop down and fill the space. The lower room
had no windows or doors other than the second-floor trapdoor. Access to the second floor was by an outside stairway.
The roof of the building was made of 10″ hewn timbers covered with pine clapboards. The existing records show that no
prisoner ever escaped from the jail.

The courthouse and most of the records burned in 1872, and in 1873 the county seat was moved to the town of Trinity by act of the legislature. In 1874, however, the county seat was moved by the voters to Pennington, named for an early settler, Hugh Pennington. Unfortunately, the courthouse burned again, this time in 1876. During and after the Civil War, the counties were overrun with land swindlers, highwaymen, and murderers. Law enforcement broke down, and the torching of courthouses to destroy records was commonplace. The description of the jail in Pennington is almost identical to that of the one in Sumpter.

In 1881 the Trinity Lumber Company was founded near a grove of blackjack oak trees, which gave the town of Groveton its name. In 1882 the Trinity and Sabine Railroad built tracks to the site, and Groveton soon teemed with sawmill workers—enough to vote for the new town to be the county seat. In 1896 a jail was built that lasted until 1938, when the New Deal's Works Progress Administration came to the area and built the substantial rock structure that is still used today.

Interviews conducted by the author: Elaine Ingram Lockhart, retired county clerk; Sheriff Brent Phillips; Peggy Sullivan, Groveton Public Library.

Other resources: *Dallas Morning News, Texas Almanac, 1998–1999;* Tyler, Barnett, and Barkley, eds., *New Handbook of Texas,* vol. 3, 355, vol. 5, 141, and vol. 6, 565, 567, 569; Kelsey and Dyal, *Courthouses of Texas;* Hensley and Hensley, *Trinity County Beginning;* Bowles, *History of Trinity County, Texas, 1827–1928.*

Tyler County (Woodville)

Tyler County was created from Liberty County in 1846 and named for Pres. John Tyler. Native Caddo and Cherokee Indians, who had been relocated from Georgia and Florida, and the Alabama-Coushatta, who had been displaced from Louisiana, occupied the area. After Texas joined the United States, Tyler County was organized, and the community of Town Bluff was made the temporary county seat. Woodville, however, was established in 1846 and named for

the second
governor
of Texas,
George T.
Wood.
Woodville
was voted
the county
seat that
same year.
    The first
settlers in
the county

Tyler County jail annex, 1936–1980, Woodville, Texas.

were mostly from the southern United States, but it was soon
found that the sandy soil was poorly suited for raising cotton.
Many of the slave owners moved on to more productive plantations, leaving those with fewer assets behind.

    After the county seat was moved to Woodville, a series of
log or wooden jails was built. In 1891, however, the county
retained architect Eugene Heiner of Houston to design a new
jail. The result was a two-story brick building very similar
to those Heiner designed and built in Montgomery and Wharton counties. In Woodville, the lockup had cells and ironwork manufactured by Diebold Safe and Lock Company. The
keep was used until 1936, when Pres. Franklin Roosevelt's
Depression-fighting Works Progress Administration came to
town to remodel the courthouse. That same year, a new jail
was put into an annex behind the remodeled courthouse, and
the old Heiner jail was torn down.

    The people of Woodville had taken very good care of their
old courthouse. According to June Maxey, in 1906 the commissioners' court, in order to minimize the bloodstains on the
floor, ordered that "no shooting be allowed in the courthouse,
in any room or hall, and the sheriff is instructed to see that this
order is carried out." Visitors should be aware that this order
is still on the books. Today a new jail has been built, and the
old lockup in the annex is used for storage. The jail cells, however, are still in place.

Interviews conducted by the author: Martha Humphus; Jack Whitmire.
Other resources: *Dallas Morning News, Texas Almanac, 1998–1999;* Metz, *Roadside History of Texas;* Tyler, Barnett, and Barkley, eds., *New Handbook of Texas,* vol. 2, 1120, and vol. 6, 538, 608, 1069.

Upshur County (Gilmer)

Upshur County was created in 1846 and named for A. P. Upshur, U.S. secretary of state, who was killed in February 1877 by the explosion of a new experimental cannon on the USS *Princeton.* The same explosion also killed Thomas W. Gilmer, for whom the county seat was named.

Two major traditional migration trails, the Cherokee Trace and the Jefferson-Dallas Road, converged in the Upshur area and were used by a constant flow of immigrants into Texas. During its earliest days, from 1839 to 1844, the county was plagued by a feud known as the Regulator-Moderator War, a dispute that took place in Shelby and Harrison counties.

Early pioneers in the county seat of Gilmer, however, had a good sense of humor about the realities of frontier life. Before the courthouse square was paved, hogs, cows, and other livestock roamed free on the streets. As a result, there were a lot of fleas in the community. Residents said that if a person picked up a handful of sand from the courtyard, half of it would jump out.

The early prosperity from cotton ended abruptly after the Civil

Upshur County jail, 1917–1936, Gilmer, Texas. Courtesy of Hays Studio Collection, Historic Upshur Museum.

War with the freeing of the slaves, who were the productive workforce. This loss of capital was not quickly remedied.

Upshur County built its first permanent jail in 1882. Until that time, the local calaboose was constantly in need of repairs, and, because of frequent escapes, each prisoner had to be restrained with leg irons that were applied and removed individually by the blacksmith. The 1882 jail was a simple one-story brick building and a rather grim place for incarceration. In 1917 the second jail was built, a two-story brick building costing thirty thousand dollars.

In 1936 the city officials ordered a new courthouse, a gift from Pres. Franklin Roosevelt's WPA. After the new courthouse, including a jail, was erected, the old 1917 lockup was converted to a city hall, and the building was expanded to include a library and a fire station. The new 1936 courthouse, designed by Elmer G. Withers, was built with a jail and sheriff's quarters on the fifth floor. In 1976 overcrowding in the facility brought about the elimination of the quarters in order to expand the prison to occupy the entire fifth floor.

Interviews conducted by the author: Mayor Everett Dean; Mary Kirby, Iris Images; Rex Shaw, county clerk; Sarah Green, *Gilmer Mirror;* Fayrene Bonebrake.

Other resources: *Dallas Morning News, Texas Almanac, 1998–1999;* Tyler, Barnett, and Barkley, eds., *New Handbook of Texas,* vol. 6, 664; Newcomb, *Indians of Texas;* Kelsey and Dyal, *Courthouses of Texas;* Loyd, *History of Upshur County.*

Upton County (Rankin)

Upton was created from Tom Green County in 1887. A town near the center of the county, Upland, was platted by Henry F. Half in 1908 and became the seat of government when the county was organized in 1910. Three important trails crossed the future Upton County: one from Chihuahua in Mexico to Arkansas, the Butterfield Overland Mail route in 1858, and the Goodnight-Loving trail in 1866.

In 1911 a courthouse and a separate two-story jail were built of limestone in Upland. As fate would have it, the very

Upton County jail, 1926–present, Rankin, Texas. Photo
courtesy of Rankin Museum.

next year, the Kansas City, Mexico, and Orient Railroad chose to follow the old Butterfield route up Centralia Draw, then went south and missed the nascent city. It is said that certain landowners would not allow the railroad to cross their land, thereby influencing the route. F. E. Rankin is supposed to have been successful in making a water well on the rail route, and the town of Rankin is named for him. A water well is an attractive asset in country where the annual rainfall is twelve inches. Within a few months, many of the folks had left Upland and moved to Rankin, putting their buildings on sleds and pulling them ten miles overland with mules to the railroad town.

The county seat remained in Upland until 1921. Meanwhile, Rankin enjoyed a miniboom when oil was discovered at McCamey, Texas, and at the Santa Rita oil well on University of Texas land in adjoining Reagan County. Rankin enjoyed great prosperity as an oil-field service center.

Rankin was made the county seat in 1921, but it was not until 1926 that a new courthouse and jail, both designed by David S. Castle, were built there. The Southern Structural Steel Company provided the cells. The two-story red brick lockup behind the courthouse, remodeled and modified, is still used.

In January 1980 Tom A. Spalding, then age ninety, said in an interview, "The jail [in 1927] was a couple of telephone poles with a chain going [from] one to the other. Going to breakfast in the morning, we would go by and see who was on the chain. It seemed that two or three of the same ones were there every morning. Then they finally done away with the chain and got a little cage sitting down there on a vacant lot."

Interviews conducted by the author: Judy Greer, Upton County Historical Society; Donna Bell, Upton County Historical Society.

Other resources: *Dallas Morning News, Texas Almanac, 1998–1999;* Tyler, Barnett, and Barkley, eds., *New Handbook of Texas,* vol. 2, 76, vol. 5, 446, and vol. 6, 662, 667; Metz, *Roadside History of Texas;* J. E. Haley, *Charles Goodnight.*

Uvalde County (Uvalde)

In January 1790 the governor of Coahuila, Juan de Ugalde, defeated three hundred Apache Indians in the Sabinal River canyon near present-day Utopia. The site, later named Canyon de Ugalde, is the origin of the anglicized "Uvalde." In 1849 the United States built Fort Inge on the Leona River at the base of a small mountain one mile south of the present town of Uvalde. The fort was one of a series established to defend against Comanche depredations and Mexican incursions from the Rio Grande.

Reading W. Black founded Uvalde. Black bought land, now the site of the town of Uvalde, on the head of the Leona River in 1852. Within a few months, he began grazing a thousand sheep, operating two rock quarries, and raising a garden; he also opened a store. In 1855 he petitioned the state legislature to create the county of Uvalde with Encino as the county seat. This accomplished, he changed the county seat's name to Uvalde. (Black, though opposed to secession, signed an oath of allegiance to the Confederacy. He was so repulsed, however, by the murder of Union sympathizer prisoners after the battle of the Nueces that he moved to Mexico. After returning to Texas in 1867, because of his Union sympathies, he was murdered in his own store by G. W. Wall, who then fled to Mexico.)

Organized in 1856, Uvalde was surrounded by an untamed realm—the lawless element—until Henry W. Baylor Sr. became sheriff after the 1884 murder of Sheriff King Fisher in

Uvalde County jail, 1899–1967, Uvalde, Texas. Photo courtesy of Sheriff Kenneth Kelley.

San Antonio. In 1890 Baylor married the daughter of Reading W. Black. Representing a new breed of law officer, Baylor served until 1906. Sheriff Baylor's firm and unremitting pursuit of lawbreakers brought one of the most lawless areas of Texas under control, earned the respect of all, and established standards for law enforcement for Texas in the twentieth century.

Uvalde County's first permanent jail was a rock building built on Main Street on the town hall plaza in the mid-1880s. The structure had two stories and the usual crenellations around the top. In those days, apprehension was swiftly followed by trial and punishment since there was little provision for expensive long-term confinement.

According to Kenneth Kelley, retired county sheriff, a new jail was built in 1899. It was an elaborate two-story brick structure at 104 East Roberts Lane. The new lockup had a gallows, which was never used. The sheriff's quarters were on the ground floor. Stewart Iron Works of Cincinnati, Ohio, manufactured the prison cells for the second floor, which housed a large cellblock with sixteen bunks for men and a four-bunk isolation cell for women or prisoners with severe mental disorders. The 1899 jail was used until 1967, when it was replaced by a new detention center on East Nopal Street. Sheriff Kelley and his family have the distinction of having lived in both jails and observing the transition from nineteenth- to twentieth-century buildings.

Interviews conducted by the author: Uvalde Chamber of Commerce; Sheriff Kenneth Kelley; Tom Schliesing; Virginia Davis; Esther Trevino, Opera House Museum.

Other resources: *Dallas Morning News, Texas Almanac, 1998–1999;* Tyler, Barnett, and Barkley, eds., *New Handbook of Texas,* vol. 1, 558, vol. 2, 1105, and vol. 6, 616, 683; Metz, *Roadside History of Texas;* Delorme Mapping, *Texas Atlas and Gazetteer;* Stovall, *Nueces Headwater Country.*

Val Verde County (Del Rio)

Val Verde County was created in 1885 and organized the same year. The name is perhaps a Spanish corruption meaning "green valley." The area has a plethora of prehistoric artifacts and pictographs, some dating back at least four thousand years.

A group of springs on San Felipe Creek, which extends two miles northeast from Del Rio, has provided precious water for Indians, Spaniards, and Americans for hundreds of years. In 1808 a Spanish mission, San Felipe del Rio, was established there. In 1857 Camp San Felipe, an outpost for Fort Clark at Bracketville, was set up. At the end of the Civil War, the village on San Felipe Creek was reestablished and given the name San Felipe del Rio to distinguish it from San Felipe in Waller County. The name was later shortened to Del Rio.

In 1885 the citizens of the new Val Verde County elected Roy Bean justice of the peace. Roy's "town" was his billiard parlor and saloon in Langtry, fifty miles west of Del Rio on the banks of the Rio Grande. This became his courtroom, and he proclaimed himself the "law west of the Pecos." Langtry was actually a work station for the Southern Pacific crews that were building track and was named for the crew foreman,

Val Verde County jail, 1888–1956, Del Rio, Texas.

although the rumor began that Bean had named it for a beautiful actress, Lillie Langtry. Lillie had a nickname—"Jersey Lily"—and Judge Bean named his bar, courtroom, and saloon the Jersey Lilly. Bean presided over the court, dispensing outlandish decisions, fines, and punishments to the consternation of county officials. He died in office in 1904. Another colorful local character was John R. Brinkley. In the 1930s he specialized in goat-gland implants on men to enhance their sexual prowess. Forced out of the United States, he set up shop cross the Rio Grande from Del Rio and advertised his treatments over a five-hundred-thousand-watt radio station, XERA, from Mexico. His Del Rio home on Qualia Drive may still be seen.

The first jail in Val Verde County was built in 1888, three years after the county's organization. The structure is on the corner of Pecan and La Soya streets in Del Rio and was designed by Jacob Larmour and A. O. Watson, who also designed the Second Empire–style courthouse. It was built of rusticated limestone by an Italian mason who was brought to America to build Fort Clark. The structure has two stories, with sheriff's quarters on the first floor and prison cells on the second. It was used until 1956, when it was replaced by a new facility.

Interviews conducted by the author: Val Verde Chamber of Commerce; Leslie Schmidt and Lavonne Schmidt.

Other resources: *Dallas Morning News, Texas Almanac, 1998–1999;* Delorme Mapping, *Texas Atlas and Gazetteer;* Tyler, Barnett, and Barkley, eds., *New Handbook of Texas,* vol. 2, 76, 578, vol. 5, 841, and vol. 6, 694; Daughtrey and Daughtrey, *Historical Markers of Val Verde County;* Kelsey and Dyal, *Courthouses of Texas;* Metz, *Roadside History of Texas;* J. W. Williams and Neighbours, *Old Texas Trails.*

Van Zandt County (Canton)

Van Zandt County was created in 1848 and named for Isaac Van Zandt, a Republic of Texas figure and Sam Houston's chargé d'affaires in Washington, advocating the annexation of Texas to the United States. In 1850, when Wood County was taken out of Van Zandt County, the county seat was changed from Jordan to Canton. Historically, the Indian tribes had extracted salt from the marshy area of Jordan's Saline for generations. The town, Jordan's Saline, was over a giant salt dome covering thirty square miles. In 1845 John Jordan began making salt there, and salt production was handed down through the years. (The company was later bought out by Morton Salt.) In 1873 the Texas and Pacific Railroad passed ten miles north of Canton and slightly north of Jordan's Saline. A new community grew up around a depot on the line called Grand Saline. The old town of Jordan's Saline is now included in Grand Saline.

John Norman built the first jail in Van Zandt County in 1853. It was a 20′ by 20′ log jail in Canton, made of 12″ "hughed" logs that lasted until 1879. E. R. Kuykendall built the second jail in Canton for thirty-seven hundred dollars. It was of 2″ by 6″ wood planks stacked flat on top of each other and nailed down with spikes set 4″ apart. The floor was of similar material, except the boards were set on edge and again nailed together with spikes. Heavy steel cages, or cells, for the prisoners were set inside the building.

In 1893 the commissioners' court planned a new jail and solicited plans from various architects. A design by architect W. C. Dodson was approved, and a contract was made with the Pauly Jail Building and Manufacturing Company to build the structure. It was to be a brick facility at a cost of $18,775. The county accepted the building in August 1894.

In 1937 Van Zandt County, as part of the Depression-era Works Project Administration, received a new courthouse, including a new jail. Architects Voelcker and Dixon designed the building in modern style with the jail on the top floor; the Southern Prison Company of San Antonio provided the cells and ironwork. The jail, though still intact in the courthouse, was retired in 1992.

Interviews conducted by the author: Sheriff Pat Burnett; Don Plemmons, Texas Historical Commission; Kathryn Sturtz, Canton Public Library.

Other resources: *Dallas Morning News, Texas Almanac, 1998–1999;* Tyler, Barnett, and Barkley, eds., *New Handbook of Texas,* vol. 1, 962, vol. 3, 278, 1003, vol. 5, 743, and vol. 6, 707, 1003; Delorme Mapping, *Texas Atlas and Gazetteer;* Metz, *Roadside History of Texas;* Manning, *Some History of Van Zandt County;* M. E. Hall, *History of Van Zandt County.*

Victoria County

Victoria County was one of the original twenty-three counties created by the Republic of Texas in 1836. Named for Mexican president Guadalupe Victoria, it was unique in being the sole Texas colony with a primarily Mexican population.

J. W. Williams and Kenneth F. Neighbours are convinced that, in 1528, Cabeza de Vaca spent some time in the area that was to become Victoria County. William E. Syers is of the opinion that de Vaca's miraculous cure of an Indian with an arrow wound occurred near present-day McFadden, Texas. In 1685 French explorer René Robert Cavelier, Sieur de La Salle, missed his intended landfall, the mouth of the Mississippi River, and landed at Garcitas Creek, where he founded Fort St. Louis in the wilderness of what is now southeastern Victoria County. This invasion of the Spanish Sea unleashed six land and five sea searches by Spain to stamp out the interloper. (Recent archeological discoveries in Matagorda Bay and on Garcitas Creek have confirmed the location of Fort St. Louis and pulled the shroud of obscurity from the story of La Salle's sunken ship, *La Belle*.)

In 1840, during the Republic of Texas years, four hundred Comanche warriors swept down on Victoria, killing several people and looting. They then moved on to Linville on the coast, where they ransacked houses and stores, burned the town, and killed sev-

Victoria County jail, 1885–1940, Victoria, Texas. Photo courtesy of Victoria County Historical Archives.

eral citizens who fled out onto the bay in boats to escape.
Four days later, in the battle of Plum Creek, a pursuit party
of Texans ambushed the retreating Indians and inflicted substantial casualties.

In early Texas history, Victoria seems to have been at the
crossroads of trade routes. There was a municipal ferry across
the Guadalupe River at Victoria, and by 1851 a toll bridge had
been built across the waterway.

The first jail in Victoria County was constructed about
1840 or 1845 of hewn 12″ logs. Much to the chagrin of the
sheriff, two clever citizens managed to loosen and remove
a wooden peg holding the logs together at the doorjamb and
escape through the opening. Perhaps expecting to need their
little secret if jailed again, they carefully replaced the log,
confounding authorities as to the mode of their deliverance.
The second jail, built in 1852, was a two-story building on
the square facing Glass Street. It remained in place until 1905.
The third lockup was a two-story frame calaboose also facing Glass Street. In 1869 it was moved across the street to face
on Forest Street.

In 1884 Eugene Heiner designed an attractive three-story
brick jail in the Romanesque Revival style with stilted arches
over the openings, mansard roof, and quoins at the corners.
The P. J. Pauly Company of St. Louis put up the building for
the contract price of $16,290. The jail was used until a new
keep was built in 1940; the 1884 building, however, was razed
in 1965. The 1940 jail is in the Art Deco style, designed and
built by the Southern Steel Company of San Antonio for
$116,381.88

Interviews conducted by the author: Gary Dunnam, Victoria Preservation, Inc.; Sheron Barnes, Archives and Special Collections, Library,
Victoria College/University of Houston–Victoria; Sgt. Teresa Touch-
stone, Victoria County Sheriff's Office; Charles Spurlin, Texas Historical
Commission.

Other resources: *Dallas Morning News, Texas Almanac, 1998–1999;* Tyler,
Barnett, and Barkley, eds., *New Handbook of Texas,* vol. 3, 1058, vol. 4,
209, vol. 5, 242, and vol. 6, 735, 739; Delorme Mapping, *Texas Atlas and
Gazetteer;* Westmoreland, "Battle of Plum Creek," in Connor, *Battles of
Texas;* Weddle, *Wilderness Manhunt;* J. W. Williams and Neighbours, *Old
Texas Trails;* Syers, *Texas.*

Walker County (Huntsville)

Walker County was created from Montgomery County in 1846. Before Walker County was separated, Montgomery County's 1838 jail was used for the whole area. Originally the county was named for Robert J. Walker, a U.S. senator from Mississippi who advocated the annexation of Texas into the United States. Robert Walker, however, became a Unionist, and in 1863 the Texas legislature changed the designated honoree to Samuel H. Walker, famous Texas Ranger and namesake of the Walker Colt revolver that he helped design. Huntsville had been founded in 1835 by brothers Ephraim and Pleasant Gray and was named for their hometown, Huntsville, Alabama.

The first jail in Walker County—on the west side of Sam Houston Street between Fourteenth and Fifteenth streets—was built in 1846. In 1857 it was moved to the north side of Eleventh Street between University and Avenue J. The jail was described as two dungeons on the ground floor, each 10′ by 16′. The two were separated by a shared plank partition containing a well-locked door. The floor was made of 1″ boards nailed to the oak block foundation. The walls were constructed of 12″ square hewn logs laid one on top of the other to a height of 9′. The walls were lined with 2″ oak planks, 12″ wide and nailed to the logs. The second story was of similar 12″ hewn logs and had jailer's quarters framed in and covered with weatherboarding, which included the dungeons. The door was double, the first of wood and the second of iron made by

Walker County jail, 1935–1982, Huntsville, Texas. Photo by Stanley Gilbert. From the author's collection.

Harvey Randolph, blacksmith. They opened into the jailer's quarters. When the building was completed, John S. Besser was paid $350 for the job. In 1848 Walker County, specifically Huntsville, was picked by the legislature as the site of the Texas State Penitentiary, which began operation in 1849.

A second jail, built in 1857, was on Cedar Street, now Eleventh Street. After the Civil War, four white men were tried for the murder of Sam Jenkins, a former slave. At the trial, sympathizers in the courtroom suddenly gave the prisoners weapons; a shootout ensued, and the armed prisoners made a clean getaway. This incident brought on three months of local martial-law enforcement.

In 1874 a third jail was built on the southeast corner of block 1, lot 1. A fourth jail, date unknown, was constructed on Main Street, now University Street. The fifth lockup, built in 1938, was a two-story, buff-colored brick building half a block from the courthouse. Architect Harry D. Payne designed the facility, and the contractor was Eckert-Burton Construction Company. Jailer's quarters were on the first floor. The prison was on the second floor, and Southern Prison Company of San Antonio provided the cells and ironwork. That jail was used until 1982; the prison cells, however, are still intact on the second floor of the old building.

Interviews conducted by the author: Paula V. Randolph, Huntsville Public Library; James D. Patton, Walker County Historical Commission; Kari French; Mrs. E. L. Van Horn.

Other resources: *Dallas Morning News, Texas Almanac, 1998–1999;* Tyler, Barnett, and Barkley, eds., *New Handbook of Texas,* vol. 2, 110, vol. 3, 793, vol. 5, 599, 601, and vol. 6, 799; W. P. Webb, *Texas Rangers;* Hosley, *Colt;* Newcomb, *Indians of Texas;* Crews, *Huntsville and Walker County, Texas.*

Waller County (Hempstead)

Waller County is named for Edwin Waller, Republic of Texas leader, signer of the Texas Declaration of Independence, and original resident of Austin's colony in 1820. In 1821 Jared Groce built a ferry across the Brazos River at a place that became known as Groce's Landing. Sam Houston's army camped near the spot on the west side of the river from

Waller County jail, 1896–1975, Hempstead, Texas. Photo courtesy of Lora Wasicek.

March 31 to April 14, 1836, before continuing on to San Jacinto.

When the county was organized in 1873, Hempstead was made the county seat. R. R. Peebles and his wife, Mary Ann Calvit Groce Peebles, founded Hempstead in 1856, and the Houston and Texas Central Railroad arrived in 1858.

The years of Reconstruction were troublesome indeed. After the war, Gen. George Armstrong Custer was stationed near Hempstead with four thousand troops. After 1873, the newly elected county officials passed the most curious ordinance of all time, the "deadly weapons act," which stated that all firearms must be forfeited to the county and then would be sold at public auction. This ingenious bit of firearms regulation was seldom enforced. Usually the owner of a forfeited weapon was able to buy back his piece at auction; meanwhile, the county reaped the profits from the sale of stolen goods.

By the turn of the century, Hempstead was generally known as "Six-Shooter Junction." The train station on the tracks was perhaps the most dangerous place in town. Locals tell a story about a drunk who got on the train in Houston without a ticket. When the conductor asked him where he thought he was going without a ticket, he replied, "I'sh goin' to hell." The conductor let him off in Hempstead.

In 1873 the county commissioners advertised for contractors to bid on the construction of a two-story frame jail to be 36' by 36' and painted white. The Ahrenbeck Brothers won the bid at $2,850. The building was later used as the first Waller County public school.

In 1879 a new 36' by 31' two-story brick lockup was built. The first contractor, G. A. Reidel of Austin, was released from his contract, and Foster and Company completed the facility. The structure was destroyed by fire in 1895. Following the fire, in 1896, a contract was let to the Diebold Safe and Lock Company to build a two-story red brick jail with beige brick trim. The sheriff's quarters were on the first floor; the prisoners, on the second floor.

During her childhood, Laura Wasicek lived in the jail for ten years when her father was sheriff and remembers her mother cooking for the inmates. Two of the prisoners, trusties, would baby-sit with her when her mother was out of the house. She says that they were in the jail most of their lives and considered it their second home. The building was replaced in 1975.

Interviews conducted by the author: Laura Wasicek; Angel Paris, deputy county clerk; Richard Senasac, Texas Historical Commission.

Other resources: *Dallas Morning News, Texas Almanac, 1998–1999;* Tyler, Barnett, and Barkley, eds., *New Handbook of Texas,* vol. 3, 349, 552, and vol. 6, 809; Waller County Historical Survey Committee, *History of Waller County;* Bruce, *Lillie of Six-shooter Junction;* Map Ink, Military History of Texas Map; Metz, *Roadside History of Texas.*

Ward County (Monahans)

The Spanish visited the Ward County area in 1583 in the process of exploring the Rio Grande. That year, on returning from New Mexico, Antonio de Espejo turned eastward to the Pecos River and followed it downriver, passing through present-day Ward County. As barren as the country appears, it probably supported aboriginal life for twelve thousand years. Many artifacts—pottery, projectile points, petroglyphs, and pictographs—have been found here. Surprisingly, the Monahans sand dunes (now Monahans Sandhills State Park) contain fresh water just five to seven feet below ground. Pools may stand in places between the dunes, providing water for a variety of animals. The small Havard shin oaks *(Quercus havardii),* seldom as much as four feet tall, have roots that plunge thirty feet into the earth and produce an abundance of acorns.

The county was created from Tom Green County in 1887 and named for Thomas W. Ward, soldier in the 1835 siege of Bexar. Ward lost a leg to a cannonball in that battle and was treated in New Orleans, where he was fitted with a peg leg. Later he moved to Houston and contracted with the Allen brothers to build the first capitol building in Houston.

Ward County was organized in 1892, and the town of Barstow was made the county seat. That same year, the first courthouse and jail were constructed. In spite of the scant rainfall (twelve inches per year), orchards and vineyards flourished, watered from the Pecos River until the earthen dam was washed away in a flood. In 1920 oil was discovered, and that changed everything. In 1938 the county seat was moved to Monahans, a town that began in 1881 as a water stop for the Texas and Pacific Railroad. In 1940 a new courthouse with a jail on the top floor was completed in Monahans. The lockup is no longer in the courthouse but has been moved out in compliance with mandates from the Commission for Jail Standards.

Interviews: Pat V. Finley, county clerk; Elizabeth Heath, chair, Ward County Historical Commission.

Other resources: *Dallas Morning News, Texas Almanac, 1998–1999;* Tyler, Barnett, and Barkley, eds., *New Handbook of Texas,* vol. 1, 791, vol. 4, 398, and vol. 6, 821; Reading, *Arrows over Texas;* Newcomb, *Indians of Texas;* Metz, *Roadside History of Texas.*

Washington County (Brenham)

Washington County, named for George Washington, was one of the original twenty-three counties formed by the Republic of Texas in 1836. Stephen F. Austin obtained ratification from the Mexican government agreement with his father, Moses Austin, to settle three hundred families on lands between the Lavaca and San Jacinto rivers and north of the San Antonio Road to twenty miles inland from the Gulf of Mexico. The first settlement was at Washington-on-the-Brazos, one mile below the junction of the Navasota and the Brazos rivers. The site became a center of political activity and a military headquarters. When the convention of 1836 met there, delegates adopted the Texas Declaration of Independence on March 2, 1836, and drew up the Texas Constitution. The town was evacuated shortly after, however, as news came of the approach of General Santa Anna's army. After the battle of San Jacinto, Washington-on-the-Brazos was declared the county seat of the new Washington County. In 1843 a three-way election between Brenham, Independence, and Mount Vernon made Brenham the permanent county seat.

In 1842, during Pres. Sam Houston's second term, the capital of Texas was moved from Austin to Washington-on-the-Brazos because of periodic Mexican invasions. It remained there through Pres. Anson Jones's administration until the annexation of Texas to the United States in 1845, when Austin was named the capital of the new state.

The earliest jail in Washington County was in Independence. In 1830 an adobe, later stuccoed, building served as a lockup under the Mexican authorities. It continued as a detention center until the late 1840s, when it became a law office. There is no information about county jails from this date until the one that was built in the 1920s.

In 1923, when the commissioners' court decided that the county needed a new jail, Southern Structural Steel Company of San Antonio submitted a plan. The county negotiated a trade of property with the chamber of commerce so that it owned a lot on Quitman Street (now Commerce Street). The new three-story brick-and-steel building was completed that year for thirty-eight thousand dollars. The jail would serve Washington County until after World War II.

Interviews conducted by the author: Wilfred Dietrich, Texas Historical Commission; Burnie Parker; Esther Lockett, Brenham Heritage Museum.

Other resources: *Dallas Morning News, Texas Almanac, 1998–1999;* Tyler, Barnett, and Barkley, eds., *New Handbook of Texas,* vol. 1, 293, vol. 3, 823, vol. 4, 1141, and vol. 6, 834.

Webb County (Laredo)

Webb County was created in 1848 from Nueces and Bexar counties. It was named for James Webb, veteran of the War of 1812, who became a lawyer in Virginia and moved to Houston in 1838. He became a friend of Pres. Mirabeau B. Lamar and, as a consequence, became secretary of the treasury and then secretary of state.

The first settler in Webb County was Tomás Sánchez, who began ranching near a ford of the Rio Grande on the road from Monterrey to San Antonio. It was 1755, and he named the place Laredo. Frequent raids by the Comanche Indians worsened during the period following the Mexican War of Independence.

After Texas Independence, the Republic of the Rio Grande was born in 1840. The idea was that the states of Tamaulipas, Nuevo Leon, and Coahuila (three northern Mexican states that were granted self-government under the Mexican constitution of 1824) would form a confederation to win their independence from Mexico. Encouraged by the success of the Texas Revolution, the leaders of the movement, known as Federalists, met in Laredo in January 1840, declared independence, and claimed the territory north to the Medina and Nueces rivers in Texas. Antonio Canales was made commander in chief of the forces. Unfortunately, Canales was no Sam Houston. Gen. Mariano Arista soundly defeated Canales's army in March 1840 near

Webb County jail, 1902–1937, Laredo, Texas. Photo courtesy of Yolanda Parker and the Nick Sanchez Collection, Institute of Texas Cultures, University of Texas–San Antonio.

Morales in Coahuila, Mexico. Canales surrendered to the Centralists in November and, being a survivor and a man of flexible convictions, was made an officer in the Centralist army.

In 1881 Webb County built a two-story brick jail at 1100 Farragut Street in Laredo. Reflecting the custom of the time, the building had crenellations around the top and miniature towers at each corner. A new jail was built in 1902 and was once again fortresslike with battlements and a central tower in a partial third story; the contractors were the Jeffries and Johnson Company. This jail remained in service until replaced by a nearby modern lockup in 1937. The architect for the 1937 jail was J. W. Beretta of San Antonio, and the builder was W. A. Martinez of Laredo.

Interviews conducted by the author: Rose Trevino, Texas Historical Commission; Elsa Navarro, Webb County Heritage Foundation; Nora Benavides, Webb County Historical Association.

Other resources: *Dallas Morning News, Texas Almanac, 1998–1999;* Tyler, Barnett, and Barkley, eds., *New Handbook of Texas,* vol. 4, 75, vol. 5, 357, and vol. 6, 862, 864; Webb County Heritage Foundation, *Laredo Legacies.*

Wharton County (Wharton)

Wharton County was created in 1846 and named for the brothers John A. and William H. Wharton, both lawyers in early Texas. William H. Wharton was at the battle of Velasco and signed the final surrender. Settlers, part of Stephen F. Austin's Old Three Hundred families, moved into Wharton County as early as 1823. Many of them came from the South and brought along slaves to set up plantations.

Roads in the area were terrible, but the Buffalo Bayou, Brazos, and Colorado Railroad eventually built into the county to capitalize on the movement of commodities. The Civil War, supported by nearly 100 percent of the population, had a devastating effect on the old system. The sudden loss of capital from freeing the slaves and the decline of the value of land, which was no longer productive, would mean years of agonizing adjustment.

Wharton County jail, 1888–1936, Wharton, Texas. Photo courtesy of David Bucek and the Wharton County Historical Museum.

In the absence of a jail in the early days of Wharton County, punishments for minor crimes were often extreme. Slaves in particular were subject to whippings. Leg irons were a standard method of restraint, and the blacksmith charged $3.50 to apply or remove the irons. Citizens were paid $1.50 daily to guard a prisoner, so it soon became economically good judgment to build a jail.

The first lockup was built in 1854. It was a 24' by 28' log structure and consisted of two stories. Its brick foundation was 3' wide and 18" high. The windows were closed with a network of iron bars. Located on Residence Street, the jail was used for thirty-five years before it was replaced and sold to George Quinan Rust, who remodeled it into a residence. In 1861 modifications were made to add brick to the first floor. The building remained a residence until 1955.

In 1888 architect Eugene Heiner of Houston designed a new jail and courthouse in High Victorian Italianate style. The keep was a large two-storied, solid brick building with cells provided by Diebold Safe and Lock Company. The cost of construction was eight thousand dollars. The jail remained in use until 1936; in 1940 it was remodeled and expanded to accommodate county offices.

In 1936 a new county jail was built on Fulton Street. This three-story brick facility, designed by Hedrick and Lindsley of Houston, had sheriff's quarters in half of the first floor, while prison cells manufactured by Southern Prison Company were on the second floor. The structure was used until 1996, when a new prison was provided for county prisoners.

Interviews conducted by the author: David Bucek, architectural historian; Chief Deputy Sheriff Bill Copeland; Delia Castillo, Wharton County Historical Museum; A. C. Shelton, Wharton County Historical Commission.

Other resources: *Dallas Morning News, Texas Almanac, 1998–1999;* Tyler, Barnett, and Barkley, eds., *New Handbook of Texas,* vol. 1, 297, and vol. 6, 907, 908; Kelsey and Dyal, *Courthouses of Texas;* Wharton County Historical Commission, *Wharton County Pictorial History, 1846–1946,* vol. 1; A. L. Williams, *History of Wharton County;* W. Robinson, *People's Architecture.*

Wheeler County (Wheeler)

Wheeler County, named for pioneer Royal T. Wheeler, chief justice of the Texas Supreme Court, was created in 1876 and organized in 1879. Once organized, Mobeetie became the first county seat. Mobeetie began in 1874 as a supply store for buffalo hunters on the headwaters of Sweetwater Creek. In 1875 the U.S. Army established Fort Elliott nearby to ensure that the Indians remained on the reservation and to protect the trail drivers headed for markets in Kansas. Mobeetie, supposedly the Indian word for "sweet water," soon became the usual riotous frontier town, providing entertainment of all sorts. At one point the contingent at Fort Elliott included Lt. Henry O. Flipper, the first black graduate of the U.S. Military Academy. Flipper served much of his military career at Texas posts.

Mobeetie was frequented by certain noted persons, including Bat Masterson, Charles Goodnight, and Temple Lea Houston, son of Gen. Sam Houston. Houston's prowess as a trial attorney was demonstrated the time a judge appointed him to represent a prisoner accused of horse stealing. The culprit had been caught while sitting on the horse in question. The judge told Houston to take his client into the other room and give him some good advice. When the bailiff came into the room, he found only Houston and a chair under an open window. When threatened with a contempt citation, Houston replied that the only good advice he could think of was "to climb out of the window."

The very first jail in Wheeler County was the guardhouse at Fort Elliott. A U.S. marshal once arrested a dozen cattlemen

Wheeler County jail, 1886–1908, Mobeetie, Texas.

for evading the tax on chewing tobacco. The judge found them all innocent. Furious at the lack of cooperation from the county commissioners and the judge, the marshal arrested them all again and put them in the guardhouse at Fort Elliott. Lieutenant Flipper quietly released the prisoners.

According to Sallie B. Harris of the Old Mobeetie Restoration Committee, the next jail was a one-story, 10′ by 10′ box that was 8′ tall. In 1880 a sandstone courthouse, designed by Simon Nevillewere, was built. It included a jail on the second floor that was designed by John S. Thomas. The contract for construction was given to J. N. Miller. Unfortunately, the sandstone was assembled with inferior mortar and soon fell apart. Obviously the jail could not be used, so in 1886 a separate sandstone jail, built by Italian stonemasons, was completed near the courthouse. The lockup had cells on the second floor manufactured by Pauly Jail Manufacturing Company. A vote in November 1907 moved the county seat to Wheeler. The Pauly jail cells were installed in the new county lockup there, and a new wood-frame courthouse was built.

The fourth county jail was built in Wheeler and completed in 1909. Constructed in the castle style, it was a two-story building with two towers topped by crenellations on the front corners. The lockup was used until the completion of a fifth jail in 1929. That facility, still in use today, was made of red brick with white trim and contains sheriff's offices on the first floor. The venerable 1886 Pauly jail cells, with modifications, are still in place. The 1886 jail in Mobeetie is now serving as a museum.

Interview conducted by the author: Bobbye Hill and Sallie B. Harris, Old Mobeetie Texas Association.

Other resources: *Dallas Morning News, Texas Almanac, 1998–1999;* Tyler, Barnett, and Barkley, eds., *New Handbook of Texas,* vol. 2, 1099, vol. 3, 720, vol. 4, 784, and vol. 5, 916, 917; Fowler, "Jailhouse Museums"; Tise, *Texas County Sheriffs;* Porter, *Memory Cups of Panhandle Pioneers.*

Wichita County (Wichita Falls)

The area of the future Wichita County was the territory of the Caddoan Indians, mostly agricultural people, until the middle of the eighteenth century. Wichita County was created in 1858 and named for the Indian tribe by that name. The Red River forms the entire northern boundary of the county, and the Wichita River flows through the southern part. In 1837 John A. Scott of Mississippi had bought certificates for Texas land that included the falls area. Years later, in 1876, members of his family found them and engaged an agent to plat a town at the falls. When the Fort Worth and Denver City Railroad rolled through in 1882, providing a connection to the outer world, the future of Wichita Falls as a commercial center was ensured.

The presence of oil in area water wells had been detected as early as 1901, so it was no surprise when the first oil well was successfully drilled in 1911. The young town then became such a rowdy oil boomtown that two

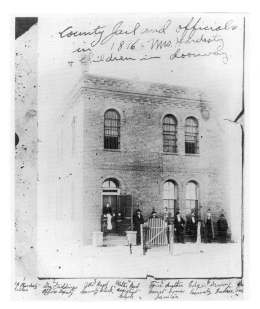

Wichita County jail, 1890–1912, Wichita Falls, Texas. Photo from "Wichita Falls, Where Enterprise and Opportunity Meet" by Nancy Hansen. Courtesy of Wichita County Jail and Officials, 1896, Wichita Falls Museum and Art Center, Lester Jones Photography Collection.

dozen Texas Rangers were stationed there until things calmed down.

The first jail was on the northwest corner of Lamar and Seventh streets and was made of 2″ by 4″ wood planks laid flat, stacked, and nailed to each other. It was used until 1890, when a substantial two-story brick jail was completed on the northeast corner of the courthouse square. The 1890 jail had sheriff's quarters on the first floor and a gallows at the top of the stairwell leading to the second floor. In 1912 a new jail was completed on the northwest corner of the courthouse square at a cost of $20,742. In 1925 an annex was added to the 1912 jail, which kept the facility in use until 1962, when a completely new lockup was finished.

Interviews conducted by the author: Ralph Harvey, Wichita County Archives; Lita Watson, Wichita County Archives; Jannis Hayers, Texas Historical Commission; Jeff Desborough, Wichita Falls Museum.

Other resources: *Dallas Morning News, Texas Almanac, 1998–1999;* Kelsey and Dyal, *Courthouses of Texas;* Metz, *Roadside History of Texas;* Tyler, Barnett, and Barkley, eds., *New Handbook of Texas,* vol. 6, 952, 955; Wichita County Archives, Louise Kelly Collection.

Wilbarger County (Vernon)

Wilbarger County, bordered on the north by the Red River and Oklahoma, was created in 1858 and organized in 1881. The Pease River crosses the county and flows into the Red River north of Vernon. Because of hostile Indians, the area was not settled until after the conclusion of the Red River War, which forced the Indians onto reservations in Oklahoma. In 1879 Jonathan Doan established a trading post and store for trail drivers, twelve and a half miles north of present-day Vernon, near the Red River crossing. This was the Western Trail, and between 1879 and 1895 six million head of cattle would cross the river at that point. Settlers not involved in the trail drives made a living collecting the bones of the slaughtered buffalo from the surrounding prairies, which brought twenty-two dollars per ton when shipped back East for making fertilizer.

The county was named for Josiah P. and Mathias Wilbarger, brothers who settled in Austin's colony in 1832 on

the Colo-
rado River.
In 1833,
while part
of a survey
party, four
miles east
of Austin,
Josiah P.
Wilbarger
and others
were at-
tacked by

Wilbarger County jail, 1912–1993, Vernon, Texas.

Indians. Josiah was wounded three times, scalped, and left
for dead. His story of rescue and recovery is remarkable (see
Wilbarger, *Indian Depredations in Texas,* 7).

The first jail in Wilbarger County was a two-story building
of hewn cottonwood logs that were 8″ thick. The building
was 14′ by 18′ with a stone foundation that rose 4″ above the
ground. The first floor was 8′ from floor to ceiling and had no
door except for a 3′ by 3′ trapdoor in the second story. There
were two 8″ by 24″ windows with ¾″ bars. An outside stairway led to the second floor, where there was a removable ladder to the dungeon. The building cost one thousand dollars
and was used until 1912.

In 1912 the county built a more up-to-date and humane
jail—a two-story masonry building with crenellated towers at
the corners and modest ornamental cornices around the edges.
As usual, the cells were on the second floor, while the sheriff's
quarters were situated on the ground floor. A few years later,
an addition provided more space for the lockup. This facility
was used until 1993. Although the 1912 cells are still intact,
Agnes Morgan now uses the building as the Jailhouse Village
Antique Shop.

Interviews conducted by the author: Sandra Sullivan, assistant county
clerk; Letha Reed, Texas Historical Commission; Agnes Morgan.

Other resources: Wilbarger, *Indian Depredations in Texas; Dallas Morn-
ing News, Texas Almanac, 1998–1999;* Kelsey and Dyal, *Courthouses of Texas;*
Ross and Rouse, *Early-day History of Wilbarger County;* Tyler, Barnett, and
Barkley, eds., *New Handbook of Texas,* vol. 2, 660, and vol. 6, 894, 965.

Willacy County (Raymondville)

The Spanish explored the future Willacy County as early as 1519, when Alonso Álvarez de Piñeda, sailing westward, mapped the northern coast of the Gulf of Mexico. He sailed south to Vera Cruz, where he skirmished with Cortez, who considered all of Mexico his territory. Returning north, de Piñeda anchored his ships at the mouth of the Rio Grande. He and his men spent forty days there refurbishing their fleet and exploring inland before returning to Spain.

Willacy County was part of the disputed territory south of the Nueces River until after the 1848 Treaty of Guadalupe Hidalgo ended the Mexican War. Gen. Zachary Taylor crossed the Arroyo Colorado at Paso Real in extreme southeastern Willacy County as he marched his troops to Mexico. A feature of interest there is La Sal Vieja, a historic rock salt deposit west of Raymondville that provided prehistoric Indians as well as modern northern Mexicans with salt as recently as the mid-twentieth century. Roads across the country were scarce. There was an obscure branch of the San Antonio Road, and in 1921 a trade route ran from Matamoros to San Patricio.

Willacy County was created in 1911, and Sarita, now the county seat of Kenedy County, was made the county seat. When Kenedy County was created from Willacy in 1921, Willacy County was reorganized, and Raymondville became the seat of government. Edward Burleson Raymond had established Raymondville, first known as Raymond Town, in 1902. As a former employee of the King Ranch, he and Henrietta King sold the lots in the newly platted village.

In 1921, after reorganization, the county built a three-story red brick courthouse in Classical Revival Style with a jail on the third floor. In 1976 the county jail was moved across the street into a new building with the sheriff's office. The 1921 courthouse remains in service, and the former lockup is currently used for storage.

Interviews conducted by the author: Lila Patina, secretary to County Judge Simon Salinas; Hilda C. Small, veterans service office.

Other resources: *Dallas Morning News, Texas Almanac, 1998–1999;* Tyler, Barnett, and Barkley, eds., *New Handbook of Texas,* vol. 1, 259, vol. 3, 1067, vol. 4, 8, vol. 5, 960, and vol. 6, 974; Syers, *Texas;* Delorme Mapping, *Texas Atlas and Gazetteer;* Horgan, *Great River.*

Williamson County (Georgetown)

Williamson County was generally the area of the Tonkawa Indians until the Comanches fought their way into dominance. Warfare between the Tonkawa, the Cherokee, and the Comanches, as well as disease, reduced the ranks of the Tonkawa.

The county was created and organized in 1848 and named for Robert M. Williamson. Williamson, "three legged Willie," was crippled as a child. He was fitted with a wooden leg at the knee, leading to the sobriquet. In 1835 he was a delegate to "the Consultation" and later organized three companies of Rangers. He participated in the battle of San Jacinto, and, as Republic of Texas judge of the Third Judicial District, was therefore a member of the supreme court of Texas.

The Córdova Rebellion, whose fulcrum was really in Nacogdoches, reached as far west as Williamson County. In 1838 Vicente Córdova of Nacogdoches had organized an Indian and Mexican alliance supported by Mexico to overthrow the Texas government. In the spring of 1839 a group of Indians and Mexicans with Manuel Flores, a long-time Mexican agent, was in the process of providing arms and assistance to the Indians in Texas. When attacked on the North San Gabriel River by Rangers under James O. Rice, Flores was killed, and the Texans captured horses, powder, and lead from the Indians. Documents found on Flores left little doubt about Mexico's complicity in

Williamson County jail, 1888–1989, Georgetown, Texas.

the plot to arm and support an uprising. The battle ended a major threat and is said to have been the most important Indian fight in the history of the Texas Republic.

According to Ralph Love, of a fourth-generation family of Williamson County, the first jail was a Conestoga wagon turned upside down for confining miscreants. The second lockup was a room in the log courthouse, and the third jail was a two-story frame building. The fourth, built in 1888, is a striking two-story limestone fortress with crenulations around the roof. The T-shaped footprint of the building is typical of many jails of a later period. The Southern Prison Company of San Antonio remodeled the jail in 1934 and provided new cells. The lockup was used until 1989, when it was replaced.

Interviews conducted by the author: Bobby Gutierrez, Williamson County constable; Ralph Love, Georgetown Public Library.

Other resources: *Dallas Morning News, Texas Almanac, 1998–1999;* Tyler, Barnett, and Barkley, eds., *New Handbook of Texas,* vol. 2, 324, 1036, and vol. 6, 992; Metz, *Roadside History of Texas;* W. P. Webb, *Texas Rangers;* Dabney, "Rule of Law vs. Mr. Colt."

Wilson County (Floresville)

Named for James Charles Wilson, an Englishman who came to Texas in 1837, Wilson County was created and organized in 1860. Wilson was a member of the Somerville expedition in the fall of 1842 and the ill-fated Mier expedition in the spring of 1843. He survived the Black Bean episode and later escaped by bribing a jailer.

Alonso de León explored the area during one of his three trips to Texas in search of La Salle's Fort St. Louis. J. W. Williams and Kenneth Neighbours, in *Old Texas Trails,* are confident that de León passed near Floresville and crossed certain identifiable creeks southeast of the future Floresville site.

The town of Floresville was founded in 1867 on two hundred acres donated by Josefa Augustina Flores de Abrego, whose family had come to New Spain in the early eighteenth century. Against incredible dangers and odds, the family established a large, successful ranch on the San Antonio River in the future Wilson County. Floresville was named for the founder of this pioneer family, Francisco Antonio Flores de

Wilson County jail, 1887–1974, Floresville, Texas. Photo by Stanley Gilbert. From the author's collection.

Abrego II. In 1873 the citizens voted to make Floresville the county seat.

The first jail in Wilson County, date unknown, was a red stone building built on lot 2 of block 11 for $5,000. The second jail, built in 1887, was designed by San Antonio architect James Riely Gordon and is still standing. B. R. Reid won the contract to build a white brick structure for $14,000. Quarters for the sheriff were ample. The living room, parlor, dining room, and kitchen were on the ground floor in the front of the building; two bedrooms on the second floor were completely separated from the second-floor prison area. Prefabricated cell blocks, built by Pauly Jail Building and Manufacturing Company, were delivered and installed in the rear portion of the second floor. The jail contained a gallows, used once but then declared unsatisfactory since the "drop" was insufficient. Details are missing. The building is described as Italianate and Second Empire in style. In 1936 both the jail and the courthouse underwent renovations, and the original brick was covered with plaster. The jail was used until 1974, giving it one of the longest service records in Texas.

Interviews conducted by the author: Eve Martinez, county clerk; Gene Maeckel, Wilson County Historical Commission.

Other resources: *Dallas Morning News, Texas Almanac, 1998–1999;* Tyler, Barnett, and Barkley, eds., *New Handbook of Texas,* vol. 4, 1006, 1010, and vol. 6, 715; Kelsey and Dyal, *Courthouses of Texas;* J. W. Williams and Neighbours, *Old Texas Trails;* Delorme Mapping, *Texas Atlas and Gazetteer.*

Winkler County (Kermit)

The Texas legislature created Winkler County from Tom Green County in 1887. It was named for Judge Clinton McKamy Winkler, a colonel in the Confederate army, a member of the Texas legislature, and a justice of the court of civil appeals. Kermit, the county seat, began as a supply community for the several ranches in the area. It was named for Kermit Roosevelt, son of Pres. Theodore Roosevelt, who had made a hunting trip in the area.

Winkler County contains part of the geological feature known as the Monahans Sandhills, an interrupted band of sand dunes that reaches from southeast New Mexico to northeast Ward County. The dunes are constantly changing in location and configuration. Interestingly, water may be found by digging four to six feet into the sand.

The story is that there was very little crime in the beginning. The rare theft of a cow or horse was abruptly dealt with—to the disadvantage of the culprit. All of this complacency would end with the discovery of oil seven miles southwest of Kermit at a spot later known as Wink. The first jail, constructed in August 1927, was actually built in Wink. It was a small 12′ by 18′ board-and-batten shack that was so unimpressive that the sheriff thoughtfully labeled it "JAIL," with the additional caution—"KEEP OUT"—for the unwary. After the discovery of oil, Wink became an instant boomtown with the inevitable gamblers, crooks, and prostitutes. Prohibition had only a slight effect on the availability of alcohol.

With new oil riches and increased work and business in the courthouse, a contract was signed in January 1929 for the construction of a larger courthouse and jail. Architect David S. Castle designed a four-story sandstone-and-brick building that was built on the courthouse square by C. S. Oats and Son of Abilene. The building cost $198,380, which would be paid for by warrants, the last courthouse in Texas to be so financed. The fourth floor included a jail, as well as quarters for the sheriff. The lockup had three rooms for cages provided by Southern Prison Company. The jail was remodeled in 1963 and continued in service until 1995.

Interviews conducted by the author: Bonnie Leck, Winkler county judge; Sheriff Robert L. Roberts Jr.; Evelyn Milligan, Wink city clerk.

Other resources: *Dallas Morning News, Texas Almanac, 1998–1999;* Tyler, Barnett, and Barkley, eds., *New Handbook of Texas,* vol. 3, 1075, and vol. 6, 1021, 1022; Kelsey and Dyal, *Courthouses of Texas;* Metz, *Roadside History of Texas.*

Wise County (Decatur)

Wise County was established and organized in 1856. It was named for Henry A. Wise, a U.S. congressman from Virginia who supported the annexation of Texas. The Wichita Indians lived in the area until about 1835. In addition, there was a small group of friendly Delaware Indians under Chief Jim Ned, who had been included in the peace treaty negotiated by Sam Houston with the Cherokee. The first county seat was called Bishop's Hill, which was later changed to Taylorsville in honor of Zachary Taylor. The surveyor who laid out the county seat changed the name to Decatur to honor navy hero Commodore Stephen Decatur. The Butterfield Overland Mail, that brief venture on the eve of the Civil War, at first bypassed Decatur. The route was changed, however, in 1860, when Decatur promised road improvements and bridge construction.

The first jail in Wise County was a limestone house in Decatur, completed about 1859, that also served as the sheriff's residence. The actual jail was underground in the cellar and accessed solely from the outside. Light and ventilation were not features of the dun-

Wise County first jail, 1859–1883, Decatur, Texas.

geon. Meals were provided by a dumbwaiter from the outside on the east end of the house.

The Civil War brought on an unhappy event similar to the Great Hanging at Gainesville. A number of Union sympathizers in Wise County were accused of anti-Confederate activities, and in 1865 five were tried by a dubious court and hanged. The whole process was challenged by a group of more than two hundred people, who were driven off by the "authorities" in the name of law and order.

The second jail was built in 1883. It was a two-story brick building across from the northwest corner of the courthouse square. Rosalie Gregg of the Wise County Historical Commission says that, when her grandfather was sheriff of Wise County from 1884 to 1888, he put a "bull's-eye" peephole in the wall so that he could watch the prisoners without their knowing it. The lockup was used until after World War II, when it was replaced by a new facility.

Interviews conducted by the author: L. B. McDonald, county judge; Rosalie Gregg, Wise County Historical Commission.

Other resources: *Dallas Morning News, Texas Almanac, 1998–1999;* Tyler, Barnett, and Barkley, eds., *New Handbook of Texas,* vol. 6, 1028; Metz, *Roadside History of Texas;* Bobo, *Ramblings of a Country Doctor;* Gregg, *Wise County History.*

Wood County (Quitman)

The Texas legislature created and organized Wood County in 1850. The area had been the domain of the Caddo Indians, a peaceful agricultural group for centuries before the time of Anglo expansion. The county was named for George T. Wood, the second governor of the recently annexed State of Texas. The county seat was named for John Quitman, a Mississippian who had recruited a militia and brought it to help Texas win independence from Mexico. Much to its disappointment, the militia arrived two days after the battle of San Jacinto. Quitman was present during the ensuing negotiations with Mexico and was an advocate of returning Santa Anna to Mexico; he may have had some influence on Sam

Houston to do so. Quitman fought in the Mexican War as a brigadier general under Gen. Zachary Taylor and was at the battle of Monterey.

People from the southeastern United States, many of whom brought their slaves with them, constituted the greater part of the early population of Quitman County. The onset of the Civil War soon after the organization of the county and the subsequent Reconstruction era put Wood County at an economic disadvantage that would prevail until the end of the nineteenth century. Nevertheless, in 1884 Wood County built its first permanent jail. It was an attractive two-story brick building in Victorian style with exterior cornices of decorative brickwork. In 1927 the county built a new court-house, designed by C. H. Leinbach, on the square. The three-story edifice was in Classic Revival style with a lockup in the basement.

The Great Depression was a financially unkind period, mitigated somewhat by federal programs such as the Civil Conservation Corp and the Works Progress Administration. In 1938 the latter built a new facility on the same site as the original 1884 jail. Rural electrification came in 1938, and the discovery of oil in the county in 1941 offset troublesome unemployment in other sectors of the economy.

Interviews conducted by the author: Lou Malloy; Rodney Mize, Wood County Sheriff's Department; Dorothy Demonigny, Quitman City Library.

Other resources: *Dallas Morning News, Texas Almanac, 1998–1999;* Tyler, Barnett, and Barkley, eds., *New Handbook of Texas,* vol. 5, 395, 396, and vol. 6, 1061; Shaw, *Wood County, 1850–1900.*

Yoakum County (Plains)

Yoakum County was organized in 1907, and Plains was chosen as the county seat. Plains had been established in 1905 by J. W. Luna as a town around his store on Sulfur Draw, a gullywash that runs through the middle of the county. With a mere twelve inches of annual rainfall, the county is mostly ranch land with an occasional farm raising cotton or

Yoakum County jail, 1926–1950, Plains, Texas.

sorghum. In 1935 oil was discovered in the southern part of the county, and by 1939 the oil boomtown of Denver City had been established.

The county, on the extreme western edge of the Texas Panhandle, with New Mexico forming its western border, was named for Henderson Yoakum, a lawyer and a veteran of both the Cherokee War and the Mexican War. He practiced law in Huntsville and became a director of the state penitentiary there. The location of the territory meant that it was not explored by the early Spanish expeditions that mostly followed the Rio Grande up to Santa Fe. Even today there are no railroads in the county, and before the Anglo immigration, it must have been a beautiful, endless plain of tall prairie grass with numerous herds of buffalo.

When the county was first organized, there was no available jail, so prisoners were regularly chained to the windmill on the courthouse square. In 1908 a frame courthouse and lockup were built. They were used until the courthouse burned in 1924. A new brick courthouse with a jail attached was built in 1926. In 1950 architect Wyatt C. Hedrick designed a new courthouse and lockup for the square. The jail was attached to the courthouse by an overhead walkway.

Interviews conducted by the author: Dallas Brewer, county judge; Mary Jo St. Romain.

Other resources: *Dallas Morning News, Texas Almanac, 1998–1999;* Tyler, Barnett, and Barkley, eds., *New Handbook of Texas,* vol. 5, 225, and vol. 6, 1122; Kelsey and Dyal, *Courthouses of Texas.*

Young County (Graham)

Young County was created in 1856 and organized the same year. It was named for William C. Young, who arrived in Texas in 1837. He served variously as sheriff, district attorney, Confederate cavalryman, and U.S. marshal. The town of Belknap grew up around Fort Belknap and was chosen as the county seat. Fort Belknap was first an army post and later a stage stop in the brief history of the Butterfield Overland Mail (1858–1861) before it fell victim to the Civil War. The army, of course, abandoned the post in 1861 but returned briefly in 1867.

In 1854 Texas made an early try at the business of Indian reservations. One of the two that were formed was the Brazos Indian Reservation, about four miles west of the present city of Graham. The reservation, 36,000 acres along the Brazos River, was well received by several of the more peaceful tribes since the army protected them from their old enemy, the Comanche. The confrontations between Indian agency officials and the intractable white anti-Indian settlers, however, ultimately doomed the experiment. The reservation was closed within five years.

Young County was the scene of the famous Warren Wagon Train Massacre near Salt Creek in 1871. About one hundred Indians under four chiefs slipped off of the reservation and ambushed freighters eight miles east of Salt Creek. They killed the wagon master and six teamsters before retreating to the Fort Sill Reservation. Gen. William Tecumseh Sherman and an es-

Young County jail, 1921–1950, Graham, Texas.

cort of troopers on an inspection tour had passed within half a mile of the hidden Indians. That evening, one of the teamsters who escaped the attack reported the incident to Col. Ranald Mackenzie and General Sherman at Fort Richardson. An angry Sherman went to Fort Sill and personally arrested the four chiefs. (The chiefs were found guilty of murder in Jacksboro civil court and sentenced to hang. The death sentence was commuted, however, and they were finally paroled in 1873 by Reconstruction Gov. Edmund J. Davis.) There is very little doubt that the incident hardened the army's attitude toward the Indians; in fact, it may have been a determining event. Mackenzie became obsessed and pursued the Indians relentlessly, culminating with the final devastating raid in 1875 on the Indians in Palo Duro Canyon.

In 1874 the county was reorganized, and Graham, founded the year before, was made the county seat. The first jail in the new Young County was built in 1874. The small building was made of logs armored with thousands of nails to prevent prisoners from sawing their way out. That lockup was replaced in 1878 by a two-story stone building. When the stone structure began to deteriorate, it was replaced in 1921 by a three-story brick jail, which was still in use after World War II.

Interview conducted by the author: Dorman Holub.
Other resources: *Dallas Morning News, Texas Almanac, 1998–1999;* Tyler, Barnett, and Barkley, eds., *New Handbook of Texas,* vol. 1, 468, 714, and vol. 6, 829, 1130; Crouch, *History of Young County, Texas.*

Zapata County (Zapata)

Zapata County was created from Starr and Webb counties in 1858 and organized that same year. It was named for Col. Antonio de Zapata, one of the military leaders of the ill-fated Republic of the Rio Grande Revolution of 1839. The earliest settlement in the area that was to become Webb, Zapata, and Starr counties was established by José Vázquez Borrego in 1750. The town, located on the east bank of the Rio Grande above Laredo, was called Dolores. The community was abandoned because of Indian depredations, however, and not reestablished until 1830. Meanwhile, at old Dolores, the area of the ferry crossing became an important horse and cattle ranch, and a town named Carrizo, later called Zapata, was established.

At the time of the Texas Revolution, Mexico was divided politically into the Centralists, headed by Santa Anna, and the Federalists, who wanted to return the government to the original constitution of 1824. Encouraged by the Texans' success, the Mexican Federalists held a convention near Zapata and Laredo in December 1840; they elected a president and appointed military leaders with the avowed intention of overthrowing the Centralist government. Antonio Zapata was second-in-command of the army under Antonio Canales. Unfortunately, Zapata was captured in the first battle at Morales, Coahuila, in March 1840. When Zapata refused to repudiate his political convictions, he was executed. His head was displayed for three days as a warning to would-be revolutionaries.

The town of Zapata built a courthouse and jail in 1900. The keep had only six cells, and Hector Lopez, justice of the peace, recalls that most of the work was done by the sheriff, who put the offenders in jail and released them in due time.

In 1953 the U.S. government completed the Falcon Dam on the Rio Grande, flooding Old Zapata. After removal of the citizens to New Zapata by the U.S. government, a new courthouse was built with a jail in the basement. The lockup, however, has now been moved into a different building.

Interviews conducted by the author: Evaristo Botello, Col. José Antonio Zapata Museum; Hector Lopez, justice of the peace.

Other resources: *Dallas Morning News, Texas Almanac, 1998–1999;* Tyler, Barnett, and Barkley, eds., *New Handbook of Texas,* vol. 2, 671, vol. 5, 537, and vol. 6, 1143; Metz, *Roadside History of Texas;* Crouch, *History of Young County, Texas;* Webb County Heritage Foundation, *Laredo Legacies;* Horgan, *Great River.*

Zavala County (Crystal City)

Zavala County, named for Lorenzo de Zavala, who was born in Mérida, Yucatan, was created in 1858 and organized in 1884. Zavala was a well-educated youth who soon began to agitate for democratic changes, an activity for which he was imprisoned. While incarcerated, he read medical books and was soon considered a skilled physician. He studied and learned English in a similar manner. After release from prison, he came to Texas and was one of the signers of the Texas Declaration of Independence. He was the first interim vice president of the republic from March 1836 to October 1836 and narrowly escaped capture by Santa Anna as the Texas government fled from Morgan's Point across the bay to Galveston.

The town of Batesville began on the ranch of Elijah A. Bates, who, with his brothers, dammed the Leona River and dug an irrigation canal for supplying water to 500 acres, which they then sold in two-acre plots. A substantial community called Bates Ditch built up around the cabin where the Bates brothers lived. When the county was organized in 1884, Bates Ditch became the county seat, and the name of the town was changed to Batesville.

The first courthouse and jail were built on the town square in 1884. The architect, J. C. Breeding, was paid $250, and a G. Thompson was awarded the building contract by promising to build the courthouse with locally fired brick from Leona River clay. The two-story jail, however, was frame, and, judging from one picture, had an outside stairway to the second floor, typical of dungeon construction.

Early in the twentieth century, after artesian water was discovered in the area, developers Groos and Buckingham bought 10,000 acres of land and divided it into farm tracts. Crystal City was platted, and the area became the Winter Garden district. In 1928, after the county seat was moved to Crystal City, a two-story brick courthouse with a jail on the top floor was built on the square. It was used until 1970, when a modern building was constructed at the same location.

Interviews conducted by the author: Marcel Valdez, Texas Agricultural Extension Service; Virginia Davis.

Other resources: *Dallas Morning News, Texas Almanac, 1998–1999;* Tyler, Barnett, and Barkley, eds., *New Handbook of Texas,* vol. 1, 415, vol. 2, 430, and vol. 6, 1147, 1149; Kelsey and Dyal, *Courthouses of Texas;* Zavala County Historical Commission, *Now and Then in Zavala County.*

Appendix A

Jail Contractors

Contractor (alphabetical order)	Home	County
Ahrenbeck Bros.		Waller
Aiken, E. L.		Dickens
Aiken and Carnett		Motley
Anderson, J. W.		Johnson
Andrews, R.		McLennan
Bailey, Burns, and Fitzpatrick		Shackelford
Baker and McDaniel		Panola
Balfanz Construction	Abilene	Irion
Bartlett, Joseph		Live Oak
Brem, John		Franklin
Breneman, H. L.		Lamar
Brooks, Samuel Wallace		Hidalgo, Starr
Brown, James		Kaufman
Chamberlain, A. D.		Fannin
Clicknor, E. C.		Hockley
Cobb, Dan		Gaines
Courtney, James A.		Bandera
Davey and Schott		Edwards
Diebold Company	Camden, Oh.	Brewster
Doughty, L. R.		Henderson
Eckert–Burton Construction Co.		Walker
Ervin, James		Austin
Ewing and McGee Construction Co.		Jim Hogg
Falls City Construction	Louisville, Ky.	Pecos, Jeff Davis
Gifford, Z. D.		Sutton
Gordon Jones Construction	San Antonio	Nueces
Green & Nichols	Lampasas	Mills
Hackney, F. N.		Cooke
Haney, J. N.		Hood
Hankamer, Charles		Chambers
Harris, P. H.	Waco	McLennan
Hefner, A. J.		Hunt

Contractor (alphabetical order)	Home	County
Herron, A.		Guadalupe
Hodges, T. S.		Schleicher
Hull Brothers	Dallas	Austin
Jackson and Arnold		Milam
Jeffries and Johnson		Webb
Jenkins, William		Jeff Davis
Johnson Construction Company		Coryell
Janssen Bros. Company		DeWitt
Jones, H. N.		San Patricio
Kane and Co.		Gonzales
Kauhl, C. J.		Limestone
Kuykendall, E. R.		Van Zandt
King, Z., and Sons Company	Cleveland, Oh	Karnes
Kohlert, Viggo		San Patricio
Lambie, C. S.		Hutchinson
Lewman, M. J. Company		Hardin
Martin and Moodie		Brown, Comanche, Irion
Martin, Byrnes, and Johnson		Caldwell, Palo Pinto Calhoun, Potter Callahan, Reeves Taylor Concho, Llano Medina, Nolan
Martin and Moore		Newton
Martinez, W. A.		Webb
Masters, T. D.		Hopkins
Maupin, F. C.		Dawson
McButler and Co.	Lubbock	Bailey
McCowan, J. W.		McLennan
McDermott, J. C.		Denton
McKenzie and Pearce		Carson
McKenzie Construction Co.	San Antonio	Falls
Miller, A.		Stephens
Millikin, J. H., and Co.		Callahan, Howard
Minor Lewis and C. S. Johnson		Galveston
Moody and Ellis		Montgomery
Myers and Johnson		Nolan
Norman, John		Van Zandt
Northcraft and Donelson	San Marcos	Lee
Northcraft, Edward		Falls, Dewitt
Oats, C. S., and Son	Abilene	Winkler
Pickett and Mead		Lavaca

Contractor (alphabetical order)	Home	County
Priess, C. F., and Brother Builders		Gillespie
Raegner, John & John Walch		Gillespie
Reauseaux and Hines		Kaufman
Reid and Sutherland Company		Nueces
Reid, B. R.		Wilson
Rice, W. R.		Lynn
Robb and Wilson Company		Leon
Robertson, Thomas B.		Pecos
Sonnefield and Emmons		Hopkins, Callahan
Schmidt, Ludwig		Gillespie
Schultze, F.		Fayette
Shell, H. H.	Lubbock	Lubbock
Smith, J. N.		Floyd
Solon and Wickens		Hartley
Strain, Risley, and Swinburn		Jack
Suggs Construction		Taylor
Templeton and Cannon	San Angelo	Jack
Thomas, J. S.	Ft. Worth	Clay
Thomas and Werner		Tarrant
Twing, E. L. Company	San Antonio	Smith
Vaughn, C. W.		Titus
Vickers, G. F. and W.S.		Burnet
Vickery and Haynes	Kimble County	Menard
Wallace, J. C., and D. H. Love		Freestone
Williams, B. T.		Childress
Wilson, R. B.		Shelby
Woodward, J. T.		Burnet
Wright, L. R.		Franklin
Yarborough Construction		Polk

Appendix B

Jail and Courthouse Architects

Adams and Adams
  Kerr Co. courthouse and jail
Andrewartha and Wahrenberger
  Fayette Co. jail, 1881
Ayres, Atlee Bernard, San
  Antonio, 1874–1969
  Cameron Co. jail, 1913
  Hidalgo Co. jail, 1908
  Jim Wells Co. courthouse,
  1912
  Kleberg Co. courthouse and
  jail, 1913
  Refugio Co. courthouse, 1919
Ayres, Robert, 1898–1977
  (Ayres joined his father,
  Atlee Bernard, in 1921)
Becker and Dixon
  Andrews Co. jail, 1930
Beckman, Albert Felix, San
  Antonio
  Maverick Co. jail
Beretta, J. W., San Antonio
  Webb Co. jail, 1937
Berry and Hatch
  Moore Co. courthouse and
  jail
Berry, J. C., Kerr, and Kerr
  Carson Co. jail, 1909
Bliss, Stanley W.
  Starr Co. courthouse and jail
Breeding, J. C.
  Zavala Co. courthouse and
  jail, 1884
Buetell and Hardie, El Paso

Hudspeth Co. courthouse
  and jail, 1917
Burnett, George
  Montague Co. courthouse
  and jail, 1912
Carnes, J. N.
  Panola Co. jail, 1890
Castle, David, Abilene
  Irion Co. jail
  Taylor Co. jail
  Winkler Co. courthouse and
  jail
Clayton and Lynch, Galveston
  Anderson Co. jail
Dawson, Alonzo N.
  Archer Co. courthouse, 1892
  Johnson Co. jail, 1884
  Sabine Co. courthouse, 1906
Deitz, J. E.
  LaVaca Co. jail, 1881
  Liberty Co. jail
Dodson, W. C.
  Coryell Co. courthouse, 1897
  Denton Co. courthouse,
  1895
  Hill Co. courthouse, 1889
  Hood Co. courthouse, 1889
  Hunt Co. courthouse
  Lampasas Co. courthouse,
  1883
  Van Zandt Co., 1893
  Fannin Co. courthouse, 1889
  Henderson Co. jail
  Parker Co. courthouse, 1885

Williamson Co. jail
Dudley, W. W.
  Coleman Co. courthouse,
  1884
Dumas, J. B.
  Mills Co. jail, 1888
Easterwood, Birch D.
  Coryell County jail, 1934
Flanders, J. E.
  Brooks Co. courthouse, 1914
  Caldwell Co. courthouse,
  1894
  Callahan Co. jail, 1898
  Gillespie Co. courthouse,
  1882
  Goliad Co. courthouse, 1894
  Irion Co. jail, 1886
  Kaufman Co. jail, 1884
  Kendall Co. courthouse
  (façade only), 1910
  Live Oak Co. courthouse,
  1919
  Navarro Co. courthouse, 1905
  Presidio Co. courthouse,
  1886
  Shackelford Co. courthouse,
  1883
  Wilson Co. courthouse, 1884
Gibson, John Joseph Emmett
  Shelby Co.
Giles, Alfred, San Antonio,
  1853–1920
  Bandera Co. jail
  Brooks Co. jail
  Presidio Co. jail
Gordon, James Riely, San Anto-
  nio, 1863–1937
  Aransas Co. jail
  Bexar Co. courthouse, 1892
  Brazoria Co., courthouse,
  1894
  Brown Co. jail
  Comal Co. courthouse, 1898
  Comanche Co. jail
  Ellis Co. courthouse, 1897

Erath Co. courthouse, 1892
Fayette Co. courthouse, 1890
Gonzales Co. courthouse,
1894
Harrison Co. courthouse,
1900
Hopkins Co. courthouse,
1895
Lee Co. courthouse, 1897
McLennan Co. courthouse,
1901
Victoria Co. courthouse,
1892
Wilson Co. jail
Wise Co. courthouse, 1897
Gordon, James Riely, and Laub
  Nueces Co. jail, 1892
Haney, J. N.
  Hood Co.
Haynes, S. B., Lubbock
  Lubbock jail, 1931
Hedrick, Wyatt C., Fort Worth
  Harris Co. jail, 1927
  Wharton Co. jail
  Yoakum Co. courthouse and
  jail, 1950
Heiner, Eugene T., Houston,
  1852–1901
  Bastrop Co., 1891
  Bee Co., 1893
  Brazoria Co. courthouse,
  1897
  Burleson Co., jail, c. 1887
  Coleman Co. jail, 1890
  Colorado Co. jail, 1890
  Galveston Co. jail, 1878
  Gonzales Co. jail, 1887
  Harris Co. jail, 1880, 1895
  Huntsville Penitentiary,
  1901
  Jefferson Co. jail, courthouse,
  1892
  Montgomery Co. jail, 1891
  Smith Co. jail, 1881
  Tarrant Co. jail, 1884

Heiner, Eugene T. (*continued*)
   Tyler Co. jail, 1891
   Victoria Co. jail, 1886
   Wharton Co. jail, 1888
Hendricks and Lindsley,
   Houston
   Wharton Co. jail, 1931
Hester, Blum E., Houston
   Houston Co. courthouse and
   jail, 1939
Hodges, Thomas
   Caldwell Co. jail, 1910
Hull, F. B. and W. S.
   Llano Co. jail, 1895
Ingraham, W. P.
   Coryell Co. jail, 1875
Kane, J. J.
   Cook Co. jail, 1884
Kaufman, W. R.
   Gray Co. courthouse and
   jail
Kirsch, R. G.
   Hemphill Co.
Lamar, G. L.
   Briscoe Co. jail, 1894
Larmour, Jacob, and Klerke,
   E. H., 1822–1901
   Milam Co. jail, 1875
   Travis Co. jail, 1876
Larmour, Jacob, and Watson,
   A. O.
   Concho Co.
   Val Verde Co. jail, 1888
Leinbach, C. H.
   Foard Co. jail
McButler and Co., Lubbock
   Bailey Co. courthouse and
   jail, 1925
McClearn, J. E.
   Real Co. courthouse and jail,
   1918
McDonald and Co., Austin
   McCulloch Co.
McGinnis, W. A.
   Lamar Co. jail, 1874
Meador, W. C.

Newton Co. jail, 1936
Northcroft, Edward
   Hays Co. jail, 1885
Orlopp and Kusener, Dallas
   Dallas Co. courthouse and
   jail, 1892
Overbeck, H. A., Dallas
   Dallas Co. criminal courts
   bldg., 1915
Page, Harvey L., San Antonio
   Nueces Co. courthouse and
   jail, 1915
Page, Southerland, and Page,
   Houston
   Fannin Co. jail, 1941
   Travis Co. courthouse and
   jail, 1931
Parker and Rittenberry
   Sherman Co. courthouse,
   1922
Payne, Harry D., Houston
   Matagorda Co. jail, 1931
   Walker Co. jail
Phelps, Henry T., San Antonio
   Atascosa Co. jail, 1915
   Jim Hogg jail, 1913
   LaSalle Co. courthouse and
   jail, 1931
Preston, J. N., and Son,
   Austin
   Bell Co. jail
Rice, W. M.
   Lipscomb Co. jail, 1916
Rice, W. R.
   Lynn Co. courthouse and
   jail, 1916
Richardson, Jack
   Pecos Co. jail, 1913
Risser, C.
   Parmer Co. jail, 1917
Ritenour and Wood,
   Sherman
   Fannin Co. jail, 1885
   Lamar Co.
Rocke, M. M., Big Spring
   Howard Co. courthouse and

jail, 1907

Roquemore, O. G.
    Hartley Co. jail, 1906

Ruffini, Frederick E., Austin,
    ?–1885
    Burnet Co. jail, 1884
    Collin Co. jail, 1882
    Comal Co. jail, 1878
    Limestone Co. jail, 1880
    Robertson Co. jail, 1882

Ruffini, Oscar, San Angelo,
    1858–1957
    Crockett Co. jail
    Menard Co. jail
    Reagan Co. courthouse and
    jail, 1911
    Sutton Co. courthouse and
    jail, 1882
    Tom Green Co. jail

Sanguinet and Messer
    Lamar Co. courthouse and
    jail, 1917

Sanguinet (Marshall) and Staats
    (Carl), Fort Worth, 1859–
    1936
    Dawson Co. jail, 1917
    Tarrant Co. jail, 1918

Simpson, John P.
    Fannin Co. jail

Smith, J. W.
    Shelby Co. jail, 1950

Smith and Praeger
    Hopkins Co. jail, 1926

Sphar, J. Weatherford
    Stephens Co. jail, 1877

Stone, Fred C., and Babin, A.
    Jefferson Co. courthouse and
    jail, 1932

Taylor, Harry R.
    Bowie Co. jail, 1891

Thomas, John (of Thomas and
    Woerner), Fort Worth
    Shackelford Co. jail, 1878

Thurmon, L. L.
    Franklin Co. jail, 1912

Jeff Davis Co. courthouse and
    jail, 1910

Townes, Wm. C.
    Hutchinson Co. courthouse
    and jail, 1928

Townes and Funk
    Castro Co. jail, 1940
    Childress Co. jail, 1939
    Potter Co. courthouse and
    jail, 1932

Townes, Lightfoot, and Funk
    Potter Co. courthouse and
    jail, 1906

Voelcker and Dixon
    Jack Co. jail, 1940
    Midland Co. jail, 1909
    Van Zandt Co. jail, 1937

Wahrenberger and Beckman,
    San Antonio
    Maverick Co. courthouse and
    jail, 1886

Waller, M. L., Fort Worth
    Crosby Co. jail, 1914

Weidner, Charles W.
    Hamilton Co. jail, 1938

White, David, and Campbell,
    G. S.
    Taylor Co. (Abilene) jail, 1931

White, Emory S.
    Polk Co. jail, 1940

White, H. M.
    Calhoun Co., 1896

Wilson, William H.
    Red River Co. jail, 1887

Withers, Elmer George, Fort
    Worth, 1881–1938
    Ector Co. courthouse and
    jail, 1938
    Jones Co. jail, 1910
    Upshur Co. courthouse and
    jail, 1936

Zoeller, Philip, and S. F. Sten-
    deback
    Kendall Co. courthouse, 1870

Appendix C

Jail Equipment Companies

Alamo Iron Works, San Antonio, Tex.
  Edwards, 1895
Allen, Gerald B., St. Louis, Mo.
  Shackelford, 1878
Champion Iron and Fence, Canton, Ohio
  Fannin, 1885
★Decatur Iron and Steel, Decatur, Ala.
Diebold Safe and Lock, Canton, Ohio
  Blanco, 1893
  Borden, 1896
  Brewster, 1887
  Chambers, 1894
  Coleman, 1890
  Grimes, 1897
  Mills, 1888
  Sherman, 1889
  Tyler, 1891
  Wharton, 1888

Folger Adams, Joliet, Ill.
  Hutchinson, 1928

★Freid Co.

Herring Hall Safe and Lock, St. Louis, Mo.
  Briscoe, 1894

King Iron Bridge, Cleveland, Ohio
  Smith, 1881, jail

King, Z., and Sons, Cleveland, Ohio
  Karnes, 1876, 1877

Myers, F. E., Covington, Ky.
  Panola, 1891
  Titus, 1917, jail

Pauly Jail Manufacturing, St. Louis, Mo.
  Anderson, 1879
  Aransas, 1890
  Armstrong, 1894
  Ball, 1893
  Bastrop, 1891
  Burleson, 1887
  Collingsworth, 1930
  Comal, 1878
  Coryell, 1897
  Dallas, 1915
  Delta, 1889
  DeWitt, 1877
  Donley, 1903
  Eastland, 1897
  Ellis, 1874
  Galveston, 1890
  Hall, 1890, 1915
  Hardeman, 1890

Note: An asterix marks the companies for which no further information was found.

Pauly Jail Manufacturing (*cont.*)
    Hartley, 1906
    Henderson, 1877, 1924
    Hood, 1885
    Kendall, 1884
    Lamar, 1874, 1917
    Lavaca, 1885
    Lipscomb, 1916
    Lubbock, courthouse and jail, 1916
    Martin, 1885
    Montague, 1912
    Nolan, 1927
    Palo Pinto, 1880 (remodeled in 1907)
    Red River, 1887
    Refugio, 1919
    Smith, 1915
    Stonewall, 1890
    Sutton, 1890
    Wheeler, 1886

Snead and Co. Iron Works, Gonzales, Tex.
    Gonzales, 1897

Southern Structural Steel, San Antonio, Tex.
    Anderson, 1930
    Angelina, jail, 1926
    Archer, jail, 1890
    Atascosa, jail, 1915
    Bailey, 1905
    Bee, 1936
    Brooks, 1913
    Childress, 1939

    Cochran, 1926
    Coke, 1907
    Coryell, 1930
    Cottle, 1921
    DeWitt, 1917
    Erath, 1905
    Floyd, 1925
    Gains, 1919
    Gregg, courthouse and jail, 1932
    Hardeman, 1905
    Hunt, 1929
    Jones, 1941
    Kendall, 1921
    Kimble, 1904
    Midland, 1909
    Nueces, 1915
    Parmer, 1917
    Potter, 1906
    Real, 1918
    Sabine 1803
    Smith, 1881, 1905
    Taylor, 1931
    Terry, 1825
    Van Zandt, 1937
    Wharton, 1936
    Winkler, 1929
Stuart Iron Works, Cincinnati, Ohio
    Uvalde
★Van Duran, Cleveland, Ohio
Virginia Bridge and Iron Co., Roanoke, Va.
    Henderson, 1874
Wilson, R. B., Center, Texas
    Shelby, 1886

Bibliography

Addison, Malcolm Henry. *Reminiscences of Burleson County, Texas*. Caldwell, Tex.: Burleson County Historical Survey Committee, 1971.

Almond, Phyllis Whitt, and Sarah Oatman Franklin. *Cobwebs and Cornerstones: A History of Llano's Business Districts*. Llano, Tex.: Junior Women's Culture Club, 1976.

Ambrose, Stephen E. *Undaunted Courage: Meriwether Lewis, Thomas Jefferson, and the Opening of the American West*. New York: Simon and Schuster, 1996.

Archambeau, Ernest R., ed. *Old Tascosa, 1886–1888*. Canyon, Tex.: Panhandle-Plains Historical Society, 1966.

Arrington, Fred. *A History of Dickens County: Ranches and Rolling Plains*. Wichita Falls, Tex.: Nortex Offset Publications, 1971.

Astride the Old San Antonio Road: A History of Burleson County, Texas. Caldwell, Tex.: Burleson County Historical Society, 1980.

Atascosa County History. Pleasanton, Tex.: Atascosa History Committee, 1984.

Baker, John Walter. *A History of Robertson County, Texas*. Waco, Tex.: Texian Press, 1970.

Barfoot, Jessie Laurie. "A History of McCulloch County, Texas." Master's thesis, University of Texas at Austin, 1937.

Barkley, Mary Starr. *History of Travis County and Austin, 1839–1899*. Waco, Tex.: Texian Press, 1963.

Barkley, Roy R., and Mark F. Odintz. *Portable Handbook of Texas*. Austin: Texas State Historical Association, 2000.

Bateman, Audray, and Katherine Hart. *Waterloo Scrapbook*. Austin: Friends of the Austin Public Library, 1970.

Bates, Jack W., James E. Riney, and Maurice G. Fortin. *Inventory of County Records: Schleicher County Courthouse, Eldorado, Texas*. Denton: Texas County Records Inventory Project, North Texas State University, 1979.

Batte, Lelia McAnally. *History of Milam County, Texas*. San Antonio: Naylor, 1956.

Bay, Betty. *Historic Brownsville: Original Townsite Guide*. Brownsville: Brownsville Historical Association, 1980.

Bennett, Carmen Taylor. *Our Roots Grow Deep: A History of Cottle County*. Flydada, Tex.: Blanco Offset Printing, 1970.

Bennett, Robert. *Kerr County, Texas, 1856–1956*. San Antonio: Naylor, 1956.

"Bicentennial Commemorative History of Nacogdoches." Nacogdoches, Tex.: Nacogdoches Jaycees, 1976.

Bishop, Lorene, and Melba Coursey. *In the Life and Lives of Brown County People*, 2d ed. Brownwood, Tex.: Brown County Historical Society, 1988.

Block, Viola. *A History of Johnson County and Surrounding Areas*. Waco, Tex.: Texian Press, 1970.

Bobo, Zack. *Ramblings of a Country Doctor: An Informal Autobiography after Eighty Years of Living and Fifty-five Years of Practice*. Dallas: Southwest Offset, 1977.

Bolton, Herbert Eugene. *Texas in the Middle Eighteenth Century: Studies in Spanish Colonial History and Administration*. New York: Russell and Russell, 1962.

Bowles, Flora Gatlin. *History of Trinity County, Texas, 1827–1928*. Groveton, Tex.: Groveton Independent School, 1966.
———. *A No-man's Land Becomes a County*. Goldthwaite, Tex.: Eagle Press, 1978.

Bridges, Clarence Allen. *History of Denton, Texas: From Its Beginning to 1960*. Waco, Tex.: Texian Press, 1978.

Browder, Virginia. *Donley County: Land o' Promise*. Quanah, Tex.: Nortex Press, 1975.

Brown, Frank. *Annals of Travis County: From the Earliest Times to the Close of 1875*. N.p., 1900, 1976. Copy of typed manuscript on file at Austin History Center.

Brown, Lawrence L. *The Episcopal Church in Texas*. Austin: Church Historical Society, 1963.

Bruce, Florence Guild. *Lillie of Six-shooter Junction: The Amazing Story of Lillie Drennan and Hempstead, Texas.* San Antonio: Naylor, 1946.

Bullard, Lucille Blackburn. *Marion County, Texas, 1860–1870.* Jefferson, Tex.: L. B. Bullard, 1965.

Calvert, Robert A., and Arnoldo De León. *The History of Texas,* 2d ed. Wheeling, Ill.: Harlan Davidson, 1996.

Campbell, Harry H. *The Early History of Motley County.* San Antonio: Naylor, 1958.

Campbell, J. C. *Scenes of Granbury and Hood County.* Granbury, Tex.: CAMMAC Agency, 1975.

Casto, Stanley D. *Settlement of the Cibolo-Nueces Strip: A Partial History of La Salle County.* Hillsboro, Tex.: Hill Junior College Press, 1969.

Castro County Historical Commission. *Castro County, 1891–1981.* Dallas: Taylor, 1981.

Catton, Bruce, and James McPherson. *The American Heritage New History of the Civil War.* New York: Viking, 1996.

Cave, Edward. *Kaufman, a Pictorial History, 1840–1980: Over Twenty-five Years in Research.* N.p., 1981.

Clarke, Joe. *Inventory of County Records: Tyler County Courthouse, Woodville, Texas.* Denton: Texas County Records Inventory Project, North Texas State University, 1981.

Clarke, Mary Whatley. *The Palo Pinto Story.* Fort Worth: Manney, 1956.

Conger, Roger N., Rupert N. Richardson, and Melvin C. Warren. *Frontier Forts of Texas.* Waco, Tex.: Texian Press, 1966.

Connor, Seymour V. *Battles of Texas.* Waco, Tex.: Texian Press, 1967.

Cowden, Craig M. *Historical Texas County Jails.* Austin: Texas Architectural Foundation, 1980.

Cox, Mary L. *History of Hale County, Texas.* Plainview, Tex., 1937.

Cox, Mike. *Texas Ranger Tales: Stories That Need Telling.* Plano: Republic of Texas Press, 1997.

Crawford, Leta. *A History of Irion County.* N.p., 1966.

Crews, D'Anne McAdams. *Huntsville and Walker County, Texas: A Bicentennial History.* Huntsville, Tex.: Sam Houston State University Press, 1976.

Crocchiola, Stanley Francis. *The Dalhart, Texas, Story.* Nazareth, Tex. 1975.

Crouch, Carrie Johnson. *A History of Young County, Texas.* Austin: Texas State Historical Association, 1956. First published in 1937 as *Young County.*

Cunningham, Eugene. *Triggernometry: A Gallery of Gunfighters, with Technical Notes on Leather Slapping as a Fine Art, Gathered from Many a Loose-Holstered Expert over the Years.* Caldwell, Idaho: Caxton Printers, 1941.

Dabney, Robert Lewis, Jr. "The Rule of Law vs. Mr. Colt," *Houston Lawyer* 36(4) (Jan.–Feb. 1999): 10.

Daggett, Marsha Lea, ed. *Pecos County History.* 2 vols. Canyon, Tex.: Staked Plains Press, 1984.

Dalrymple, Edwin; Ruth Fowler, and Phyllis Whitt Almond. *Inventory of County Records, Llano, Texas.* Austin: Texas State Library, 1979.

Daughtrey, Robert E., and Elizabeth D. Daughtrey. *Historical Markers of Val Verde County.* Del Rio, Tex.: Val Verde County Historical Commission, 1986.

Davis, Joe Tom. *Historic Towns of Texas: Houston, Texana, Helena, Egypt, East Columbia, West Columbia, Matagorda.* Austin: Eakin Press, 1992.

Davis, William C. *Three Roads to the Alamo: The Lives and Fortunes of David Crockett, James Bowie, and William Barret Travis.* New York: HarperCollins, 1998.

Day, James M. *The Texas Almanac, 1857–1873: A Compendium of Texas History.* Waco, Tex.: Texian Press, 1967.

Deaf Smith County Historical Society. *The Land and Its People: Deaf Smith County, Texas.* Hereford, Tex.: Deaf Smith County Historical Society, 1982.

Debo, Darrell. *Burnet County History.* Burnet, Tex.: Eakin Press, 1979.

Dickens County: Its Land and People. Dickens, Tex.: Dickens County Historical Commission and Dickens County Book Committee, 1986.

Didear, Hedwig Krell. *A History of Karnes County and Old Helena*. Austin: San Felipe Press, 1969.

Douthitt, Katherine. *Romance and Dim Trails: A History of Clay County*. Dallas: W. T. Tardy, 1938.

Downie, Alice Evans. *Terrell County, Texas; Its Past, Its People: A Compilation, Pictures of, and Writings by or about People, Places, and Events in Terrell County*. Sanderson, Tex.: Terrell County Heritage Commission, 1978.

Earle, J. P. *History of Clay County and Northwest Texas*. Austin: Brick Row Book Shop, 1963.

Eaton, John. "The Sutton County Jail." Story submitted to the Texas Historical Commission for a historical marker, 1974.

Eddins, Roy, ed. *History of Falls County, Texas*. Marlin, Tex.: Old Settlers and Veterans Association of Falls County, Texas, 1947.

Ehrle, Michael G. *The Childress County Story*. Childress, Tex.: Arrow Printing, 1971.

Erwin, Allen A. *The Southwest of John Horton Slaughter, 1841–1922: Pioneer Cattleman and Trail-Driver of Texas, the Pecos, and Arizona, and Sheriff of Tombstone*. Glendale, Calif.: Arthur H. Clark, 1965.

Ezell, Camp. *Historical Story of Bee County, Texas*. Beeville, Tex.: Beeville Publishing, 1973.

Fehrenbach, T. R. *Lone Star: A History of Texas and the Texans*. New York: Macmillan, 1968.

Ferguson, Clarence. *And the Clock Struck Ten*. Waco, Tex.: Texian Press, 1995.

Fisher, Ovie Clark. *It Occurred in Kimble*. Houston: Anson Jones Press, 1937.

Flores, Dan L. *Caprock Canyonlands: Journeys into the Heart of the Southern Plains*. Austin: University of Texas Press, 1990.

Fowler, Gene. "Jailhouse Museums," *Texas Highways* (Oct. 1997), p. 34.

Frantz, Joe Berthram, Mike Cox, and Roger A. Griffin. *Lure of the Land: Texas County Maps and the History of Settlement*. College Station: Texas A&M University Press, 1988.

Friedrichs, Irene Hohmann. *History of Goliad.* Victoria, Tex.:
    Regal Printers, 1961.

Fry, Tillie Badu Moss. "A History of Llano County, Texas."
    Master's thesis, University of Texas–Austin, 1943.

Gandy, William Harley. "A History of Montgomery County,
    Texas." Master's thesis, University of Houston, 1952.

Gates, James Young, and H. B. Fox. *A History of Leon County.*
    Centerville, Tex.: *Leon County News,* 1936.

Gilbert, Randal B. "Jails of Smith County." *Chronicles of Smith
    County* 28(1) (Summer 1989).

Gillett, James B., and Milo Milton Quaife. *Six Years with the
    Texas Rangers, 1875–1881.* New Haven, Conn.: Yale Uni-
    versity Press, 1925.

Glimpses of Newton County History, comp. Newton County
    Historical Commission. Burnet, Tex.: Nortex Press, 1982.

Gray County Heritage. Pampa, Tex.: Gray County History
    Book Committee, 1985.

Gray, Frank S. *Pioneering in Southwest Texas: True Stories of
    Early Day Experiences in Edwards and Adjoining Counties.*
    Austin: Steck, 1949.

Greene, A. C. *The Santa Clause Bank Robbery.* New York:
    Knopf, 1972.

———. *Texas Sketches.* Dallas: Taylor, 1985.

Greene, Shirley Brooks. *When Rio Grande City Was Young:
    Buildings of Old Rio Grande City,* 2d ed. Austin: Pan Ameri-
    can University, 1987.

Gregg, Rosalie, ed. *Wise County History: A Link with the Past.*
    Decatur, Tex.: Nortex Press, 1975.

Griffin, John Howard. *Land of the High Sky: History of Midland
    County of West Texas from 1849 to the Present.* Midland, Tex.:
    First National Bank of Midland, 1959.

Gurasich, Marj A. *A History of the Harris County Sheriff's De-
    partment, 1836–1984.* Houston: Harris County Sheriff's
    Deputies Association, 1984.

Hadeler, Glenn. "Mason County Hoodoo Wars," http://
    www.texfiles.com/texashistory/hoodoowar.htm.

Haley, James Evetts. *Charles Goodnight: Cowman and Plainsman.*
    Norman: University of Oklahoma Press, 1949.

Haley, James L. *Texas, An Album of History.* Garden City, N.Y.: Doubleday, 1985.

———. *Texas: from the Frontier to Spindletop.* New York: St. Martin's Press, 1985.

Hall, Claude Vaden. *The Early History of Floyd County.* Canyon, Tex.: Panhandle-Plains Historical Society, 1947.

Hall, Margaret Elizabeth. *A History of Van Zandt County.* Austin: Jenkins, 1976.

Haltom, R. W. *History and Description of Angelina County, Texas.* 1888. Reprint, Austin: Pemberton, 1969.

Hanna, Betty. *Doodle Bugs and Cactus Berries: A Historical Sketch of Stephens County.* Austin: Nortex Press, 1975.

Hansford County Historical Commission. *Hansford County, Texas: Covering the Lives of Its Citizens, Their Hopes, Dreams, Failures, and Successes.* Dallas: Taylor, 1980.

Harris, Cyril M. *Dictionary of Architecture and Construction,* 3d ed. New York: McGraw Hill, 2000.

Harrison, W. Walworth. *History of Greenville and Hunt County, Texas.* Waco, Tex.: Texian Press, 1976.

Hart, Herbert M. *Old Forts of the Southwest.* Seattle: Superior, 1964.

Hartsfield, Loy W. "A History of Stephens County, Texas," Master's thesis, University of Texas–Austin, 1929.

Haven, Charles Tower, and Frank A. Belden. *A History of the Colt Revolver and the Other Arms Made by Colt's Patent Fire Arms Manufacturing Company from 1836 to 1940.* New York: W. Morrow, 1940.

Havins, Thomas Robert. *Something about Brown: A History of Brown County, Texas.* Brownwood, Tex.: Banner Print Co., 1958.

Hawkins, Edna Davis. *History of Ellis County.* Waco, Tex.: Ellis County History Workshop, 1972.

Hemphill County Preservation Committee. *Hemphill County History.* Dallas: Taylor, 1985.

Hensley, Patricia B., and Joseph W. Hensley. *Trinity County Beginnings.* Groveton, Tex.: Trinity County Book Committee, 1986.

Hicks, B. F., and Dan T. Bolin. *Early Days in Franklin County.* Mount Vernon: Northeast Texas Publishing, 1998.

Hines, Pauline. *Newton County Nuggets: A Collection of True Stories by Newton County Folk.* Newton, Tex.: Newton County Historical Commission, 1986.

Historic Frio County, 1871–1971. Pearshall, Tex.: Frio County Centennial Corporation, 1971.

Historical Montage of Tom Green County: Representative Papers of Historical Interest about People, Places, and Things Presented to the Society. San Angelo, Tex.: Anchor, 1987.

History of Cass County, Texas, comp. Nita Mac Jaynes and Willard G. Jaynes. Linden, Tex.: Cass County Historical Society, 1972.

History of Crosby County, comp. Crosby County Pioneer Memorial Museum. Crosbyton, Tex.: Crosby County Historical Commission, 1978.

History of Freestone County, Texas. Fairfield, Tex.: Freestone County Historical Commission, 1978.

History of Grimes County. Navasota, Tex.: Grimes County Historical Commission, 1982.

History of Leon County, Texas. Dallas: Curtis Media, 1986.

History of Palo Pinto County: Word-of-Mouth Family History, Palo Pinto, Texas. Palo Pinto, Tex.: Palo Pinto Historical Association, 1978.

History of Schleicher County. Schleicher County Historical Society. San Angelo, Tex.: Anchor, 1979.

History of Stonewall County. Stonewall, Tex.: Stonewall County Historical Commission, 1979.

History of Waller County. Waller, Tex.: Waller County Historical Survey Committee, 1973.

Hodge, Floy Crandall. *A History of Fannin County, Featuring Pioneer Families.* Hereford, Tex.: Pioneer, 1966.

Hood County Museum Committee. "The Jail, A Self-Guided Tour." Booklet. Granbury, Tex.: Hood County Museum, n.d.

Hopkins County Pictorial History. Sulphur Springs, Tex.: Hopkins County Historical Commission and Hopkins County Historical Society, 1987.

Horgan, Paul. *Great River: The Rio Grande in North American History.* New York: Holt, Rinehart, and Winston, 1954.

Horton, Thomas F. *History of Jack County.* Jacksboro, Tex.: Gazette Print, 1933.

Hosley, William. *Colt: The Making of an American Legend.* Amherst: University of Massachusetts Press, 1996.

House, Aline. *Big Thicket: Its Heritage.* San Antonio: Naylor, 1967.

Huckabay, Ida Lasater. *Ninety-four Years in Jack County, 1854–1948.* C. 1949. Reprint, Jacksboro, Tex.: Texian Press, 1974.

Humphrey, David C. *Austin: An Illustrated History.* Northridge, Calif.: Windsor, 1985.

Hunter, Gladys Nevins. *Historically Speaking: Coleman County, Texas.* San Angelo, Tex.: Anchor, 1977.

Hunter, J. Marvin. *Brief History of Early Days: Mason County.* Bandera, Tex.: J. Marvin Hunter, 1929.

———. *Trail Drivers of Texas: Interesting Sketches of Early Cowboys and Their Experiences on the Range and on the Trail during the Days That Tried Men's Souls, True Narratives Related by Real Cowpunchers and Men Who Fathered the Cattle Industry in Texas.* Austin: University of Texas Press, 1985.

Hunter, Lillie Mae. *The Book of Years: A History of Dallam and Hartley Counties.* Hereford, Tex.: Pioneer, 1969.

———. *The Moving Finger.* Borger, Tex.: Plains Print Co., 1956.

Hurn, Eugene W. *Clay County: A Half-century in Photographs (1873–1950).* Henrietta, Tex.: Clay County Historical Society in Cooperation with Clay County Historical Commission and Clay County Commissioners' Court, 1984.

Huson, Hobart. 1953–1955. *Refugio: A Comprehensive History of Refugio County from Aboriginal Times to 1953.* 2 vols. Woodsboro, Tex.: Rooke Foundation.

Hutto, John R. *Howard County in the Making: Personalities, Business Institutions, and Other Contributing Factors in the Development of a Progressive West Texas Community from Open Frontier.* Big Springs, Tex.: Jordan's, 1938.

Indianola Scrap Book: Fiftieth Anniversary of the Storm of August 20, 1986, ed. and comp. *Victoria Advocate.* 1936.

Reprint, Port Lavaca, Tex.: Calhoun County Historical
   Survey Committee, 1974.

Ingmire, Frances Terry. *Archives and Pioneers of Hunt County,
   Texas*. Creve Coeur, Mo.: Ingmire, 1975.

Jones, Charles Neilson. *Early Days in Cooke County, Texas,
   1848–1873*. Gainesville, Tex.: Cooke County Heritage
   Society, 1977.

Jones, Julia. *Lee County: Historical and Descriptive*. Houston:
   Gulf Coast Baptist Print, 1945.

Jones, William Moses. *Texas History Carved in Stone*. Houston:
   Monument, 1958.

Jordan, Gilbert John. *Yesterday in Texas Hill Country*. College
   Station: Texas A&M University Press, 1979.

Jordan-Bychkov, Terry G. *Texas Log Buildings: A Folk Architecture*. Austin: University of Texas Press, 1978.

Josephy, Alvin M., Jr. *500 Nations: An Illustrated History of
   North American Indians*. New York: Knopf, 1994.

Jurney, Richard Loyall. *History of Titus County, Texas*. Dallas:
   Royal, 1961.

Kellner, Marjorie. *Wagons, Ho!: A History of Real County,
   Texas*. Dallas: Curtis Media, 1995.

Kelsey, Mavis Parrott, and Donald H. Dyal. *The Courthouses
   of Texas: A Guide*. College Station: Texas A&M University
   Press, 1993.

Kemerer, Frank R. *William Wayne Justice: A Judicial Biography*.
   Austin: University of Texas Press, 1991.

Kemp, Mary E., and Billie R. Bell. *Pictorial History of Parker
   County, 1850–1985*. Weatherford, Tex.: Parker County Historical Commission, 1985.

Key, Della Tyler. *In the Cattle Country: History of Potter County*.
   Amarillo: Tyler-Berkeley, 1961.

King County Historical Society. *King County: Windmills and
   Barbed Wire*. Quanah, Tex.: Nortex Press, 1976.

Kingston, Michael T., Ruth Harris, and Erma Bailey, eds.
   Texas Almanac and State Industrial Guide, 1984–1985. Dallas:
   A. H. Belo, 1983.

Kinsall, A. Ray. *Fort Duncan: Frontier Outpost on the Rio Grande:
   A Sesquicentennial Celebration Edition Compendium*. Piedras
   Negras, Coahuila, Mexico: A. R. Kinsall, 1999.

Kirkland, Forrest, and William W. Newcomb. *Rock Art of Texas Indians*. Austin: University of Texas Press, 1967.

Kirkpatrick, A. Y. *Early Settlers' Life in Texas and the Organization of Hill County*. Waco, Tex.: Texian Press, c. 1963.

Kleberg County, Texas: A Collection of Historical Sketches and Family Histories, comp. Kleberg County Historical Commission and American Revolution Bicentennial Heritage Project of 1976. Austin: Austin Graphics, 1979.

Knight, Oliver. *Fort Worth: Outpost on the Trinity*. 1953. Reprint, Fort Worth: Texas Christian University Press, 1990.

Knox County History Committee. *Knox County History*. Haskell, Tex.: Haskell Free Press, 1966.

Landry, Wanda A. *Outlaws in the Big Thicket*. Quanah, Tex.: Nortex Press, 1976.

Laredo Legacies: A Tribute to Our Past and a Legacy for Our Future. Laredo, Tex.: Webb County Heritage Foundation, 1995.

Le Fevre, Hazie Davis. *Concho County History, 1858–1958*. Eden, Tex.: H. D. Fevre, 1959.

Leakey, John. *Granddad and I: A Story of a Grand Old Man and Other Pioneers in Texas and the Dakotas*. Leakey, Tex., 1951.

Leathers, Frances Jane. *Through the Years: A Historical Sketch of Leon County and the Town of Oakwood*. Oakwood, Tex., 1946.

Lemburg, Dorothy, and Jane Hoerster. *Mason County Jail*. Mason County Historical Commission, n.d.

Leon County Historical Book Survey Committee, Leon County Genealogical Society, and Leon County Historical Commission. *History of Leon County, Texas*. Dallas: Curtis Media, 1986.

Lindsey, M. C. *The Trail of Years in Dawson County, Texas*. Fort Worth: J. Wallace, 1960.

Linsley, Judith Walker, and Ellen Walker Rienstra. *Beaumont, A Chronicle of Promise: An Illustrated History*. Woodlands Hills, Calif.: Windsor, 1982.

Live Oak County Centennial Association, *Live Oak County Centennial*, 1956.

Longview, Texas, Centennial: The Long View of a Hundred Years, 1870–1970. Longview, Tex.: Longview Centennial Book Committee, 1970.

Lotto, Frank. *Fayette County: Her History and Her People*. Schulenburg, Tex: Author, 1902.

Loyd, Doyal T. *A History of Upshur County,* ed. Sarah Green. Gilmer, Tex., 1966.

Ludeman, Annette Martin. *La Salle: La Salle County, South Texas Brush Country, 1856–1975*. Quanah, Tex.: Nortex Press, 1975.

Malsch, Brownson. *Indianola: The Mother of Western Texas*. Austin: State House Press, 1988.

Manney, Mrs. H. J. *Kinney County: Account of Kinney County*. New World Study, 1907.

Manning, Wentworth. *Some History of Van Zandt County*. 1919. Reprint, Winston-Salem, N.C.: Hunter, 1977.

Marshall, Nida A., and Johanna Eurich. *Once upon a Time*. Anchorage: Anchorage Museum of History and Art, 1993.

Martin, James C., and Robert Sidney Martin. *Maps of Texas and the Southwest, 1513–1900*. Albuquerque: University of New Mexico Press, 1984.

Mayhall, Mildred P. *Indian Wars of Texas*. Waco, Tex.: Texian Press, 1965.

McAllen, Margaret H. *The Heritage Sampler: Selections from the Rich and Colorful History of the Rio Grande Valley*. Edinburg, Tex.: New Santander, Press, 1991.

———. "Jewel of the Rio Grande." Booklet. McAllen, Tex.: Hidalgo County Historical Museum, 1992.

McCollum, Irene. *Discover Bastrop's Historic Old Jail: Pine and Water Street*. Bastrop, Tex.: Bastrop Chamber of Commerce, 1987.

McComb, David. *Houston: A History*. Austin: University of Texas Press, 1981.

McDonald, Archie P. *The Old Stone Fort*. Austin: Texas State Historical Association, 1981.

McGuire, James. *Iwonski in Texas: Painter and Citizen*. San Antonio: San Antonio Museum Association, 1976.

McKay, Mrs. Arch, and Mrs. H. A. Spellings. *A History of Jefferson, Marion County, Texas, 1836–1936,* 3d ed. N.p., 1930s.

McKellar, Jo Ann Littlejohn. *The History of Daingerfield, Texas*. N.p., 1966.

Mears, Mildred Watkins. *Coryell County Scrapbook*. Waco,
    Tex.: Texian Press, 1963.

Memorial and Biographical History of Dallas County, Texas. Chi-
    cago: Lewis, 1892.

Menard County Historical Society. *Menard County History:
    An Anthology*. San Angelo, Tex.: Anchor, 1982.

Menn, Alfred E. *The Cuero and DeWitt County Story*. Cuero,
    Tex.: A. E. Menn, 1955.

Merriman, Walter W. *Once upon a Time in Throckmorton*. N.p.,
    1996.

Metz, Leon Claire. *El Paso Chronicles: A Record of Historical
    Events in El Paso, Texas*. El Paso: Mangan Books, 1993.

————. *Roadside History of Texas*. Missoula, Mont.: Mountain
    Press, 1994.

Military History of Texas Map. Norman, Okla.: Map Ink, n.d.

Montgomery, Robin Navarro. *A History of Montgomery County*.
    Austin: Jenkins, 1975.

Morrill, Clifford R.. *History of El Paso Division of the Southern
    Pacific Railroad Company*. N.p., 1923; rev. Hugh B. Wilson,
    El Paso, 1970.

Moseley, Laurie. *Somervell County Centennial 1875–1975*. Glen
    Rose, Tex.: Somervell County Centennial Association, His-
    torical Booklet Commission, 1975.

Moursund, John S. *Blanco County History*. Burnet, Tex.: Nor-
    tex Press, 1979.

Nacogdoches Historical Society. *Nacogdoches, Texas Centennial,
    1716–1936*. Nacogdoches, Tex.: Nacogdoches Historical
    Society, 1936.

Nacogdoches Jaycees. *The Bicentennial Commemorative History of
    Nacogdoches*. Nacogdoches, Tex.: Nacogdoches Jaycees, 1976.

Navarro County Historical Society. *Navarro County History*.
    Wolfe City, Tex.: Henington, 1991.

Neely, Pamela. "Jail for Milam County," *Junior Historian* 26
    (Sept. 1965).

Neville, Alexander White. *Backward Glances*, ed. Skipper
    Steely. Paris, Tex.: Wright Press, 1983.

Newcomb, William W. *The Indians of Texas: From Prehistoric to
    Modern Times*. Austin: University of Texas Press, 1961.

Neyland, James. *The Anderson County Courthouse: A History.* Available from the Anderson County Historical Commission, Palestine, Texas.

Noble, Harry P. *As Noble as It Gets.* Waco, Tex.: Texian Press, 1999.

Noviskie, Diana, and B. T. Noviskie. *History of the Austin County Jail.* N.p., n.d.

Now and Then in Zavala County: A History of Zavala County. Crystal City, Tex.: Zavala County Historical Commission, 1985.

Nunn, William Curtis. *Somervell: Story of a Texas County.* Fort Worth: Texas Christian University Press, 1975.

Oatman, Wilburn. *Llano, Gem of the Hill Country: A History of Llano County, Texas,* edited by author's children after author's death. Hereford, Tex.: Pioneer Book Publishers, 1970.

O'Banion, Maurine M. "The History of Caldwell County." Master's thesis, University of Texas–Austin, 1931.

Orren, G. G. "History of Hopkins County." Master's thesis, East Texas State University, Commerce, Tex., 1938.

Outlaws and Gunfighters of Texas Map. Norman, Okla.: Map Ink, 1996.

Palo Pinto County Historical Commission. *History of Palo Pinto County, Texas.* Dallas: Curtis Media, 1986.

Partlow, Miriam. *Liberty, Liberty County, and the Atascosito District.* Austin: Pemberton Press, 1974.

Patterson, Bessie. *A History of Deaf Smith County.* Hereford, Tex.: Pioneer, 1964.

Patterson, Cyril Leone. *Nixon, Gonzales County, Texas: A Progressive Diversified Agricultural Haven.* San Antonio: Sid Murray and Son, 1938.

Patton, Jack, and John Rosenfield. *Texas History Movies.* Dallas: P. J. M. Publishing, 1985.

Pennington, May Amanda Williams. *The History of Brenham and Washington County.* San Antonio: Naylor, 1949.

Phillips, John Neal. *Running with Bonnie and Clyde: The Ten Fast Years of Ralph Fults.* Norman: University of Oklahoma Press, 1996.

Pickle, Joe. *Getting Started: Howard County's First Twenty-five Years.* Austin: Nortex Press, 1980.

Pictorial History of Parker County. Weatherford, Tex.: Parker County Historical Commission, 1985.

Pierce, Burnett Cecil. "Titus County, Texas: Its Background and History in Ante-Bellum Days." Master's thesis, University of Colorado, 1932.

Pierce, Gerald C. *Texas under Arms: The Camps, Posts, Forts, and Military Towns of the Republic of Texas, 1836–1848.* Austin: Encino Press, 1969.

Polk, Stella Gipson. *Mason and Mason County: A History.* Burnet, Tex.: Nortex Press, 1980.

Pool, William C., Edward Triggs, and Lance Wren. *Historical Atlas of Texas.* Austin: Encino Press, 1975.

Porter, Millie Jones. *Memory Cups of Panhandle Pioneers.* Clarendon, Tex.: Clarendon Press, 1945.

Potts, Marisue B. *Motley County Roundup: Over One Hundred Years of Gathering; A Centennial History,* 2d ed. Floydada, Tex.: M. Potts, 1991.

Pritchett, Jewell G., and Erma B. Black. *Kent County and Its People.* Rotan, Tex.: *Rotan Advance,* 1983.

Ramsdell, Charles William. *Reconstruction in Texas.* 1910. Reprint, Gloucester, Mass.: P. Smith, 1964.

Randel, Jo Stuart, and Hobart Ebey Stocking. *A Time to Purpose: A Chronicle of Carson County.* Hereford, Tex.: Pioneer Book Publishers, 1966–1972.

Rawson, Gertrude K. *New Braunfels: A Story of Triumph in Texas.* New Braunfels, Tex.: Zeitung Publishing, 1932.

Reading, Robert S. *Arrows over Texas.* San Antonio: Naylor, 1960.

Roach, Hattie Joplin. *The Hills of Cherokee: Historical Sketches of Life in Cherokee County, Texas.* Rusk, Tex., 1952.

Robinson, Charles M. *Frontier Forts of Texas.* Houston: Lone Star Books, 1986.

Robinson, Willard. *Gone from Texas: Our Lost Architectural Heritage.* College Station: Texas A&M University Press, 1981.

————. *The People's Architecture: Texas Courthouses, Jails, and Municipal Buildings.* Austin: Texas State Historical Association, 1983.

Robinson, Willard, and Todd Webb. *Texas Public Buildings of the Nineteenth Century.* Austin: University of Texas Press, 1974.

Rocksprings Women's Club Historical Committee. *History of Edwards County.* San Angelo, Tex.: Anchor, 1984.

Roemer, Ferdinand. *Texas; with Particular Reference to German Immigration and the Physical Appearance of the Country; Described through Personal Observation, by Dr. Ferdinand Roemer,* trans. Oswald Mueller. San Antonio: Standard Printing, 1935.

Ross, Charles P., and T. L. Rouse. *Early-day History of Wilbarger County.* Vernon, Tex.: Vernon Times, 1933.

Rundell, Walter. *Early Texas Oil: A Photographic History, 1866–1936.* College Station: Texas A&M University Press, 1977.

Russell, Traylor. *Story of Titus County, Texas.* Waco, Tex.: W. M. Morrison, 1965.

San Patricio County News, comp. "Early History of San Patricio County," Stinton, Tex., 1934.

Scardino, Barrie. *Clayton's Galveston: The Architecture of Nicholas J. Clayton and His Contemporaries.* College Station: Texas A&M University Press, 2000.

Schaadt, Robert L. *The History of Hardin County, Texas.* Dallas: Curtis Media, 1991.

Schmidt, Charles Frank. *History of Washington County.* San Antonio: Naylor, 1949.

Scobee, Barry. *Fort Davis, Texas, 1583–1960.* Fort Davis, Tex.: privately printed, 1963.

Scott, Zelma. *A History of Coryell County, Texas.* Austin: Texas State Historical Association, 1965.

Settle, S. E. "Early Days in Callahan County." West Texas Historical Association *Yearbook* 12 (1936).

Shaw, Virgil B. *Wood County, 1850–1900.* Quitman, Tex.: Wood County Historical Society, 1976.

Sheffy, Lester F. *West Texas Historical Association Yearbook* 6 (June 1930).

Shifting Sands of Calhoun County, Texas, The. Port Lavaca, Tex.: Calhoun County Historical Commission, 1974.

Shrimpton, Ann Worley. *Texas Spur* (Apr. 4, 1991).

Smith, Alex Morton. *The First One Hundred Years in Cooke County.* San Antonio: Naylor, 1955.

Smythe, Henry. *Historical Sketch of Parker County and Weatherford, Texas.* St. Louis: L. C. Lavat Printer, 1877.

Sonnichsen, Charles L. *I'll Die before I'll Run: The Story of the Great Feuds of Texas.* New York: Devin-Adair, 1962.

Spencer, Artemesia Lucille Brison. *The Camp County Story.* Fort Worth: Branch-Smith, 1974.

Spikes, Nellie Witt, and Temple Ann Ellis. *Through the Years: A History of Crosby County, Texas.* San Antonio: Naylor, 1952.

St. Clair, Gladys Annelle. *A History of Hopkins County, Texas.* Austin, 1965.

Stanley, Francis. *Rodeo Town (Canadian, Texas).* Denver: World Press, 1953.

Sterling, William Warren. *Trails and Trials of a Texas Ranger.* 1959. Reprint, Norman: University of Oklahoma Press, 1968.

Stieghorst, Junann J. *Bay City and Matagorda County.* Austin: Pemberton Press, 1965.

Stovall, Allan A. *Breaks of the Balcones: A Regional History,* ed. Wanda Pope and Allan Stovall. Barksdale, Tex., 1967.

————. *Nueces Headwater Country: A Regional History.* San Antonio: Naylor, 1959.

Stroud, Martha Sue. *Gateway to Texas: History of Red River County.* Austin: Nortex Press, 1997.

Syers, William Edward. *Texas: The Beginning, 1519–1834.* Waco, Tex.: Texian Press, 1978.

Tarpley, Fred. *Jefferson: Riverport to the Southwest.* Austin: Eakin Press, 1983.

Taylor, Ira T. *The Cavalcade of Jackson County.* San Antonio: Naylor, 1938.

Taylor, William C. *A History of Clay County.* Austin: Jenkins, 1974.

Texas Almanac and State Industrial Guide, 1996–1997. Dallas: *Dallas Morning News,* 1997.

Texas Almanac and State Industrial Guide, 1998–1999. Dallas: *Dallas Morning News,* 1999.

Texas Atlas and Gazetteer: Detailed Maps of the Entire State.
    Freeport, Me.: DeLorme Mapping, 1995.

Texas Permian Historical Society. "Odessa, Tex.: Diamond
    Jubilee, 1886–1961." N.p., 1961.

Thompson, Cecilia. *History of Marfa and Presidio County, 1535–*
    1946. Austin: Nortex Press, 1985.

Thonhoff, Robert H. *The First Ranch in Texas.* 1964. Reprint,
    Karnes City, Tex.: Old Helena Foundation, 1968.

———. "Historic Helena: Birthplace of Karnes County."
    Karnes City Citation (Apr. 1 and Apr. 8, 1965).

———. "Karnes County Courthouse Centennial Tribute."
    Karnes City Citation (Oct. 19, 1994).

Tidwell, Laura Knowlton. *Dimmit County Mesquite Roots.*
    Austin: Wind River Press, 1984.

Tise, Sammy. *Texas County Sheriffs.* Albuquerque: Oakwood,
    1989.

Tom Green County Historical Society. *Historical Montage of*
    Tom Green County: Representative Papers of Historical Interest
    about People, Places, and Things Presented to the Society. San
    Angelo, Tex.: Anchor, 1987.

Turner, Hicks A. *I Remember Callahan: A History of Callahan*
    County, Texas. Stillwater, Tex.: Western Pub., 1986.

Tyler, George W., and Charles M. Ramsdell. *History of Bell*
    County. San Antonio: Naylor, 1936.

Tyler, Paula E., and Ronnie C. Tyler. *Texas Museums: A*
    Guidebook. Austin: University of Texas Press, 1983.

Tyler, Ronnie C., Douglas E. Barnett, and Roy R. Barkley,
    eds. *New Handbook of Texas.* 6 vols. Austin: Texas State
    Historical Association, 1996.

Van Bavel, Margaret Lips. *The Birth and Death of Bonneville.*
    Austin: Nortex Press, 1986.

Wallace, Ernest. *Ranald S. Mackenzie on the Texas Frontier.*
    College Station: Texas A&M University Press, 1993.

Walter, Ray A. *A History of Limestone County.* Austin: Von
    Boeckmann-Jones, 1959.

Wax, Ted A. *Dead Man on the Bayou?: Western History's Best*
    Kept Secret Finally Revealed. Gonzales, La.: T. A. Wax, 1988.

Webb, Todd, and Willard B. Robinson. *Texas Public Buildings*
    of the Nineteenth Century. Austin: University of Texas Press,
    1974.

Webb, Walter Prescott. *Texas Rangers: A Century of Frontier Defense,* 2d ed. Austin: University of Texas Press, 1965.

Weddle, Robert S. *The French Thorn: Rival Explorers in the Spanish Sea, 1682–1762.* College Station: Texas A&M University Press, 1991.

———. *Wilderness Manhunt: The Spanish Search for La Salle.* Austin: University of Texas Press, 1973.

Weed, Bobby. "Mellie Ruth Smith Weed," *Bandera County Historian* 20(1) (Spring 1998).

Weems, John Edward. *Austin, 1839–1889.* Austin: John Weems, 1989.

Weinert, Willie Mae. *An Authentic History of Guadalupe County.* Seguin, Tex.: *Seguin Enterprise,* 1951.

Welch, June Rayfield. *Historic Sites of Texas.* Dallas: G. L. A. Press, 1972.

Werner, Vance R. *History of the Buildings and the People of Old Town Cameron.* Rockdale, Tex.: *Rockdale Reporter,* 1974.

West Texas Historical Association Yearbook 1. Abilene, Tex.: West Texas Historical Association, 1925.

Wharton County Historical Commission. *Wharton County Pictorial History, 1846–1946: Our First One Hundred Years.* Austin: Eakin Press, 1993.

Wiggins, Gary, and Stephen W. Sylvia. *Dance and Brothers: Gunmakers of the Confederacy.* Orange County, Va.: Moss, 1986.

Wilbarger, John W. *Indian Depredations in Texas.* Austin: Pemberton Press, 1967.

Williams, Annie Lee. *A History of Wharton County.* Austin: Von Boeckmann-Jones, 1964.

Williams, Clayton W., and Ernest Wallace. *Texas' Last Frontier: Fort Stockton and the Trans-Pecos, 1861–1895.* College Station: Texas A&M University Press, 1982.

Williams, Howard C. *Gateway to Texas: The History of Orange and Orange County,* 2d ed. Orange, Tex.: Heritage House Museum of Orange, 1988.

Williams, Jesse W., and Kenneth F. Neighbours. *Old Texas Trails.* Burnet, Tex.: Eakin Press, 1979.

Wilson, Hugh B. *Southern Pacific Lines: The Galveston, Harrisburg, and San Antonio Railway: A Brief History of El Paso Division, 1881–1925.* Golden, Colo.: Southern Pacific, 1977.

Work Projects Administration in the State of Texas. *Houston: A History and Guide.* Houston: Anson Jones Press, 1942.

Workers of the Writers' Program of the Works Progress Administration in the State of Texas. *Houston: A History and a Guide.* Houston: Anson Jones Press, 1942.

Wortham, Louis J. *A History of Texas: From Wilderness to Commonwealth.* Fort Worth: Wortham-Molyneaux, 1924.

Zachary, Juanita Daniel. *A History of Rural Taylor County.* Burnet, Tex.: Nortex Press, 1980.

Index

Comanche Indians: Adobe Walls
fights, 175; Bandera Co., 29; Comanche Co., 81; Council House
Fight in San Antonio, 37; Crosby
Co., 89; Floyd Co., 120–21;
Foard Co., 122; Fort Parker raid,
213; Gaines Co., 129; Ken Co.,
193; Linnville raid, 56; Llano Co.,
216; McCulloch Co., 229–30;
Menard Co., 235–36; Meusebach-Comanche Peace Treaty,
134; Moore Co., 246; Navarro
Co., 251; Pease River battle, 150–
51; Plum Creek battle, 55, 339;
Sterling Co., 308; Swisher Co.,
312; Throckmorton Co., 320;
Victoria Co., 338–39; women
and children as prisoners of, 49
Comancheros, 120
Comanche Springs, 266
Comfort, Tex., 194
Concho County, 82–83
Concho River, 82, 323
conditions, jail: attempts to legislate,
7–8; Blanco Co., 39; Brazos Co.,
46; doctor's complaint about, 205;
medical services, 97; post-WWII
deterioration of, 10; sanitation, 6,
217
Connell, Ed. F., 97
Conner, Lincoln, 273
Conrey, John, 179
Conroe, Tex., 245
Constitution of 1824, 365
construction methods and materials,
4–5, 9–14. See also individual
counties
Consultation of 1835 in Brazoria
Co., 44
Cook, James, 68
Cook, Joseph Thomas, 67
Cooke, Capt. W. G., 83
Cooke County, 83–84
Cook's Fort, Tex., 67–68
Cooley, Scott, 54
Coonskin (Coldspring), Tex., 290
Cooper, Tex., 97–98
Cora, Tex., 81
Córdoba, Vicente, 68, 289, 355
Córdoba Rebellion, 286, 355
Cornett, J. T., 249
Corpus Christi, Tex., 198, 215, 256–57

Corsicana, Tex., 251–52
Cortina, Juan Nepomuceno, 60–61
Coryell, James, 84
Coryell County, 5–6, 84–86
Cottle, George W., 86
Cottle County, 86–87
Cotulla, Tex., 205–206
Council House Fight, 37
counties in Texas, historical develop-
ment, 3
courthouses and jail construction
considerations, 8–9. See also indi-
vidual counties
Courthouses of Texas (Kelsey and
Dyal), 279
Courtney, James A., 30
Cousins, Al, 159
Cousins, Bob, 159
Cox, Helen Brady, 165
Crane, Tex., 87–88
Crane, William Carey, 87
Crane County, 87–88
Crawford, John C., 45
Creager, Donald C., 218
Cresswell Ranch, 257
Crockett, Davy, 170
Crockett, Tex., 170–71
Crockett County, 88–89
Crosby, Stephen, 89
Crosby County, 89–90
Crosbyton, Tex., 89–90
Cross L Ranch, 146
Crowell, George T., 122
Crowell, Tex., 122–23
Crystal City, Tex., 365–66
Cuero, Tex., 100–101
Culberson County, 91
Currie, Jim, 156
Curry Comb Ranch, 132

Daingerfield, Capt. London, 247
Daingerfield, Tex., 247–48
Dalhart, Tex., 92–93
Dallam County, 92–93
Dallas, George M., 93
Dallas, Tex., 93–95
Dallas County, 93–95
Dalton Gang, 196
Danby (criminal), 249
Dance Brothers, 45
Daugherty, Matt, 99
Davey and Schott, 110
Davidson, Will, 288

Davidson Creek, 52
Davis, E. J., 7
Davis, Edmund, 101
Davis, Henry Clay, 305
Davis, W. O., 84
Davis (Jefferson), Tex., 64
Davis Landing, 305
Dawson, Nicholas M., 95
Dawson County, 95
Deaf Smith County, 96–97
Dean, J. M., 271
Decatur, Cmdr. Stephen, 359
Decatur, Tex., 359–60
Deitz, J. E., 207
DeKalb, Tex., 42
Delaware Creek, 278
Delaware Indians, 359
Del Rio, Tex., 335–36
Delta County, 97–98
Denman Springs (Lufkin), Tex., 20
Denton, John Bunyan, 99
Denton, Tex., 98–100
Denton County, 98–100
Denver City, Tex., 361
Denver City and Fort Worth Rail-
road, 92
Department of Corrections (TDC),
10
Depression, Great, jail construction
effects of, 9. See also Public
Works Administration (PWA)
DeWitt, Green, 100
DeWitt colony, 100, 138
DeWitt County, 100–101
Diamond Tail Ranch, 77
Dickens, J., 101
Dickens, Tex., 101–103
Dickens County, 101–103
Diebold, Karl, 13
Diebold Safe and Lock Company,
Appendix C
Dildime, J. E. K., 39
Dimmit County, 103–104
Dimmitt, Phillip, 103
Dimmitt, Tex., 65–66
Dimmitt, Rev. W. C., 65
Dixon, William "Billy," 175
Dixon and Staley, 238
Doan, Jonathan, 352
Dodson, W. C., 165, 231–32, 337
Dog Town (Tilden), Tex., 233
Dolores, Tex., 364
Donelson, George W., 209